ORATIONS

GEORGE F. HOAR

ORATIONS

FROM HOMER TO
WILLIAM MCKINLEY

EDITED BY

MAYO W. HAZELTINE, A.M.

ILLUSTRATED

IN TWENTY-FIVE VOLUMES

VOL. XX

NEW YORK

P. F. COLLIER AND SON
MCMII

CONTENTS

VOLUME TWENTY

ARNOLD
Lecture on Emerson... 8321
Lecture on Numbers; or the Majority and the Remnant.. 8347

HALE
New England Culture.. 8374
Sons of Massachusetts.. 8388

GRANT
Inaugural Address.. 8399
Speech at Warren, Ohio.. 8403

PHELPS
Farewell Address.. 8407

HAYES
Campaign Speech... 8412

ARGYLL
Welcome to Garrison.. 8423

SHERMAN
On Silver Coinage and Treasury Notes............................. 8429
Great Speech on the Financial Situation........................... 8441

MEAGHER
"Sword Speech"... 8453
An Indictment of the Whigs.. 8463
Hope for Ireland.. 8468
The Glory of Ireland.. 8471
The Orators of Ireland.. 8477

MORTON
On the Issues of 1868... 8486
On Reconstruction... 8501

SMITH
The Evolution of the Dominion... 8530

i

GROW

    On Manila.. 8541

HILL

    On the Perils of the Nation.. 8557

HUGHES

    The Cause of Freedom.. 8568

MAX MULLER

    The Impassable Barrier Between Brutes and Man............. 8580
    On Some Lessons of Antiquity.. 8588

HIGGINSON

    Decoration Day Address at Mount Auburn Cemetery......... 8599
    Oration upon Grant... 8603
    For Self-Respect and Self-Protection................................ 8610

CURTIS

    On the Spoils System and the Progress of Civil Service
        Reform.. 8627
    His Sovereignty Under his Hat.. 8649
    The Duty of the American Scholar..................................... 8651
    Oration at Concord... 8668
    Eulogy of Wendell Phillips.. 8699

COX

    The Beauties of Diplomacy... 8721
    Revival of American Shipping... 8730

KING

    On the Privilege and Duties of Patriotism.......................... 8748

ARNOLD

MATTHEW ARNOLD, a distinguished English essayist and poet, was born at Laleham, near Staines, January 24, 1822. He was the oldest son of Dr. Thomas Arnold, of Rugby. He was educated at Winchester, Rugby (where he won the Rugby prize poem), and Balliol College, Oxford (where he won the Newdigate prize). He graduated with distinguished honors in 1844, and was elected a fellow of Oriel. For four years he served as private secretary to Lord Lansdowne, and in 1851 was appointed lay inspector of schools, a thankless and onerous office, which he filled with conscientious fidelity for thirty-five years. He was several times sent by his government to inquire into the state of education in France, Holland, and Germany, and his reports, full of keen observations, pregnant suggestions, and trenchant criticisms, attracted wide attention. In 1857 he was made professor of poetry at Oxford, and his lectures on the translation of Homer and other topics are among the classics of literary criticism. He held his Oxford professorship for ten years. In 1883 a pension of £250 was conferred on him, and he came to America to lecture. His death occurred April 18, 1888, at Liverpool, where he had gone to meet his daughter, who had married an American. Outwardly somewhat cold and formal, he is shown by his letters and the testimony of his friends to have been one of the most gentle and lovable of men. He was animated by noble ideals and faithful to the guiding light of a broad and liberal religious philosophy. As a poet he is more and more recognized as one of the chief galaxy of the Victorian age. As a critic he has been called the Sainte-Beuve of English letters and many of his felicitous phrases have become current quotations. His works are comprised in about forty volumes, including " Poems " (1853-4); " Essays in Criticism " (1865); " Lectures on the Study of Celtic Literature " and " New Poems " (1867); " Culture and Anarchy " (1869); " St. Paul and Protestantism " (1870); " Literature and Dogma " (1872); " Discourses on America " (1885).

LECTURE ON EMERSON

FORTY years ago, when I was an undergraduate at Oxford, voices were in the air there which haunt my memory still. Happy the man who in that susceptible season of youth hears such voices! they are a possession to him forever. No such voices as those which we heard in our youth at Oxford are sounding there now. Oxford has more criti-

cism now, more knowledge, more light; but such voices as
those of our youth it has no longer. The name of Cardinal
Newman is a great name to the imagination still; his genius
and his style are still things of power. But he is over eighty
years old; he is in the Oratory at Birmingham; he has
adopted, for the doubts and difficulties which beset men's
minds to-day, a solution which, to speak frankly, is impossible.
Forty years ago he was in the very prime of life; he was
close at hand to us at Oxford; he was preaching in St. Mary's
pulpit every Sunday; he seemed about to transform and to
renew what was for us the most national and natural institution in the world, the Church of England. Who could
resist the charm of that spiritual apparition, gliding in the dim
afternoon light through the aisles of St. Mary's, rising into
the pulpit, and then, in the most entrancing of voices, breaking the silence with words and thoughts which were a religious
music,— subtle, sweet, mournful? I seem to hear him still,
saying: "After the fever of life, after wearinesses and sick-
nesses, fightings and despondings, languor and fretfulness,
struggling and succeeding; after all the changes and chances
of this troubled, unhealthy state,— at length comes death, at
length the white throne of God, at length the beatific vision."
Or, if we followed him back to his seclusion at Littlemore,
that dreary village by the London road, and to the house of
retreat and the church which he built there,— a mean house
such as Paul might have lived in when he was tent-making at
Ephesus, a church plain and thinly sown with worshippers,—
who could resist him there either, welcoming back to the
severe joys of church fellowship, and of daily worship and
prayer, the firstlings of a generation which had well-nigh
forgotten them? Again I seem to hear him: "The season is
chill and dark, and the breath of the morning is damp, and

worshippers are few; but all this befits those who are by their profession penitents and mourners, watchers and pilgrims. More dear to them that loneliness, more cheerful that severity, and more bright that gloom, than all those aids and appliances of luxury by which men nowadays attempt to make prayer less disagreeable to them.   True faith does not covet comforts; they who realize that awful day, when they shall see him face to face whose eyes are as a flame of fire, will as little bargain to pray pleasantly now as they will think of doing so then."

Somewhere or other I have spoken of those "last enchantments of the Middle Age" which Oxford sheds around us, and here they were!   But there were other voices sounding in our ear besides Newman's.   There was the puissant voice of Carlyle; so sorely strained, over-used, and mis-used since, but then fresh, comparatively sound, and reaching our hearts with true, pathetic eloquence.   Who can forget the emotion of receiving in its first freshness such a sentence as that sentence of Carlyle upon Edward Irving, then just dead: "Scotland sent him forth a herculean man, our mad Babylon wore and wasted him with all her engines,— and it took her twelve years!"   A greater voice still,— the greatest voice of the century,— came to us in those youthful years through Carlyle: the voice of Goethe.   To this day,— such is the force of youthful associations,— I read the "Wilhelm Meister" with more pleasure in Carlyle's translation than in the original.   The large, liberal view of human life in "Wilhelm Meister," how novel it was to the Englishman in those days! and it was salutary, too, and educative for him, doubtless, as well as novel.   But what moved us most in "Wilhelm Meister" was that which, after all, will always move the young most,— the poetry, the eloquence.   Never, surely, was Carlyle's prose so beautiful and pure as in his rendering of the Youths' dirge over Mignon! — "Well is our treasure now laid up, the fair image of the past. Here sleeps it in the marble, undecaying; in your hearts, also, it lives, it works. Travel, travel, back into life! Take along with you this holy earnestness, for earnestness alone makes life eternity." Here we had the voice of the great Goethe; — not the stiff, and hindered, and frigid, and factitious Goethe who speaks to us too often from those sixty volumes of his, but of the great Goethe, and the true one.

And besides those voices, there came to us in that old Oxford time a voice also from this side of the Atlantic, — a clear and pure voice, which for my ear, at any rate, brought a strain as new, and moving, and unforgetable, as the strain of Newman, or Carlyle, or Goethe. Mr. Lowell has well described the apparition of Emerson to your young generation here, in that distant time of which I am speaking, and of his workings upon them. He was your Newman, your man of soul and genius visible to you in the flesh, speaking to your bodily ears, a present object for your heart and imagination. That is surely the most potent of all influences! nothing can come up to it. To us at Oxford Emerson was but a voice speaking from three thousand miles away. But so well he spoke, that from that time forth Boston Bay and Concord were names invested to my ear with a sentiment akin to that which invests for me the names of Oxford and of Weimar; and snatches of Emerson's strain fixed themselves in my mind as imperishably as any of the eloquent words which I have been just now quoting. "Then dies the man in you; then once more perish the buds of art, poetry, and science, as they have died already in a thousand thousand men." "What Plato has thought, he may think; what a saint has felt, he may feel; what at any time has befallen any man, he can understand." "Trust thyself! every heart vibrates to that iron string. Accept the place the divine Providence has found for you, the society of your contemporaries, the connection of events. Great men have always done so, and confided themselves childlike to the genius of their age; betraying their perception that the Eternal was stirring at their heart, working through their hands, predominating in all their being. And we are now men, and must accept in the highest spirit the same transcendent destiny; and not pinched in a corner, not cowards fleeing before a revolution, but redeemers and benefactors, pious aspirants to be noble clay plastic under the Almighty effort, let us advance and advance on chaos and the dark!" These lofty sentences of Emerson, and a hundred others of like strain, I never have lost out of my memory; I never can lose them.

At last I find myself in Emerson's own country, and looking upon Boston Bay. Naturally I revert to the friend of my youth. It is not always pleasant to ask oneself questions about the friends of one's youth; they cannot always well support it. Carylye, for instance, in my judgment, cannot well support such a return upon him. Yet we should make the return; we should part with our illusions, we should know the truth. When I come to this country, where Emerson now counts for so much, and where such high claims are made for him, I pull myself together, and ask myself what the truth about this object of my youthful admiration really is. Improper elements often come into our estimate of men. We have lately see a German critic make Goethe the greatest of all poets, because Germany is now the greatest of military powers, and wants a poet to match. Then, too, America is a young country; and young countries, like young persons, are

apt sometimes to evince in their literary judgments a want
of scale and measure. I set myself, therefore, resolutely to
come at a real estimate of Emerson, and with a leaning even
to strictness rather than to indulgence. That is the safer
course. Time has no indulgence; any veils of illusion which
we may have left around an object because we loved it Time
is sure to strip away.

I was reading the other day a notice of Emerson by a serious and interesting American critic. Fifty or sixty passages
in Emerson's poems, says this critic,— who had doubtless
himself been nourished on Emerson's writings, and held them
justly dear,— fifty or sixty passages from Emerson's poems
have already entered into English speech as matter of familiar
and universally current quotation. Here is a specimen of
that personal sort of estimate which, for my part, even in
speaking of authors dear to me, I would try to avoid. What
is the kind of phrase of which we may fairly say that it has
entered into English speech as matter of familiar quotation?
Such a phrase, surely, as the "Patience on a monument" of
Shakespeare; as the "Darkness visible" of Milton; as the
"Where ignorance is bliss" of Gray. Of not one single
passage in Emerson's poetry can it be truly said that it has
become a familiar quotation like phrases of this kind. It is
not enough that it should be familiar to his admirers, familiar
in New England, familiar even throughout the United States;
it must be familiar to all readers and lovers of English poetry.
Of not more than one or two passages in Emerson's poetry
can it, I think, be truly said, that they stand ever present in
the memory of even many lovers of English poetry. A great
number of passages from his poetry are no doubt perfectly
familiar to the mind and lips of the critic whom I have mentioned, and perhaps a wide circle of American readers.

But this is a very different thing from being matter of universal quotation, like the phrases of the legitimate poets.

And, in truth, one of the legitimate poets, Emerson, in my opinion, is not. His poetry is interesting, it makes one think; but it is not the poetry of one of the born poets. I say it of him with reluctance, although I am sure that he would have said it of himself; but I say it with reluctance, because I dislike giving pain to his admirers, and because all my own wish, too, is to say of him what is favorable. But I regard myself, not as speaking to please Emerson's admirers, not as speaking to please myself; but rather, I repeat, as communing with time and nature concerning the productions of this beautiful and rare spirit, and as resigning what of him is by their unalterable decree touched with caducity, in order the better to mark and secure that in him which is immortal.

Milton says that poetry ought to be simple, sensuous, impassioned. Well, Emerson's poetry is seldom either simple, or sensuous, or impassioned. In general it lacks directness; it lacks concreteness; it lacks energy. His grammar is often embarrassed; in particular, the want of clearly-marked distinction between the subject and the object of his sentence is a frequent cause of obscurity in him. A poem which shall be a plain, forcible, inevitable whole he hardly ever produces. Such good work as the noble lines graven on the Concord Monument is the exception with him; such ineffective work as the " Fourth of July Ode " or the " Boston Hymn " is the rule. Even passages and single lines of thorough plainness and commanding force are rare in his poetry. They exist, of course; but when we meet with them they give us a slight shock of surprise, so little has Emerson

accustomed us to them. Let me have the pleasure of quoting
one or two of these exceptional passages:

> " So nigh is grandeur to our dust,
> So near is God to man,
> When duty whispers low, Thou must,
> The youth replies, I can."

Or again this:

> " Though love repine and reason chafe,
> There came a voice without reply:
> ' 'Tis man's perdition to be safe,
> When for the truth he ought to die.' "

Excellent! but how seldom do we get from him a strain
blown so clearly and firmly! Take another passage where
his strain has not only clearness, it has also grace and
beauty:

> " And ever, when the happy child
> In May beholds the blooming wild,
> And hears in heaven the bluebird sing,
> ' Onward,' he cries, ' your baskets bring!
> In the next field is air more mild,
> And in yon hazy west is Eden's balmier spring.' "

In the style and cadence here there is a reminiscence, I
think, of Gray; at any rate the pureness, grace, and beauty
of these lines are worthy even of Gray. But Gray holds his
high rank as a poet, not merely by the beauty and grace of
passages in his poems; not merely by a diction generally
pure in an age of impure diction: he holds it, above all, by
the power and skill with which the evolution of his poems
is conducted. Here is his grand superiority to Collins,
whose diction in his best poem, the " Ode to Evening," is
purer than Gray's; but then the " Ode to Evening " is like
a river which loses itself in the sand, whereas Gray's best
poems have an evolution sure and satisfying. Emerson's
" Mayday," from which I just now quoted, has no real evo-

lution at all; it is a series of observations. And, in general, his poems have no evolution. Take, for example, his "Titmouse." Here he has an excellent subject; and his observation of nature, moreover, is always marvellously close and fine. But compare what he makes of his meeting with his titmouse with what Cowper or Burns makes of the like kind of incident! One never quite arrives at learning what the titmouse actually did for him at all, though one feels a strong interest and desire to learn it; but one is reduced to guessing, and cannot be quite sure that after all one has guessed right. He is not plain and concrete enough,— in other words, not poet enough,— to be able to tell us. And a failure of this kind goes through almost all his verse, keeps him amid symbolism and allusion and the fringes of things, and, in spite of his spiritual power, deeply impairs his poetic value. Through the inestimable virtue of concreteness, a simple poem like "The Bridge" of Longfellow, or the "School Days" of Mr. Whittier, is of more poetic worth, perhaps, than all the verse of Emerson.

I do not, then, place Emerson among the great poets. But I go further, and say that I do not place him among the great writers, the great men of letters. Who are the great men of letters? They are men like Cicero, Plato, Bacon, Pascal, Swift, Voltaire,— writers with, in the first place, a genius and instinct for style; writers whose prose is by a kind of native necessity true and sound. Now the style of Emerson, like the style of his transcendentalist friends and of the "Dial" so continually,— the style of Emerson is capable of falling into a strain like this, which I take from the beginning of his "Essay on Love:" "Every soul is a celestial being to every other soul. The heart has its sabbaths and jubilees, in which the world appears as a hymeneal feast, and all natural sounds and the circle of the seasons are erotic odes and dances." Emerson altered this sentence in the later editions. Like Wordsworth, he was in later life fond of altering; and in general his later alterations, like those of Wordsworth, are not improvements. He softened the passage in question, however, though without really mending it. I quote it in its original and strongly marked form. Arthur Stanley used to relate that about the year 1840, being in conversation with some Americans in quarantine at Malta, and thinking to please them, he declared his warm admiration for Emerson's "Essays," then recently published. However, the Americans shook their heads, and told him that for home taste Emerson was decidedly too "greeny." We will hope, for their sakes, that the sort of thing they had in their heads was such writing as I have just quoted. Unsound it is, indeed, and in a style almost impossible to a born man of letters.

It is a curious thing, that quality of style which marks the great writer, the born man of letters. It resides in the whole tissue of his work, and of his work regarded as a composition for literary purposes. Brilliant and powerful passages in a man's writings do not prove his possession of it; it lies in their whole tissue. Emerson has passages of noble and pathetic eloquence, such as those which I quoted at the beginning; he has passages of shrewd and felicitous wit; he has crisp epigram; he has passages of exquisitely touched observation of nature. Yet he is not a great writer; his style has not the requisite wholeness of good tissue. Even Carlyle is not, in my judgment, a great writer. He has surpassingly powerful qualities of expression, far more powerful than Emerson's, and reminding one of the gifts of expression of the great poets,— of even Shakespeare himself.

What Emerson so admirably says of Carlyle's " devouring eyes and portraying hand," " those thirsty eyes, those portrait-eating, portrait-painting eyes of thine, those fatal perceptions," is thoroughly true.   What a description is Carlyle's of the first publisher of " Sartor Resartus," " to whom the idea of a new edition of Sartor is frightful, or rather ludicrous, unimaginable; " of this poor Fraser, in whose " wonderful world of Tory pamphleteers, Conservative Younger-brothers, Regent Street loungers, Crockford gamblers, Irish Jesuits, drunken reporters, and miscellaneous unclean persons (whom nitre and much soap will not wash clean), not a soul has expressed the smallest wish that way! "   What a portrait, again, of the well-beloved John Sterling! " One, and the best, of a small class extant here, who, nigh drowning in a black wreck of infidelity (lighted up by some glare of radicalism only, now growing dim too), and about to perish, saved themselves into a Coleridgian shovel-hattedness." What touches in the invitation of Emerson to London! " You shall see blockheads by the million; Pickwick himself shall be visible,— innocent young Dickens, reserved for a questionable fate.   The great Wordsworth shall talk till you yourself pronounce him to be a bore. Southey's complexion is still healthy mahogany brown, with a fleece of white hair, and eyes that seem running at full gallop.   Leigh Hunt, man of genius in the shape of a cockney, is my near neighbor, with good humor and no common sense; old Rogers with his pale head, white, bare, and cold as snow, with those large blue eyes, cruel, sorrowful, and that sardonic shelf chin."   How inimitable it all is! And finally, for one must not go on forever, this version of a London Sunday, with the public-houses closed during the hours of divine service! " It is silent Sunday; the populace not

yet admitted to their beer shops, till the respectabilities con-
clude their rubric mummeries,— a much more audacious
feat than beer." Yet even Carlyle is not, in my judgment,
to be called a great writer; one cannot think of ranking him
with men like Cicero and Plato and Swift and Voltaire.
Emerson freely promises to Carlyle immortality for his his-
tories. They will not have it. Why? Because the materials
furnished to him by that devouring eye of his, and that portraying hand, were not wrought in and subdued by him to
what his work, regarded as a composition for literary purposes, required. Occurring in conversation, breaking out in
familiar correspondence, they are magnificent, inimitable;
nothing more is required of them; thus thrown out anyhow,
they serve their turn and fulfil their function. And, therefore, I should not wonder if really Carlyle lived, in the long
run, by such an invaluable record as that correspondence
between him and Emerson, of which we owe the publication
to Mr. Charles Norton,— by this and not by his works, as
Johnson lives in Boswell, not by his works. For Carlyle's
sallies, as the staple of a literary work, become wearisome;
and as time more and more applies to Carlyle's works its
stringent test, this will be felt more and more. Shakespeare,
Molière, Swift,— they, too, had, like Carlyle, the devouring
eye and the portraying hand. But they are great literary
masters, they are supreme writers, because they knew how
to work into a literary composition their materials, and to
subdue them to the purposes of literary effect. Carlyle is
too wilful for this, too turbid, too vehement.

You will think I deal in nothing but negatives. I have
been saying that Emerson is not one of the great poets, the
great writers. He has not their quality of style. He is,
however, the propounder of a philosophy. The Platonic dia-

logues afford us the example of exquisite literary form and treatment given to philosophical ideas. Plato is at once a great literary man and a great philosopher. If we speak carefully, we cannot call Aristotle or Spinoza or Kant great literary men, or their productions great literary works. But their work is arranged with such constructive power that they build a philosophy, and are justly called great philosophical writers. Emerson cannot, I think, be called with justice a great philosophical writer. He cannot build; his arrangement of philosophical ideas has no progress in it, no evolution; he does not construct a philosophy. Emerson himself knew the defects of his method, or rather want of method, very well; indeed, he and Carlyle criticise themselves and one another in a way which leaves little for any one else to do in the way of formulating their defects. Carlyle formulates perfectly the defects of his friend's poetic and literary production when he says of the " Dial: " " For me it is too ethereal, speculative, theoretic; I will have all things condense themselves, take shape and body, if they are to have my sympathy." And, speaking of Emerson's orations, he says: " I long to see some concrete thing, some event, man's life, American forest, or piece of creation, which this Emerson loves and wonders at, well ' Emersonized,' — depictured by Emerson, filled with the life of Emerson, and cast forth from him, then to live by itself. If these orations balk me of this, how profitable soever they may be for others, I will not love them." Emerson himself formulates perfectly the defect of his own philosophical productions when he speaks of his "formidable tendency to the lapidary style. I build my house of boulders." " Here I sit and read and write," he says again, "with very little system, and, as far as regards composition, with the most fragmentary result; paragraphs incomprehensible, each sentence an infinitely repellent particle." Nothing can be truer; and the work of a Spinoza or Kant, of the men who stand as great philosophical writers, does not proceed in this wise.

Some people will tell you that Emerson's poetry, indeed, is too abstract, and his philosophy too vague, but that his best work is his "English Traits." The "English Traits" are beyond question very pleasant reading. It is easy to praise them, easy to commend the author of them. But I insist on always trying Emerson's work by the highest standards. I esteem him too much to try his work by any other. Tried by the highest standards, and compared with the work of the excellent markers and recorders of the traits of human life,— of writers like Montaigne, La Bruyère, Addison,—the "English Traits" will not stand the comparison. Emerson's observation has not the disinterested quality of the observation of these masters. It is the observation of a man systematically benevolent, as Hawthorne's observation in "Our Old Home" is the work of a man chagrined. Hawthorne's literary talent is of the first order. His subjects are generally not to me subjects of the highest interest; but his literary talent is of the first order, the finest, I think, which America has yet produced,— finer, by much, than Emerson's. Yet "Our Old Home" is not a masterpiece any more than "English Traits." In neither of them is the observer disinterested enough. The author's attitude in each of these cases can easily be understood and defended. Hawthorne was a sensitive man, so situated in England that he was perpetually in contact with the British Philistine; and the British Philistine is a trying personage. Emerson's systematic benevolence comes from what he himself calls somewhere his "persistent optimism;" and his persistent optimism is the root of his greatness and the source of his charm. But still let us keep our literary conscience true, and judge every kind of literary work by the laws really proper to it. The kind of work attempted in the "English Traits" and in "Our Old Home" is work which cannot be done perfectly with a bias such as that given by Emerson's optimism or by Hawthorne's chagrin. Consequently, neither "English Traits" nor "Our Old Home" is a work of perfection in its kind.

Not with the Miltons and Grays, not with the Platos and Spinozas, not with the Swifts and Voltaires, not with the Montaignes and Addisons, can we rank Emerson. His work of various kinds, when one compares it with the work done in a corresponding kind by these masters, fails to stand the comparison. No man could see this clearer than Emerson himself. It is hard not to feel despondency when we contemplate our failures and shortcomings; and Emerson, the least self-flattering and the most modest of men, saw so plainly what was lacking to him that he had his moments of despondency. "Alas, my friend," he writes in reply to Carlyle, who had exhorted him to creative work,— "Alas, my friend, I can do no such gay thing as you say. I do not belong to the poets, but only to a low department of literature,— the reporters; suburban men." He deprecated his friend's praise; praise "generous to a fault," he calls it; praise "generous to the shaming of me,— cold, fastidious, ebbing person that I am. Already in a former letter you had said too much good of my poor little arid book, which is as sand to my eyes. I can only say that I heartily wish the book were better; and I must try and deserve so much favor from the kind gods by a bolder and truer living in the months to come,— such as may perchance one day release and invigorate this cramp hand of mine. When I see how much work is to be done;

what room for a poet, for any spiritualist, in this great, intelligent, sensual, and avaricious America,— I lament my fumbling fingers and stammering tongue." Again, as late as 1870, he writes to Carlyle; "There is no example of constancy like yours, and it always stings my stupor into temporary recovery and wonderful resolution to accept the noble challenge. But 'the strong hours conquer us;' and I am the victim of miscellany,— miscellany of designs, vast debility, and procrastination." The forlorn note belonging to the phrase, "vast debility," recalls that saddest and most discouraged of writers, the author of "Obermann," Senancour, with whom Emerson has in truth a certain kinship. He has, in common with Senancour, his pureness, his passion for nature, his single eye; and here we find him confessing, like Senancour, a sense in himself of sterility and impotence.

And now I think I have cleared the ground. I have given up to envious time as much of Emerson as time can fairly expect ever to obtain. We have not in Emerson a great poet, a great writer, a great philosophy maker. His relation to us is not that of one of those personages; yet it is a relation of, I think, even superior importance. His relation to us is more like that of the Roman emperor Marcus Aurelius. Marcus Aurelius is not a great writer, a great philosophy maker; he is the friend and aider of those who would live in the spirit. Emerson is the same. He is the friend and aider of those who would live in the spirit. All the points in thinking which are necessary for this purpose he takes; but he does not combine them into a system, or present them as a regular philosophy. Combined in a system by a man with the requisite talent for this kind of thing, they would be less useful than as Emerson gives them to us; and the man with the talent so to systematize them would be less impressive than Emerson. They do very well as they now stand;—like "boulders," as he says;—in "paragraphs incompressible, each sentence an infinitely repellent particle." In such sentences his main points recur again and again, and become fixed in the memory.

We all know them. First and foremost, character. Character is everything. "That which all things tend to educe,—which freedom, cultivation, intercourse, revolutions, go to form and deliver,—is character." Character and self-reliance. "Trust thyself! every heart vibrates to that iron string." And yet we have our being in a not ourselves. "There is a power above and behind us, and we are the channels of its communications." But our lives must be pitched higher. "Life must be lived on a higher plane; we must go up to a higher platform, to which we are always invited to ascend; there the whole scene changes." The good we need is forever close to us, though we attain it not. "On the brink of the waters of life and truth, we are miserably dying." This good is close to us, moreover, in our daily life, and in the familiar, homely places. "The unremitting retention of simple and high sentiments in obscure duties,—that is the maxim for us. Let us be poised and wise, and our own to-day. Let us treat the men and women well,—treat them as if they were real; perhaps they are. Men live in their fancy, like drunkards whose hands are too soft and tremulous for successful labor. I settle myself ever firmer in the creed, that we should not postpone and refer and wish, but do broad justice where we are, by whomsoever we deal with; accepting our actual companions and circumstances, however humble or odious, as the mystic officials to whom the universe has delegated its whole pleasure for us. Massachusetts, Connecticut

River, and Boston Bay, you think paltry places, and the ear loves names of foreign and classic topography. But here we are; and if we will tarry a little we may come to learn that here is best. See to it only that thyself is here." Furthermore, the good is close to us all. "I resist the scepticism of our education and of our educated men. I do not believe that the differences of opinion and character in men are organic. I do not recognize, besides the class of the good and the wise, a permanent class of sceptics, or a class of conservatives, or of malignants, or of materialists. I do not believe in the classes. Every man has a call of the power to do something unique." Exclusiveness is deadly. "The exclusive in social life does not see that he excludes himself from enjoyment in the attempt to appropriate it. The exclusionist in religion does not see that he shuts the door of heaven on himself in striving to shut out others. Treat men as pawns and ninepins, and you shall suffer as well as they. If you leave out their heart you shall lose your own. The selfish man suffers more from his selfishness than he from whom that selfishness withholds some important benefit." A sound nature will be inclined to refuse ease and self-indulgence. "To live with some rigor of temperance, or some extreme of generosity, seems to be an asceticism which common good nature would appoint to those who are at ease and in plenty, in sign that they feel a brotherhood with the great multitude of suffering men." Compensation, finally, is the great law of life; it is everywhere, it is sure, and there is no escape from it. This is that "law alive and beautiful, which works over our heads and under our feet. Pitiless, it avails itself of our success when we obey it, and of our ruin when we contravene it. We are all secret believers in it. It rewards actions after their nature. The reward of a thing well done is to have done it. The thief steals from himself, the swindler swindles himself. You must pay at last your own debt."

This is tonic indeed! And let no one object that it is too general; that more practical, positive direction is what we want; that Emerson's optimism, self-reliance, and indifference to favorable conditions for our life and growth have in them something of danger. "Trust thyself;" "what attracts my attention shall have it;" "though thou shouldst walk the world over thou shalt not be able to find a condition inopportune or ignoble;" "what we call vulgar society is that society whose poetry is not yet written, but which you shall presently make as enviable and renowned as any." With maxims like these, we surely, it may be said, run some risk of being made too well satisfied with our own actual self and state, however crude and imperfect they may be. "Trust thyself?" It may be said that the common American or Englishman is more than enough disposed already to trust himself. I often reply, when our sectarians are praised for following conscience: Our people are very good in following their conscience; where they are not so good is in ascertaining whether their conscience tells them right. "What attracts my attention shall have it?" Well, that is our people's plea when they run after the Salvation Army, and desire Messrs. Moody and Sankey. "Thou shalt not be able to find a condition inopportune or ignoble?" But think of the turn of the good people of our race for producing a life of hideousness and immense *ennui;* think of that specimen of your own New England life which Mr. Howells gives us in one of his charming stories which I was reading lately; think of the life of that rugged New England farm in " The Lady of the Aroostook;" think of Deacon Blood, and Aunt Maria, and the straight-backed chairs with black horse-hair seats, and Ezra

Perkins with perfect self-reliance depositing his travellers in the snow! I can truly say that in the little which I have seen of the life of New England, I am more struck with what has been achieved than with the crudeness and failure. But no doubt there is still a great deal of crudeness also. Your own novelists say there is, and I suppose they say true. In the new England, as in the old, our people have to learn, I suppose, not that their modes of life are beautiful and excellent already; they have rather to learn that they must transform them.

To adopt this line of objection to Emerson's deliverances would, however, be unjust. In the first place, Emerson's points are in themselves true, if understood in a certain high sense; they are true and fruitful. And the right work to be done, at the hour when he appeared, was to affirm them generally and absolutely. Only thus could he break through the hard and fast barrier of narrow, fixed ideas, which he found confronting him, and win an entrance for new ideas. Had he attempted developments which may now strike us as expedient, he would have excited fierce antagonism, and probably effected little or nothing. The time might come for doing other work later, but the work which Emerson did was the right work to be done then.

In the second place, strong as was Emerson's optimism, and unconquerable as was his belief in a good result to emerge from all which he saw going on around him, no misanthropical satirist ever saw shortcomings and absurdities more clearly than he did, or exposed them more courageously. When he sees "the meanness," as he calls it, "of American politics," he congratulates Washington on being "long already happily dead," on being "wrapt in his shroud and forever safe." With how firm a touch he delineates the faults of your two great political parties of forty years ago! The Democrats, he says, " have not at heart the ends which give to the name of democracy what hope and virtue are in it. The spirit of our American radicalism is destructive and aimless; it is not loving; it has no ulterior and divine ends, but is destructive only out of hatred and selfishness. On the other side, the conservative party, composed of the most moderate, able, and cultivated part of the population, is timid, and merely defensive of property. It vindicates no right, it aspires to no real good, it brands no crime, it proposes no generous policy. From neither party, when in power, has the world any benefit to expect in science, art, or humanity, at all commensurate with the resources of the nation." Then with what subtle though kindly irony he follows the gradual withdrawal in New England, in the last half century, of tender consciences from the social organizations,— the bent for experiments such as that of Brook Farm and the like,— follows it in all its " dissidence of dissent and Protestantism of the Protestant religion!" He even loves to rally the New Englander on his philanthropical activity, and to find his beneficence and its institutions a bore! " Your miscellaneous popular charities, the education at college of fools, the building of meeting-houses to the vain end to which many of these now stand, alms to sots, and the thousandfold relief societies, — though I confess with shame that I sometimes succumb and give the dollar, yet it is a wicked dollar, which by and by I shall have the manhood to withhold." " Our Sunday schools and churches and pauper societies are yokes to the neck. We pain ourselves to please nobody. There are natural ways of arriving at the same ends at which these aim, but do not arrive." " Nature does not like our benevolence or our learning much better than she likes our frauds and wars. When we come out of the caucus, or the bank, or the Abolition convention, or the temperance meeting, or the Transcendental club, into the fields and woods, she says to us: "So hot, my little sir?'"

Yes, truly, his insight is admirable; his truth is precious. Yet the secret of his effect is not even in these; it is in his temper. It is in the hopeful, serene, beautiful temper wherewith these, in Emerson, are indissolubly joined; in which they work, and have their being. He says himself: "We judge of a man's wisdom by his hope, knowing that the perception of the inexhaustibleness of nature is an immortal youth." If this be so, how wise is Emerson! for never had man such a sense of the inexhaustibleness of nature, and such hope. It was the ground of his being; it never failed him. Even when he is sadly avowing the imperfection of his literary power and resources, lamenting his fumbling fingers and stammering tongue, he adds: "Yet, as I tell you, I am very easy in my mind and never dream of suicide. My whole philosophy, which is very real, teaches acquiescence and optimism. Sure I am that the right word will be spoken, though I cut out my tongue." In his old age, with friends dying and life failing, his tone of cheerful, forward-looking hope is still the same. "A multitude of young men are growing up here of high promise, and I compare gladly the social poverty of my youth with the power on which these draw." His abiding word for us, the word by which being dead he yet speaks to us, is this: "That which befits us, embosomed in beauty and wonder as we are, is cheerfulness and courage, and the endeavor to realize our aspirations. Shall not the heart, which has received so much, trust the power by which it lives?"

One can scarcely overrate the importance of thus holding

fast to happiness and hope. It gives to Emerson's work an invaluable virtue. As Wordsworth's poetry is, in my judgment, the most important work done in verse, in our language, during the present century, so Emerson's "Essays" are, I think, the most important work done in prose. His work is more important than Carlyle's. Let us be just to Carlyle, provoking though he often is. Not only has he that genius of his which makes Emerson say truly of his letters, that "they savor always of eternity." More than this may be said of him. The scope and upshot of his teaching are true; "his guiding genius," to quote Emerson again, is really "his moral sense, his perception of the sole importance of truth and justice." But consider Carlyle's temper, as we have been considering Emerson's! Take his own account of it! "Perhaps London is the proper place for me after all, seeing all places are improper: who knows? Meanwhile, I lead a most dyspeptic, solitary, self-shrouded life; consuming, if possible in silence, my considerable daily allotment of pain; glad when any strength is left in me for writing, which is the only use I can see in myself,— too rare a case of late. The ground of my existence is black as death; too black, when all void too; but at times there paint themselves on it pictures of gold, and rainbow, and lightning; all the brighter for the black ground, I suppose. Withal, I am very much of a fool."— No, not a fool, but turbid and morbid, wilful and perverse. "We judge of a man's wisdom by his hope."

Carlyle's perverse attitude towards happiness cuts him off from hope. He fiercely attacks the desire for happiness; his grand point in "Sartor," his secret in which the soul may find rest, is that one shall cease to desire happiness, that one should learn to say to one self: "What if thou wert born and predestined not to be happy, but to be unhappy!" He is wrong; Saint Augustine is the better philosopher, who says: "Act we must in pursuance of what gives us most delight." Epictetus and Augustine can be severe moralists enough; but both of them know and frankly say that the desire for happiness is the root and ground of man's being. Tell him and show him that he places his happiness wrong, that he seeks for delight where delight will never be really found; then you illumine and further him. But you only confuse him by telling him to cease to desire happiness: and you will not tell him this unless you are already confused yourself.

Carlyle preached the dignity of labor, the necessity of righteousness, the love of veracity, the hatred of shams. He is said by many people to be a great teacher, a great helper for us, because he does so. But what is the due and eternal result of labor, righteousness, veracity? — Happiness. And how are we drawn to them by one who, instead of making us feel that with them is happiness, tells us that perhaps we were predestined not to be happy but to be unhappy?

You will find, in especial, many earnest preachers of our popular religion to be fervent in their praise and admiration of Carlyle. His insistence on labor, righteousness, and veracity, pleases them; his contempt for happiness pleases them too. I read the other day a tract against smoking, although I do not happen to be a smoker myself. "Smoking," said the tract, "is liked because it gives agreeable sensations. Now it is a positive objection to a thing that it gives agreeable sensations. An earnest man will expressly avoid what gives agreeable sensations." Shortly afterwards I was inspecting a school, and I found the children reading a piece of poetry on the common theme that we are here to-day and gone to-morrow. I shall soon be gone, the speaker in this poem was made to say,—

> "And I shall be glad to go,
> For the world at best is a dreary place,
> And my life is getting low."

How usual a language of popular religion that is, on our side of the Atlantic at any rate! But then our popular religion, in disparaging happiness here below, knows very well what it is after. It has its eye on a happiness in a future life above the clouds, in the New Jerusalem, to be won by disliking and rejecting happiness here on earth. And so long as this ideal stands fast, it is very well. But for very many it now stands fast no longer; for Carlyle, at any rate, it had failed and vanished. Happiness in labor, righteousness, and veracity,— in the life of the spirit,— here was a gospel still for Carlyle to preach, and to help others by preaching. But he baffled them and himself by preferring the paradox that we are not born for happiness at all.

Happiness in labor, righteousness, and veracity; in all the life of the spirit; happiness and eternal hope; — that was Emerson's gospel. I hear it said that Emerson was too sanguine; that the actual generation in America is not turning out so well as he expected. Very likely he was too sanguine as to the near future; in this country it is difficult not to be too sanguine. Very possibly the present generation may prove unworthy of his high hopes; even several generations succeeding this may prove unworthy of them. But by his conviction that in the life of the spirit is happiness, and by his hope that this life of the spirit will come more and more to be sanely understood, and to prevail, and to work for happiness,— by this conviction and hope Emerson was great, and he will surely prove in the end to have been right in them. In this country it is difficult, as I said, not to be sanguine. Very many of your writers are over-sanguine, and on the wrong grounds. But you have two men who in what they have written show their sanguineness in a line where courage and hope are just, where they are also infinitely important, but where they are not easy. The two men are Franklin and Emerson.[1] These two are, I think, the most distinctively and honorably American of your writers; they are the most original and the most valuable. Wise men everywhere know that we must keep up our courage and hope; they know that hope is, as Wordsworth well says,—

> " The paramount duty which Heaven lays,
> For its own honor, on man's suffering heart."

But the very word " duty " points to an effort and a struggle to maintain our hope unbroken. Franklin and Emerson maintained theirs with a convincing ease, an inspiring joy. Franklin's confidence in the happiness with which industry, honesty, and economy will crown the life of this work-day world, is such that he runs over with felicity. With a like felicity does Emerson run over, when he contemplates the happiness eternally attached to the true life in the spirit. You

---

[1] I found with pleasure that this conjunction of Emerson's name with Franklin's had already occurred to an accomplished writer and delightful man, a friend of Emerson, left almost the sole survivor, alas! of the famous literary generation of Boston,—Dr. Oliver Wendell Holmes. Dr. Holmes has kindly allowed me to print here the ingenious and interesting lines, hitherto unpublished, in which he speaks of Emerson thus:

> " Where in the realm of thought, whose air is song,
> Does he, the Buddha of the West, belong?
> He seems a wingéd Franklin, sweetly wise,
> Born to unlock the secret of the skies;
> And which the nobler calling—if 'tis fair
> Terrestrial with celestial to compare—
> To guide the storm-cloud's elemental flame,
> Or walk the chambers whence the lightning came
> Amidst the sources of its subtile fire,
> And steal their effluence for his lips and lyre? "

cannot prize him too much, nor heed him too diligently. He has lessons for both the branches of our race. I figure him to my mind as visible upon earth still, as still standing here by Boston Bay, or at his own Concord, in his habit as he lived, but of heightened stature and shining feature, with one hand stretched out towards the east, to our laden and laboring England; the other towards the ever-growing west, to his own dearly-loved America,—"great, intelligent, sensual, avaricious America." To us he shows for guidance his lucid freedom, his cheerfulness and hope; to you his dignity, delicacy, serenity, elevation.

LECTURE ON NUMBERS; OR THE MAJORITY AND THE REMNANT

THERE is a characteristic saying of Dr. Johnson: "Patriotism is the last refuge of a scoundrel." The saying is cynical, many will even call it brutal; yet it has in it something of plain, robust sense and truth. We do often see men passing themselves off as patriots, who are in truth scoundrels; we meet with talk and proceedings laying claim to patriotism, which are these gentlemen's last refuge. We may all of us agree in praying to be delivered from patriots and patriotism of this sort. Short of such, there is undoubtedly, sheltering itself under the fine name of patriotism, a good deal of self-flattery and self-delusion which is mischievous. "Things are what they are, and the consequences of them will be what they will be; why, then, should we desire to be deceived?" In that uncompromising sentence of Bishop Butler's is surely the right and salutary maxim for both individuals and nations.

Yet there is an honorable patriotism which we should satisfy if we can, and should seek to have on our side. At home
I have said so much of the characters of our society and the
prospects of our civilization, that I can hardly escape the like
topic elsewhere. Speaking in America, I cannot well avoid
saying something about the prospects of society in the United
States. It is a topic where one is apt to touch people's
patriotic feelings. No one will accuse me of having flattered
the patriotism of that great country of English people on the
other side of the Atlantic, amongst whom I was born. Here,
so many miles from home, I begin to reflect with tender con-
trition, that perhaps I have not,— I will not say flattered the
patriotism of my own countrymen enough, but regarded it
enough. Perhaps that is one reason why I have produced so
very little effect upon them. It was a fault of youth and
inexperience. But it would be unpardonable to come in
advanced life and repeat the same error here. You will not
expect impossibilities of me. You will not expect me to say
that things are not what, in my judgment, they are, and
that the consequences of them will not be what they will be.
I should make nothing of it; I should be a too palpable failure.
But I confess that I should be glad if in what I say here I
could engage American patriotism on my side, instead of rousing it against me. And it so happens that the paramount
thoughts which your great country raises in my mind are
really and truly of a kind to please, I think, any true American patriot, rather than to offend him.

The vast scale of things here, the extent of your country,
your numbers, the rapidity of your increase, strike the imagination, and are a common topic for admiring remark. Our
great orator, Mr. Bright, is never weary of telling us how
many acres of land you have at your disposal, how many

bushels of grain you produce, how many millions you are, how many more millions you will be presently, and what a capital thing this is for you. Now, though I do not always agree with Mr. Bright, I find myself agreeing with him here. I think your number afford a very real and important ground for satisfaction.

Not that your great numbers, or indeed great numbers of men, anywhere, are likely to be all good, or even to have the majority good. "The majority are bad," said one of the wise men of Greece; but he was a pagan. Much to the same effect, however, is the famous sentence of the New Testament: "Many are called, few chosen." This appears a hard saying; frequent are the endeavors to elude it, to attenuate its severity. But turn it how you will, manipulate it as you will, the few, as Cardinal Newman well says, can never mean the many. Perhaps you will say that the majority is, sometimes, good; that its impulses are good generally, and its action is good occasionally. Yes, but it lacks principle, it lacks persistence; if to-day its good impulses prevail, they succumb to-morrow; sometimes it goes right, but it is very apt to go wrong. Even a popular orator, or a popular journalist, will hardly say that the multitude may be trusted to have its judgment generally just, and its action generally virtuous. It may be better, it is better, that the body of the people, with all its faults, should act for itself, and control its own affairs, than that it should be set aside as ignorant and incapable, and have its affairs managed for it by a so-called superior class, possessing property and intelligence. Property and intelligence cannot be trusted to show a sound majority themselves; the exercise of power by the people tends to educate the people. But still, the world being what it is, we must surely expect the aims and doings of the majority of men to be at present very faulty, and this in a numerous community no less than in a small one. So much we must certainly, I think, concede to the sages and to the saints.

Sages and saints are apt to be severe, it is true; apt to take a gloomy view of the society in which they live, and to prognosticate evil to it. But then it must be added that their prognostications are very apt to turn out right. Plato's account of the most gifted and brilliant community of the ancient world, of that Athens of his to which we all owe so much, is despondent enough. "There is but a very small remnant," he says, "of honest followers of wisdom, and they who are of these few, and who have tasted how sweet and blessed a possession is wisdom, and who can fully see, moreover, the madness of the multitude, and that there is no one, we may say, whose action in public matters is sound, and no ally for whosoever would help the just, what," asks Plato, "are they to do? They may be compared," says Plato, "to a man who has fallen among wild beasts; he will not be one of them, but he is too unaided to make head against them; and before he can do any good to society or his friends, he will be overwhelmed and perish uselessly. When he considers this, he will resolve to keep still, and to mind his own business; as it were standing aside under a wall in a storm of dust and hurricane of driving wind; and he will endure to behold the rest filled with iniquity, if only he himself may live his life clear of injustice and of impiety, and depart, when his time comes, in mild and gracious mood, with fair hope."

Plato's picture here of democratic Athens is certainly gloomy enough. We may be sure the mass of his contemporaries would have pronounced it to be monstrously overcharged. We ourselves, if we had been living then, should most of us have by no means seen things as Plato saw them. No, if we had seen Athens even nearer its end than when Plato wrote the strong words which I have been quoting, Athens in the very last days of Plato's life, we should most of us probably have considered that things were not going badly with Athens. There is a long sixteen years' administration,— the administration of Eubulus,— which fills the last years of Plato's life, and the middle years of the fourth century before Christ. A temperate German historian thus describes Athens during this ministry of Eubulus: "The grandeur and loftiness of Attic democracy had vanished, while all the pernicious germs contained in it were fully developed. A life of comfort and a craving for amusement were encouraged in every way, and the interest of the citizens was withdrawn from serious things. Conversation became more and more superficial and frivolous. Famous courtesans formed the chief topic of talk; the new inventions of Thearion, the leading pastry-cook in Athens, were hailed with loud applause; and the witty sayings which had been uttered in gay circles were repeated about town as matters of prime importance."

No doubt, if we had been living then to witness this, we should from time to time have shaken our heads gravely, and said how sad it all was. But most of us would not, I think, have been very seriously disquieted by it. On the other hand, we should have found many things in the Athens of Eubulus to gratify us. "The democrats," says the same historian whom I have just quoted, "saw in Eubulus one of their own set at the head of affairs;" and I suppose no good democrat would see that without pleasure. Moreover, Eubulus was of popular character. In one respect he seems to have resembled your own "heathen Chinee;" he had "guileless ways," says our historian, "in which the citizens took pleasure." He was also a good speaker, a thorough man of business; and, above all, he was very skilful in matters of finance. His administration was both popular and prosperous. We should certainly have said, most of us, if we had encountered somebody announcing his resolve to stand aside under a wall during such an administration, that he was a goose for his pains; and if he had called it "a falling among wild beasts" to have to live with his fellow citizens who had confidence in Eubulus, their country, and themselves, we should have esteemed him very impertinent.

Yes; and yet at the close of that administration of Eubulus came the collapse, and the end of Athens as an independent state. And it was to the fault of Athens herself that the collapse was owing. Plato was right after all; the majority were bad, and the remnant were impotent.

So fared it with that famous Athenian state, with the brilliant people of art and intellect. Now let us turn to the people of religion. We have heard Plato speaking of the very small remnant which honestly sought wisdom. The remnant! it is the word of the Hebrew prophets also, and especially is it the word of the greatest of them all, Isaiah. Not used with the despondency of Plato, used with far other power informing it, and with a far other future awaiting it, filled with fire, filled with hope, filled with faith, filled with joy, this term itself, the remnant, is yet Isaiah's term as well as Plato's. The texts are familiar to all Christendom. "Though thy people Israel be as the sand of the sea, only a remnant of them shall return." Even this remnant, a tenth of the whole, if so it may be, shall have to come back into the purging fire, and be again cleared and further reduced there. But nevertheless,

" as a terebinth-tree, and as an oak, whose substance is in them, though they be cut down, so the stock of that burned tenth shall be a holy seed."

Yes, the small remnant should be a holy seed; but the great majority, as in democratic Athens, so in the kingdoms of the Hebrew nation, were unsound, and their state was doomed. This was Isaiah's point. The actual commonwealth of the "drunkards" and the "blind," as he calls them, in Israel and Judah, of the dissolute grandees and gross and foolish common people, of the great majority, must perish; its perishing was the necessary stage towards a happier future. And Isaiah was right, as Plato was right. No doubt to most of us, if we had been there to see it, the kingdom of Ephraim or of Judah, the society of Samaria and Jerusalem, would have seemed to contain a great deal else besides dissolute grandees and foolish common people. No doubt we should have thought parts of their policy serious, and some of their alliances promising. No doubt, when we read the Hebrew prophets now, with the larger and more patient temper of a different race and an augmented experience, we often feel the blame and invective to be too absolute. Nevertheless, as to his grand point, Isaiah, I say, was right. The majority in the Jewish state, whatever they might think or say, whatever their guides and flatterers might think or say, the majority were unsound, and their unsoundness must be their ruin.

Isaiah, however, does not make his remnant confine itself, like Plato's, to standing aside under a wall during this life and then departing in mild temper and good hope when the time for departure comes; Isaiah's remnant saves the state. Undoubtedly he means to represent it as doing so. Undoubtedly he imagines his prince of the house of David who is to be born within a year's time, his royal and victorious Immanuel, he imagines him witnessing as a child the chastisement of Ephraim and the extirpation of the bad majority there; then witnessing as a youth the chastisement of Judah and the extirpation of the bad majority there also; but finally, in mature life, reigning over a state renewed, preserved, and enlarged, a greater and happier kingdom of the chosen people.

Undoubtedly Isaiah conceives his remnant in this wise; undoubtedly he imagined for it a part which, in strict truth, it did not play, and could not play. So manifest was the non-fulfilment of his prophecy, taken strictly, that ardent souls feeding upon his words had to wrest them from their natural meaning, and to say that Isaiah directly meant something which he did not directly mean. Isaiah, like Plato, with inspired insight, foresaw that the world before his eyes, the world of actual life, the state and city of the unsound majority, could not stand. Unlike Plato, Isaiah announced with faith and joy a leader and a remnant certain to supersede them. But he put the leader's coming, and he put the success of the leader's and the remnant's work far, far too soon; and his conception, in this respect, is fantastic. Plato betook himself for the bringing in of righteousness to a visionary republic in the clouds; Isaiah,— and it is the immortal glory of him and of his race to have done so,— brought it in upon earth. But Immanuel and his reign, for the eighth century before Christ, were fantastic. For the kingdom of Judah they were fantastic. Immanuel and the remnant could not come to reign under the conditions there and then offered to them; the thing was impossible.

The reason of the impossibility is quite simple. The scale of things, in petty states like Judah and Athens, is too small; the numbers are too scanty. Admit that for the world, as we hitherto know it, what the philosophers and prophets say is true: that the majority are unsound. Even in communities with exceptional gifts, even in the Jewish state, the Athenian state, the majority are unsound. But there is "the remnant." Now the important thing, as regards states such as Judah and Athens, is not that the remnant bears but a small proportion to the majority; the remnant always bears a small proportion to the majority. The grave thing for states like Judah and Athens is, that the remnant must in positive bulk be so small, and therefore so powerless for reform. To be a voice outside the state, speaking to mankind or to the future, perhaps shaking the actual state to pieces in doing so, one man will suffice. But to reform the state in order to save it, to preserve it by changing it, a body of workers is needed as well as a leader; a considerable body of workers, placed at many points, and operating in many directions. This considerable body of workers for good is what is wanting in petty states such as were Athens and Judah. It is said that the Athenian state had in all but 350,000 inhabitants. It is calculated that the population of the kingdom of Judah did not exceed a million and a quarter. The scale of things, I say, is here too small, the numbers are too scanty, to give us a remnant capable of saving and perpetuating the community. The remnant, in these cases, may influence the world and the future, may transcend the state and survive it; but it cannot possibly transform the state and perpetuate the state; for such a work it is numerically too feeble.

Plato saw the impossibility. Isaiah refused to accept it, but facts were too strong for him. The Jewish state could not be renewed and saved, and he was wrong in thinking that it could. And therefore I call his grand point this other, where he was altogether right: that the actual world of the unsound majority, though it fancied itself solid, and though most men might call it solid, could not stand. Let us read him again and again, until we fix in our minds this true conviction of his, to edify us whenever we see such a world existing: his indestructible conviction that such a world, with its prosperities, idolatries, oppression, luxury, pleasures, drunkards, careless women, governing classes, systems of policy, strong alliances, shall come to nought and pass away; that nothing can save it. Let us do homage, also, to his indestructible conviction that states are saved by their righteous remnant, however clearly we may at the same time recognize that his own building on this conviction was premature.

That, however, matters to us little. For how different is the scale of things in the modern states to which we belong, how far greater are the numbers! It is impossible to overrate the importance of the new element introduced into our calculations by increasing the size of the remnant. And in our great modern states, where the scale of things is so large, it does seem as if the remnant might be so increased as to become an actual power, even though the majority be unsound. Then the lover of wisdom may come out from under his wall, the lover of goodness will not be alone among the wild beasts. To enable the remnant to succeed, a large strengthening of its numbers is everything.

Here is good hope for us, not only, as for Plato's recluse, in departing this life, but while we live and work in it. Only, before we dwell too much on this hope, it is advisable to make sure that we have earned the right to entertain it. We have earned the right to entertain it, only when we are at one with the philosophers and prophets in their conviction respecting the world which now is, the world of the unsound majority; when we feel what they mean, and when we go thoroughly along with them in it. Most of us, as I have said already, would by no means have been with them when they were here in life, and most of us are not really with them now. What is saving? Our institutions, says an American; the British constitution, says an Englishman; the civilizing mission of France, says a Frenchman. But Plato and the sages, when they are asked what is saving, answer: "To love righteousness and to be convinced of the unprofitableness of iniquity." And Isaiah and the prophets, when they are asked the same question, answer to just the same effect: that what is saving is to "order one's conversation right;" to "cease to do evil;" to "delight in the law of the Eternal;" and to "make one's study in it all day long."

The worst of it is, that this loving of righteousness and this delighting in the law of the Eternal sound rather vague to us. Not that they are vague really; indeed, they are less vague than American institutions, or the British constitution, or the civilizing mission of France. But the phrases sound vague because of the quantity of matters they cover. The thing is to have a brief but adequate enumeration of these matters. The New Testament tells us how righteousness is composed. In England and America we have been brought up in familiarity with the New Testament. And so, before Mr. Bradlaugh on our side of the water, and the congress of American Freethinkers on yours, banish it from our education and memory, let us take from the New Testament a text showing what it is that both Plato and the prophets mean when they tell us that we ought to love righteousness and to make our study in the law of the Eternal, but that the unsound majority do nothing of the kind. A score of texts offer themselves in a moment. Here is one which will serve very well: " Whatsoever things are true, whatsoever things are elevated, whatsoever things are just, whatsoever things are pure, whatsoever things are amiable, whatsoever things are of good report; if there be any virtue, and if there be any praise; have these in your mind, let your thoughts run upon these." That is what both Plato and the prophets mean by loving righteousness, and making one's study in the law of the Eternal.

Now the matters just enumerated do not come much into the heads of most of us, I suppose, when we are thinking of politics. But the philosophers and prophets maintain that these matters, and not those of which the heads of politicians are full, do really govern politics and save or destroy states. They save or destroy them by a silent, inexorable fatality; while the politicians are making believe, plausibly and noisily, with their American institutions, British constitution, and civilizing mission of France. And because these matters are what do really govern politics and save or destroy states, Socrates maintained that in his time he and a few philosophers, who alone kept insisting on the good of righteousness and the unprofitableness of iniquity, were the only real politicians then living.

I say, if we are to derive comfort from the doctrine of the remnant (and there is a great comfort to be derived from it), we must also hold fast to the austere but true doctrine as to what really governs politics, overrides with an inexorable fatality the combinations of the so-called politicians, and saves or destroys states. Having in mind things true, things elevated, things just, things pure, things amiable, things of good report; having these in mind, studying and loving these, is what saves states.

There is nothing like positive instances to illustrate general propositions of this kind, and to make them believed. I hesitate to take an instance from America. Possibly there are some people who think that already, on a former occasion, I have said enough about America without duly seeing and knowing it. So I will take my instances from England, and from England's neighbor and old co-mate in history, France. The instance from England I will take first. I will take it from the grave topic of England's relations with Ireland. I am not going to reproach either England or Ireland. To reproach Ireland here would probably be indiscreet. As to England, anything I may have to say against my own countrymen I prefer to say at home; America is the last place where I should care to say it. However, I have no wish or intention now to reproach either the English or the Irish. But I want to show you from England's relations with Ireland how right the philosophers and prophets are. Every one knows that there has been conquest and confiscation in Ireland. So there has elsewhere. Every one knows that the conquest and the confiscation have been attended with cupidity, oppression, and ill-usage. So they have elsewhere. "Whatsoever things are just" are not exactly the study, so far as I know, of conquerors and confiscators anywhere; certainly they were not the study of the English conquerors of Ireland. A failure in justice is a source of danger to states. But it may be made up for and got over; it has been made up for and got over in many communities. England's confiscations in Ireland are a thing of the past; the penal laws against Catholics are a thing of the past; much has been done to make up for the old failure in justice; Englishmen generally think that it has been pretty well made up for, and that Irishmen ought to think so too. And politicians invent Land Acts for curing the last results of the old failure in justice, for insuring the contentment of the Irish with us, and for consolidating

the Union: and are surprised and plaintive if it is not con-
solidated. But now see how much more serious people are
the philosophers and prophets than the politicians. Whatsoever things are amiable! — the failure in amiability, too, is
a source of danger and insecurity to states, as well as the failure in justice. And we English are not amiable, or at any
rate, what in this case comes to the same thing, do not appear
so. The politicians never thought of that! Quite outside
their combinations lies this hindrance, tending to make their
most elaborate combinations ineffectual. Thus the joint
operation of two moral causes together,— the sort of causes
which politicians do not seriously regard,— tells against the
designs of the politicians with what seems to be an almost
inexorable fatality. If there were not the failure in amiability, perhaps the original failure in justice might by this time
have been got over; if there had not been the failure in justice,
perhaps the failure in amiability might not have mattered
much. The two failures together create a difficulty almost
insurmountable. Public men in England keep saying that
it will be got over. I hope that it will be got over, and that
the union between England and Ireland may become as solid
as that between England and Scotland. But it will not
become solid by means of the contrivances of the mere politician, or without the intervention of moral causes of concord
to heal the mischief wrought by moral causes of division.
Everything, in this case, depends upon the "remnant," its
numbers and its powers of action.

My second instance is even more important. It is so important, and its reach is so wide, that I must go into it with some
little fulness. The instance is taken from France. To
France I have always felt myself powerfully drawn. People
in England often accuse me of liking France and things

French far too well.   At all events I have paid special regard to them, and am always glad to confess how much I owe to them. M. Sainte-Beuve wrote to me in the last years of his life: " Vous avez traversé notre vie et notre littérature par une ligne intérieure, profonde, qui fait les initiés, et que vous ne perdrez jamais." [1]   I wish I could think that this friendly testimony of that accomplished and charming man, one of my chief benefactors, were fully deserved.   But I have pride and pleasure in quoting it; and I quote it to bear me out in saying, that whatever opinion I may express about France, I have at least been a not inattentive observer of that great country, and anything but a hostile one.

The question was once asked by the town clerk of Ephesus: " What man is there that knoweth not how that the city of the Ephesians is a worshipper of the great goddess Diana? " Now really, when one looks at the popular literature of the French at this moment,— their popular novels, popular stage plays, popular newspapers,— and at the life which this literature of theirs is the index, one is tempted to make a goddess out of a word of their own, and then, like the town clerk of Ephesus, to ask: " What man is there that knoweth not how that the city of the French is a worshipper of the great goddess Lubricity? "   Or rather, as Greek is the classic and euphonious language for names of gods and goddesses, let us take her name from the Greek Testament, and call her the goddess Aselgeia.   That goddess has always been a sufficient power amongst mankind, and her worship was generally supposed to need restraining rather than encouraging.   But here is now a whole popular literature, nay, and art too, in France at her service! stimulations and suggestions by her and to her

---

[1] "You have passed through our life and literature by a deep inner line, which confers initiation, and which you will never lose."

meet one in it at every turn. She is becoming the great recognized power there; never was anything like it. M. Renan himself seems half inclined to apologize for not having paid her more attention. "Nature cares nothing for chastity," says he; "*Les frivoles ont peutêtre raison.*"[1] Men even of this force salute her; but the allegiance now paid to her, in France, by the popular novel, the popular newspaper, the popular play, is, one may say, boundless.

I have no wish at all to preach to the French; no intention whatever, in what I now say, to upbraid or wound them. I simply lay my finger on a fact in their present condition; a fact insufficiently noticed, as it seems to me, and yet extremely potent for mischief. It is well worth while to trace the manner of its growth and action.

The French have always had a leaning to the goddess of whom we speak, and have been willing enough to let the world know of their leaning, to pride themselves on their Gaulish salt, their gallantry, and so on. But things have come to their present head gradually. Catholicism was an obstacle; the serious element in the nation was another obstacle. But now just see the course which things have taken, and how they all, one may say, have worked together for this goddess. First, there was the original Gaul, the basis of the French nation; the Gaul, gay, sociable, quick of sentiment, quick of perception; apt, however, very apt, to be presumptuous and puffed up. Then came the Roman conquest, and from this we get a new personage, the Gallo-Latin; with the Gaulish qualities for a basis, but with Latin order, reason, lucidity, added, and also Latin sensuality. Finally, we have the Frankish conquest and the Frenchman. The Frenchman proper is the Gallo-Latin, with Frankish or Germanic qualities added and

---

[1] "The gay people are perhaps in the right."

infused. No mixture could be better. The Germans have plenty of faults, but in this combination they seem not to have taken hold; the Germans seem to have given of their seriousness and honesty to the conquered Gallo-Latin, and not of their brutality. And mediæval France, which exhibits the combination and balance, under the influence then exercised by Catholicism, of Gaulish quickness and gaiety with Latin rationality and German seriousness, offers to our view the soundest and the most attractive stage, perhaps, in all French history.

But the balance could not be maintained; at any rate, it was not maintained. Mediæval Catholicism lost its virtue. The serious Germanic races made the Reformation, feeling that without it there was no safety and continuance for those moral ideas which they loved and which were the ground of their being. France did not go with the Reformation; the Germanic qualities in her were not strong enough to make her go with it. " France did not want a reformation which was a moral one," [1] is Michelet's account of the matter. Let us put the case more favorably for her, and say that perhaps, with her quick perception, France caught sense, from the very outset, of that intellectual unsoundness and incompleteness in the Reformation, which is now so visible. But, at any rate, the Reformation did not carry France with it; and the Germanic side in the Frenchman, his Germanic qualities, thus received a check. They subsisted, however, in good force still; the new knowledge and new ideas, brought by the revival of letters, gave an animating stimulus; and in the seventeenth century the Gaulish gaiety and quickness of France, the Latin rationality, and the still subsisting German seriousness, all combining under the puissant breath of the Renascence, pro-

---

[1] " La France ne voulait pas de réforme morale."

duced a literature, the strongest, the most substantial and the most serious which the French have ever succeeded in producing, and which has, indeed, consummate and splendid excellences.

Still, the Germanic side in the Frenchman had received a check, and in the next century this side became quite attenuated. The Germanic steadiness and seriousness gave way more and more; the Gaulish salt, the Gaulish gaiety, quickness, sentiment, and sociability, the Latin rationality, prevailed more and more, and had the field nearly to themselves. They produced a brilliant and most efficacious literature,— the French literature of the eighteenth century. The goddess Aselgeia had her part in it; it was a literature to be praised with reserve; it was, above all, a revolutionary literature. But European institutions were then in such a superannuated condition, straightforward and just perception, free thought and rationality, were at such a discount, that the brilliant French literature in which these qualities predominated, and which by their predominance was made revolutionary, had in the eighteenth century a great mission to fulfil, and fulfilled it victoriously.

The mission is fulfilled, but meanwhile the Germanic quality in the Frenchman seems pretty nearly to have died out, and the Gallo-Latin in him has quite got the upper hand. Of course there are individuals and groups who are to be excepted; I will allow any number of exceptions you please; and in the mass of the French people, which works and is silent, there may be treasures of resource. But taking the Frenchman who is commonly in view — the usual type of speaking, doing, vocal, visible Frenchman — we may say, and he will probably be not at all displeased at our saying, that the German in him has nearly died out, and the Gallo-Latin has quite got the upper hand. For us, however, this means that the chief source of seriousness and of moral ideas is failing and drying up in him, and that what remains are the sources of Gaulish salt, and quickness, and sentiment, and sociability, and sensuality, and rationality. And, of course, the play and working of these qualities is altered by their being no longer in combination with a dose of German seriousness, but left to work by themselves. Left to work by themselves, they give us what we call the *homme sensuel moyen,* the average sensual man. The highest art, the art which by its height, depth, and gravity possesses religiousness,— such as the Greeks had, the art of Pindar and Phidias; such as the Italians had, the art of Dante and Michael Angelo,— this art, with the training which it gives and the standard which it sets up, the French have never had. On the other hand, they had a dose of German seriousness, a Germanic bent for ideas of moral duty, which neither the Greeks had, nor the Italians. But if this dies out, what is left is the *homme sensuel moyen.* This average sensual man has his very advantageous qualities. He has his gaiety, quickness, sentiment, sociability, rationality. He has his horror of sour strictness, false restraint, hypocrisy, obscurantism, cretinism, and the rest of it. And this is very well; but on the serious, moral side he is almost ludicrously insufficient. Fine sentiments about his dignity and his honor and his heart, about the dignity and the honor and the heart of France, and his adoration of her, do duty for him here; grandiose phrases about the spectacle offered in France and in the French republic of the ideal for our race, of the *épanouissement de l'élite de l'humanité.*[1] In M. Victor Hugo we have (his worshippers must forgive me for saying so) the average sensual man impassioned and grandiloquent;

[1] The coming into blow of the choice flower of humanity.

in M. Zola we have the average sensual man going near the ground. "Happy the son," cries M. Victor Hugo, "of whom one can say, 'He has consoled his mother!' Happy the poet of whom one can say, 'He has consoled his country!'" The French themselves, even when they are severest, call this kind of thing by only the mild name of emphasis, "*emphase*,"— other people call it fustian. And a surly Johnson will growl out in answer, at one time, that "Patriotism is the last refuge of a scoundrel;" at another time, that fine sentiments about "me mère" are the last refuge of a scoundrel. But what they really are is the creed which in France the average sensual man rehearses, to do duty for serious moral ideas. And, as the result, we have a popular literature and a popular art serving, as has been already said, the goddess Aselgeia.

Such an art and literature easily make their way everywhere. In England and America the French literature of the seventeenth century is peculiarly fitted to do great good, and nothing but good; it can hardly be too much studied by us. And it is studied by us very little. The French literature of the eighteenth century, also, has qualities to do us much good, and we are not likely to take harm from its other qualities; we may study it to our great profit and advantage. And it is studied by us very little. The higher French literature of the present day has more knowledge and a wider range than its great predecessors, but less soundness and perfection, and it exerts much less influence than they did. Action and influence are now with the lower literature of France, with the popular literature in the service of the goddess Aselgeia. And this popular modern French literature, and the art which corresponds to it, bid fair to make their way in England and America far better than their predecessors. They appeal to instincts so universal and accessible; they appeal, people are beginning boldly to say, to Nature herself.   Few things have lately struck me more than M. Renan's dictum, which I have already quoted, about what used to be called the virtue of chastity.   The dictum occurs in his very interesting autobiography published but the other day.   M. Renan, whose genius I unfeignedly admire, is, I need hardly say, a man of the most perfect propriety of life; he has told us so himself.   He was brought up for a priest, and he thinks it would not have been in good taste for him to become a free liver.   But this abstinence is a mere matter of personal delicacy, a display of good and correct taste on his own part in his own very special circumstances.   "Nature," he cries, "cares nothing about chastity."   What a slap in the face to the sticklers for "Whatsoever things are pure!"

I have had to take a long sweep to arrive at the point which I wished to reach.   If we are to enjoy the benefit, I said, of the comfortable doctrine of the remnant, we must be capable of receiving also, and of holding fast, the hard doctrine of the unsoundness of the majority, and of the certainty that the unsoundness of the majority, if it is not withstood and remedied, must be their ruin.   And therefore, even though a gifted man like M. Renan may be so carried away by the tide of opinion in France where he lives, as to say that nature cares nothing about chastity, and to see with amused indulgence the worship of the great goddess Lubricity, let us stand fast, and say that her worship is against nature, human nature, and that it is ruin.   For this is the test of its being against human nature, that for human societies it is ruin.   And the test is one from which there is no escape, as from the old tests in such matters there may be.   For if you allege that it is the will of God that we should be pure, the sceptical Gallo-Latins will tell you that they do not know any such person.   And in

like manner, if it is said that those who serve the goddess
Aselgeia shall not inherit the kingdom of God, the Gallo-
Latin may tell you that he does not believe in any such place.
But that the sure tendency and upshot of things establishes
that the service of the goddess Aselgeia is ruin, that her followers are marred and stunted by it and disqualified for the
ideal society of the future, is an infallible test to employ.

The saints admonish us to let our thoughts run upon whatsoever things are pure, if we would inherit the kingdom of
God; and the divine Plato tells us that we have within us a
many-headed beast and a man, and that by dissoluteness we
feed and strengthen the beast in us and starve the man; and
finally, following the divine Plato among the sages at a humble distance, comes the prosaic and unfashionable Paley, and
says in his precise way that " this vice has a tendency, which
other species of vice have not so directly, to unsettle and
weaken the powers of the understanding; as well as, I think,
in a greater degree than other vices, to render the heart thoroughly corrupt." True; and once admitted and fostered, it
eats like a canker, and with difficulty can ever be brought to
let go its hold again, but forever tightens it. Hardness and
insolence come in its train; an insolence which grows until it
ends by exasperating and alienating everybody; a hardness
which grows until the man can at last scarcely take pleasure
in anything, outside the service of his goddess, except cupidity
and greed, and cannot be touched with emotion by any language except fustian. Such are the fruits of the worship of
the great goddess Aselgeia.

So, instead of saying that nature cares nothing about chastity, let us say that human nature, our nature, cares about it
a great deal. Let us say that, by her present popular literature, France gives proof that she is suffering from a dangerous

and perhaps fatal disease; and that it is not clericalism which is the real enemy to the French so much as their goddess; and if they can none of them see this themselves, it is only a sign of how far the disease has gone, and the case is so much the worse. The case is so much the worse; and for men in such case to be so vehemently busy about clerical and dynastic intrigues at home, and about alliances and colonial acquisitions and purifications of the flag abroad, might well make one borrow of the prophets and exclaim, "Surely ye are perverse!" perverse to neglect your really pressing matters for those secondary ones. And when the ingenious and inexhaustible M. Blowitz, of our great London "Times," who sees everybody and knows everything, when he expounds the springs of politics and the causes of the fall and success of ministries, and the combinations which have not been tried but should be, and takes upon him the mystery of things in the way with which we are so familiar,—to this wise man himself one is often tempted, again, to say with the prophets: "Yet the Eternal also is wise, and will not call back his words." M. Blowitz is not the only wise one; the Eternal has his wisdom also, and somehow or other it is always the Eternal's wisdom which at last carries the day. The Eternal has attached to certain moral causes the safety or the ruin of states, and the present popular literature of France is a sign that she has a most dangerous moral disease.

Now if the disease goes on and increases, then, whatever sagacious advice M. Blowitz may give, and whatever political combinations may be tried, and whether France gets colonies or not, and whether she allies herself with this nation or with that, things will only go from bad to worse with her; she will more and more lose her powers of soul and spirit, her intellectual productiveness, her skill in counsel, her might for war,

her formidableness as a foe, her value as an ally, and the life
of that famous state will be more and more impaired, until it
perish. And this is that hard but true doctrine of the sages
and prophets, of the inexorable fatality of operation, in moral
failure of the unsound majority, to impair and destroy states.
But we will not talk or think of destruction for a state with
such gifts and graces as France, and which has had such a
place in history, and to which we, many of us, owe so much
delight and so much good. And yet if France had no greater
numbers than the Athens of Plato or the Judah of Isaiah, I
do not see how she could well escape out of the throttling
arms of her goddess and recover. She must recover through
a powerful and profound renewal, a great inward change,
brought about by " the remnant " amongst her people; and,
for this, a remnant small in numbers would not suffice. But
in a France of thirty-five millions, who shall set bounds to the
numbers of the remnant, or to its effectualness and power of
victory?

In these United States (for I come round to the United
States at last) you are fifty millions and more. I suppose that,
as in England, as in France, as everywhere, so likewise
here, the majority of people doubt very much whether the
majority is unsound; or, rather, they have no doubt at all
about the matter, they are sure that it is not unsound. But
let us consent to-night to remain to the end in the ideas of the
sages and prophets whom we have been following all along;
and let us suppose that in the present actual stage of the world,
as in all the stages through which the world has passed
hitherto, the majority is and must be in general unsound
everywhere,— even in the United States, even here in New
York itself. Where is the failure. I have already, in the
past, speculated in the abstract about you, perhaps, too much.

But I suppose that in a democratic community like this, with its newness, its magnitude, its strength, its life of business, its sheer freedom and equality, the danger is in the absence of the discipline of respect; in hardness and materialism, exaggeration and boastfulness; in a false smartness, a false audacity, a want of soul and delicacy. "Whatsoever things are elevated,"— whatsoever things are nobly serious, have true elevation,— that perhaps, in our catalogue of maxims which are to possess the mind, is the maxim which points to where the failure of the unsound majority, in a great democracy like yours, will probably lie. At any rate let us for the moment agree to suppose so. And the philosophers and the prophets, whom I at any rate am disposed to believe, and who say that moral causes govern the standing and the falling of states, will tell us that the failure to mind whatsoever things are elevated must impair with an inexorable fatality the life of a nation, just as the failure to mind whatsoever things are just, or whatsoever things are amiable, or whatsoever things are pure, will impair it; and that if the failure to mind whatsoever things are elevated should be real in your American democracy, and should grow into a disease, and take firm hold on you, then the life of even these great United States must inevitably suffer and be impaired more and more, until it perish.

Then from this hard doctrine we will betake ourselves to the more comfortable doctrine of the remnant. "The remnant shall return;" shall "convert and be healed" itself first, and shall then recover the unsound majority. And you are fifty millions and growing apace. What a remnant yours may be, surely! A remnant of how great numbers, how mighty strength, how irresistible efficacy! Yet we must not go too fast, either, nor make too sure of our efficacious remnant. Mere multitude will not give us a saving remnant with certainty. The Assyrian empire had multitude, the Roman empire had multitude; yet neither the one nor the other could produce a sufficing remnant any more than Athens or Judah could produce it, and both Assyria and Rome perished like Athens and Judah.

But you are something more than a people of fifty millions. You are fifty millions mainly sprung, as we in England are mainly sprung, from that German stock which has faults indeed,— faults which have diminished the extent of its influence, diminished its power of attraction and the interest of its history, and which seems moreover just now, from all I can see and hear, to be passing through a not very happy moment, morally, in Germany proper. Yet of the German stock it is, I think, true, as my father said more than fifty years ago, that it has been a stock " of the most moral races of men that the world has yet seen, with the soundest laws, the least violent passions, the fairest domestic and civil virtues." You come, therefore, of about the best parentage which a modern nation can have. Then you have had, as we in England have also had, but more entirely than we and more exclusively, the Puritan discipline. Certainly I am not blind to the faults of that discipline. Certainly I do not wish it to remain in possession of the field forever, or too long. But as a stage and a discipline, and as means for enabling that poor inattentive and immoral creature, man, to love and appropriate and make part of his being divine ideas, on which he could not otherwise have laid or kept hold, the discipline of Puritanism has been invaluable; and the more I read history, the more I see of mankind, the more I recognize its value. Well, then, you are not merely a multitude of fifty millions; you are fifty millions sprung from this excellent Germanic stock, having passed through this excellent Puritan discipline, and set in this enviable and unbounded country. Even supposing, therefore, that by the necessity of things your majority must in the present stage of the world probably be unsound, what a remnant, I say,— what an incomparable, all-transforming remnant,— you may fairly hope with your numbers, if things go happily, to have!

HALE

EDWARD EVERETT HALE, a distinguished American Unitarian clergyman, was born in Boston, Massachusetts, April 3, 1822, and educated at Harvard University. While preparing himself to enter the Unitarian ministry he taught for two years in the Boston Latin School and in 1842 was licensed to preach. From 1846 to 1856 he was pastor of the Church of the Unity in Worcester, Massachusetts, and pastor of the South Congregational (Unitarian) Church in Boston, 1856-1900. Throughout his entire career he has been active in philanthropic and educational movements. He edited " Old and New," a monthly magazine, 1869-75, and from 1886 to the present has edited " Lend a Hand," a journal of organized charity. In 1870 he published " Ten Times One is Ten," a story which led to the formation of many charitable clubs throughout the United States. As a writer of short stories he has gained a very extended reputation, the most noted of these being " The Man Without a Country," which at the time of its issue in 1863 did very much to stimulate a feeling of patriotism; " In His Name," " My Double and How He Undid Me." He has been a voluminous as well as versatile writer and among his many books may be named " The Ingham Papers " (1869); " His Level Best and Other Stories " (1870); " Ups and Downs," a novel (1871); " Philip Nolan's Friends " (1876); " Franklin in France " (1887); " Life of Washington " (1887); " For Fifty Years," a collection of verse (1893); " A New England Boyhood," autobiographic in its nature (1893); " Lowell and His Friends " (1899). His collected works are issued in twelve volumes.

NEW ENGLAND CULTURE

ADDRESS AT THE BANQUET OF THE NEW ENGLAND SOCIETY, DECEMBER 22, 1876

MR. PRESIDENT AND GENTLEMEN,— You seem to have a very frank way of talking about each other among yourselves here. I observe that I am the first stranger who has crossed the river, which, I recollect Edward Winslow says, divides the continent of New England from the continent of America, and, as a stranger, it is my pleasure and duty at once to express the thanks and congratulations of the invited guests here for the distinguished care which has been taken on this occasion outdoors to make us feel entirely at home. As I came down in the snow-storm, I could not help feeling that Elder Brewster, and William Bradford, and Carver, and Winslow, could not have done better than this in Plymouth; and, indeed, as I ate my pork and beans just now, I felt that the gospel of New England is extending beyond the Connecticut to other nations, and that what is good to eat and drink in Boston is good to eat and drink even here on this benighted point at Delmonico's.

When you talk to us about "culture," that is rather a dangerous word. I am always a little afraid of the word "culture." I recollect the very brightest squib that I read in the late election campaign — and, as the President says, gentlemen, I am going to respect the proprieties of the occasion. It was sent to one of the journals from the western reserve, and the writer, who, if I have rightly guessed his name, is one of the most brilliant of our younger poets, was descanting on the Chinook vocabulary, in which a Chinook calls an Englishman a Chinchog to this day, in memory of King George. And this writer says that when they have a young chief whose war-paint is very perfect, whose blanket is thoroughly embroidered, whose leggins are tied up with exactly the right colors, and who has the right kind of a star upon his forehead and cheeks, but who never took a scalp, never fired an arrow, and never smelled powder, but was always found at home in the lodges whenever there was anything that scented of war — he says the Chinooks called that man by the name of "Boston Cultus."

Well, now, gentlemen, what are you laughing at? Why do you laugh? Some of you had Boston fathers, and more of you had Boston mothers. Why do you laugh? Ah! you

have seen these people, as I have seen them, as everybody
has seen them — people who sat in Parker's and discussed
every movement of the campaign in the late war, and told
us that it was all wrong, that we were going to the bad, but
who never shouldered a musket. They are people who tell
us that the emigration, that the Pope of Rome, or the German element, or the Irish element, is going to play the dogs
with our social system, and yet they never met an emigrant
on the wharf or had a word of comfort to say to a foreigner.
We have those people in Boston. You may not have them
in New York, and I am very glad if you have not; but if
you are so fortunate, it is the only place on God's earth
where I have not found such people. But there is another
kind of culture which began even before there was any
Boston — for there was such a day as that. There were
ten years in the history of this world, ten long years, too,
before Boston existed, and those are the years between
Plymouth Rock and the day when some unfortunate men,
not able to get to Plymouth Rock, stopped and founded that
city. This earlier culture is a culture not of the school-
house, or of the tract, but a culture as well of the church,
of history, of the town meeting, as John Adams says; that
nobler culture to which my friend on the right has alluded
when he says that it is born of the Spirit of God — the culture which has made New England, which is born of God,
and which it is our mission to carry over the world.

In the very heart of that culture — representing it, as I
think, in a very striking way, half way back to the day we
celebrate — Ezra Styles, one of the old Connecticut men,
published a semi-centennial address. It seems strange that
they should have centennials then, but they had. He published a semi-centennial address in the middle of the last

century, on the condition of New England, and the prospects before her. He prophesied what New England was to be in the year 1852. He calculated the population descending from the twenty thousand men who emigrated in the beginning, and he calculated it with great accuracy.

He said: " There will be seven million men, women and children, descended from the men who came over with Winslow and with Winthrop," and it proved that he was perfectly right. He went on to sketch the future of New England when these seven million should crowd her hillsides, her valleys, her farms, and her shops all over the four States of New England. For it didn't occur to him, as he looked forward, that one man of them all would ever go west of Connecticut, or west of Massachusetts.

He cast his horoscope for a population of seven million people living in the old New England States, in the midst of this century. He did not read, as my friend here does, the missionary spirit of New England. He did not know that they would be willing to go across the arm of the ocean which separated the continent of New England from the continent of America. All the same, gentlemen, seven million people are somewhere, and they have not forgotten the true lessons which make New England what she is. They tell me there are more men of New England descent in San Francisco than in Boston to-day. All of those carried with them their mothers' lessons, and they mean their mothers' lessons shall bear fruit away out in Oregon, in California, in South Carolina, in Louisiana.

They have those mothers' lessons to teach them to do something of what we are trying to do at home in this matter. We have been so fortunate in New England in this centennial year that we are able to dedicate a noble monument of the past to the eternal memory of the Pilgrim principle. We have been so fortunate that we are able to consecrate the old South Meeting House in Boston to the cause of fostering this Pilgrim principle, that it may be from this time forward a monument, not of one branch of the Christian religion, not of one sect or another, but of that universal religion, that universal patriotism, which has made America and which shall maintain America.

For myself, I count it providential that in this centennial year of years this venerable monument, that monument whose bricks and rafters are all eloquent of religion and liberty, that that monument has passed from the possession of one sect and one State to belong to the whole nation, to be consecrated to American liberty, and to nothing but American liberty.

I need not say — for it is taken for granted when such things are spoken of — that when it was necessary for New England to act at once for the security of this great monument, we had the active aid and hearty assistance of the people of New York, who came to us and helped us and carried that thing right through. I am surrounded here with the people who had to do with the preservation of that great monument for the benefit of the history of this country forever.

Let me say, in one word, what purposes it is proposed this great monument shall serve, for I think they are entirely in line with what we are to consider to-night. We propose to establish here what I might fairly call a university for the study of the true history of this country. And we propose, in the first place, to make that monument of the past a great Santa Croce, containing the statues and portraits of the men who have made this country what it is. Then we propose to establish an institute for the people of America, from Maine to San Francisco, the people of every national- ity and every name; and we hope that such societies as this, and all others interested in the progress and preserva- tion of the interests of our country, will aid us in the work.

For we believe that the great necessity of this hour is that higher education in which this people shall know God's work with man. We hope that the Forefathers' societies, the Sam Adams' clubs, the Centennial clubs over the land, shall make the State more proud of its fathers, and more sure of the lessons which they lived. We mean by the spoken voice and by the most popular printed word, circu- lated everywhere, to instil into this land that old lesson of New England culture. We stand by the side of those of you who believe in compulsory education. We desire, in looking to the future, that the determination shall be made here by us, as it has been in England, that every child born on American soil shall learn to read and write.

But there is a great deal more to be taught than that. There is a great deal which the common school does not teach and cannot teach, when it teaches men to read. We not only want to teach them to read, but we want to teach them what is worth reading. And we want to instil the principles by which the nation lives. We have got to create in those who came from the other side of the water the same loyalty to the whole of American principles that each man feels to his native country.

What is this constitution for which we have been fight- ing, and which must be preserved? It is a most delicate mutual adjustment of the powers and rights of a nation, among and because of the powers and rights of thirty or forty States. It exists because they exist. That it may stand, you need all their mutual rivalries, you need every sentiment of local pride, you need every symbol and laurel of their old victories and honors. You need just this homestead feeling which to-night we are cherishing.

But that balance is lost, that whole system is thrown out of gear, if the seven million people of foreign parentage here are indifferent to the record of New York as they are to that of Illinois, to that of Illinois as to that of Louisiana, to that of Louisiana as to that of Maine; if they have no local pride; if to them the names of Montgomery, of John Hancock, of Samuel Adams, have no meaning, no association with the past. Unless they also acquire this local feeling, unless they share the pride and reverence of the native American for the State in which he is born, for the history which is his glory, all these delicate balances and combinations are worthless, all your revolving planets fall into your sun! It is the national education in the patriotism of the Fathers, an education addressing itself to every man, woman and child, from Katahdin to the Golden Gate — it is this, and only this, which will insure the perpetuity of your Republic.

Now, gentlemen, if you would like to try an experiment in this matter, go into one of your public schools, next week, and ask what Saratoga was, and you will be told it is a great watering place, where people go to spend money. You will find there is not one in ten who will be able to tell you that there the Hessian was crushed, and foreign bayonets forever driven from the soil of New York. Ask about Brandywine, the place where La Fayette shed his young blood, where a little handful of American troops were defeated, yet, although they were defeated, broke the force of the English army for one critical year. Put the word Brandywine in one of your public schools, and you will see that the pupils laugh at the funny conjunction of the words "brandy" and "wine," but they can tell you nothing about the history which made the name famous. It seems to me it is dangerous to have your children growing up in such ignorance of the past.

How much did they know here about the day when, a short time since, you celebrated the battle of Haarlem Heights, where the British were shown that to land on American soil was not everything? Is it quite safe for your children to grow up in ignorance of your past, while you are looking down upon the century of the future? The great institution we are hoping for in the future is to carry this New England culture above the mere mathematics of life, and to incorporate into all education that nobler culture which made the men who made the revolution, which made the men who have sustained this country.

We shall ask for the solid assistance of all the Forefathers' stock in the country to carry out this great work of national education, and I am quite sure, from what I have seen here to-night, that we shall not ask in vain.

I ought to apologize for speaking so long. I am conscious of the fact that I am a fraud, and I am nothing but a fraud. The truth is, gentlemen (I say this as I am sitting down), I have no business to be here at all. I am not a Pilgrim, nor the son of a Pilgrim, nor the grandson of a Pilgrim; there is not one drop of Pilgrim blood in my veins. I am a "forefather" myself (for I have six children), but I am not the son of a forefather. I had one father; most men have; I have two grandfathers, I have four great-grand-fathers, but I have not four fathers. I want to explain, now, how all this happened, because something is due to me before you put me out of the room. Like most men, I had eight great-great-grandfathers — so have you; so have you. If you run it up, I have got sixty-four great-grandfathers of the grandfathers of my grandfathers, and I have sixty-four great-grandmothers of the grandmothers of my grandmothers. There were one hundred and twenty-eight of these people the day the " Mayflower " sailed. There were one hundred and twenty-eight of them in England eager to come over here, looking forward to this moment, gentlemen, when we meet here at Delmonico's, and they were hoping and praying, every man of them and every woman of them, that I might be here at this table to-night, and they meant me to be; and every one of them would have come here in the " Mayflower " but for Miles Standish, as I will explain. The " Mayflower," you know, started from Holland. They had to go to Holland first to learn the Dutch language. They started from Holland, and they came along the English Channel and stopped at Plymouth in England. They stopped there to get the last edition of the London " Times " for that day, in order that they might bring over early copies to the New York " Tribune " and New York " World."

These ancestors of mine, the legend says, were all on the dock at Plymouth waiting for them. It was a bad night, a very bad night. It fogged as it can only fog in England. They waited on the wharf there two hours, as you wait at the Brooklyn and Jersey ferries, for the " Mayflower " to come along. Methinks I see her now, the " Mayflower " of a forlorn hope, freighted with the prospect of a fertile State and bound across an unknown sea. Her dark and weather-beaten form looms wearily from the deep, when the pilot brings her up at the Plymouth dock, and a hundred and twenty-eight of my ancestors press forward. They were handsome men and fair women. When they all pressed forward, Miles Standish was on hand and met them. He was on board and looked at them. He went back to the governor, and said, " Here are one hundred and twenty-eight of as fine emigrants as I ever saw." " Well," Governor Carver said, " the capacity of the vessel, as prescribed in the emigrant act, is already exceeded." Miles Standish said, " I think we could let them in." The governor said, " No, they cannot come in." Miles Standish went back to the gangway, and said, " You are handsome men, but you can't come in ; " and they had to stand there, every man and every woman of them.

That is the unfortunate reason why I had no ancestors at the landing of the Pilgrims. But my ancestors looked westward still. They stayed in England, praying that they might come, and when Winthrop, ten years afterwards, sailed, he took them all on board, and, if the little State of Massachusetts has done anything to carry out the principles of the men who landed on Plymouth Rock ·in 1620, why, some little part of the credit is due to my humble ancestry.

SONS OF MASSACHUSETTS

FROM AN ORATION DELIVERED AT BOSTON, JULY 5, 1897

I HAVE sometimes feared that in his own city John Hancock is not honored as he should be. Woe to the city which neglects the memory of its great men! I heard with dismay a few days ago that the Sons of the Revolution have not money enough to pay for the bronze statue of Hancock which they have ordered. Why, thanks to Hancock and to the men behind him, there is money enough in Boston to pay for fifty statues in gold to his memory, if the people of to-day understand what independence means to them!

Here was John Hancock, a young merchant of fashion, of family and of wealth — things which in those days were highly considered in Boston. He was surrounded by all the temptations which surround young men of fashion, of family, and of wealth in a provincial city, and Boston was then a provincial city. As things go in such cities, the nephew of a rich merchant surrounded with every indulgence, is not apt to throw himself into what is called rebellion against his king. But such a young gentleman as that, after the lines of rebellion are fairly drawn, when all the world knows what he means, accepts what are the critical positions of selectman and of a Boston member of the House of Assembly.

That means that, at the age of twenty-nine, he accepts the lead of Sam Adams, who is already laying his large plans for the independence of this empire. The royal governors are surprised and distressed. In ways known to such men from that time to this time, they try to separate Hancock from his alliance with the people. He is offered this, and he is offered that, and he refuses the offers. And so, after the battle of Lexington, when George III offers a pardon to almost everybody else in Massachusetts, the two great exceptions are Samuel Adams and John Hancock.

The day when the young Hancock was chosen into the General Assembly, John and Sam Adams happened to meet on the mall at the head of Winter street. They walked up and down the mall, and as they came in sight of Hancock's elegant mansion, the older man said to the younger: "This town has done a wise thing to-day; they have made that young man's fortune their own." And John Adams says more than once that John Hancock was one of the younger men whom Samuel Adams, so to speak, took in training as soon as he saw their ability to serve the Commonwealth. When one remembers that others in the same company were the second Josiah Quincy and Joseph Warren, one sees how great is the compliment implied. There is not a youngster of us all who might not be proud to have been selected as a special friend of freedom, and a possible martyr in her cause, by such a leader as Samuel Adams.

In later life, when there was time to quarrel, the master and his pupil parted. For thirteen years Hancock and Adams were not friends, although George III had written their names in the same line, and so writing, had helped their immortality. But, really, that quarrel is very little to you and me. Because Hancock was a rich man and lived in a palace, and Adams was a poor man, who lived by the scanty profits of his retail shop, we can well see that there might have been petty issues which should part them in daily life. No matter for that. For nothing can part them in the great record of history. That record is that the older man conceived of the Declaration of Independence, and that the younger man, though he had a rope around his neck, was the first to sign that Declaration. Showy and pompous in his daily life, if you please, but he knew the responsibilities of wealth so well that in time of famine, brought on by King George, his agents had the charge of the relief of three hundred families. Short-sighted as to etiquette in his dealings with Washington, you say? But this is because he has the honor of Massachusetts at heart. He will not, by any etiquette, let Massachusetts take a lower place than belongs to her.

John Adams named George Washington, the Virginia colonel, to the command of the American army just before Warren died at Bunker Hill. John Adams writes privately, what he did not say in public, that up to that time, the services and the sacrifices of John Hancock in the cause of the nation had been immeasurably beyond those of George Washington. Time has gone by, and there is fame enough for both of them. But you and I are not going to forget that, when the moment for battle came, and the blow was to be struck which should declare independence, our own John Hancock, bone of our bone and blood of our blood, was found worthy to be named by the side of George Washington.

And by way of showing that wealth is not always vulgar, and that the man of the largest wealth may still be the truest servant of the people, it is worth while to say, in passing, of these two leaders whose names have thus come down together in the history of this day, that George Washington was the richest man in Virginia and John Hancock the richest man in Massachusetts. Such men were not ashamed nor afraid of the probable honor of being the first martyrs when they committed themselves as the fast friends of America.

Massachusetts may refuse her statues if she doubts as to the achievements of her sons, but she does not doubt nor refuse such an honor when it is proposed for John Hancock.

In those days men were praised when they made sacrifices for the nation. Nay, States and towns expected to make sacrifices! I see, now, to my disgust, that every State is expected to stand for itself, and to forget that it is one member of a nation. Hancock knew better. On that great occasion when Washington prepared to bombard and burn Boston, Hancock wrote in words which we will inscribe on the base of his statue: "All my property is there, but may God crown your attempt with success. I most heartily wish it, though individually I may be the greatest sufferer." Such is the motto of statesmen, of States and of their senators.

Mr. Choate said of Virginia that she was "the mother of great men and was not unmindful of her children." The remark is eminently true. But I am apt to think that Massachusetts, the leader in the Revolution, mother of great men, is sometimes unmindful of her children. The truth is that in the birthright of every son of Massachusetts he inherits the duty which is a privilege, or the privilege which is a duty, that first of all he must live to the glory of God. A Massachusetts boy or a Massachusetts man, a Massachusetts girl or a Massachusetts woman, must not live for himself alone — no, nor for herself alone. First of all we live for the common good and for the public service. I say this is ingrain in our make-up; it is a part of our birthright privilege. And so it is that you shall have a man like Robert Treat Paine, a Massachusetts lawyer, who is taken from his daily duty to go to Philadelphia and engage in the direct work of treason. He is sent there, and he goes there; openly and before the world he "devises war against the king." This is the definition of treason.

It is a pity if we forget such men; if we do not, on these great occasions of history or of ceremony, repeat their names and commemorate their service. Here is your type, then, of the Massachusetts lawyer. In that remarkable case in which these people, hot with rebellion, decided the right and wrong of the Boston massacre by the calm methods of a civic trial, Paine appears on the one side and his friend Quincy on the other. He signs the Declaration of Independence; he is the first attorney-general of Massachusetts; he is a judge in the superior court.

I do not wonder, and I do not complain, if, after a century, this honored name brings up, first, the memory of another honored Robert Treat Paine, of our own fellow citizens, who is drawn by the determination to serve mankind into the homes of the poorest, in his relief of those most unfortunate. And further back, such is the magic of song that a thousand men will sing:

"Ne'er shall the sons of Columbia be slaves,"

and shall remember the Paine who wrote those words, for one who remembers his father, the stern jurist whose name I spoke just now. But there are justly honors enough for all.

For a generation after the Declaration no one could have said or sung a word with regard to the great struggle without speaking of Joseph Warren, another of these younger men whom Samuel Adams loved. It does not seem to me that in our time he receives the tribute which is his due. Whoever else was second, the people of Massachusetts in 1775 counted Warren first. It was because they had given him the rank of a major-general in their militia that he thought it his duty to appear at the redoubt at Charlestown, where he waived the command, which was in the hands of a more experienced soldier, and where he fell. He died too soon for his own fame. In the work of those critical years, which needed courage and decision as perhaps no other years in history ever needed them, Warren had shown already that he was a leader of men. But in our time he has shown this only to those who study old archives, who disinter old letters from their graves, and then sadly ask themselves what might have been.

To the country, his loss seemed at the time almost irreparable. The language used by those who knew him, and by those who only knew about him, is the language of the most profound regret, as if the national cause in his death had sustained a great disaster. We know to-day, what they did not know, that the battle fought on St. Botolph's day, on our own hill yonder, was not only the first pitched battle of the American Revolution, but that in a certain sense it was the last. For that battle really decided the contest, as I think all military men would say. From that time till the surrender at Yorktown, no English general had the temerity to order troops to attack any military work fitly manned by Americans. From that time till the end, the war on the part of England was generally, with a few distinguished exceptions, a series of Fabian campaigns — campaigns of endurance and waiting, of hoping for a collapse which never came.

It is of such campaigns that, at the end of six years, poor Cowper sang that the English troops

> " With opium drugged,
> Snore to the murmurs of the Atlantic wave."

Such is the lesson which was taught by the " embattled farmers " who surrounded Warren when he died. But the men of their time did not understand that lesson. In that time men spoke of Bunker Hill with tears of rage. They spoke of it as I remember six and thirty years ago we spoke here of the first Bull Run. In the midst of that rage there was this pathetic sorrow, that Warren, the first man in Massachusetts, most beloved and most trusted, had lost his life. His children were adopted by the State, a monument to his memory was ordered, which the piety of other generations built. And to-day, after four generations have passed, you and I must not forget the service which had won such sorrow. His monument, thank God and our fathers, is secure!

Listen to what Daniel Webster said of him — who knew hundreds of men who had known Warren well. Daniel Webster was not used to exaggerate. And he knew what he was saying:

" But, ah! Him! the first great martyr in this great cause! Him! the premature victim of his own self-devoting heart. Him! the head of our civil councils, and the destined leader of our military bands, whom nothing brought hither but the unquenchable fire of his own spirit. Him! cut off by Providence in the hour of overwhelming anxiety and thick gloom, falling, ere he saw the star of his country rise; pouring out his generous blood, like water, before he knew whether it would fertilize a land of freedom or of bondage! How shall I struggle with the emotions that stifle the utterance of thy name! Our poor work may perish, but thine shall endure. This monument may moulder away; the solid ground it rests upon may sink down to the level of the sea, but thy memory shall not fail. Wheresoever among men a heart shall be found that beats to the transports of patriotism and liberty, its aspirations shall be to claim kindred with thy spirit."

When Washington arrived in Cambridge, at the beginning of July, 1775, he found the English army blockaded in Boston. The battle of Bunker Hill had been fought. Strong works on Prospect Hill and the other hills in Somerville made any advance of the English troops over Charlestown Neck impossible. Efficient works on Charles river blocked the passage against any boats sent from the squadron up that river. The strong fortification had been begun which, under the auspices of my friend here, has just now been restored, on the heights of Roxbury, and blocked the way for any such "military promenade" as Percy had made in April of that year. These works had been designed by Henry Knox, another of our Latin School boys.

He kept the leading bookstore in Boston, at the head of

King street, a place where English officers looked in for the latest books. He kept himself well supplied with the books on tactics and all military art; he studied these books himself while he sold them to the enemies of his country.

When Paddock, famous for the elms, left Boston for England, he recommended Knox as his successor in command of the artillery company. With such training, Knox joined Ward at Cambridge, as soon as Ward took command of the army. He recommended himself at once to Washington. By Washington's appointment, probably at Knox's own suggestion, he was sent to Ticonderoga to bring across the mountains the artillery which Ethan Allen captured there. With the arrival of that artillery, the works which he had built could be properly armed. It would have been hot shot from his cannon which would have destroyed the wooden town of Boston had it been determined, in John Adams's phrase, to "smoke the rats out of their hole."

From the first, Washington saw the ability and merits of this great man. Then, at Washington's suggestion, he was made a brigadier in the Continental army. At Washington's request, after Knox's distinguished service at Yorktown, he was made a major-general. Washington made him secretary of war and of the navy, when the nation became a nation. It is hard to say what would have become of the infant cause of independence had it not been for Henry Knox. The finest line in Dwight's "Conquest of Canaan," gives Knox his epitaph:

"And Knox created all the stores of war."

One is glad to say that the vigor of such a man is preserved generation after generation among his descendants. More than one of them has done essential service to the State.

It was a grandson of Knox who led the way in the naval attacks of the nation in the capture of Fort Fisher and of Mobile.

I must leave to some other orator, better equipped for his task than I am, to give the whole of this sacred hour on some future Fourth of July to the memory of Samuel Adams, the father of American independence. He, too, like Hancock, was so eager in later life that Massachusetts should not lose one leaf from her laurel crown that he was coy and doubtful when the constitution of the nation was brought to him for his approval. Yet here, too, it is to be said that, when the moment came for the great decision, Adams was willing to sacrifice his own pride for the welfare of the whole. His decision saved the constitution. He was too great a man to sacrifice Massachusetts on the altar of "separate sovereignty."

Later generations have remembered fondly, what in commencement week is worth repeating, the subject of his master's address at Cambridge thirty years before the Revolution: "Whether it be lawful to resist the supreme magistrate, if the Commonwealth cannot otherwise be preserved."

I am fond of thinking that from that moment forward Adams must have called together around him the younger men of Boston, perhaps in some social club of which we have forgotten the name, in which they were indoctrinated with the eternal principles of home rule, in which they learned the catechism of independence. Samuel Adams saw, I should say, before any other public man saw, that the colonies were in fact independent. It is a pity that in our anniversary orations we do not always recollect this. The Declaration which we celebrate to-day was a declaration of past history and present truth. "These united colonies are, and of right ought to be, free and independent States."

It is not the declaration of a future which one hopes for, as the people of Crete to-day might declare that they will be independent to-morrow and in the future. It is the declaration of what has been for generations, of what is on this Fourth of July, 1776, of what shall be till time shall end. The State of Massachusetts was independent under its old charter. It coined its own money, it made its own wars, it signed its own treaties of peace. When King Philip, who could call more men into the field than the colony of Massachusetts could, attacked her, Massachusetts fought with him and conquered him. And when some friends in England asked why Massachusetts had not sent to England for assistance, Massachusetts proudly replied that England had no business in the affair. In fact, England did not send an ounce of powder or lead for that death struggle. Even after William III, who knew what power was, and who meant to hold it in his hands — after he sent us the second charter, the colony taught every successive governor that he was dependent upon Massachusetts. Every judge and every governor must receive his salary from the Massachusetts treasury.

And when she chose, Massachusetts erected monuments to her friends in Westminster Abbey. There were the vestiges of a certain royal dignity; the lion and the unicorn were on the town house; the crown and the mitre were in King's chapel. But the crown could not search a house unless the colony granted the writ of assistance.

That is what the Declaration of Independence expresses in those central words: "These united colonies are, and of right ought to be, free and independent States."

> "Daughter am I in my mother's house,
> But mistress in my own."

John Adams himself has left to us the history of his time, in which he filled a place so large. Impetuous even to audacity, a magnificent hater, he made enemies with the greatest ease. It was once said of the Adams family that "they never turn their backs on any but their friends." It has followed with John Adams that he, also, has not had the honor that he deserved. He was not in the ranks of battle, but in debate and in diplomacy he showed that fight was in him, to the very sole of his foot, if he were sure that he was in the right.

When the English commissioner, Oswald, sent the treaty of peace home from Paris, he said: "If we had not given way in the article of the fishery, we should have had no treaty at all. Mr. Adams . . . declared that he would never put his hand to any treaty if the restraints proposed were not dispensed with."

They asked Adams what he would do if they insisted on these restraints. "Fight twenty years more," he said. Seventy-eight years after, his illustrious grandson had to write in much the same strain to the minister of the same nation. And yet there have been men called statesmen in America who have offered to cede these rights of free fishing in the ocean as they might give away a cigar stub!

John Adams was no such man as that. Unfortunately for him, and for his country, therefore, he was jealous of other men; he suspected other men. He suspected Franklin; he suspected Jay, both as pure patriots as ever lived. But no man ever suspected him of swerving from his country's cause, in his own interest or in that of any other man. The country first — the country second — the country always! Such men as that do not need statues for their memorial! But all the more they deserve them.

Now I come to Benjamin Franklin. An accomplished scholar, born in Germany, once asked me why in Boston we were so chary of our honors to Benjamin Franklin, seeing Boston is best known by half the world as Franklin's birth-place. I could only say, as I said just now, that we had so many great men to commemorate that we could not say half we would about any of them. But it was a poor apology.

Franklin is the oldest of our signers of the Declaration. At the time of Sam Adams's birth, Franklin is leaving Boston for his Philadelphia home. Fifty-three years after, as a representative of Pennsylvania, he signs the Declaration in what my friend, the old writing-master, Mr. Jonathan Snelling, used to call in one of his writing book copies the "Boston style of writing."

In the same year he crossed the ocean to France, and arrived in Paris just before Christmas. Lord Stormont, the English ambassador, at once reported his arrival in England, to be told in reply by his chief, Lord North, that he need not distress himself "about the movements of an old man of seventy." But before the old man of seventy had done with France he had dictated the treaty of independence. He had compelled George III — the Brummagem Louis XIV — to surrender half his empire, and by far the better half, as it has proved.

So majestic was Franklin's diplomacy that when the English ministry compelled the House of Commons to ratify the treaty, it was openly said that America had seven negotiators to make it, while the King of England had none.

So was it that the town of Boston — will the mayor let me say the Latin School? — sent the diplomatist to Europe who crowned the work of independence, as in Samuel Adams she had kept at home the far-seeing statesman who began it. These are our jewels!

Far in advance of all other men in the work of independence are the two greatest men yet born in America — Washington and Franklin. Two men who honored each other, absolutely and without jealousy. One, in America, established independence; one, in Europe, made independence possible. The croakers tell us that in government by democracy the people cannot find their true leaders, and do not trust them when found. Tell me in what oligarchy, in what empire, was ever a people so loyal to a leader, in good report and in evil fortune, as the people of America to Washington? And in what empire or in what oligarchy has any nation ever found a diplomatist who is to be named on the same day with Benjamin Franklin?

Of leaders in lower rank I must not speak even to name them. First, second and last, here is the old Puritan sense of duty — the present service of the present God. It is in the hunger of Valley Forge; it is in the wilderness tramp under Arnold; it is in the injustice of Newburgh, when the war was done. Duty first! To serve where God has placed me!

And when the field of such service is their own field the triumph is simply magnificent.

I must not even attempt to describe the work of Massachusetts at sea in the War of Independence. Enough to say that the treaty of peace was forced on England by seven years of losses at sea. Her enemy was Massachusetts. In the year 1777 King George employed 45,000 men in the English navy, in all oceans of the world. In the same year New England employed against him 80,000 men upon the Atlantic alone. Of these nine tenths were from Massachusetts.

Remember that, through the war, America had more men

on the sea fighting the King than Washington ever commanded on the land.   Of these sea kings, nine tenths, at least, were from Massachusetts.   From first to last more than 3,000 prizes were taken from the English merchant marine by the American cruisers and privateers, most of them by the men of Massachusetts.   And here is the reason why, when the war ended, the merchants of London insisted that it should end — the same men who, when it began, were hounding Lord North and George III to their ruin.

GRANT

ULYSSES S. GRANT, soldier, statesman, and the eighteenth President of the United States, was born at Point Pleasant, Ohio, April 27, 1822. He was the oldest of six children and spent his boyhood on his father's farm. He attended the village school and was appointed to the United States Military Academy in 1839, where he was noted for proficiency in mathematics and horsemanship. He graduated in 1843 and, in 1845, joined the army of occupation under General Taylor in Mexico. He served with distinction during the Mexican war and was twice brevetted. In 1848 he returned to Pascagoula, Mississippi, with his regiment; and on August 22 of that year married Miss Julia B. Dent at St. Louis. After five years of service at various army posts he received his commission as captain on August 5, 1853, and the following year resigned and settled on a small farm near St. Louis. In 1860 he removed to Galena, Illinois, and became a clerk in his father's hardware and leather store. At the beginning of the civil war he offered his services to the national government but no answer to his letter was ever received. On June 17, 1861, he was appointed colonel of the Twenty-first Illinois Regiment of infantry. Throughout the war he displayed the highest skill and was promoted to the supreme command of the Union forces. As a man and as a soldier he was possessed of the finest traits of character. He combined with self-reliance and fertility of resource a moral and physical courage equal to all emergencies. In 1866 General Grant served as secretary of war under President Johnson, during the temporary suspension of Secretary Stanton. He was nominated for the presidency at Chicago May 20, 1868, and was elected over the Democratic nominee, Horatio Seymour, of New York. He was nominated for a second term June 5, 1872, and was again elected. His first administration was characterized by the inauguration of many important reforms. The national debt was reduced over $450,000,000 and the balance of trade changed from $130,000,000 against this country to $130,000,000 in its favor.

On retiring from the presidency in 1877, General Grant made a tour around the world and was everywhere received with honors usually accorded only to royalty. In 1880 his name was again presented at the Republican national convention, but he did not receive the party's nomination. In 1881 he took up his residence in New York and became a partner in the banking house of Grant & Ward. The failure of this firm in 1884 made him a bankrupt, but on March 4, 1885, Congress created him a general on the retired list, thus restoring him to his former rank. He died on Mount McGregor, New York, July 23, 1885, from cancer at the root of the tongue. His contributions to literature consist of his " Memoirs " and several articles on the war, written for the " North American Review " and the " Century " Magazine.

INAUGURAL ADDRESS

DELIVERED MARCH 4, 1873

FELLOW CITIZENS,— Under Providence I have been called a second time to act as Executive over this great nation. It has been my endeavor in the past to maintain all the laws, and, as far as lay in my power, to act for the best interests of the whole people. My best efforts will be given in the same direction in the future, aided, I trust, by my four years' experience in the office.

When my first term of the office of chief executive began, the country had not recovered from the effects of a great internal revolution, and three of the former States of the Union had not been restored to their federal relations.

It seemed to me wise that no new questions should be raised so long as that condition of affairs existed. Therefore, the past four years, so far as I could control events, have been consumed in the effort to restore harmony, public credit, commerce and all the arts of peace and progress. It is my firm conviction that the civilized world is tending toward republicanism, or government by the people, through their chosen representatives, and that our own great Republic is destined to be the guiding star to all others.

Under our Republic we support an army less than that of any European power of any standing, and a navy less than that of either of at least five of them. There could be no extension of territory on the continent which would call for an increase of this force, but rather might such extension enable us to diminish it.

The theory of government changes with years of progress. Now that the telegraph is made available for communicating thought, together with rapid transit by steam, all parts of the continent are made contiguous for all purposes of government, and communication between the extreme limits of the country made easier than it was throughout the old thirteen States at the beginning of our national existence.

The effects of the late civil strife have been to free the slave and make him a citizen. Yet he is not possessed of the civil rights which citizenship should carry with it. This is wrong, and should be corrected. To this correction I stand committed, so far as executive influence can avail.

Social equality is not a subject to be legislated upon, nor shall I ask that anything be done to advance the social status of the colored man, except to give him a fair chance to develop what good there is in him, give him access to the schools, and when he travels, let him feel assured that his conduct will regulate the treatment and fare he will receive.

The States lately at war with the general government are now happily rehabilitated, and no executive control is exercised in any one of them that would not be exercised in any other State under like circumstances.

In the first year of the past administration the proposition came up for the admission of Santo Domingo as a Territory of the Union. It was not a question of my seeking, but was a proposition from the people of Santo Domingo, and which I entertained. I believe now, as I did then, that it was for the best interest of this country, for the people of Santo Domingo, and all concerned, that the proposition should be received favorably. It was, however, rejected, constitutionally, and therefore the subject was never brought up again by me.

In future, while I hold my present office, the subject of acquisition of territory must have the support of the people before I will recommend any proposition looking to such acquisition. I say here, however, that I do not share in the apprehension, held by many, as to the danger of governments becoming weakened and destroyed by reason of their extension of territory. Commerce, education, and rapid transit of thought and matter by telegraph and steam have changed all this. Rather do I believe that our Great Maker is preparing the world in his own good time to become one nation, speaking one language, and when armies and navies will no longer be required.

My efforts in the future will be directed to the restoration of good feeling between the different sections of our common country; to the restoration of our currency to a fixed value as compared with the world's standard of values — gold — and, if possible, to a par with it; to the construction of cheap routes of transit throughout the land, to the end that the products of all may find a market and leave a living remuneration to the producer; to the maintenance of friendly relations with all our neighbors, and with distant nations; to the re-establishment of our commerce, and share in the carrying-trade upon the ocean; to the encouragement of such manufacturing industries as can be economically pursued in this country, to the end that the exports of home products and industries may pay for our imports, the only sure method of returning to, and permanently maintaining, a specie basis; to the elevation of labor; and by a humane course to bring the aborigines of the country under the benign influence of education and civilization. It is either this, or war to extermination.

Wars of extermination, engaged in by people pursuing

commerce and all industrial pursuits, are expensive even against the weakest people, and are demoralizing and wicked. Our superiority of strength and advantages of civilization should make us lenient toward the Indian. The wrong inflicted upon him should be taken into account, and the balance placed to his credit. The moral view of the question should be considered, and the question asked: Cannot the Indian be made a useful and productive member of society, by proper teaching and treatment? If the effort is made in good faith, we will stand better before the civilized nations of the earth, and in our own consciences, for having made it.

All these things are not to be accomplished by one individual, but they will receive my support, and such recommendations to Congress as will, in my judgment, best serve to carry them into effect. I beg your support and hearty encouragement.

It has been, and is, my earnest desire to correct abuses that have grown up in the civil service of the country. To secure this reformation, rules regulating methods of appointment and promotion were established, and have been tried. My efforts for such reformation shall be continued to the best of my judgment. The spirit of the rules adopted will be maintained.

I acknowledge before this assembly, representing, as it does, every section of our country, the obligation I am under to my countrymen for the great honor they have conferred on me, by returning me to the highest office within their gift, and the further obligation resting on me to tender to them the best services within my power. This I promise, looking forward with the greatest anxiety to the day when I shall be released from responsibilities that at times are almost overwhelming, and from which I have scarcely had a respite since the eventful firing upon Fort Sumter, in April, 1861, to the present day. My services were then tendered and accepted under the first call for troops growing out of that event.

I did not ask for place or position, and was entirely without influence, or the acquaintance of persons of influence, but was resolved to perform my part in a struggle threatening the very existence of the nation. I performed a conscientious duty without asking promotion or command, and without a revengeful feeling toward any section or individual.

Notwithstanding this, throughout the war, and from my candidacy for my present office in 1868, to the close of the last presidential campaign, I have been the subject of abuse and slander never equalled in political history, which to-day I feel I can afford to disregard in view of your verdict, which I gratefully accept as my vindication.

SPEECH AT WARREN, OHIO

[At Warren, Ohio, on the 28th of September, 1880, the Honorable Roscoe Conkling addressed a Republican mass meeting and General U. S. Grant presided. Before introducing the senator, General Grant said:]

IN view of the known character of the speaker who is to address you to-day, and his long public career, and association with the leading statesmen of this country for the past twenty years, it would not be becoming in me to detain you with many remarks of my own. But it may be proper for me to account to you on the first occasion of my presiding at political meetings for the faith that is in me.

I am a Republican, as the two great political parties are now divided, because the Republican party is a national party seeking the greatest good for the greatest number of citizens. There is not a precinct in this vast nation where a Democrat cannot cast his ballot and have it counted as cast. No matter what the prominence of the opposite party, he can proclaim his political opinions, even if he is only one among a thousand, without fear and without proscription on account of his opinions. There are fourteen States, and localities in some other States, where Republicans have not this privilege.

This is one reason why I am a Republican. But I am a Republican for many other reasons. The Republican party assures protection to life and property, the public credit, and the payment of the debts of the government, State, county, or municipality so far as it can control. The Democratic party does not promise this; if it does, it has broken its promises to the extent of hundreds of millions, as many northern Democrats can testify to their sorrow. I am a Republican, as between the existing parties, because it fosters the production of the field and farm, and of manufactories, and it encourages the general education of the poor as well as the rich.

The Democratic party discourages all these when in absolute power. The Republican party is a party of progress, and of liberty toward its opponents. It encourages the poor to strive to better their children, to enable them to compete successfully with their more fortunate associates, and, in fine, it secures an entire equality before the law of every citizen, no matter what his race, nationality, or previous condition. It tolerates no privileged class. Every one has the opportunity to make himself all he is capable of.

Ladies and gentlemen, do you believe this can be truthfully said in the greater part of fourteen of the States of this Union to-day which the Democratic party control absolutely? The Republican party is a party of principles; the same principles prevailing wherever it has a foothold.

The Democratic party is united in but one thing, and that is in getting control of the government in all its branches. It is for internal improvement at the expense of the government in one section and against this in another. It favors repudiation of solemn obligations in one section and honest payment of its debts in another, where public opinion will not tolerate any other view. It favors fiat money in one place and good money in another. Finally, it favors the pooling of all issues not favored by the Republicans, to the end that it may secure the one principle upon which the party is a most harmonious unit, namely, getting control of the government in all its branches.

I have been in some part of every State lately in rebellion within the last year. I was most hospitably received at every place where I stopped. My receptions were not by the Union class alone, but by all classes, without distinction. I had a free talk with many who were against me in war, and who have been against the Republican party ever since. They were, in all instances, reasonable men, judged by what they said. I believed then, and believe now, that they sincerely want a break-up in this "Solid South" political condition. They see that it is to their pecuniary interest, as well as to their happiness, that there should be harmony and confidence between all sections. They want to break away from the slavery which binds them to a party name. They want a pretext that enough of them can unite upon to make it respectable. Once started, the Solid South will go as

Ku-Kluxism did before, as is so admirably told by Judge Tourgee in his "Fool's Errand." When the break comes, those who start it will be astonished to find how many of their friends have been in favor of it for a long time, and have only been waiting to see some one take the lead. This desirable solution can only be attained by the defeat, and continued defeat, of the Democratic party as now constituted.

PHELPS

EDWARD JOHN PHELPS, an American lawyer and diplomat, was born at Middlebury, Vermont, July 11, 1822, and graduated at Middlebury College in the class of 1840. In 1843 he was admitted to the Vermont bar and two years later removed to Burlington. In 1851 he was appointed second comptroller of the United States Treasury. In 1880 he was elected president of the American Bar Association and was nominated as Democratic governor of Vermont, but failed of election. The following year he became professor of law at Yale University. In 1885 he was sent to England as minister and remained at the Court of St. James for five years. In 1893 he was one of the counsel of the United States government in the court of arbitration in the Bering Sea controversy, where he served with distinction. On his return he again began to instruct in law at Yale University.

FAREWELL ADDRESS

MY LORD MAYOR, MY LORDS, AND GENTLE-MEN,— I am sure you will not be surprised to be told that the poor words at my command do not enable me to respond adequately to your most kind greeting, nor the too flattering words which have fallen from my friend, the Lord Mayor, and from my distinguished colleague, the Lord Chancellor. But you will do me the justice to believe that my feelings are not the less sincere and hearty if I cannot put them into language. I am under a very great obligation to your Lordship not merely for the honor of meeting this evening an assembly more distinguished I apprehend than it appears to me has often assembled under one roof, but especially for the opportunity of meeting under such pleasant circumstances so many of those to whom I have become so warmly attached, and from whom I am so sorry to part.

It is rather a pleasant coincidence to me that about the first hospitality that was offered me after my arrival in England came from my friend, the Lord Mayor, who was at the time one of the sheriffs of London. I hope it is no disparagement to my countrymen to say that under existing circumstances the first place that I felt it my duty to visit was the Old Bailey criminal court. I had there the pleasure of being entertained by my friend, the Lord Mayor. And it happens also that it was in this room almost four years ago at a dinner given to her Majesty's judges by my friend, Sir Robert Fowler, then Lord Mayor, whose genial face I see before me, that I appeared for the first time on any public occasion in England and addressed my first words to an English company. It seems to me a fortunate propriety that my last public words should be spoken under the same hospitable roof, the home of the chief magistrate of the city of London. Nor can I ever forget the cordial and generous reception that was then accorded, not to myself personally, for I was altogether a stranger, but to the representative of my country. It struck what has proved to the keynote of my relations here. It indicated to me at the outset how warm and hearty was the feeling of Englishmen toward America.

And it gave me to understand, what I was not slow to accept and believe, that I was accredited not merely from one government to the other, but from the people of America to the people of England — that the American minister was not expected to be merely a diplomatic functionary shrouded in reticence and retirement, jealously watching over doubtful relations, and carefully guarding against anticipated dangers; but that he was to be the guest of his kinsmen—one of themselves — the messenger of the sympathy and good will, the mutual and warm regard and esteem that bind together the two great nations of the same race, and make them one in all the fair

humanities of life. The suggestion that met me at the thresh-
old has not proved to be mistaken. The promise then held
out has been generously fulfilled. Ever since and through
all my intercourse here I have received, in all quarters, from
all classes with whom I have come in contact, under all circumstances and in all vicissitudes, a uniform and widely varied
kindness far beyond what I had personally the least claim to.
And I am glad of this public opportunity to acknowledge it in
the most emphatic manner.

My relations with the successive governments I have had
to do with have been at all times most fortunate and agreeable,
and quite beyond those I have been happy in feeling always
that the English people had a claim upon the American minister for all kind and friendly offices in his power, and upon his
presence and voice on all occasions when they could be
thought to further any good work.

And so I have gone in and out among you these four years
and have come to know you well. I have taken part in many
gratifying public functions; I have been the guest at many
homes; and my heart has gone out with yours in memorable
jubilee of that sovereign lady whom all Englishmen love and
all Americans honor. I have stood with you by some unfor-
gotten grave; I have shared in many joys; and I have tried as
well as I could through it all, in my small way, to promote
constantly a better understanding, a fuller and more accurate
knowledge, a more genuine sympathy between the people of
the two countries.

And this leads me to say a word on the nature of these
relations. The moral intercourse between the governments
is most important to be maintained, and its value is not to be
overlooked or disregarded. But the real significance of the
attitude of nations depends in these days upon the feelings

which the general intelligence of their inhabitants entertain toward each other. The time has long passed when kings or rulers can involve their nations in hostilities to gratify their own ambition or caprice. There can be no war nowadays between civilized nations, nor any peace that is not hollow and delusive unless sustained and backed up by the sentiment of the people who are parties to it. Before nations can quarrel their inhabitants must seek war. The men of our race are not likely to become hostile until they begin to misunderstand each other. There are no dragon's teeth so prolific as mutual misunderstandings. It is in the great and constantly increasing intercourse between England and America, in its reciprocities, and its amenities, that the security against misunderstanding must be found. While that continues, they cannot be otherwise than friendly. Unlucky incidents may sometimes happen; interests may conflict; mistakes may be made on one side or on the other, and sharp words may occasionally be spoken by unguarded or ignorant tongues. The man who makes no mistakes does not usually make anything. The nation that comes to be without fault will have reached the millenium, and will have little further concern with the storm-swept geography of this imperfect world. But these things are all ephemeral; they do not touch the great heart of either people; they float for a moment on the surface and in the wind, and then they disappear and are gone — " in the deep bosom of the ocean buried."

I do not know, sir, who may be my successor, but I venture to assure you that he will be an American gentleman, fit by character and capacity to be the medium of communication between our countries; and an American gentleman, when you come to know him, generally turns out to be a not very distant kinsman of an English gentleman. I need not bespeak for him a kindly reception. I know he will receive it for his country's sake and his own.

" Farewell," sir, is a word often lightly uttered and readily forgotten. But when it marks the rounding-off and completion of a chapter in life, the severance of ties many and cherished, of the parting with many friends at once — especially when it is spoken among the lengthening shadows of the western light — it sticks somewhat in the throat. It becomes, indeed, " the word that makes us linger." But it does not prompt many other words. It is best expressed in few. Not much can be added to the old English word " Good-by." You are not sending me away empty-handed or alone. I go freighted with happy memories — inexhaustible and unalloyed — of England, its warm-hearted people, and their measureless kindness. Spirits more than twain will cross with me, messengers of your good will. Happy the nation that can thus speed its parting guest! Fortunate the guest who has found his welcome almost an adoption, and whose farewell leaves half his heart behind!

HAYES

RUTHERFORD BIRCHARD HAYES, the nineteenth president of the United States, was born in Delaware, Ohio, October 4, 1822, and educated at Kenyon College. He studied law at Harvard University and began the practice of his profession at Fremont, Ohio, removing to Cincinnati in 1849, and being city solicitor there, 1858-61. In June, 1861, he entered the federal army as major of an Ohio regiment and served in many engagements, being wounded at the battle of South Mountain. He resigned from the army in June, 1865, with the rank of brevet major-general. He entered Congress in December, 1865, resigning his seat in 1867 to become governor of Ohio. He held this office for two terms, and after being defeated as a congressional candidate in 1872 was in 1875 elected governor of Ohio for the third time. In 1876 he was nominated by the Republican party as their candidate for the presidency, Samuel Tilden being the Democratic candidate. The campaign resulted in a disputed election, the entire electoral votes of South Carolina, Florida, and Louisiana, and one of those of Oregon being claimed by both sides. To settle the dispute an electoral commission was appointed, which on March 2, 1877, announced that Hayes had been duly elected. President Hayes's administration was a dignified if not especially brilliant one, and his choice of ministers to foreign courts was notably excellent. At the close of his four years of office he retired to Fremont, Ohio, where he died, January 17, 1893.

CAMPAIGN SPEECH

DELIVERED AT LEBANON, OHIO, AUGUST 5, 1867

THE military bill and amendments are peace-offerings. We should accept them as such, and place ourselves upon them as the starting point from which to meet future political issues as they arise.

"Like other southern men, I naturally sought alliance with the Democratic party, merely because it was opposed to the Republican party. But, as far as I can judge, there is nothing tangible about it, except the issues that were staked upon the war and lost. Finding nothing to take hold of except prejudice, which cannot be worked into good for any one,

(8412)

it is proper and right that I should seek some standpoint from which good may be done."

Quotations like these from prominent Democratic politicians, from rebel soldiers, and from influential rebel newspapers, might be multiplied indefinitely. Enough have been given to show how completely and how exactly the Reconstruction Acts have met the evil to be remedied in the South. My friend, Mr. Hassaurek, in his admirable speech at Columbus, did not estimate too highly the fruits of these measures. Said he:

"And, sir, this remedy at once effected the desired cure. The poor contraband is no longer the persecuted outlaw whom incurable rebels might kick and kill with impunity; but he at once became 'our colored fellow citizen,' in whose well-being his former master takes the liveliest interest. Thus, by bringing the negro under the American system, we have completed his emancipation. He has ceased to be a pariah. From an outcast he has been transformed into a human being, invested with the great national attribute of self-protection, and the re-establishment of peace, and order, and security, the revival of business and trade, and the restoration of the southern States on the basis of loyalty and equal justice to all, will be the happy results of this astonishing metamorphosis, provided the party which has inaugurated this policy remains in power to carry it out."

The Peace Democracy generally throughout the North oppose this measure. In Ohio they oppose it especially because it commits the people of the nation in favor of manhood suffrage. They tell us that if it is wise and just to entrust the ballot to colored men in the District of Columbia, in the Territories, and in the rebel States, it is also just and wise that they should have it in Ohio and in the other States of the North.

Union men do not question this reasoning, but if it is

urged as an objection to the plan of Congress, we reply: There are now within the limits of the United States about five millions of colored people. They are not aliens or strangers. They are here not by the choice of themselves or of their ancestors. They are here by the misfortune of their fathers and the crime of ours. Their labor, privations, and sufferings, unpaid and unrequited, have cleared and redeemed one third of the inhabited territory of the Union. Their toil has added to the resources and wealth of the nation untold millions. Whether we prefer it or not, they are our countrymen, and will remain so forever.

They are more than countrymen — they are citizens. Free colored people were citizens of the colonies. The constitution of the United States, formed by our fathers, created no disabilities on account of color. By the acts of our fathers and of ourselves, they bear equally the burdens and are required to discharge the highest duties of citizens. They are compelled to pay taxes and to bear arms. They fought side by side with their white countrymen in the great struggle for independence, and in the recent war for the Union. In the revolutionary contest, colored men bore an honorable part, from the Boston massacre, in 1770, to the surrender of Cornwallis, in 1781. Bancroft says: "Their names may be read on the pension rolls of the country side by side with those of other soldiers of the revolution."

In the war of 1812, General Jackson issued an order complimenting the colored men of his army engaged in the defence of New Orleans. I need not speak of their number enrolled and accepted them among her defenders to the or of their services in the war of the rebellion. The nation number of about two hundred thousand, and in the new regular army act, passed at the close of the rebellion, by the

votes of Democrats and Union men alike, in the Senate
and in the House, and by the assent of the President, regi-
ments of colored men, cavalry and infantry, form part of the
standing army of the Republic.

In the navy, colored American sailors have fought side by
side with white men from the days of Paul Jones to the
victory of the " Kearsarge " over the rebel pirate "Alabama."
Colored men will, in the future as in the past, in all times
of national peril, be our fellow soldiers. Taxpayers, countrymen, fellow citizens, and fellow soldiers, the colored men
of America have been and will be. It is now too late for the
adversaries of nationality and human rights to undertake to
deprive these taxpayers, freemen, citizens, and soldiers of
the right to vote.

Slaves were never voters. It was bad enough that our
fathers, for the sake of union, were compelled to allow masters to reckon three fifths of their slaves for representation,
without adding slave suffrage to the other privileges of the
slaveholder. But free colored men were always voters in
many of the colonies, and in several of the States, North and
South, after independence was achieved. They voted for
members of the Congress which declared independence, and
for members of every Congress prior to the adoption of the
federal constitution; for the members of the convention
which framed the constitution ; for the members of many of
the State conventions which ratified it, and for every president from Washington to Lincoln.

Our government has been called the white man's government. Not so. It is not the government of any class, or
sect, or nationality, or race. It is a government founded on
the consent of the governed, and Mr. Broomall, of Pennsylvania, therefore properly calls it " the government of the

governed." It is not the government of the native born, or
of the foreign born, of the rich man, or of the poor man, of
the white man, or of the colored man — it is the government
of the freeman. And when colored men were made citizens,
soldiers, and freemen, by our consent and votes, we were
estopped from denying to them the right of suffrage.

General Sherman was right when he said, in his Atlanta
letter, of 1864: " If you admit the negro to this struggle
for any purpose, he has a right to stay in for all; and, when
the fight is over, the hand that drops the musket cannot be
denied the ballot."

Even our adversaries are compelled to admit the Jeffer-
sonian rule, that " the man who pays taxes and who fights
for the country is entitled to vote."

Mr. Pendleton, in his speech against the enlistment of
colored soldiers, gave up the whole controversy. He said:
" Gentlemen tell us that these colored men are ready, with
their strong arms and their brave hearts, to maintain the
supremacy of the constitution, and to defend the integrity
of the Union, which in our hands to-day is in peril. What
is that constitution? It provides that every child of the
Republic, every citizen of the land is before the law the equal
of every other. It provides for all of them trial by jury,
free speech, free press, entire protection for life and liberty
and property. It goes further. It secures to every citizen
the right of suffrage, the right to hold office, the right to
aspire to every office or agency by which the government is
carried on. Every man called upon to do military duty,
every man required to take up arms in its defence, is by its
provisions entitled to vote, and a competent aspirant for
every office in the government."

The truth is, impartial manhood suffrage is already practically decided. It is now merely a question of time. In the eleven rebel States, in five of the New England States, and in a number of the northwestern States, there is no organized party able to successfully oppose impartial suffrage. The Democratic party of more than half of the States are ready to concede its justice and expediency. The " Boston Post," the able organ of the New England Democracy, says:

" Color ought to have no more to do with the matter (voting) than size. Only establish a right standard, and then apply it impartially. A rule of that sort is too firmly fixed in justice and equality to be shaken. It commends itself too clearly to the good sentiment of the entire body of our countrymen to be successfully traversed by objections. Once let this principle be fairly presented to the people of the several States, with the knowledge on their part that they alone are to have the disposal and settlement of it, and we sincerely believe it would not be long before it would be adopted by every State in the Union."

The New York " World," the ablest Democratic newspaper in the Union, says:

" Democrats in the North, as well as the South, should be fully alive to the importance of the new element thrust into the politics of the country. We suppose it to be morally certain that the new constitution of the State of New York, to be framed this year, will confer the elective franchise upon all adult male negroes. We have no faith in the success of any efforts to shut the negro element out of politics. It is the part of wisdom frankly to accept the situation, and get beforehand with the Radicals in gaining an ascendancy over the negro mind."

The Chicago " Times," the influential organ of the northwestern Democracy, says:

" The word ' white ' is not found in any of the original constitutions, save only that of South Carolina. In every

other State negroes, who possessed the qualifications that
were required impartially of all men, were admitted to vote,
and many of that race did vote, in the southern as well as in
the northern States. And, moreover, they voted the Democratic ticket, for it was the Democratic party of that day
which affirmed their right in that respect upon an impartial
basis with white men. All Democrats cannot, even at this
day, have forgotten the statement of General Jackson, that
he was supported for the presidency by negro voters in the
State of Tennessee.

" The doctrine of impartial suffrage is one of the earliest
and most essential doctrines of Democracy. It is the affirma-
tion of the right of every man who is made a partaker of the
burdens of the State to be represented by his own consent or
vote in its government. It is the first principle upon which
all true republican government rests. It is the basis upon
which the liberties of America will be preserved, if they are
preserved at all. The Democratic party must return from
its driftings, and stand again upon the immutable rock of
principles."

In Ohio the leaders of the Peace Democracy intend to
carry on one more campaign on the old and rotten platform
of prejudice against colored people. They seek in this way
to divert attention from the record they made during the
war of the rebellion. But the great facts of our recent history are against them. The principles of the fathers, reason,
religion, and the spirit of the age are against them.

The plain and monstrous inconsistency and injustice of
excluding one seventh of our population from all participation in a government founded on the consent of the governed
in this land of free discussion is simply impossible. No such
absurdity and wrong can be permanent. Impartial suffrage
will carry the day. No low prejudice will long be able to
induce American citizens to deny to a weak people their best
means of self-protection for the unmanly reason that they
are weak. Chief Justice Chase expressed the true sentiment

when he said "the American nation cannot afford to do the smallest injustice to the humblest and feeblest of her children."

Much has been said of the antagonism which exists between the different races of men. But difference of religion, difference of nationality, difference of language, and difference of rank and privileges are quite as fruitful causes of antagonism and war as difference of race. The bitter strifes between Christians and Jews, between Catholics and Protestants, between Englishmen and Irishmen, between aristocracy and the masses, are only too familiar. What causes increase and aggravate these antagonisms, and what are the measures which diminish and prevent them ought to be equally familiar. Under the partial and unjust laws of the nations of the Old World men of one nationality were allowed to oppress those of another; men of one faith had rights which were denied to men of a different faith; men of one rank or caste enjoyed special privileges which were not granted to men of another. Under these systems peace was impossible and strife perpetual. But under just and equal laws in the United States, Jews, Protestants, and Catholics, Englishmen and Irishmen, the former aristocrat and the masses of the people, dwell and mingle harmoniously together. The uniform lesson of history is that unjust and partial laws increase and create antagonism, while justice and equality are the sure foundation of prosperity and peace.

Impartial suffrage secures also popular education. Nothing has given the careful observer of events in the South more gratification than the progress which is there going on in the establishment of schools. The colored people, who as slaves were debarred from education, regard the right to learn as one of the highest privileges of freemen. The ballot gives them the power to secure that privilege. All parties and all public men in the South agree that, if colored men vote, ample provision must be made in the reorganization of every State for free schools. The ignorance of the masses, whites as well as blacks, is one of the most discouraging features of southern society. If congressional reconstruction succeeds, there will be free schools for all. The colored people will see that their children attend them. We need indulge in no fears that the white people will be left behind. Impartial suffrage, then, means popular intelligence; it means progress; it means loyalty; it means harmony between the North and the South, and between the whites and the colored people.

The Union party believes that the general welfare requires that measures should be adopted which will work great change in the South. Our adversaries are accustomed to talk of the rebellion as an affair which began when the rebels attacked Fort Sumter in 1861, and which ended when Lee surrendered to Grant in 1865. It is true that the attempt by force of arms to destroy the United States began and ended during the administration of Mr. Lincoln. But the causes, the principles, and the motives which produced the rebellion are of an older date than the generation which suffered from the fruit they bore, and their influence and power are likely to last long after that generation passes away. Ever since armed rebellion failed, a large party in the South have struggled to make participation in the rebellion honorable and loyalty to the Union dishonorable. The lost cause with them is the honored cause. In society, in business, and in politics, devotion to treason is the test of merit, the passport to preferment. They wish to return to the old state of things — an oligarchy of race and the sovereignty of States.

To defeat this purpose, to secure the rights of man, and to perpetuate the national Union, are the objects of the congressional plan of reconstruction. That plan has the hearty support of the great generals (so far as their opinions are known) — of Grant, of Thomas, of Sheridan, of Howard — who led the armies of the Union which conquered the rebellion. The statesmen most trusted by Mr. Lincoln and by the loyal people of the country during the war also support it. The supreme court of the United States, upon formal application and after solemn argument, refuse to interfere with its execution. The loyal press of the country, which did so much in the time of need to uphold the patriot cause, without exception, are in favor of the plan.

In the South, as we have seen, the lessons of the war and the events occurring since the war have made converts of thousands of the bravest and of the ablest of those who opposed the national cause. General Longstreet, a soldier second to no living corps commander of the rebel army, calls it "a peace-offering," and advises the South in good faith to organize under it. Unrepentant rebels and unconverted Peace Democrats oppose it, just as they opposed the measures which destroyed slavery and saved the nation.

Opposition to whatever the nation approves seems to be the policy of the representative men of the Peace Democracy. Defeat and failure comprise their whole political history. In laboring to overthrow reconstruction they are probably destined to further defeat and further failure. I know not how it may be in other States, but if I am not greatly mistaken as to the mind of the loyal people of Ohio, they mean to trust power in the hands of no man who, during the awful struggle for the nation's life, proved unfaithful to the cause of liberty and of Union. They will continue to exclude from the administration of the government those who prominently opposed the war, until every question arising out of the rebellion relating to the integrity of the nation and to human rights shall have been firmly settled on the basis of impartial justice.

They mean that the State of Ohio, in this great progress, " whose leading object is to elevate the condition of men, to lift artificial weights from all shoulders, to clear the paths of laudable pursuits for all, to afford all an unfettered start and a fair chance in the race of life," shall tread no step backward.

Penetrated and sustained by a conviction that in this contest the Union party of Ohio is doing battle for the right, I enter upon my part of the labors of the canvass with undoubting confidence that the goodness of the cause will supply the weakness of its advocates, and command in the result that triumphant success which I believe it deserves.

ARGYLL

GEORGE JOHN DOUGLAS CAMPBELL, eighth Duke of Argyll, a distinguished Scotch scientist, theologian, and statesman, was born April 30, 1823, and educated privately. In 1842 he wrote "A Letter to the Peers from a Peer's Son," treating of the struggle which ended in disruption. In 1847 he published his "Presbytery Examined" and two years later succeeded his father. From 1853 to 1855 he was lord privy seal, serving in the same capacity from 1859 to 1866, and again in 1880 and 1881. From 1855 to 1858 he was postmaster-general, and was secretary of state for India from 1868 till 1874. He resigned the keepership of the privy seal in 1881 in disapproval of the Irish land bill. He was also opposed to home rule. Among other honorary posts, he was lord-lieutenant of Argyllshire, chancellor of the University of St. Andrews, trustee of the British Museum, and elder brother of Trinity House. He took a great interest in science, but was thoroughly conservative and opposed to the doctrine of evolution. He died September 28, 1900. His best known publications were "The Reign of Law" (1866); "Primeval Man" (1869); "Iona" (1871); "The Eastern Question" (1876); "Unity of Nature" (1884); "Scotland as It Was and Is" (1887); "Unseen Foundations of Society" (1893); "Poems" (1894); "Philosophy of Belief" (1896).

WELCOME TO GARRISON

MR. CHAIRMAN, LADIES, AND GENTLEMEN, — It is hard to follow an address of such extraordinary beauty, simplicity, and power; but it now becomes my duty at your command, sir, to move an address of hearty congratulation to our distinguished guest, William Lloyd Garrison. Sir, this country is from time to time honored by the presence of many distinguished and of a few illustrious men; but for the most part we are contented to receive them with that private cordiality and hospitality with which, I trust, we shall always receive strangers who visit our shores. The people of this country are not pre-eminently an emotional people; they are not naturally fond of public demonstrations; and it is only upon rare occasions that we give, or can give, such a reception as that we see here this

day. There must be something peculiar in the cause which
a man has served, in the service which he has rendered, and
in our own relations with the people whom he represents, to
justify or to account for such a reception. As regards the
cause, it is not too much to say that the cause of negro
emancipation in the United States of America has been the
greatest cause which, in ancient or in modern times, has been
pleaded at the bar of the moral judgment of mankind. I
know that to some this will sound as the language of exaggerated feeling; but I can only say that I have expressed
myself in language which I believe conveys the literal truth.

I have, indeed, often heard it said in deprecation of the
amount of interest which was bestowed in this country on the
cause of negro emancipation in America, that we are apt to
forget the forms of suffering which are immediately at our
own doors, over which we have some control, and to express
exaggerated feeling as to the forms of suffering with which
we have nothing to do, and for which we are not responsible.
I have never objected to that language in so far as it might
tend to recall us to the duties which lie immediately around
us, and in so far as it might tend to make us feel the forgetful-
ness of which we are sometimes guilty, of the misery and
poverty in our own country; but, on the other hand, I will
never admit — for I think it would be confounding great
moral distinctions — that the miseries which arise by way of
natural consequence out of the poverty and the vices of mankind, are to be compared with those miseries which are the
direct result of positive law and of a positive institution,
giving to man property in man. It is true, also, that there
have been forms of servitude — meaning thereby compulsory
labor — against which we do not entertain the same feelings
of hostility and horror with which we have regarded slavery in

America. Although we rejoiced at the cessation of serfdom
in Russia, what person felt in regard to that condition of
things as we all felt in regard to negro slavery in America?
Undoubtedly the condition of compulsory servitude has been
a stage in the progress of mankind, and we rejoice that that
stage has been passed; but with regard to negro slavery in
America, it was not one, but many circumstances, which constituted its peculiar aggravation and horror. It was a system
of which it may be truly said, that it was twice cursed. It
cursed him who served, and it cursed him that owned the
slave. When we recollect the insuperable temptations which
that system held out to maintain in a state of degradation
and ignorance a whole race of mankind; the horrors of the
internal slave-trade, more widely demoralizing, in my opinion,
than the foreign slave-trade itself; the violence which was
done to the sanctities of domestic life; the corrupting effect
which it was having upon the very churches of Christianity,—
when we recollect all these things, we can fully estimate the
evil from which my distinguished friend and his coadjutors
have at last redeemed their country. It was not only the
slave States which were concerned in the guilt of slavery; it
had struck its roots deep in the free States of North America.
And what are the free States of North America? I think we
may say with truth that America is a country which seems
destined by Almighty God to test the question, what man
can do best for himself under the most favorable conditions
of external circumstances; possessing a vast territory of the
greatest wealth with the greatest natural capabilities of
improvement, peopled by the most energetic races of Europe,
free to take with them all that is best, or at least much that
is best, of the more ancient civilizations of the world, and
free to leave behind them as much as they may think evil of

the traditions of the past, who is there with a heart in his breast, or for that matter with a head on his shoulders, who does not look with intense interest to the conduct of that great experiment, and who does not rejoice with a joy unspeakable in events which have freed their young and noble life from the taint and the curse of slavery?

If such be the cause, what are we to say of the man and of the services which he has rendered to that cause? We honor Mr. Garrison, in the first place, for the immense pluck and courage which he displayed. Sir, you have truly said that there is no comparison between the contests in which he had to fight and the most bitter contests of our own public life. In looking back, no doubt, to the contest which was maintained in this country some thirty-five years ago against slavery in our colonies, we may recollect that Clarkson and Wilberforce were denounced as fanatics, and had to encounter much opprobrium; but it must not be forgotten that, so far as regards the entwining of the roots of slavery into the social system, in the opinions and interests of mankind, there was no comparison whatever between the circumstances of that contest here and those which attended it in America. The number of persons who in this country were enlisted on the side of slavery by personal interest was always comparatively few; whilst, in attacking slavery at its headquarters in the United States, Mr. Garrison had to encounter the fiercest passions which could be roused. That is, indeed, a tremendous sea which runs upon the surface of the human mind when the storms of passion and of self-interest run counter to the secret currents of conscience and the sense of right. Such was the stormy sea on which Mr. Garrison embarked at first — if I may use the simile — almost in a one-oared boat. He stood alone. And so in our reception this day of Mr.

Garrison, we are entitled to think of him as representing the increased power and force which is exerted in our own times by the moral opinions of mankind. It is true, indeed, that we have lately seen some of the most tremendous and bloody wars which history records; and I, for one, must admit that the time has not yet come — it is not even yet in sight — when we can beat our swords into plowshares and our spears into pruning-hooks; but if we look to the great events to which I have referred, we shall see that in our own time the march of great battalions has generally been in the wake of the march of great principles, that in the freedom of Italy, in the consolidation of Germany, and still more in the recent contest in America, we are to look to the triumphs of opinion as, in the main, the triumphs which have been won. I can understand the joy which must be felt by a great sovereign, or by a great general, when standing amidst the heaps of slain he can feel that he has won the independence of a country, or, still better, has established the independence of a race. We can all, however, understand still better the joy of him who, like our distinguished friend, after years of obloquy and oppression, and being denounced as the fanatical supporter of extreme opinions, finds himself acknowledged at last by his countrymen and the world as the prophet and apostle of a triumphant and accepted cause.

One word in regard to the nation which Mr. Garrison represents. Let us remember with joy and thankfulness that only a few years ago the present reception could not have been given to Mr. Garrison. He was then not the representative of a people, of a country, or of a government. He was the representative only of a party in the United States, and I have always held that public receptions or meetings in foreign countries, or at least in other countries, for I will not call

America a foreign country — I mean public assemblies or conventions taking part with particular parties of another country, are sometimes almost as apt to do as much harm as good. Now, thank God, Mr. Garrison appears before us as the representative of the United States; freedom is now the policy of the government and the assured policy of the country, and we can to-day accept and welcome Mr. Garrison, not merely as the liberator of the slaves, but as the representative also of the American government. This country desires to maintain with the American people not merely relations of amity and peace; it desires to have their friendship and affection. It is not merely that that country has sprung from us in former times. It is that it is still to a great extent springing from England. It is hardly possible to go into any house of the farming class in that part of the country with which I am particularly connected without being told that a brother or a sister, a daughter or a son, has gone to the United States of America, and is flourishing in the free States of Ohio or Illinois. I think we ought to feel, every one of us, that in going to America we are going only to a second home. Such are the relations which I trust we shall see established between the two countries. Surely it is time to forget ancient differences — differences dating from the days of Burgoyne's retreat or our failure before the ramparts of New Orleans. I maintain that there is hardly an Englishman in this country — I am sure there is no one in this room — who is not almost as proud of Washington as he is of Wellington, the memory of both belonging indeed to the common heritage of our race. Therefore, on all these grounds — on the ground of the cause of which he was the great champion, of the peculiar services which he has rendered to that cause, and of the people whom he represents, we desire to give Mr. Garrison a hearty welcome.

SHERMAN

JOHN SHERMAN was born at Lancaster, Ohio, May 10, 1823. He was not sent to college, but received a fairly good academic education. He studied law and was admitted to the bar at the age of twenty-one. He joined the Whig party, and was a delegate to the National Whig Conventions in 1848 and 1852. He took part in the organization of the Republican party, and in 1855 presided over the first Republican Convention held in his native State. He was a representative in Congress from March 4, 1855, to March, 1861, and was the Republican candidate for Speaker in 1859–60. He was sent to the Federal Senate in 1861 to succeed Salmon P. Chase, and was re-elected in 1866 and 1872. He was Secretary of the Treasury under President Hayes from 1877 to 1881. On March 4, of the year last named, he again took a seat in the Senate and was re-elected in 1886 and 1892. He was a prominent candidate for the Presidency in several Republican National Conventions. On March 4, 1897, he became Secretary of State in the McKinley administration, but did not long retain the office. He died in 1900.

ON SILVER COINAGE AND TREASURY NOTES

UNITED STATES SENATE, JUNE 5, 1890

I APPROACH the discussion of this bill and the kindred bills and amendments pending in the two Houses with unaffected diffidence. No problem is submitted to us of equal importance and difficulty. Our action will affect the value of all the property of the people of the United States, and the wages of labor of every kind, and our trade and commerce with all the world. In the consideration of such a question we should not be controlled by previous opinions or bound by local interests, but with the lights of experience and full knowledge of all the complicated

(8429)

facts involved, give to the subject the best judgment which imperfect human nature allows. With the wide diversity of opinion that prevails, each of us must make concessions in order to secure such a measure as will accomplish the objects sought for without impairing the public credit or the general interests of our people. This is no time for visionary theories of political economy. We must deal with facts as we find them and not as we wish them. We must aim at results based upon practical experience, for what has been probably will be. The best prophet of the future is the past.

To know what measures ought to be adopted we should have a clear conception of what we wish to accomplish. I believe a majority of the Senate desire, first, to provide an increase of money to meet the increasing wants of our rapidly growing country and population, and to supply the reduction in our circulation caused by the retiring of national banknotes; second, to increase the market value of silver not only in the United States but in the world, in the belief that this is essential to the success of any measure proposed, and in the hope that our efforts will advance silver to its legal ratio with gold, and induce the great commercial nations to join with us in maintaining the legal parity of the two metals, or in agreeing with us in a new ratio of their relative value; and third, to secure a genuine bimetallic standard, one that will not demonetize gold or cause it to be hoarded or exported, but that will establish both gold and silver as standards of value not only in the United States, but among all the civilized nations of the world.

Believing that these are the chief objects aimed at by us all, and that we differ only as to the best means to obtain them, I will discuss the pending propositions to test how far they tend, in my opinion, to promote or defeat these objects.

And, first, as to the amount of currency necessary to meet the wants of the people. . . .

It is a fact that there has been a constant increase of currency. It is a fact which must be constantly borne in mind. If any evils now exist such as have been so often stated, such as falling prices, increased mortgages, contentions between capital and labor, decreasing value of silver, increased relative value of gold, they must be attributed to some other cause than our insufficient supply of circulation, for not only has the circulation increased in these twelve years eighty per cent, while our population has only increased thirty-six per cent, but it has all been maintained at the gold standard, which, it is plain, has been greatly advanced in purchasing power. If the value of money is tested by its amount, by numerals, according to the favorite theory of the Senator from Nevada (Mr. Jones), then surely we ought to be on the high road of prosperity, for these numerals have increased in twelve years from $805,000,000 to $1,405,000,000 in October last, and to $1,420,000,000 on the first of this month. This single fact disposes of the claim that insufficient currency is the cause of the woes, real and imaginary, that have been depicted, and compel us to look to other causes for the evils complained of.

I admit that prices for agricultural productions have been abnormally low, and that the farmers of the United States have suffered greatly from this cause. But this depression of prices is easily accounted for by the greatly increased amount of agricultural production, the wonderful development of agricultural implements, the opening of vast regions of new and fertile fields in the West, the reduced cost of transportation, the doubling of the miles of railroads, and the quadrupling capacity of railroads and steamboats for transportation, and the new-fangled forms of trusts and combinations which monopolize nearly all the productions of the farms and workshops of our country, reducing the price to the producer and in some cases increasing the cost to the consumer. All these causes co-operate to reduce prices of farm products. No one of them can be traced to an insufficient currency, now larger in amount in proportion to population than ever before in our history.

But to these causes of a domestic character must be added others, over which we have no control. The same wonderful development of industry has been going on in other parts of the globe. In Russia, especially in Southern Russia, vast regions have been opened to the commerce of the world. Railroads have been built, mines have been opened, exhaustless supplies of petroleum have been found, and all these are competitors with us in supplying the wants of Europe for food, metals, heat, and light. India, with its teeming millions of poorly paid laborers, is competing with our farmers, and their products are transported to market over thousands of miles of railroads constructed by English capital, or by swift steamers through the Red Sea and the Suez Canal, reaching directly the people of Europe whom we formerly supplied with food. No wonder, then, that our agriculture is depressed by low prices, caused by competition with new rivals and agencies.

Any one who can overlook these causes and attribute low prices to a want of domestic currency, that has increased and is increasing continually, must be blind to the great forces that in recent times throughout the world are tending by improved methods and modern inventions to lessen the prices of all commodities. . . .

These fluctuations depend upon the law of supply and demand, involving facts too numerous to state, but rarely depending on the volume of money in circulation. An increase of currency can have no effect to advance prices unless we cheapen and degrade it by making it less valuable; and if that is the intention now, the direct and honest way is to put fewer grains of gold or silver in our dollar. This was the old way, by clipping the coin, adding base metal.

If we want a cheaper dollar we have the clear constitutional right to put in it 15 grains of gold instead of 23, or 300 grains of silver instead of 412½, but you have no power to say how many bushels of wheat the new dollar shall buy. You can, if you choose, cheapen the dollar under your power to coin money, and thus enable a debtor to pay his debts with fewer grains of silver or gold, under the pretext that gold or silver has risen in value, but in this way you would destroy all forms of credit and make it impossible for nations or individuals to borrow money for a period of time. It is a species of repudiation.

The best standard of value is one that measures for the longest period its equivalent in other products. Its relative value may vary from time to time. If it falls, the creditor loses; if it increases, the debtor loses; and these changes are the chances of all trade and commerce and all loaning and borrowing. The duty of the government is performed when it coins money and provides convenient credit representatives of coin. The purchasing power of money for other commodities depends upon changing conditions over which the government has no control. Even its power to issue paper money has been denied until recently, but this may be considered as settled by the recent decisions of the Supreme Court in the legal-tender cases. All that Congress ought to do is to provide a sufficient amount of money, either of coin or its equivalent of paper money, to meet the current wants of business. This it has done in the twelve years last passed at a ratio of increase far in excess of any in our previous history. . . .

Under the law of February, 1878, the purchase of $2,000,000 worth of silver bullion a month has by coinage produced annually an average of nearly $3,000,000 a month for a period of twelve years, but this amount, in view of the retirement of the banknotes, will not increase our currency in proportion to our increase in population. If our present currency is estimated at $1,400,000,000, and our population is increasing at the ratio of 3 per cent per annum, it would require $42,000,000 increased circulation each year to keep pace with the increase of population; but as the increase of population is accompanied by a still greater ratio of increase of wealth and business, it was thought that an immediate increase of circulation might be obtained by larger purchases of silver bullion to an amount sufficient to make good the retirement of banknotes, and keep pace with the growth of population. Assuming that $54,000,000 a year of additional circulation is needed upon this basis, that amount is provided for in this bill by the issue of Treasury notes in exchange for bullion at the market price. I see no objection to this proposition, but believe that Treasury notes based upon silver bullion purchased in this way will be as safe a foundation for paper money as can be conceived.

Experience shows that silver coin will not circulate to any considerable amount. Only about one silver dollar to each inhabitant is maintained in circulation with all the efforts made by the Treasury Department, but silver certificates, the representatives of this coin, pass current without question, and are maintained at par in gold by being received by the government for all purposes and redeemed if called for. I do not fear to give to these notes every sanction and value that the United States can confer. I do not object to their being made a legal tender for all debts, public or private. I believe that if they are to be issued they ought to be issued as money, with all the sanction and authority that the government can possibly confer. While I believe the amount to be issued is greater than is necessary, yet in view of the retirement of banknotes I yielded my objections to the increase beyond $4,000,000. As an expedient to provide increased circulation it is far preferable to free coinage of silver or any proposition that has been made to provide some other security than United States bonds for bank circulation. I believe it will accomplish the first object proposed, a gradual and steady increase of the current money of the country. . . .

What then can we do to arrest the fall of silver and to advance its market value? I know of but two expedients. One is to purchase bullion in large quantities as the basis and security of Treasury notes, as proposed by this bill. The other is to adopt the single standard of silver, and take the chances for its rise or fall in the markets of the world. I have already stated the probable results of the hoarding of bullion. By purchasing in the open market our domestic production of silver and hoarding it in the Treasury we withdraw so much from the supply of the world, and thus maintain or increase the price of the remaining silver production of the world. It is not idle in our vaults, but is represented by certificates in active circulation. Sixteen ounces of silver bullion may not be worth one ounce of gold, still one dollar's worth of silver bullion is worth one dollar of gold.

What will be the effect of the free coinage of silver? It is said that it will at once advance silver to par with gold at the ratio of 16 to 1. I deny it. The attempt will bring us to the single standard of the cheaper metal. When we advertise that we will buy all the silver of the world at that ratio and pay in Treasury notes, our notes will have the precise value of 371¼ grains of pure silver, but the silver will have no higher value in the markets of the world. If, now, that amount of silver can be purchased at 80 cents, then gold will be worth $1.25 in the new standard. All labor, property, and commodities will advance in nominal value, but their purchasing power in other commodities will not increase. If you make the yard 30 inches long instead of 36 you must purchase more yards for a coat or a dress, but do not lessen the cost of the coat or the dress. You may by free coinage, by a species of confiscation, reduce the burden of a debt, but you cannot change the relative value of gold or silver, or any object of human desire. The only result is to demonetize gold and to cause it to be hoarded or exported. The cheaper metal fills the channels of circulation and the dearer metal commands a premium.

If experience is needed to prove so plain an axiom we have it in our own history. At the beginning of our National Government we fixed the value of gold and silver as 1 to 15. Gold was undervalued and fled the country to where an ounce of gold was worth 15¼ ounces of silver. Congress, in 1834, endeavored to rectify this by making the ratio 1 to 16, but by this silver was undervalued.

Sixteen ounces of silver were worth more than 1 ounce of gold, and silver disappeared. Congress, in 1853, adopted another expedient to secure the value of both metals as money. By this expedient gold is the standard and silver the subsidiary coin, containing confessedly silver of less value in the market than the gold coin, but maintained at the parity of gold coin by the government. . . .

But it is said that those of us who demand the gold standard, or paper money always equal to gold, are the representatives of capital, money-changers, bondholders, Shylocks, who want to grind and oppress the people. This kind of argument I hoped would never find its way into the Senate Chamber. It is the cry of the demagogue, without the slightest foundation. All these classes can take care of themselves. They are the men who make their profits out of the depreciation of money. They can mark up the price of their property to meet changing standards. They can protect themselves by gold contracts. In proportion to their wealth they have less money on hand than any other class. They have already protected themselves to a great extent by converting the great body of the securities in which they deal into gold bonds, and they hold the gold of the country, which you cannot change in value. They are not, as a rule, the creditors of the country.

The great creditors are savings banks, insurance companies, widows and orphans, and provident farmers, and business men on a small scale. The great operators are the great borrowers and owe more than is due them. Their credit is their capital and they need not have even money enough to pay their rent.

But how will this change affect the great mass of our fellow citizens who depend upon their daily labor? A dollar to them means so much food, clothing, and rent. If you cheapen the dollar it will buy less of these. You may say they will get more dollars for their labor, but all experience shows that labor and land are the last to feel the change in monetary standards, and the same resistance will be made to an advance of wages on the silver standard as on the gold standard, and when the advance is won it will be found that the purchasing power of the new dollar is less than the old. No principle of political economy is better established than that the producing classes are the first to suffer and the last to gain by monetary changes.

I might apply this argument to the farmer, the merchant, the professional man, and to all classes except the speculator or the debtor who wishes to lessen the burden of his obligations; but it is not necessary.

It is sometimes said that all this is a false alarm, that our demand for silver will absorb all that will be offered and bring it to par with gold at the old ratio. I have no faith in such a miracle. If they really thought so, many would lose their interest in the question. What they want is a cheaper dollar that would pay debts easier. Others do not want either silver or gold, but want numbers, numerals, the fruit of the printing-press, to be fixed every year by Congress as we do an appropriation bill.

Now, sir, I am willing to do all I can with safety even to taking great risks to increase the value of silver to gold at the old ratio, and to supply paper substitutes for both for circulation, but there is one immutable, unchangeable, ever-existing condition, that the paper substitute must always have the same purchasing power as gold and silver coin, maintained at their legal ratio with each other. I feel a conviction, as strong as the human mind can have that the free coinage of silver now by the United States will be a grave mistake and a misfortune to all classes and conditions of our fellow citizens. I also have a hope and belief, but far from a certainty, that the measure proposed for the purchase of silver bullion to a limited amount, and the issue of Treasury notes for it, will bring silver and gold to the old ratio, and will lead to an agreement with other commercial nations to maintain the free coinage of both metals.

And now, sir, I want to state in conclusion, without any purpose to bind myself to detail, that I will vote for any measure that will, in my judgment, secure a genuine bimetallic standard—one that will not demonetize gold or cause it to be hoarded or exported, but will establish both silver and gold as common standards and maintain them at a fixed ratio, not only in the United States but among all the nations of the world. The principles adopted by the Acts of 1853 and 1875 have been sustained by experience and should be adhered to. In pursuance of them I would receive into the Treasury of the United States all the gold and silver produced in our country at their market value, not at a speculative or forced value, but at their value in the markets of the world. And for the convenience of our people I would represent them by Treasury notes to an amount not exceeding their cost. I would confer upon these notes all the use, qualities, and attributes that we can confer within our constitutional power, and support and maintain them as money by coining the silver and gold as needed upon the present legal ratios, and by a pledge of all the revenues of the government and all the wealth and credit of the United States. And I would proclaim to all our readiness, by international negotiations or treaties, to bring about an agreement among nations for common units of value and of weights and measures for all the productions of the world.

This hope of philosophers and statesmen is now nearer realization than ever before. If we could contribute to this result it would tend to promote commerce and intercourse, trade and travel, peace and harmony among nations. It would be in line with the civilization of our age. It is by such measures statesmen may keep pace with the marvellous inventions, improvements, and discoveries which have quadrupled the capacity of man for production, made lightning subservient to his will, revealed to him new agencies of power hidden in the earth, and opened up to his enterprise all the dark places of the world. The people of the United States boast that they have done their full share in all this development; that they have grown in population, wealth, and strength; that they are the richest of nations, with untarnished credit, a model and example of self-government without kings or princes or lords. Surely this is no time for a radical change of public policy which seems to have no motive except to reduce the burden of obligations freely taken, a change likely to impair our public credit and produce disorder and confusion in all monetary transactions. Others may see reasons for this change, but I prefer to stand by the standards of value that come to us with the approval and sanction of every party that has administered the government since its beginning.

GREAT SPEECH ON THE FINANCIAL SITUATION

DELIVERED IN THE UNITED STATES SENATE, DECEMBER 31, 1895

MR. PRESIDENT,— I intend to do what I have rarely if ever done in the Senate, read a speech to this body. I have felt that on account of the importance of the subject-matter and the necessity of brevity it would be better for me to reduce my remarks to writing, and I have done so in order to save the time of the Senate more than for any other purpose.

The President, in his annual message to Congress, confined himself to two important subjects, one our foreign relations and the other the condition of our national finances. He followed it by another message on the application of the Monroe doctrine to the controversy between Great Britain and Venezuela.

While Congress has heartily, perhaps too hastily, but with entire unanimity, supported him in maintaining the interests and honor of our country in the field of diplomacy, it has not and will not approve his recommendations on the more important subject of our financial policy and especially of our currency. He has mistaken the cause of our present financial condition in attributing it to the demand for gold for United States notes instead of to the deficiency of revenue caused by the legislation of the last Congress. He places the effect before the cause. He proposes as a remedy the conversion of the United States notes and the treasury notes into interest-bearing bonds, thus increasing the interest-bearing debt nearly $500,000,000. He proposes a line of public policy that will produce a sharp contraction of our currency, add greatly to the burden of existing debts, and arrest the progress of almost every American industry which now competes with foreign productions.

The President is supported in these views by Mr. Carlisle, his able secretary of the treasury, in his report to Congress. It is with diffidence I undertake to controvert their opinions; but my convictions are so strong that they are in error that I hope the strength of the facts I will submit to the Senate will convince it that the true line of public policy is to supply the government with ample means to meet current expenditures and to pay each year a portion of the public debt. The gold reserve provided for the redemption of United States notes can then be easily maintained without cost except the loss of interest on the gold in the treasury, but with a saving of interest on United States notes and treasury notes of five times the interest lost by the gold held in reserve. A vastly greater benefit than saving interest is secured to our people by a national paper currency at par with coin supported by the credit of the United States and redeemed on demand in coin at the treasury in the principal city of the United States.

The only difficulty in the way of an easy maintenance of our notes at par with coin is the fact that during this administration the revenues of the government have not been sufficient to meet the expenditures authorized by Congress. If Congress had provided necessary revenue, or if the President and Mr. Carlisle had refused to expend appropriations not mandatory in form, but permissive, so as to confine expenditures within receipts, they would have had no difficulty with the reserve. This would have been a stalwart act in harmony with the President's character and plainly within his power.

All appropriations which are not provided to carry into effect existing law are permissive, but not mandatory, and his refusal to expend money in excess of the revenues of the government would not only be justified by public policy, but would have been heartily approved by the people of the United States. He knew as well as any one that since the close of the civil war to the date of his inauguration the expenditures of the government had been less than its receipts. I have here a table which shows the receipts and expenditures each year from 1866 to 1893. . . .

From this official statement it appears that each and every year during that long period there was a surplus, which was applied to the reduction of the public debt bearing interest. . . .

The President, in his recent annual message, complains that the law of October 6, 1890, known as the McKinley Act, was "inefficient for the purposes of revenue." That law, though it largely reduced taxation by placing many articles on the free list and granted a bounty for the production of sugar, yet did not reduce revenues below expenditures, but provided a surplus of $37,239,762.57 June 30, 1891, and $9,914,453.66 June 30, 1892, and $2,341,674.29 on the 30th of June, 1893, when Mr. Cleveland was President and a Democratic majority in both Houses of Congress had been elected, all pledged to repeal the McKinley Act and to reduce duties. That the McKinley Act did not produce more revenue in 1893 and 1894 is not a matter of surprise. Any tariff law denounced by the party in power, with a promise to repeal it and to reduce duties, would prevent importations under the old law and thus lower the revenue. Early in December, 1893, at the first regular session of Congress during Mr. Cleveland's term, a bill was formulated, and as soon as practicable passed the House of Representatives.

That bill met the hearty approval of the President. If it had become a law as originally presented, the deficiency in revenue would have been much greater than now; but conservative Democratic senators with the aid of Republican senators, greatly improved the House bill, added other duties and changed the scope of the measure. With these amendments it became a law. The President refused to sign it, expressing his opposition to the Senate amendments, and yet now supports it when deficiencies have been greatly increased, when the public debt is increasing, and doubts are expressed as to the ability of the government to maintain its notes at par with coin. The President makes no mention in his message of these deficiencies; no mention of the issue of interest-bearing bonds to meet them. The secretary of the treasury is more frank in his statement. He reports a deficiency of $69,803,260.58 during the fiscal year ended June 30, 1894, and for the year ended June 30, 1895, $42,805,223.18, and for the six months prior to December 1, 1895, $17,613,539.24; in all, $130,221,023.

No complaint was made that the McKinley law "was inefficient for the purposes of revenue" when the Wilson bill was pending. The objection to the McKinley law was that it was a "protective tariff," and the Wilson bill was a "revenue tariff." I have a statement showing the receipts and expenditures under each law each month, the McKinley law from its passage to the election of Cleveland, and the Wilson law from its passage to December 1, 1895. During the twenty-five months of the McKinley law the average monthly surplus was $1,129,821. During the existence of the Wilson law the average monthly deficiency was $4,699,603. If the

McKinley law was, in the opinion of the President, inefficient for revenue, he should have said of the Wilson law that
it was bounteous in deficiencies. . . .

I could pursue the analysis of these two laws further, but
I have said enough to explain the preference by the President
of the Wilson bill. He believes in large importations at the
lowest cost, without regard to the industries and labor of our
countrymen, while I believe in a careful discrimination and
the imposition of such duties on articles that compete with
home productions as will diversify our employments and
protect and foster impartially all industries, whether of the
farm, the workshop, the mine, the forest, or the sea. I have
not been satisfied with any tariff law made during my public
life, though I have shared in framing many. I prefer a law
that will impartially protect and encourage all home industries, and regard the McKinley law as infinitely better than
the Wilson law, which I believe is the cause of all the evils
which we now encounter by adverse balance of trade, by
exportation of gold and derangement of our monetary system. The Wilson law has produced a deficiency in every
hour and day that it has been on the statute book, while the
McKinley law has always produced a surplus until after the
incoming of this administration, and if administrated since
that time by friendly agents would have furnished the government all the revenue needed.

The deficiency of revenue was the primary cause of the
demand for gold for United States notes. The gold hoarded
for resumption purposes was not separated from the money
received for current revenue, and this revenue being insuffi-
c'ent to meet expenses, the gold accumulated for redemption
purposes was drawn upon to make good deficiencies. This
created a doubt of the ability of the government to maintain

the parity of United States notes with coin, and led to their presentation for redemption in coin. The draft on the treasury for coin during this administration has been greater than the amount of deficiency of revenue during the same period. In every aspect in which the subject presents itself to my mind I come to no other conclusion than that the deficiency of revenue and the consequent encroachment upon the redemption fund is the cause of our present financial condition and that the only remedies are either a radical reduction of expenditures or an increase of taxation, and perhaps both. I do not believe that the condition requires a suspension of public works or a postponement of measures now in progress to strengthen the army and navy. . . .

Such a deficiency is discreditable to the United States, with its vast wealth and resources. There is no difficulty in collecting for taxation all and more money than is necessary for its expenditures. It is humiliating to read in the newspapers of the day that our government is negotiating for money from associated bankers, and, like a distressed debtor in view of bankruptcy, is offered by a friendly power its accumulated gold to relieve us from our supposed financial distress. The true remedy is to supply additional revenue by taxation in some form, and, until this can be effected, to borrow from the people of the United States enough money to cover past and future deficiencies. This done, gold will readily be exchanged for United States notes, as was done from January, 1879, to the election of Mr. Cleveland. . . .

The President complains that the notes are presented and paid, reissued, and paid again and again, making a continuous circuit. When did this circuit commence? The only answer is, when this administration, supported by the last Congress, created a deficiency. Why does the circuit continue? It is because the deficiency continues. The government resorts to the financial policy of Micawber. It gives its bonds and thinks the debt paid. But the circuit continues. The money received for current revenue is paid to cover deficiencies and is returned for gold, and then more bonds. The secretary hopes that in two or three years there will be no deficiency. What is the ground for this hope? It is that a new administration will provide more revenue, and then the circuit will be broken. Why not apply the remedy now?

If deficiencies occur Congress should immediately supply the means to meet them, and Congress, and not the administration, must be the judge of the mode and manner of relief. The invasion and misapplication of the resumption fund is of infinitely greater injury to our people than the imposition of ten times the amount of taxation.

It is said that the law for their continued reissue is mandatory. That is not a fair construction of the law. The plain meaning of it is the redemption of the notes shall not cause their cancellation. They are placed on the footing of bank notes. What solvent bank would reissue its notes when there was a run upon it? It would hold them until the demand ceased. The government ought to exercise the same prudence. The President is of the opinion that the United States notes and treasury notes should be retired and give place to bank notes. This is a question for Congress to decide. It is certainly not of that opinion now, nor was the last Congress of that opinion. Outside of a few large cities where banking facilities are abundant and business is conducted by checks and commercial paper, there is no desire for the retirement of national paper money. It is not right for the executive authorities to discredit this money by using it for current deficiencies. It was the use and dispersion of the redemption fund that created the circle of which he complains.

I believe that under existing law the aggregate sum of United States notes and treasury notes issued under the act of 1890, amounting to about $460,000,000 can be easily maintained at par with coin if the two amendments I have mentioned are adopted by Congress. These notes are a legal tender for all debts, public or private. They are a debt of the United States without interest and without other material cost to the government than the interest on the cost of the coin or bullion held in the treasury to redeem them. They are preferred by the people to any other form of paper money that has been devised. They have all the sanctions of law and all the security that has been or can be given to our bonds. They have the pledge of the public faith that they will be redeemed in coin. The substitution of these notes for State-bank paper money was one of the greatest benefits that has resulted from the Civil War. These notes have all the sanction, protection, and security that has been or can be given to our national bank notes, with the added benefit that the large saving derived from them inures to the people of the United States instead of to the bankers.

Another reason, founded upon belief, is that the national banking system could not long endure if the United States notes were withdrawn. I will not on this occasion discuss this, nor any other of the numerous financial questions involved, such as the policy of requiring the duties on imports to be paid in gold Imports are purchased with gold, are paid for in gold, and we may require gold for duties. The disposition of silver certificates is a much more serious problem. They are in express terms redeemable in silver dollars. Ought they not to be redeemed by silver dollars? While the silver dollars are maintained at par with gold it would seem that there was no injustice in paying the silver dollars for silver certificates. Then comes up the question of free coinage of silver, which I regard as the most dangerous policy.

All these are vital questions I do not wish to mingle with the pressing recommendation of the President in his last annual message "that authority be given the secretary of the treasury to issue bonds of the United States bearing a low rate of interest payable by their terms in gold for the purpose of maintaining a sufficient gold reserve and also for the redemption and cancellation of outstanding United States notes and the treasury notes issued for the purchase of silver under the law of 1890." He recommends the exchange of gold interest-bearing bonds for the legal-tender notes of the United States, and the substitution of national bank notes as our only currency.

He is supported in this by large and influential classes of our fellow citizens, most of them engaged in banking or classed as capitalists. Their arguments mainly rest upon the difficulties encountered by this administration in maintaining a reserve in coin to redeem United States notes. They forget that during a period of fourteen years when the revenues of the government exceeded expenditures and when the public debt was being reduced with unexampled rapidity there was no difficulty in maintaining our notes at par with coin. There is scarcely a doubt but that in all conditions of trade or finance, except the contingency of war, the whole mass of United States notes and treasury notes now in circulation can be maintained at par with coin if it is supported by a reserve of gold coin or bullion or silver bullion at market value in due proportions equal to one third or one fourth of the amount of such notes.

A careful study of the systems of banking currency and coinage adopted by the principal nations of Europe convinces me that our system, when cured of a few defects developed by time, founded upon the bimetallic coinage of gold and silver maintained at par with each other, with free national banks established in every city and town of importance in the United States, issuing their notes secured beyond doubt by United States bonds or some equivalent security, redeemable on demand in United States notes, and the issue of an amount of United States notes and treasury notes equal to the amount now outstanding, with provision for a ratable increase with the increase of population, always redeemable in coin and supported by an ample reserve of coin in the treasury, not to be invaded by deficiencies of revenue, and separated by the sub-treasury system from all connection with the receipts and expenditures of the government — such a system would make our money current in commercial circles in every land and clime, better than the best that now exists in Europe, better than that of Great Britain, which now holds the purse-string of the world.

It is not given to man to foresee with certainty the future; but if we may judge the future by the past, the growth and progress of our country will continue, the diversity and extent of our industries will expand, the vast plains of our broad territory will be teeming with population. The rapid growth of our cities, unexampled in the history of mankind, will continue. A century spans the life of this Republic; what will the next century do? I have seen great changes in my life, but those who come after us will see greater changes still. I may on some proper occasion hereafter give the reasons for my faith in our present financial system. All I ask now is that you will not disturb it with your deficiencies, you will not rob it of its safeguards, you will not return to the days of wildcat money, you will not lessen the savings of prudent labor or the accumulations of the rich. Time makes all things even. Let us give to the executive authorities ample means to meet the appropriations you have made, but let us strengthen rather than weaken our monetary system, which lies at the foundation of our prosperity and progress.

MEAGHER

THOMAS FRANCIS MEAGHER, an Irish soldier and revolutionist, was the son of a retired merchant and was born in Waterford, Ireland, August 3, 1823. After obtaining an education at the Jesuit College of Clongowes Wood and Stonyhurst College, Lancashire, he went to Dublin in 1844 with the intention of studying law, but speedily relinquished it for politics. He espoused the cause of Ireland with the greatest enthusiasm, and in a fiery speech on July 28 of that year deprecated the idea that the use of arms was immoral and declared the sword to be a sacred weapon. For this he was styled by Thackeray "Meagher of the Sword." On the 5th of March, 1848, he made a vehement speech before a meeting of the Irish confederation, asserting that Irishmen were justified in saying to the government, "If you do not give us a parliament in which to state our grievances, we shall state them by arms and force." He was arrested for sedition a few days later and tried at Dublin without a verdict being obtained. Undismayed by this warning, Meagher travelled about Ireland in the following July attempting to organize a revolution, but was again arrested. In October he was brought to trial at Clonmel and after six days' deliberation was adjudged guilty of high treason and sentenced to be hanged, drawn, and quartered. His sentence being commuted to penal servitude for life, he was banished to Tasmania, where considerable liberty appears to have been allowed him. In 1852 he escaped to the United States, where for two years he came frequently before the public as a lecturer, his fiery eloquence and his handsome features together making a great impression upon his hearers. He took up the study of law again and was admitted to the New York bar in 1855, but at the opening of the civil war promptly gave up his professional duties, and, organizing a company of zouave volunteers, served at their head in the Federal army. In 1862 he was appointed brigadier-general and distinguished himself by bravery at Antietam and other battle-fields. In 1866 he was appointed governor of Montana *pro tempore*, and while occupying this position was drowned in the Missouri River, near Fort Benton, Montana, July 1, 1867, by accidentally falling from the deck of a steamboat. Meagher was an extremely impulsive, recklessly courageous character, whose oratory was of the most fiery description. His writings include " Speeches on the Legislative Independence of Ireland " (1853); " Recollections of Ireland and the Irish; " " Last Days of the Sixty-Ninth in Virginia " (1861).

(8452)

"SWORD SPEECH"

DELIVERED IN CONCILIATION HALL, DUBLIN, JULY 20, 1846

M Y LORD MAYOR,— I will commence as Mr. Mit-
chel concluded, by an allusion to the Whigs.

I fully concur with my friend, that the most
comprehensive measures which the Whig minister may propose will fail to lift this country up to that position which
she has the right to occupy and the power to maintain. A
Whig minister, I admit, may improve the province — he
will not restore the nation. Franchises, tenant-compensation
bills, liberal appointments, may ameliorate — they will not
exalt. They may meet the necessities — they will not call
forth the abilities of the country. The errors of the past
may be repaired — the hopes of the future will not be fulfilled. With a vote in one pocket, a lease in the other, and
full "justice" before him at the petty sessions — in the
shape of a "restored magistrate" — the humblest peasant
may be told that he is free; but, my lord, he will not have
the character of a freeman — his spirit to dare, his energy
to act. From the stateliest mansion, down to the poorest
cottage in the land, the inactivity, the meanness, the debasement, which provincialism engenders, will be perceptible.

These are not the crude sentiments of youth, though the
mere commercial politician, who has deduced his ideas of
self-government from the table of imports and exports, may
satirize them as such. Age has uttered them, my lord, and
the experience of eighty years has preached them to the
people. A few weeks since, and there stood in the court of
queen's bench an old and venerable man, to teach the coun-

try the lessons he had learned, in this youth, beneath the portico of the Irish Senate House, and which, during a long life, he had treasured in his heart as the costliest legacy a true citizen could bequeath the land that gave him birth.

What said this aged orator?

"National independence does not necessarily lead to national virtue and happiness; but reason and experience demonstrate that public spirit and general happiness are looked for in vain under the withering influence of provincial subjection. The very consciousness of being dependent on another power, for advancement in the scale of national being, weighs down the spirit of a people, manacles the efforts of genius, depresses the energies of virtue, blunts the sense of common glory and common good, and produces an insulated selfishness of character, the surest mark of debasement in the individual, and mortality in the State."

My lord, it was once said by an eminent citizen of Rome, the elder Pliny, that "we owe our youth and manhood to our country, but our declining age to ourselves." This may have been the maxim of the Roman — it is not the maxim of the Irish patriot. One might have thought that the anxieties, the labors, the vicissitudes of a long career, had dimmed the fire which burned in the heart of the illustrious old man whose words I have cited; but now, almost from the shadow of death, he comes forth with the vigor of youth and the authority of age, to serve the country — in the defence of which he once bore arms — by an example, my lord, that must shame the coward, rouse the sluggard, and stimulate the bold.

These sentiments have sunk deep into the public mind. They are recited as the national creed. Whilst these sentiments inspire the people, I have no fear for the national cause — I do not dread the venal influence of the Whigs. Inspired by such sentiments, the people of this country will look beyond the mere redress of existing wrongs, and strive for the attainment of future power.

A good government may, indeed, redress the grievances of an injured people; but a strong people can alone build up a great nation. To be strong, a people must be self-reliant, self-ruled, self-sustained. The dependence of one people upon another, even for the benefits of legislation, is the deepest source of national weakness.

By an unnatural law it exempts a people from their just duties,— their just responsibilities. When you exempt a people from these duties, from these responsibilities, you generate in them a distrust in their own powers. Thus you enervate, if you do not utterly destroy, that spirit which a sense of these responsibilities is sure to inspire, and which the fulfilment of these duties never fails to invigorate. Where this spirit does not actuate, the country may be tranquil — it will not be prosperous. It may exist — it will not thrive. It may hold together — it will not advance. Peace it may enjoy — for peace and serfdom are compatible. But, my lord, it will neither accumulate wealth, nor win a character. It will neither benefit mankind by the enterprise of its merchants, nor instruct mankind by the examples of its statesmen. I make these observations, for it is the custom of some moderate politicians to say, that when the Whigs have accomplished the " pacification " of the country, there will be little or no necessity for Repeal.

My lord, there is something else, there is everything else, to be done when the work of " pacification " has been accomplished — and here it is hardly necessary to observe, that the prosperity of a country is, perhaps, the sole guarantee for its tranquillity, and that the more universal the prosperity, the more permanent will be the repose.

But the Whigs will enrich as well as pacify! Grant it, my lord. Then do I conceive that the necessity for Repeal will augment. Great interests demand great safeguards. The prosperity of a nation requires the protection of a senate. Hereafter a national senate may require the protection of a national army.

So much for the extraordinary affluence with which we are threatened; and which, it is said by gentlemen on the opposite shore of the Irish Sea, will crush this association, and clamor for Irish nationality, in a sepulchre of gold. This prediction, however, is feebly sustained by the ministerial programme that has lately appeared. On the evening of the sixteenth the Whig premier, in answer to a question that was put to him by the member for Finsbury, Mr. Duncombe, is reported to have made this consolatory announcement: —

"We consider that the social grievances of Ireland are those which are most prominent — and to which it is most likely to be in our power to afford, not a complete and immediate remedy, but some remedy, some kind of improvement, so that some kind of hope may be entertained that, some ten or twelve years hence, the country will, by the measures we undertake, be in a far better state with respect to the frightful destitution and misery which now prevails in that country. We have that practical object in view."

After that most consolatory announcement, my lord, let those who have the patience of Job and the poverty of Lazarus, continue in good faith " to wait on Providence and the Whigs " — continue to entertain " some kind of hope " that if not " a complete and immediate remedy," at least " some remedy," " some improvement " will place this country in " a far better state " than it is at present, " some ten or twelve years hence." After that, let those who prefer the

periodical boons of a Whig government to that which would
be the abiding blessing of an Irish Parliament — let those
who deny to Ireland what they assert for Poland — let those
who would inflict, as Henry Grattan said, an eternal dis-
ability upon this country, to which Providence has assigned
the largest facilities for power — let those who would ratify
the " base swap," as Mr. Shiel once stigmatized the Act of
Union, and would stamp perfection upon that deed of per-
fidy — let such men

> ———— " Plod on in sluggish misery,
> Rotting from sire to sire, from age to age,
> Proud of their trampled nature."

But we, my lord, who are assembled in this hall, and in
whose hearts the Union has not bred the slave's disease — we
who have not been imperialized — we are here, with the
hope to undo that work, which, forty-six years ago, dishon-
ored the ancient peerage, and subjugated the people of our
country.

My lord, to assist the people of Ireland to undo that work,
I came to this hall. I came to repeal the Act of Union, I
came here for nothing else. Upon every other question, I feel
myself at perfect liberty to differ from each and every one
of you. Upon questions of finance, questions of religious
character, questions of an educational character, questions of
municipal policy, questions that may arise from the proceedings of the legislature; upon all these questions, I feel
myself at perfect liberty to differ from each and every one
of you.

Yet more, my lord, I maintain that it is my right to express
my opinion upon each of these questions, if necessary. The
right of free discussion I have here upheld. In the exercise of that right I have differed, sometimes, from the leader

of this association, and would do so again. That right I will not abandon — I shall maintain it to the last. In doing so, let me not be told that I seek to undermine the influence of the leader of this association and am insensible to his services. My lord, I am grateful for his services, and will uphold his just influence. This is the first time I have spoken in these terms of that illustrious man, in this hall. I did not do so before — I felt it was unnecessary. I hate unnecessary praise — I scorn to receive it, I scorn to bestow it.

No, my lord, I am not ungrateful to the man who struck the fetters off my arms, whilst I was yet a child, and by whose influence, my father — the first Catholic who did so for two hundred years — sat, for the last two years, in the civic chair of an ancient city. But, my lord, the same God who gave to that great man the power to strike down an odious ascendancy in this country, and enable him to institute in this land the glorious law of religious equality; the same God gave to me a mind that is my own — a mind that has not been mortgaged to the opinions of any man or any set of men, a mind that I was to use, and not surrender.

My lord, in the exercise of that right, which I have here endeavored to uphold — a right which this association should preserve inviolate, if it desires not to become a despotism. In the exercise of that right, I have differed from Mr. O'Connell on previous occasions, and differ from him now. I do not agree with him in the opinion he entertains of my friend, Charles Gavan Duffy — that man whom I am proud, indeed, to call my friend — though he is a "convicted conspirator," and suffered for you in Richmond prison. I do not think he is a "maligner." I do not think he has lost, or deserves to lose, the public favor. I have no more connection with the "Nation" than I have with the "Times." I, therefore, feel

no delicacy in appearing here this day in defence of its principles, with which I avow myself identified. My lord, it is
to me a source of true delight and honest pride to speak this
day in defence of that great journal. I do not fear to assume
the position. Exalted though it be, it is easy to maintain it.
The character of that journal is above reproach. The ability
that sustains it has won a European fame. The genius of
which it is the offspring, the truth of which it is the oracle,
have been recognized, my lord, by friends and foes.

I care not how it may be assailed — I care not howsoever
great may be the talent, howsoever high may be the position,
of those who now consider it their duty to impeach its writings — I do think that it has won too splendid a reputation
to lose the influence it has acquired. The people, whose
enthusiasm has been kindled by the impetuous fire of its
verse, and whose sentiments have been ennobled by the earnest purity of its teaching, will not ratify the censure that has
been pronounced upon it in this hall.

Truth will have its day of triumph, as well as its day of
trial; and I foresee that the fearless patriotism which, in those
pages, has braved the prejudices of the day, to enunciate grand
truths, will triumph in the end. My lord, such do I believe
to be the character, such do I anticipate will be the fate of
the principles that are now impeached. This brings me to
what may be called the "question of the day." Before I
enter upon that question, however, I will allude to one observation which fell from the honorable member for Kilkenny,
and which may be said to refer to those who expressed
an opinion that has been construed into a declaration of
war.

The honorable gentleman said — in reference, I presume,
to those who dissented from the resolutions of Monday — that

"those who were loudest in their declarations of war, were usually the most backward in acting up to these declarations."

My lord, I do not find fault with the honorable gentleman for giving expression to a very ordinary saying, but this I will say, that I did not volunteer the opinion he condemns — to the declaration of that opinion I was forced. You left me no alternative — I should compromise my opinion, or avow it. To be honest, I avowed it. I did not do so to brag, as they say. We have had too much of that "bragging" in Ireland. I would be the last to imitate the custom. Well, I dissented from those "peace resolutions" as they are called. Why so? In the first place, my lord, I conceive that there was not the least necessity for them. No member of this association suggested an appeal to arms. No member of this association advised it. No member of this association would be so infatuated as to do so.

In the existing circumstances of the country an excitement to arms would be senseless and wicked because irrational. To talk nowadays of repealing the Act of Union by force of arms would be to rhapsodize. If the attempt were made it would be a decided failure. There might be a riot in the street — there would be no revolution in the country. The secretary, Mr. Crean, will far more effectually promote the cause of repeal, by registering votes in Green street than registering firearms in the head police office. Conciliation Hall on Burg Quay, is more impregnable than a rebel camp on Vinegar Hill. The hustings at Dundalk will be more successfully stormed than the magazine in the park. The registry club, the reading room, the polling booths, these are the only positions in the country we can occupy. Voters' certificates, books, pamphlets, newspapers, these are the only weapons we can employ. Therefore, my lord, I cast my vote in favor of the peaceful policy of this association. It is the only policy we can adopt. If that policy be pursued with truth, with courage, with fixed determination of purpose, I firmly believe it will succeed.

But, my lord, I dissented from the resolutions before us, for other reasons. I stated the first, I now come to the second. I dissented from them, for I felt, that, by assenting to them, I should have pledged myself to the unqualified repudiation of physical force in all countries, at all times, and under every circumstance. This I could not do. For, my lord, I do not abhor the use of arms in the vindication of national rights. There are times when arms will alone suffice, and when political ameliorations call for a drop of blood, and many thousand drops of blood. Opinion, I admit, will operate against opinion. But, as the honorable member for Kilkenny has observed, force must be used against force. The soldier is proof against an argument, but he is not proof against a bullet. The man that will listen to reason, let him be reasoned with; but it is the weaponed arm of the patriot that can alone prevail against battalioned despotism.

Then, my lord, I do not condemn the use of arms as immoral, nor do I conceive it profane to say, that the King of heaven — the Lord of hosts! the God of battles! bestows his benediction upon those who unsheathe the sword in the hour of a nation's peril.

From that evening on which, in the valley of Bethulia he nerved the arm of the Jewish girl to smite the drunken tyrant in his tent, down to this day, in which he has blessed the insurgent chivalry of the Belgian priest, his Almighty hand hath ever been stretched forth from his throne of light, to consecrate the flag of freedom, to bless the patriot's sword! Be it in the defence, or be it in the assertion of a people's liberty, I hail the sword as a sacred weapon; and if, my lord, it has sometimes taken the shape of the serpent and reddened the shroud of the oppressor with too deep a dye, like the anointed rod of the high priest, it has at other times, and as often, blossomed into celestial flowers to deck the freeman's brow.

Abhor the sword — stigmatize the sword? No, my lord, for, in the passes of the Tyrol, it cut to pieces the banner of the Bavarian, and, through those cragged passes, struck a path to fame for the peasant insurrectionist of Insprück!

Abhor the sword — stigmatize the sword? No, my lord, for at its blow, a giant nation started from the waters of the Atlantic, and by its redeeming magic, and in the quivering of its crimson light, the crippled colony sprang into the attitude of a proud Republic — prosperous, limitless, and invincible!

Abhor the sword — stigmatize the sword? No, my lord, for it swept the Dutch marauders out of the fine old towns of Belgium, scourged them back to their own phlegmatic swamps, and knocked their flag and sceptre, their laws and bayonets into the sluggish waters of the Scheldt.

My lord, I learned that it was the right of a nation to govern herself, not in this hall, but upon the ramparts of Antwerp. This, the first article of a nation's creed, I learned upon those ramparts, where freedom was justly estimated, and the possession of the precious gift was purchased by the effusion of generous blood.

My lord, I honor the Belgians, I admire the Belgians, I love the Belgians, for their enthusiasm, their courage, their success, and I, for one, will not stigmatize, for I do not abhor, the means by which they obtained a citizen king, a chamber of deputies.

AN INDICTMENT OF THE WHIGS

DELIVERED IN THE THEATRE ROYAL, GALWAY, FEBRUARY 14, 1847

GENTLEMEN,—You saw the men who voted for the Whig candidate on Saturday. Did they advance to the hustings like men who felt they had a country and were conscious that their votes would be recorded for her liberty? No, they went there like slaves—insensible to the dictates of patriotism—insensible to the crushing calamities of their country—insensible to its thrilling invocations for redress.

The troops, under the armed guardianship of which they were driven to utter sentence against the independence of their country, proclaimed the cause for which their venal franchise was compelled. Did not the proud escort that attended the tenants of Lord Clanricarde to the court-house proclaim that to the supremacy of England those venal tenants sacrificed their souls?

The troops that were arrayed against your right to petition upon the field of Clontarf were fit companions indeed for the slaves who were herded together to vote against your right to legislate. Those men might as well have voted in manacles.

But if their hands were free their souls were fettered; and if they wore not the garb of convicts they exhibited all the debasement of criminals. Yet these men had illustrious models of depravity—models selected from the brightest page of Irish history, as some Whig orator would designate the narrative of the Union.

They had Fitzgibbon—they had Castlereagh—the titled miscreants who purchased English coronets by the destruction

of the Irish senate. Castlereagh purchased something else—
an English grave.

This, at least, was a privilege to Ireland—to be exempt
from the contamination of the dust which, when breathing,
had drenched our senate with corruption and our land with
blood. Let England still claim such treasures, and let no
Irish traitor—no tenant of Clanricarde—rot beneath the soil
in which the bones of Swift, of Tone, and Davis, have been
laid to rest.

Turn from this soiled and revolting picture, and contemplate the reverse. You saw the men who voted for the Repeal candidate. Did they register their votes under the sabres
of hussars? No; they voted for their country, and were
therefore under no obligation to the liveried champions of the
English flag. They went up to the hustings like honest citizens, and were protected, not by the musket of the soldier,
but by the arm of the God of Hosts. Their souls were as
untrammelled as their limbs, and, recording their votes, they
were distinguished for the manliness which men who love
freedom can alone exhibit. They voted like men who knew
well that the scheme of the Whigs is to soothe this country
into degradation, and they looked like men who scorned to
be soothed for that purpose—scorned the vile scheme that
would prostrate this country by patronage—scorned the vile
scheme that would perpetuate the Union by making it prolific
in small boons.

Men of Galway, to the hustings on the morrow in the
same gallant spirit. Show no mercy to these Whigs! Swamp
them before the sun sets, and let the night fall upon the
broken flagstaff and baffled cohorts of the English minister!
Let the minister hear of his defeat on Wednesday morning,
and curse the virtue that had no price. There must be no

jubilee in Chesham Place at the expense of Irish liberty. There must be no delegate from Galway authorized to sustain the dictation of the English Commons—authorized to sustain the dictation that has been assumed to coerce, to enslave, to starve this country.

What will the Commons say when the Solicitor-General for Ireland takes his seat on the treasury bench as the Whig member for this borough? Will they say that the threat uttered by the Paymaster of the Forces has forced you to capitulate? No; I do not think they will charge you with cowardice, but I am sure they will arraign you for corruption.

They will say that venality has accomplished what battalions could not achieve, and that the money-bags of the Mint can do more for the English interest in Ireland than all the batteries of Woolwich. And, let me tell you, these money-bags have been flung across the Channel into Galway. Trust me, the Whig government will fight this battle to the last farthing.

This I sincerely believe—this I deliberately avow. I am justified in this belief, for it is notorious that the favorite weapon of the Whig government is corruption.

It is the boast of these Whigs that they alone can govern Ireland—that they can mesmerize the Irish beggars! Prove to them that this boast is a falsehood—prove to them that you will not be governed by them, and that Ireland shall be their difficulty and their scourge. What claims have these Whigs upon us? None save what corruption constitutes. Their liberal appointments? How do these appointments serve the country? How much wealth flows into Ireland by the member for Dungarvan being Master of the Mint?

Recollect this, the Whigs voted twenty milions to emancipate the Africans—they refuse to sanction a loan of sixteen millions to employ the Irish. Vote for their nominee, and you will vote against the noble proposition of the Protectionist leader. And has it come to this that you will vote for non-employment—for starvation—for deaths by the minute and inquests by the hour. Will you vote for this government of economists—this government of misers—this government of grave-diggers? Before you do so, read the advertisement on the walls of the Treasury—" Funerals supplied to all parts of the country."

That is the true way to tranquillize the country! That is the true way to hush the tumult of sedition! That is the true way to incorporate the countries and make the Union binding!

If we do not beat those Whigs out of Galway—if we do not fight them for every inch of Irish ground—if we do not drive them across the Channel—they will starve this country into a wilderness, and at the opening of the next session they will bid their royal mistress congratulate her assembled Parliament upon the successful government and the peace of Ireland. And they insist, too, that the executive of this wilderness shall be a chief of police, a poor-law commissioner. and a commissary-general.

Will you submit to this? Do you prefer a soup-kitchen to a custom-house? Do you prefer graveyards to cornfields? Do you prefer the Board of Works to a national senate? Do you prefer the insolent rule of Scotch and English officials to the beneficent legislation of Irish peers and Irish commoners? Heaven forbid that the blight which putrefied your food should infect your souls! Heaven forbid that the famine should tame you into debasement, and that the spirit which has triumphed over the prison and the scaffold should surrender to the corruptionist at last!

I asked you, a moment since, how much wealth flows into

Ireland by the member for Dungarvan being Master of the Mint? I must tell you this; there is a little stream of it always dropping through the castle yard; but sometimes there are extraordinary spring-tides—just about election times—and then that tide swells and deepens, and rises so high, and rushes so rapidly, that it frequently sweeps away the votes of the people—sweeps away their placards—sweeps away their banners—sweeps away their committee rooms—and, in the end, throws up a Whig official upon the white shore of England!

Beware of this spring-tide; it is sweeping through Galway this moment—through lane and street. Its glittering waters intoxicate and debase. The wretches who drink them fall into the current and are whirled away—the drenched and battered spoils of England.

And is this the end of all you have vowed and done? And has it come to this, that after the defiances, the resolutions, the organization of 1843, England shall plant her foot upon the neck of Ireland and exclaim: "Behold my bribed and drunken slave!"

I do not exaggerate. The battle of Ireland is being fought in Galway. If the Whigs take Galway—Ireland falls. Shall Ireland fall? Incur defeat, and you shall have her bitter curse. Win the battle, and you shall have her proud blessing. Your virtue and your victory will fire the coward and regenerate the venal—your example will be followed—the Whigs will be driven from Wexford, from Waterford, from Mallow, from Dungarvan; their bribes will be trampled in the dust, their strongest citadels be stormed, the integrity of the people shall prevail against the venality of the faction, the Union Act shall share the fate of the Penal Code, and mankind shall hail the birth, the career, the glory of an Irish nation.

HOPE FOR IRELAND

SPEECH DELIVERED FROM THE DOCK, OCTOBER 23, 1848

M Y LORDS,—It is my intention to say a few words
only. I desire that the last act of a proceeding
which has occupied so much of the public time
should be of short duration. Nor have I the indelicate wish
to close the dreary ceremony of a state prosecution with a vain
display of words.

Did I fear that hereafter, when I shall be no more, the
country I tried to serve would speak ill of me, I might indeed
avail myself of this solemn moment to vindicate my sentiments and my conduct.

But I have no such fear. The country will judge of those
sentiments and that conduct in a light far different from that
in which the jury by whom I have been convicted have viewed
them, and by the country the sentence which you, my lords,
are about to pronounce, will be remembered only as the severe
and solemn attestation of my rectitude and truth.

Whatever be the language in which that sentence be
spoken, I know that my fate will meet with sympathy, and
that my memory will be honored.

In speaking thus, my lords, accuse me not of an indecorous
presumption in the efforts I have made in a just and noble
cause. I ascribe no main importance, nor do I claim for those
efforts any high reward.

But it so happens, and it will ever happen so, that they who
have lived to serve their country—no matter how weak their
efforts may have been—are sure to receive the thanks and
blessings of its people.

With my countrymen I leave my memory, my sentiments, my acts, proudly feeling that they require no vindication from me this day. A jury of my countrymen, it is true, have found me guilty of the crime of which I stood indicted. For this I entertain not the slightest feeling of resentment toward them. Influenced as they must have been by the charge of the Lord Chief Justice, they could perhaps have found no other verdict.

What of that charge? Any strong observations on it I feel sincerely would ill befit the solemnity of this scene; but I would earnestly beseech of you, my lord—you who preside on that bench—when the passions and the prejudices of this hour have passed away, to appeal to your own conscience, and ask of it, was your charge what it ought to have been, impartial and indifferent between the subject and the Crown?

My lords, you may deem this language unbecoming in me, and perhaps it may seal my fate; but I am here to speak the truth, whatever it may cost—I am here to regret nothing I have ever done, to regret nothing I have ever said—I am here to crave with no lying lip the life I consecrate to the liberty of my country.

Far from it. Even here—here, where the thief, the libertine, the murderer, have left their footprints in the dust—here, on this spot, where the shadows of death surround me, and from which I see my early grave in an unanointed soil open to receive me—even here, encircled by these terrors, that hope which first beckoned me to the perilous sea on which I have been wrecked still consoles, animates, and enraptures me.

No; I do not despair of my poor old country—her peace, her liberty, her glory. For that country I can do no more than bid her hope. To lift this island up—to make her a benefactor to humanity instead of being, as she is now, the meanest beggar in the world—to restore to her her native powers and her ancient constitution—this has been my ambition, and this ambition has been my crime.

Judged by the law of England, I know this crime entails upon me the penalty of death; but the history of Ireland explains that crime and justifies it. Judged by that history I am no criminal, you [addressing Mr. McManus] are no criminal, you [addressing Mr. O'Donoghue] are no criminal, and we deserve no punishment; judged by that history the treason of which I stand convicted loses all its guilt, has been sanctified as a duty, and will be ennobled as a sacrifice.

With these sentiments I await the sentence of the court. I have done what I felt to be my duty. I have spoken now, as I did on every other occasion during my short life, what I felt to be the truth. I now bid farewell to the country of my birth—of my passions—of my death; a country whose misfortunes have invoked my sympathies—whose factions I sought to quell—whose intelligence I prompted to a lofty aim —whose freedom has been my fatal dream.

To that country I now offer, as a pledge of the love I bore her, and of the sincerity with which I thought and spoke and struggled for her freedom, the life of a young heart; and with that life, the hopes, the honors, the endearments of a happy, a prosperous, and honorable home.

Proceed then, my lords, with that sentence which the law directs—I am prepared to hear it—I trust I am prepared to meet its execution. I shall go, I think, with a light heart before a higher tribunal, a tribunal where a Judge of infinite goodness, as well as of infinite justice, will preside, and where, my lords, many, many of the judgments of this world will be reversed.

THE GLORY OF IRELAND

FROM AN ADDRESS DELIVERED IN THE PEOPLE'S THEATRE, VIRGINIA
CITY, ON ST. PATRICK'S DAY, 1866

ON this day, nearly thirteen hundred years ago, the
lurid fire of the Druid began to pale, and the Cross
appeared in the kindly Irish sky.   The celebration
we Irishmen make to-day is the celebration of love, of pride,
of sorrow.   Were Ireland an ill-favored country—were it
sterile, bleak, inhospitable—were there no scenes there to delight the eye and captivate the heart—were there no sweet
valleys, no laughing rivers, none of the graces and grandeur
of nature such as have inspired the melodies of Moore and
given to the pencil of Maclise some of its finest themes; had
the country no picturesque history, no great name illuminat-
ing her annals, no halls that had echoed to a superior eloquence, no fields on which heroism had fought for liberty—
were it a desert in the light of an unpropitious sun, and a
blank in the literature of the world—even so, as the place of
our birth—as the place where we first knew a mother's smile
and a father's blessing—we should love it, be jealous of it,
and cling to it all the more devotedly on account of the de-
privations with which it had been stricken.

But our love for Ireland has no such rigorous conditions to
test and vindicate it.   Heaven has been most bountiful to that
land.   As it came from the hand of God, it has all the rare
excellence that makes it a singularly favored land.   Under a
government of its own sons—partial and generous as they
would be to it—no land would be happier—no land be more
profitable to its people; for it has been endowed with all ad-

vantages—serenity of climate and wealth of soil, safe and
spacious harbors indenting the whole circle of its coast, the
more essential minerals and superabundant water—all which,
under a genial administration and favoring laws, would not
only make it prosperous, but give it greatness.

I have spoken of the means which Ireland abundantly possesses to be a strong and prosperous nation. Her intellectual
wealth is fully commensurate with her physical. The fame
of her more gifted sons revolves with the planet, and it is no
exaggeration to say that it has a recognition which is coexten-
sive with civilization. Has not the " Vicar of Wakefield "
gone round the world?

Does not Edmund Burke loom up in political history with a
stature too colossal not to be seen from every quarter of the
globe? " Lalla Rookh " has been translated, and is a volume
of gold in the land of the Fire Worshippers themselves.
Sheridan has written his name in letters of inextinguishable
light upon the desecrated temples and plundered palaces.

Never in any country was there so superb an assembly of
orators and wits, statesmen and gallant gentlemen, as the
Irish Parliament was in the few years of independence.
There was Harry Flood, of whom it was grandly said by his
great rival that, like Hercules, he failed with the distaff, but
with the thunderbolt he had the arm of a Jupiter. There
was Henry Grattan, of whom Lord Brougham declared that
no orator of any age was his equal, and who communicating
to Ireland the pentecostal fire with which he himself was
inflamed, beheld his country, to use his own magnificent
phrase, rising from her bed in the ocean and getting nearer
to the sun. There was Curran—the most thorough Irishman
of them all—the exhaustless wit, the dauntless and defiant
advocate, whose marvellous eloquence threw over the darkest

cause the most copious streams of splendor and enchantment, and who was as true to Ireland as he was to the saddest client who sought the shelter and defence of his blazing shield.

In art Maclise has won an imperial crown. Davis said of him that his pencil was as true as a sunbeam. Barry was in his studio what Burke was in the senate—a prodigy of genius. In his vast painting of the "Last Judgment" he has "shaken one world with the thunders of another."

But it is said that the educated intelligence, to say nothing of the property of Ireland, has, unless in some eccentric instances, become imperialized, and that to the independence of the country it is haughtily hostile. Here an argument is advanced against Irish independence. With me that argument goes for nothing. Shall a nation postpone her liberty in deference to an erudite slavery? Is the liberty of a nation a usurpation unless the menials of political life, the painted butterflies of fashion, varlets, harlequins, and vassals, concur in the claim?

Give me the people—the democracy—the men who till the fields, the men who build ships and cities, the men who subjugate the wilderness, train and rear it into a noble civilization, and, so far, consummate the Divine purpose of creation. From this element have some of the most powerful intellects and potentates of the world sprung. Homer, Shakespeare, Michael Angelo, the great jurists of England, the great statesmen of America, the marshals of Napoleon, were from the democracy.

Give me the people, the democracy of Ireland! Should they demand the liberty of Ireland, I shall not wait on any lord or pedant, or on any lord's or pedant's flunkey, to ratify the claim. Give me the peasantry—the reviled, scorned,

ignored peasantry of Ireland! Their wretched cabins have
been the holy shrines in which the traditions and the hopes
of Ireland have been treasured and transmitted. In the adverse days—in the days of cowardice, debasement, and despair—the spirit of Ireland has lived in them and become
immortal. In the fiercest storms they have never once
winced or wavered. In the bloodiest times they have been
dauntless and heroic. The hills of Wexford, the plains of
Kildare, the mountain passes of Wicklow—all are vital with
their desperate courage under the shock and scourge of
battle.

Never, never let the Irish heart give up the hope of seeing,
on Irish soil, the fatal destiny of centuries reversed, and a
restored nation, wisely instructed and ennobled in the school
of sorrow, planted there. Think, think, what this hope has
been to Ireland. It has been the light of her darkness, the
jewel of her poverty, the music of her tribulation, the bright
companion of her exiles. It has been the main nerve of her
industry abroad; on the field of death it has been the fire of
her heart and the magic of her flag.

Now comes the question—is this festival of love, of pride,
of sorrow, celebrated here, incompatible with Irish loyalty
in America? The question—an ignominious one—would not
surely emanate from me were it not that there are some
vicious bigots—men of small brains and smaller hearts—men
of more gall than blood—who, even here, assert that love
for Ireland, devotion to her cause, active sympathy with the
protracted contest for her redemption, involve an equivocal
allegiance to the United States.

Out upon the bastard Americanism that spews this impu-
tation on the gallant race whose blood, shed in torrents for its
inviolability and its glory, has imparted a brighter crimson

to the Stripes and made the Stars of that triumphant flag irra-
diate with a keener radiance.

I appeal not to the burning sands, the cactus-circled for-
tresses, the causeways, the volcanic heights, the gates and
towers of Mexico. Let the woods and swamps of the deadly
Chickahominy, the slopes of Malvern Hill, the waters of
the Antietam, the defiant heights of Fredericksburg, the
thickets of the Wilderness—a thousand fields, now billowed
with Irish graves, declare that love for Ireland blends in
ecstacy with loyalty to America, and that America has been
served by none more truly than by those who carried in their
impetuous hearts the memories and hopes of Ireland.

No true American looks otherwise than with full trustful-
ness and the heartiest fellowship upon such manifestations
of Irish heart, Irish piety, and Irish remembrance of the
Irish birthplace as to-day animate this city.

The true American knows, feels, and with enthusiasm declares, that of all human emotions, of all human passions,
there is not one more pure, more noble, more conducive to
good and great and glorious deeds than that which bears us
back to the spot that was the cradle of our childhood, the
playground of our boyhood, the theatre of our manhood.

Has the Holy Book a passage more deeply touching than
that which pictures to us the daughters of a captive race, in
their desolation of soul, weeping by the waters of Babylon
when they remembered their lost homes and the vanished
towers of Zion? Has profane verse a line more exquisitely
eloquent than that which tells us of the brave young Greek
—beautiful and radiant as his native land—bleeding and
dying on the plains of Latium, with his darkening eyes fixed
on Greece?

Has political history a grander incident than that of

Warren Hastings, the Dictator of India, in the midst of all his ambitious schemes—all through his struggles, his contests, his triumphs, his crimes, and splendors—ever and always cherishing in his purer heart the hope and purpose of returning to his ancestral domain and spending there in calmness and goodness the evening of his stormy life? Has our own bright poet, Moore, with all the wealth of his melody and fancy, given the world a scene in the presence of which kindlier, sweeter, holier sympathies arise than that which shows the captive girls of the East, amid all the luxuries of their perfumed and golden bondage—amid all the deadening enchantments of their voluptuous vassalage—winging their way back in tender thought to the scene of their free and spotless childhood.

It is the American who has no heart—who has no thought beyond putting a dollar out at mighty interest—who has no zest for any other book than his Easy Account or his soulless Ledger—who hates the Irish for their generous qualities, their infallible religion, and who deprecates the love of Ireland which the Irishman brings with him to America, which he cherishes here in every vicissitude of his laborious life, and with which, whether he be in rags or in purple and in fine linen, whether he be digging for gold like a drudge in Montana or spending it like an Irish prince in New York, he celebrates St. Patrick's Day.

THE ORATORS OF IRELAND

I COME to speak of those whose memories are the inalienable inheritance of my poor country, and in the possession of which — even though she sits in desolation, in "tattered weeds," and though "sharp misery has worn her to the bone "— a radiant pride tinges her pale cheek, and over her aching head rays of inextinguishable glory congregate. I come to speak of those who, with the beauty, the intrepidity, the power of the intellect that dwelt within them, rescued the country of my birth from the obscurity and inanition to which the laws of evil men had doomed her, and which, having conquered for her an interval of felicity and freedom, left her with a history which the coldest or the haughtiest of her sons will revert to with love and pride, and on which the bitterest of her calumniators cannot meditate without respect.

It is well that the story of such men should be simply told. Their grand proportions need no cunning drapery. It would be worse than useless to gild the glowing marble. Like the statues in Evadne, each has a noble history, and, dead though they be, in their presence virtue grows strong, heroism kindles in the weakest, and the guilty stand abashed.

There is an old man, with stooped shoulders, long thin arms, the sparest figure, haggard face, lips grimly set, and an eye with the searching glance of a gray eagle,— that is Henry Grattan.

What of him? He had a great cause, a great opportunity,

a great genius. The independence of Ireland — the cause.
The embarrassment of England with her colonies — the opportunity. With the magnitude of both his genius was
commensurate. He was equal to his friends — as he himself
said of his great rival, Harry Flood — and was more than
equal to his foes. When he spoke, the infirmities and deform-
ities of the man disappeared in a blaze of glory. His eloquence was more than human. " It was a combination of
cloud, whirlwind, and flame." Nothing could resist it, nothing could approach it. It conquered all or distanced all. Like
the archangel of Raphael, it was winged as well as armed.
His intellect was most noble. His heart was not less divinely
molded. Never before did so much gentleness, so much
courage, so much force, unite in one poor frame. The
brightest event in Irish history is the great event of that great
man's life. If it is the brightest, let us refer it to his genius,
his spirit, his ambition. His love of country was intense.
" He never would be satisfied as long as the meanest cottager
in Ireland had a link of the British chain clanking to his
rags." Thus he spoke, moving the Declaration of Independence. The last time he appeared in the Irish Parliament was
at midnight. He came from a sick bed. They gave him
leave to sit while he addressed the House. For a moment—
for a moment — his agony forsook him. Men beheld before
their eyes a sublime transfiguration. " I rose," said he,
" with the rising fortunes of my country — I am willing to
die with her expiring liberties." Had he been at that time
inspired with the republicanism of Wolfe Tone, his career
and glory would have been complete.

And there is a dark, dwarfish figure, with a brown rugged
face, short flat nose, an upturned earnest face, and an eye
full of black lustre, his hands upon his hips, his awkward

body swinging to and fro as though it were convulsed,—
that is John Philpot Curran!

Who, knowing anything of Ireland, had not heard of him?
Who, having heard the story of her wrongs and martyrdoms,
has failed to love that loving, gallant, glowing nature? Who,
at all familiar with the great features of his time, will refuse
to him an exalted station and the most generous homage?
In a period conspicuous for its wit, his was the brightest wit
of all. At a time when the most profuse hospitality prevailed, his was the most genial nature that flowed and
sparkled at the social board. In a crowded school of orators,
each one of whom was prominent and towering, he stood, if
not the foremost, second only to the foremost. When corruption was let loose, he stood unpurchasable and inviolate.
In a reign of terror, he was dauntless and invincible. "You
may murder," he exclaimed one day to the armed ruffians who
threatened him with their bayonets in the court house, "but
you cannot intimidate me." In the midst of devastation he
was a guardian spirit and an immortal savior. From the
beginning to the end he clung to the fortunes of his country
— gave to her his love, his labors, his sorrows, the inspiration of his courage, the exhilarating warmth and splendor of
his genius — gave them all to her in the fullest measure.
Closing our hands in prayer, and bending in reverence beside
his tomb, one regret alone may escape our lips in the contemplation of his career — that he did not die with those
whom he strove to save.

On a broken ledge of granite, against which the green
waves of the sea seem to have worked many a long day, and
in the shadow of a mountain clad in purple heath, and over
which the mist is passing, there stands, as though it grew
out of it, a massive figure — arms folded, stoutly limbed,

broad-shouldered, deep-chested, erect, well-set, staunch, massive as the granite — small head, small gray, twinkling eyes, flexible, small lips, features suffused with humor, yet lurking sagacity and purpose and a consciousness of power,— it is Daniel O'Connell!

Why say more? He himself uttered these words one day in the spring of 1843:

"I find my humble name has penetrated and become familiar along the Carpathian Mountains, and I verily believe the Autocrat of Russia has heard of him who now addresses you. Portugal has heard of it—Spain has felt it. It has been talked of in the mountains of Hungary. Coupled with it, the woes of Ireland are heard of at the sources of the Missouri. From the springs that first feed the mighty Mississippi, from the waters of the Ohio, from the summits of the Alleghanies, and the wooded banks of the Monongahela—in every part of that vast continent—from the forests of the Canadas to the morasses of New Orleans—with my name is mingled the cry for the restoration of the liberties of Ireland."

The utterance of these words was no heinous ostentation. His own importance he did not exaggerate. No one will dispute it. The celebrity of his name was measured by seas and continents. I have seen a rude likeness of him in the Australian forest—in a log hut—the owner if it a native of the forest, miles and miles aloof from the outward circle of civilization.

Nothing within the range of human capacity, in the way of revolution and administration, was to him impossible. He could easily have recovered the confiscated privileges of 1782. His dominion exceeded that of Henry Grattan, though his military resources were less ostensible. Had he willed it, he would have been crowned in 1843 and his dynasty established. Imbued with loftier aspirations still, he could have thrown the crown to the moths and worms, and, like Washington, have inaugurated the sovereignty of his people, under the code and banners of a republic.

Yet, failing to do so, and failing in other instances, and perhaps more culpably, he did much for Ireland—much for her in his earlier years—much for her before the sun of life moved downward from the zenith; and, dying, he bequeathed a memory to his country which contributes largely to that stock of wealth which no laws can confiscate, no adversary deteriorate,—a memory which those who differ from him most and censure him the most severely will, for the honor of the country, be solicitous and jealous to perpetuate.

A little nearer to us, but close to that colossal figure, stands a smaller one—one by many inches smaller, and by many degrees less impressive, yet most striking. For, though the little figure is slight, wiry, angular, the attitude is fine—one foot hastily advanced—hair swept back from the forehead, as if a wild gust had struck it—the head projecting, and eyes of a fierce black beauty darting from it—and then a white hand of the most exquisite shape, flung passionately in the air, and quivering and flashing as it threatens,—it is Richard Sheil.

Less liberally endowed with the great attributes of those who preceded him, he is nevertheless worthy of a high place in the Pantheon which they occupy. His nature less susceptible of great impressions, his integrity in political matters more questionable, his ambition decidedly less generous, nevertheless his instincts were kindred to theirs, his spirit as intrepid, his intellect as vivid, and, if less majestic, better cultivated.

Throughout a hard contest he fought with a ceaseless impetuosity, and to the victorious issue of it contributed not less by the magic of his rhetoric than by the rapid continuity of his labor. Never passive, never halting, never downcast; always on the march, ever in action, ever hopeful; communicating the enthusiasm of his genius to the thousands with whom he felt and for whom he spoke; the timid were emboldened, the sluggish were impelled; the fire, the force, or the action was sustained until for him, for his comrades, for his cause, and for an outcast race and creed proscribed the triumph was achieved. With the dethronement of a detestable ascendancy, with the enactment of the law repealing the disabilities which in the name of religion had been iniquitously imposed, his name in the history of his country is inseparably identified. He had the opportunity, the field, the ability to do more. He could have reached a loftier eminence—have left a broader effulgence above his grave. The last chapter of his life casts a shadow on those which commemorate the promise of his youth and the glory of his pride. He gathered in one harvest. In his old age he might have reaped another one and more plenteous, and then have gone to sleep, having worthily fulfilled his days.

Yet he, too, leaves a name behind which his country cannot afford to lose; which it would be unnatural for her to proscribe; which she could not injure without impoverishing the inheritance which, generation after generation, her children, reciprocating the bounty of their mother, have bounteously bequeathed.

But who is that—the last in the group—so tall, so handsome, so gay, so commanding, "with so much vivacity, frankness, chivalry in his look and bearing—with such deep brows, with so broad and white a forehead, with eyes of so intense lustre that someone whispers to us they could give expression to a face of clay?" Who else can it be but him of whom

an ecstatic sister wrote that " his cheeks had the glow of
health; his eyes, the finest in the world, the brilliancy of
genius, and yet were as soft as a tender and affectionate
heart could render them." Who else can it be but him
whose name cannot be mentioned without all that is beautiful, all that is strange, all that is sad, all that is glorious, all
that is inexplicable, in the history of our country, flashing
upon the mind half in cloud and half in glory? Who else
can it be but Richard Brinsley Sheridan?

If his nature partook of the caprices of our climate, that
nature was as fruitful and abounding as our soil. Tumbling
to destruction himself, he would stop to rescue others. Of
selfishness there was not a particle in his nature—neither in
his domestic concerns nor in his public life. He had a
thought, a word, an honest hand, for all. Cast into the
whirling current of aristocratic life, his sympathies never
swerved from the people. In him, as in Charles Fox, the
French Revolution found a resolute defender. When old
Doctor Johnson comes out against America with his pamphlet entitled, " Taxation no tyranny," Sheridan promptly
takes the side of America; dismisses the lumbersome old doctor as " the man of letters who had been drawn from obscurity by the inquisitive eye of a sovereign," and the pamphlet
itself as nothing better in sincerity or value than " a venal
birthday ode." Caressed by princes; a man of the highest
note among the notables of England; with England for his
field of action and the pedestal of his fame; he never lost
sight of Ireland—never looked with a careless or supercilious
eye upon her defects, her grievances, her destitution—never,
never shaped his sentiments and votes in her regard to suit
the vicious propensities of his patrons. That he had many
frailties his warmest admirer will not deny. But the age

in which he lived and the society of which he was the favorite was remarkable neither for the regularity of its morals nor the purity of its pleasures.

The history of Ireland is a mournful one—perhaps the saddest that has been written. From the beginning even to the end it has the deep tone of a lamentation. But, like the lamentation of the prophet, it is resonant and glowing with grand memories, the loftiest hopes, and invocations the most sublime. The genius of her children suffuses, beautifies, illuminates the sorrow of the old land. It is the inextinguishable sunshine among the clouds, the showers, the storms. And thus, through the agonies of an enduring martyrdom, we behold ever, as it were, the kindling radiance of a promised resurrection.

What are the memories of the men whom I have this moment pointed out? Are they not beams of eternal light, brightening while they penetrate the shadows of the past and the troubled· waters over which they continually play? Are they not, again, the rays of the sun coming up through the solitude of the night—effulgent promises of a distant but advancing destiny? Thus they are the life, the wealth, the glory of our country. It is well. It is beneficently ordained. It has been most bounteously vouchsafed. For never did a country stand more in need of strength, of wealth, of glory; for never was a country so impoverished, so disabled, so utterly cast down. Never did a country suffer so much—suffer so rapacious a spoliation—endure so terrible a torture. Ireland has been lashed upon the rack, and has been bleeding from every limb and pore for years, and years, and years!

Yet never did a country prove itself so exhaustless—so invincible. "The edifices of the mind are indestructible."

The sword which decimates, the fire which crumbles cities into ashes, the famine which—less discriminating than the sword, more sweeping than the fire—depopulates the land, leaves behind it a wilderness where there has been a garden, and graves where there have been buzzing hives of industry; visitations the most calamitous pass like the idle wind over those structures which the intellect has reared, and leave them, even in the desert, even among ruins, even gilding the tombs, evidences of a vitality that is invincible— evidences to the exile that the country from which he has been driven cannot be wholly lost—evidences to those of little faith that there is beyond the world a purer condition of humanity, and that all, all we witness here, is not doomed to perish!

Yes! Let the robber have his way—the incendiary his way! Let the war come—the famine come! There is a treasure they cannot seize, cannot injure, cannot deface, cannot annihilate. It is the soul—it is the soul of a country expressing itself, on the canvas, through the marble, in words of melody and transcendent power.

Is this exaggerated?—this an impious boast? The Pantheon is in ruins; but Demosthenes is not dead. The Athenian theatre is in ruins; but Euripides and Sophocles walk the earth.

Thus it is of Ireland. Thus Ireland, though in ruins, to day is great. Thus, in the glory of the men of whom I speak, my country perpetuates herself even to the end of time. "The immortal fire outlasts the organ which conveyed it, and the breath of liberty, like the word of the holy man, dies not with the prophet, but survives him."

MORTON

OLIVER PERRY MORTON, an American statesman, was born at Sauls-
bury, Indiana, August 4, 1823. After four years' apprenticeship
to the hatter's trade, he studied at Miami University, fitted himself for
the bar, and began to practise his profession at Centreville, Indiana, in
1847. In 1852 he was elected a county judge. He threw himself actively
into politics, was one of the founders of the Republican party, and in
1860 was elected lieutenant-governor of Indiana, becoming governor very
shortly on account of Governor Lane's election to the United States Senate.
Morton stoutly opposed all compromise with the Secessionists and at the
outbreak of the Civil War promptly placed large bodies of State troops
at the service of the general government. In 1862 the Democratic legislature of Indiana declined to receive the governor's message, but the subsequent withdrawal of the Republican members left both houses without
a quorum. In order to carry on the government of the State the governor
then appointed a bureau of finance, which from April, 1863, to January,
1865, made all disbursements, the legislature not being summoned within
that period. His course at this juncture was condemned by the supreme
court, but received the approval of the people, the State assuming the
obligations thus incurred. The disunionists of Indiana conspired against
his life but their plan was discovered and the leaders of the " Knights
of the Golden Circle," as the conspirators called themselves, were arrested. In 1864 Morton was elected governor, but resigned from office
in 1867 in order to enter the United States Senate, to which he was re-
elected in 1873. He wielded an extended influence in the Republican party
and made many strong speeches in behalf of its principles. He was active
in the impeachment of President Johnson, and in 1877 was a member of
the electoral commission. His death took place in Indianapolis, September 1, 1877. Although a sufferer from paralysis for the last ten years
of his life his strength and influence as a public speaker remained unaffected.

ON THE ISSUES OF 1868

DELIVERED BEFORE THE SOLDIERS AND SAILORS' UNION, WASHING-
TON, D. C., JANUARY 6, 1868

GENTLEMEN OF THE SOLDIERS AND SAIL-
ORS' UNION,—There are two ideals paramount
in the American mind antagonistic and irreconcil-
able, each struggling for the supremacy.

One is the justice and propriety of the war to put down the rebellion and preserve the integrity of the Union.

The other is the rightfulness of the rebellion and the wickedness and injustice of the government of the United States in putting it down by force of arms. The contest between these two ideas will, as in 1864, constitute the issue in 1868 and all other questions will be offshoots from them and will arrange themselves upon the one side or the other.

Whoever shall vote the so-called "Conservative" or Democratic ticket in 1868, whether he so intend it or not, will thereby indorse the rebellion; and whoever shall vote the Republican ticket will utter his voice in favor of union, liberty, and justice. Whoever believes in the justice of the war and the preservation of the Republic will be in favor of reconstruction upon such terms as will give protection to all loyal men and guaranties against future rebellion; and whoever believes in the rightfulness of the rebellion will be in favor of the immediate restoration of rebels, without condition or limitation, to civil and political rights, just as if there had been no war and nothing had happened.

The Democratic or "Conservative" party will be composed of the Northern Democracy who sympathized with secession and rebellion and of the Southern rebels, with the addition of a few recruits from the Republican party. But before entering more fully into the issues of 1868 I will glance briefly at the present condition of affairs.

There is much financial embarrassment in the country, depression of labor, and stagnation of trade. Much of this can be traced directly to the unsettled and disturbed condition of the South.

The persistent and determined efforts of Southern rebels and Northern Democrats to defeat reconstruction and keep that question open for the chances of future events has greatly impaired confidence in the financial and commercial world, and keeps the business men of the country doubtful and uncertain what to do.

It is, therefore, of the first importance to the general prosperity that reconstruction be speedily settled upon principles of equality and impartial justice that shall ensure domestic tranquillity and permanent peace.

Another cause of embarrassment and distress is the great drain which has been made upon the people since the end of the war in the payment of the public debt. We now learn that more than $465,000,000 have been paid on the public debt since the 1st of August, 1865; but of this vast amount only $265,000,000 have been reported in that way, $200,-000,000 belonging to what is called the unliquidated debt, that is, debt not evidenced by notes, bonds, or certificates of indebtedness, but nevertheless a part of the public debt that should have been funded for the time being. The people would be in far better condition, and far more cheerful today, if they had only paid the interest upon this sum, and had been left free for a time to recover from the exhaustion of a protracted civil war.

The policy of extorting nearly $500,000,000 in payment of the national debt in so short a time after the end of the war is most unwise and disastrous, and cannot be justified upon any principle or theory. For several years to come the nation will be burdened with heavy taxes for State, county, and municipal purposes, growing out of the war, while the expenditures of the national government will be greatly increased by the payment of bounties, pensions, currency debts, and the innumerable expenses springing from the unsettled condition of our affairs.

While the payment, under such circumstances, of so large a portion of the public debt may excite the astonishment of other nations, it will certainly fail to excite their admiration for our good sense; and they must despise that statesmanship which would further exhaust an exhausted people, to the great detriment of their future strength and prosperity. The sum thus far paid has been collected exclusively from the loyal States, and such will be the case for the next few years; and I am in favor of waiting until the people of the South, who caused the debt to be contracted, shall be able and be required to pay some part of it themselves.

In less than ten years we shall have increased our population ten millions and more than doubled our taxable property, and can pay with ease a tax three times the aggregate of the present.

Within five years the Southern States will be reconstructed and in the enjoyment of comparative prosperity.

Within five years the increase of population, wealth, and capital will enable the government to sell at par bonds bearing a much lower rate of interest than the present, and thus consolidate and reduce the debt.

Should the government find itself at any time in possession of coin or currency that can be applied to the reduction of the debt, it should of course be promptly applied; but any attempt to pay the bonded debt in advance by heavy taxation will be unnecessary, unwise, and injurious.

I would reduce the rate of taxation to the lowest point that would defray the expenses of the government economically administered, and pay the interest and maturing obligations, and leave the principal of the bonded debt to be discharged in other and better times.

Then again, we have added to our financial troubles by the

policy inaugurated by the secretary of the treasury in the contraction of the currency, which has served to restrain commercial enterprise, paralyze trade, and keep the money market in an unsettled and feverish condition. The country is imperatively demanding the passage of a law which shall restrain the secretary from further contraction.

We want retrenchment, reform in the expenses of the government. We do not want that picayune retrenchment which will confine clerks to starving salaries and leave the great sources of expenditures unchecked. The expenses of the government are enormous, and the time has come when they can and ought to be greatly diminished. We have now an army of more than fifty thousand men, and a navy that is much larger than the country requires, and the time is at hand when both can be greatly reduced and thereby lessen our expenses many millions of dollars.

The purchase of Alaska from Russia can be justified on high political considerations and the future commercial importance of owning the northwestern part of this continent. But it is not easy to see the necessity for spending seven and one half millions of dollars in gold for the purchase of St. Thomas, a small West Indian island, which may be said to be the very birth-place of the yellow fever, and is frequently made desolate by earthquakes and hurricanes.

It is important that we should fund our national debt into a uniform bond bearing a lower rate of interest. Whether this can be done now I do not know; I hope it can. And it is desirable, if possible, that the debt should be put in such a shape that it may bear a fair share of the burdens of taxation like other property; but I can see no advantage in having the government of the United States pay taxes to the several States which have first to be collected from the people.

The principal financial scheme of the Democratic party is that the government and the treasury shall be turned over into the hands of the men who made the rebellion, and caused the debt to be contracted, and this, I suppose, upon the principle that the "hair of the dog is good for the bite;" but this I am sure is the last remedy the people intend to try.

But to return to the irrepressible conflict of ideas to which I alluded in the beginning, the palpable and direct issue will be presented in the attempt to restore the rebels unconditionally to the full enjoyment of political rights; to place in their hands exclusively the governments of the rebel States; to give them the control absolutely of the loyal men, black and white, living in those States; and the unqualified admission of their senators and representatives into Congress.

The Democratic party are not willing that political power in the rebel States shall be divided between the loyal and the disloyal, but they demand that it shall be placed exclusively in the hands of the disloyal, to whose tender mercies the true and faithful people shall be consigned without redress or appeal.

To deceive the people they are uttering false cries, and fill the land with clamor because of the alleged oppression practised upon the people of the South.   Who are those oppressed people in the South?   They are those who, less than three years ago, were in arms against the nation; who have cost us more than a half a million loyal lives, and five thousand millions of dollars; twenty-five hundred of which still remain to us as a legacy, and who have filled the land with mourning and untold suffering and sorrow.   And now we are charged with being oppressors and tyrants because they have not been admitted to full political rights; because they have not been welcomed into Congress, and because they are not allowed to butcher and drive into exile the Union men in their midst. It is contended that these rebels in the act of being conquered were remitted to all civil and political privileges; that the moment their arms were wrested from their hands upon the battle-field they had a right to run back to seats in Congress, and take part in the adjustment of all questions growing out of their rebellion, and to take charge of their several State governments the same as if there had been no war.

All these pretensions proceed upon the principle that the rebellion was right; for, if it be admitted that the rebellion was wrong, they are destitute of all sense whatever. It is only by ignoring the fact of the rebellion, or by treating it as rightful, that any man without shamefacedness can stand up and say these things.

If it be acknowledged that the rebellion was a crime, then the demand that the criminal shall without delay, punishment, condition, or security, be restored to political power and put on a level with loyal men, is to put vice and virtue upon an equality and make nonsense of notions commonly received that there is an essential difference between the good and bad actions of mankind. So you see that these questions of reconstruction all turn upon the original question as to the rightfulness of the rebellion. In the congressional plan of reconstruction Congress has gone to the extreme of mercy and conciliation by proposing to divide the power in the rebel States between the loyal and the disloyal so that each shall have protection against the other.

But a small number of men, not exceeding forty-five thousand, have been disfranchised; and they not because they were in the rebel army, but because they had once sworn to support the constitution of the United States and afterward committed perjury by going into the rebellion.

The President's decree of disfranchisement in his plan of reconstruction was far more sweeping, for it included fourteen classes of persons, numbering not less than two hundred and fifty thousand men, who were excluded from the polls in the election of delegates. The present State governments, which it is said Congress intends to overthrow, and which were formed under the President's plan, have no right to be regarded as legal governments whatever. They were formed by conventions of delegates elected in 1865 by not more than one third of the white men who had a right to vote under the President's proclamation. These delegates represented only a small minority of the white population, and the constitutions they formed were never ratified or accepted by the people, but were put in operation by the President's authority, and are in that condition to-day. They were never submitted to Congress, never received its approval; but, on the contrary, in the reconstruction acts were pronounced illegal and unauthorized. In these constitutions there are clauses prohibiting slavery and the payment of their several war debts, but when they are restored to their representation in Congress, and thus made secure in the enjoyment of political power, they will throw them off as impositions which they have only tolerated for a time, and make new ones, leaving out the obnoxious clauses on the subject of slavery and their war debts.

Congress, in conferring suffrage upon the colored men of the South, has been governed not only by high principles of equality and justice, but by an overruling necessity. A bitter and bloody experience under the President's plan of reconstruction had demonstrated that the rebels were unrepentant and unrelenting, and that loyal State governments could not be erected on the basis of the white population, and that a new loyal voting population must be raised up by enfranchising the colored men.

So that whatever views the people of the North may have had upon the propriety of admitting men who were so recently slaves to the immediate exercise of the elective franchise, they had no choice or discretion upon the subject left, but were driven to it by the conduct of the rebels and their Northern allies.

Wrapped up in this issue and in the success of the Democratic party are other issues, which will be inevitable sequences. The first of which I shall mention is the payment for the emancipated slaves. This question will have to be decided in 1868 as emphatically as if written out in the Democratic platform. The State of Maryland in her new constitution, just adopted, has provided for it in the following terms:

" Sec. 37. The General Assembly shall pass no law providing for payment by this State for slaves emancipated from servitude in this State; but they shall adopt such measures as they may deem expedient to obtain from the United States compensation for such slaves, and to receive and distribute the same equitably to the persons entitled."

It will thus be seen that Maryland has provided for this issue in her fundamental law, and we cannot doubt that one involving so many millions of dollars to her governing class will be pressed with all the zeal which love of money and rage for the destroyed " institution " can inspire.

Georgia in her constitution in 1865 gave notice that she should demand payment for her slaves by the following emphatic provision:

" The government of the United States having as a war measure proclaimed all slaves held or owned in this State emancipated from slavery, and having carried that proclamation into full practical effect: Provided, That acquiescence in the action of the government of the United States is not intended to operate as a relinquishment, or waiver, or estoppel of such claim for compensation of loss sustained by reason of the emancipation of his slaves as any citizen of Georgia may hereafter make upon the justice and magnanimity of that government."

Democratic Kentucky, a few days ago, by a joint resolution in her legislature, took steps in the same direction, which will be seen by the following report of legislative proceedings:

" Resolved by the General Assembly of Kentucky, That a select committee, composed of five members of this House and five of the Senate, be appointed, with instructions to report as soon as practicable to the General Assembly of Kentucky the assessed value of the slaves taken from citizens of Kentucky by federal executive proclamation, by acts of Congress, and by the amendment to the federal constitution (known as article 13); and also the value of such slaves taken from each county of this Commonwealth; and that said committee report what steps are necessary and proper to enable citizens of this State to obtain compensation from the federal government for said property so taken."

All the rebels of the South will be unanimous on this question and the interest at stake is so vast as to enable them to hold out great temptations in the way of corruption; and the Democratic party of the North are not only in position to meet them, but are fully committed to the justice and legality of their claims.

When, in 1866, it was proposed to amend the constitution so as to prohibit the government from making compensation for slaves, every Democratic member of Congress, I believe, in both Houses, voted against it, and throughout the North Democratic papers and orators denounced it with the utmost bitterness. And when, in 1862, the President's proclamation of emancipation appeared, and afterward, in 1864, when it was formally proposed to abolish slavery by an amendment of the constitution, the Democracy everywhere, in Congress and out of it, denounced the proclamation and amendment as unjust, wicked, and impolitic, roundly declaring " the masters should not be deprived of their slaves without due compensation made."

But were the Northern Democracy not already committed in favor of the proposition, they would when the Southern wing made it a condition readily yield acquiescence, and thus add not less than eighteen hundred millions of dollars to the public debt. Whoever believes in the rightfulness of the rebellion or gave it their sympathy must and will, if consistent, be in favor of paying for the slaves.

Another issue directly involved in the success of the Democratic party is the assumption of the rebel war debt. When Southern rebels are restored to power and take their seats in Congress does any man believe that they will vote to tax themselves and others to pay the national debt, or the interest upon it, while their own war debt is in no way provided for? They put their property and money into Confederate stocks and bonds and lost all, and the simple soul must be credulous indeed who believes that these men will voluntarily tax themselves to pay the Northern bondholder, or will act in concert with a Northern party that proposes to tax them for that purpose. They hate the Northern bondholder, and feel under no moral or political obligations to pay his debts, and will make it a condition with the Northern Democracy that they shall repudiate the national debt or consolidate their own with it. And the Northern Democracy are in position to meet them on this question also.

When it was proposed in 1866 to amend the constitution so as to prohibit the assumption of the rebel war debt, every Democrat in Congress voted against it, and their action was sustained by the party throughout the North. The Democratic party were hostile to the national debt in its inception and have always sympathized more strongly with the Southern than the Northern bondholder, and if they refuse to accede to the demands of the South in this matter it will be the first time in their history.

And I may say to the national creditors right here that the payment of their debt will depend absolutely upon the future supremacy of the "idea" that the war to suppress the rebellion and to preserve the Union was waged in a righteous cause. The antagonistic idea will never pay the debt.

Another issue immediately involved in the success of the Democratic party is the pensioning of rebel soldiers, their widows, and orphans, and placing them upon a level with the soldiers of the Union. Is it to be supposed for one moment that rebels when restored to power in the national government will levy taxes and vote money to pension Union soldiers, their widows and orphans, while their own are unprovided for and left in poverty?

This would be against human nature, and upon this they would never compromise. The elevation of the rebel soldier will follow the elevation of the Democratic party to power, as surely as the noon will follow the rising sun, and if you would comprehend what would then be the condition of the Union soldier look to his present status in the Democratic States of Kentucky and Maryland. In these States he is to-day an outcast from society. He is proscribed socially as inflexibly as if he had been an inmate of the penitentiary, and is equally proscribed in his business. If a farmer, his neighbors will not help him; if a merchant, they will not buy his goods; if a lawyer or doctor, they will not employ him; and his home has become more cruel than a foreign land, and he must go into exile for the crime of having been faithful to his country.

The military policy to be hereafter pursued in the matter of reconstruction is clearly indicated in the order promulgated by General Hancock on assuming command of the fifth military district, and as it has been presented by the President to Congress for its admiration, it is a fair subject for criticism and remark. . . .

This order is like the apples of the Dead Sea, "which are fair to the eye, but turn to ashes upon the lip." The first thing noticeable in it is that it makes no reference to the work of reconstruction or the business for which he was placed in command of the district. The position to which he was appointed was created by an act of Congress, to enable him to manage the machinery of reconstruction for the States of Louisiana and Texas, and his duties are prescribed by law; but in his introductory order he makes no mention of this business, and seems to contemplate purposes hostile to it. He was not ignorant of his business, nor did he forget it, and his omission to refer to it is significant of his purpose to defeat it.

The body of the order is devoted to the emphatic recognition of the legality and binding authority of the existing State governments in defiance and contempt of the declarations of Congress as set forth in the several acts of reconstruction. These acts of Congress are predicated upon the idea that the existing State governments are illegal, unauthorized, and have no rightful authority whatever to control the people. . . .

These different sections declare in the most positive terms that the existing State governments are illegal and unauthorized; that they do not furnish protection for life or property, and that they are made entirely subordinate to the military authority, and whatever powers they continue to exercise will be by the consent of the military commander.

But General Hancock, in open contempt of these declarations, asserts that the civil authorities do furnish adequate protection to life and property; that to preserve peace and quiet is the object of his mission, and that as a means to this great end he regards the maintenance of the civil authorities in the execution of the laws as the most efficient means under existing circumstances. He says the war is over, the civil authorities are ready and willing to perform their duties; the military power should cease to lead, and the civil administration resume its natural and rightful dominion.

Again he says, pompously: "Solemnly impressed with these views, the General announces that the great principles of American liberty still are the lawful inheritance of this people, and ever should be."

This is a very startling proposition, and quite as astonishing as the news that the "Dutch have taken Holland." Again he says: "Crimes and offences committed in this district must be referred to the consideration and judgment of the regular civil tribunals, and those tribunals will be supported in their lawful jurisdiction." Here he abjures the military power conferred upon him by Congress, recognizes the supremacy of the bogus civil authorities, and declares that he will support their tribunals in the exercise of their lawful jurisdiction. And this he says standing upon ground in New

Orleans yet moist with the blood of nearly two hundred men slaughtered in the presence and by the contrivance of these civil authorities, while the tribunals which he pledges himself to support have never brought one of the murderers to justice. If peace prevailed when he went there it was because of the bold and determined measures of Generals Sheridan, Griffin, and Mower, and not from any merit of these civil authorities, which he delights to honor, for it is a notorious fact that until General Sheridan took command there was no security for the life or property of Union men in Texas or Louisiana.

Again, says General Hancock, " The right of trial by jury, the habeas corpus, the liberty of the press, the freedom of speech, and the natural rights of persons and the rights of property must be preserved." This is a very pretty saying, but what does it mean in this connection? It means that the loyal men, white and black, shall have the right to be tried by rebel juries, which is like giving the lambs the right to be tried by the wolves. It means that rebels who have murdered Union men shall be tried by rebel juries; and when, I ask, has one of them been brought to justice?

It means that men arrested by military authority may be discharged from custody upon a writ of habeas corpus issued by a State judge, which is in direct violation of the concluding part of the third section of the act of March 2, 1867, which says, " and all interference under color of State authority with the exercise of military authority under this act shall be null and void."

I read this order of General Hancock with unmingled sorrow, and felt he had committed an error more fatal to his reputation than the loss of a battle. General Hancock is a gallant soldier, who has been wounded in the service of his country, but if he shall now lend himself to the support of the principles against which he fought, and become the ally of his enemies against his friends, his laurels, be they ever so bright, will wither, " like the tender flower beneath the simoon of the desert."

ON RECONSTRUCTION

DELIVERED IN THE UNITED STATES SENATE, JANUARY 24, 1868

M R. PRESIDENT,—If I had not been referred to by my honorable friend from Wisconsin [Mr. Doolittle] in the debate yesterday I should not desire to speak on this question, especially at this time. I fear that I shall not have the strength to say what I wish to.

The issue here to-day is the same which prevails throughout the country, which will be the issue of this canvass, and perhaps for years to come. To repeat what I have had occasion to say elsewhere, it is between two paramount ideas, each struggling for the supremacy. One is that the war to suppress the rebellion was right and just on our part; that the rebels forfeited their civil and political rights, and can only be restored to them upon such conditions as the nation may prescribe for its future safety and prosperity. The other idea is, that the rebellion was not sinful but was right; that those engaged in it forfeited no rights, civil or political, and have a right to take charge of their State governments and be restored to their representation in Congress just as if there had been no rebellion and nothing had occurred. The immediate issue before the Senate now is between the existing State governments established under the policy of the President of the United States in the rebel States and the plan of reconstruction presented by Congress.

When a surveyor first enters a new territory he endeavors to ascertain the exact latitude and longitude of a given spot, and from that can safely begin his survey; and so I will endeavor to ascertain a proposition in this debate upon which both parties are agreed, and start from that proposition. That proposition is, that at the end of the war in the spring of 1865 the rebel States were without State governments of any kind. The loyal State governments existing at the beginning of the war had been overturned by the rebels; the rebel State governments erected during the war had been overturned by our armies, and at the end of the war there were no governments of any kind existing in those States. This fact was recognized distinctly by the President of the United States in his proclamation under which the work of reconstruction was commenced in North Carolina in 1865, to which I beg leave to refer. The others were mere copies of this proclamation. In that proclamation he says:

"And whereas the rebellion, which has been waged by a portion of the people of the United States against the properly constituted authorities of the government thereof, in the most violent and revolting form, but whose organized and armed forces have now been almost entirely overcome, has in its revolutionary progress deprived the people of the State of North Carolina of all civil government."

Here the President must be allowed to speak for his party, and I shall accept this as a proposition agreed upon on both sides: that at the end of the war there were no governments of any kind existing in those States.

The fourth section of the fourth article of the constitution declares that " the United States shall guarantee to every State in this Union a republican form of government." This provision contains a vast, undefined power that has never yet been ascertained—a great supervisory power given to the United States to enable them to keep the States in their orbits, to preserve them from anarchy, revolution, and rebellion. The measure of power thus conferred upon the government of the United States can only be determined by that which is requisite to guarantee or maintain in each State a legal and republican form of government. Whatever power therefore may be necessary to enable the government of the United States thus to maintain in each State a republican form of government is conveyed by this provision.

Now, Mr. President, when the war ended and these States were found without governments of any kind, the jurisdiction of the United States under this provision of the constitution at once attached; the power to reorganize State governments to use the common word, to reconstruct, to maintain, and guarantee republican State governments in those States at once attached under this provision. Upon this proposition there is also a concurrence of the two parties. The President has distinctly recognized the application of this clause of the constitution. He has recognized the fact that its jurisdiction attached when those States were found without republican State governments, and he himself claimed to act under this clause of the constitution. I will read the preamble of the President's proclamation.

" Whereas, the fourth section of the fourth article of the constitution of the United States declares that the United States shall guarantee to every State in the Union a republican form of government, and shall protect each of them against invasion and domestic violence; and whereas, the President of the United States is by the constitution made commander-in-chief of the army and navy, as well as chief civil executive officer of the United States, and is bound by

solemn oath faithfully to execute the office of President of
the United States, and to take care that the laws be faithfully
executed; and whereas the rebellion which has been waged
by a portion of the people of the United States against the
properly constituted authorities of the government thereof
in the most violent and revolting form, but whose organized
and armed forces have now been almost entirely overcome,
has in its revolutionary progress deprived the people of the
State of North Carolina of all civil government; and whereas
it becomes necessary and proper to carry out and enforce the
obligations of the people of the United States to the people
of North Carolina in securing them in the enjoyment of a
republican form of government."

I read this, Mr. President, for the purpose of showing that
the President of the United States in his policy of reconstruction started out with a distinct recognition of the applicability
of this clause of the constitution, and that he based his system
of reconstruction upon it.   It is true that he recites in this
proclamation that he is the commander-in-chief of the army
of the United States; but at the same time he puts his plan
of reconstruction not upon the exercise of the military power
which is called to its aid, but on the execution of the guaranty
provided by the clause of the constitution to which I have
referred.   He appoints a governor for North Carolina and
for these other States, the office being civil in its character
but military in its effects.   This governor has all the power
of one of the district commanders, and in fact far greater
power than was conferred upon General Pope or General
Sheridan, or any general in command of a district; for it is
further provided:

" That the military commander of the department, and all
officers and persons in the military and naval service, aid and
assist the said provisional governor in carrying into effect
this proclamation."

We are then agreed upon the second proposition that the power of the United States to reconstruct and guarantee republican forms of government at once applied when these States were found in the condition in which they were at the end of the war. Then, sir, being agreed upon these two propositions, we are brought to the question as to the proper form of exercising this power and by whom it shall be exercised. The constitution says that " the United States shall guarantee to every State in this Union a republican form of government." By the phrase " United States " here is meant the government of the United States. The United States can only act through the government, and the clause would mean precisely the same thing if it read " the government of the United States shall guarantee to every State in this Union a republican form of government."

Then as the government of the United States is to execute this guaranty the question arises, What constitutes the government of the United States? The President does not constitute the government; the Congress does not constitute the government; the judiciary does not constitute the government: but all three together constitute the government; and as this guaranty is to be executed by the government of the United States, it follows necessarily that it must be a legislative act. The President could not assume to execute the guaranty without assuming that he was the United States within the meaning of that provision, without assuming that he was the government of the United States. Congress could not of itself assume to execute the guaranty without assuming that it was the government of the United States; nor could the judiciary without a like assumption. The act must be the act of the government and therefore it must be a legislative act, a law passed by Congress, submitted to the President for his approval, and perhaps in a proper case subject to be reviewed by the judiciary.

Mr. President, that this is necessarily the case from the simple reading of the constitution seems to me cannot be for a moment denied. The President in assuming to execute this guaranty himself is assuming to be the government of the United States, which he clearly is not, but only one of its co-ordinate branches; and, therefore, as this guaranty must be a legislative act, it follows that the attempt on the part of the President to execute the guaranty was without authority, and that the guaranty can only be executed in the form of a law, first to be passed by Congress and then to be submitted to the President for his approval; and if he does not approve it, then to be passed over his head by a majority of two thirds in each House. That law then becomes the execution of the guaranty and is the act of the government of the United States.

Mr. President, this is not an open question. I send to the secretary and ask him to read a part of the decision of the supreme court of the United States in the case of Luther vs. Borden, as reported in 7 Howard.

[The secretary read as follows

" Moreover, the constitution of the United States, as far as it has provided for an emergency of this kind, and authorized the general government to interfere in the domestic concerns of the State, has treated the subject as political in its nature and placed the power in the hands of that department.

" The fourth section of the fourth article of the constitution of the United States provides that the United States shall guarantee to every State in the Union a republican form of government, and shall protect each of them against invasions; and, upon the application of the legislature or of the executive (when the legislature cannot be convened), against domestic violence.

" Under this article of the constitution it rests with Congress to decide what government is the established one in a State. For, as the United States guarantees to each State a republican government, Congress must necessarily decide what government is established in the State before it can determine whether it is republican or not. And when the senators and representatives of a State are admitted into the councils of the Union, the authority of the government under which they are appointed as well as its republican character is recognized by the proper constitutional authority. And its decision is binding upon every other department of the government and could not be questioned in a judicial tribunal. It is true that the contest in this case did not last long enough to bring the matter to this issue; and as no senators or representatives were elected under the authority of the government of which Mr. Dorr was the head, Congress was not called upon to decide the controversy. Yet the right to decide is placed there and not in the courts."]

In this opinion of the supreme court of the United States delivered many years ago the right to execute the guaranty provided for in this clause of the constitution is placed in Congress and nowhere else, and therefore the necessary reading of the constitution is confirmed by the highest judicial authority which we have.

[Mr. Johnson: Do you read from the opinion delivered by the chief justice?]

Yes, sir; the opinion delivered by Chief Justice Taney. He decides that this power is not judicial; that it is one of the high powers conferred upon Congress; that it is not subject to be reviewed by the supreme court because it is political in its nature. It is a distinct enunciation of the doctrine that this guaranty is not to be executed by the President or by the supreme court but by the Congress of the United

States, in the form of a law to be passed by that body and to be submitted to the President for his approval; and should he disapprove it, it may become a law by being passed by a two thirds majority over his head.

Now, I will call the attention of my friend from Wisconsin to some other authority. As he has been pleased to refer to a former speech of mine to show that I am not quite consistent, I will refer to a vote given by him in 1864 on a very important provision. On the 1st of July, 1864, the Senate having under consideration, as in committee of the whole, " a bill to guarantee to certain States whose governments have been usurped or overthrown a republican form of government," Mr. Brown, of Missouri, offered an amendment to strike out all of the bill after the enacting clause and to insert a substitute, which I will ask the secretary to read.

[The secretary read as follows:
" That when the inhabitants of any State have been declared in a state of insurrection against the United States by proclamation of the President, by force and virtue of the act entitled ' An act further to provide for the collection of duties on imports, and for other purposes,' approved July 13, 1861, they shall be, and are hereby declared to be, incapable of casting any vote for electors of President or Vice-President of the United States, or of electing senators or representatives in Congress until said insurrection in said State is suppressed or abandoned, and said inhabitants have returned to their obedience to the government of the United States, and until such return to obedience shall be declared by proclamation of the President, issued by virtue of an act of Congress hereafter to be passed, authorizing the same."]

The honorable senator from Wisconsin voted for that in committee of the whole and on its final passage. I call attention to the conclusion of the amendment, which declares that they shall be—

—" incapable of casting any vote for electors of President or Vice-President of the United States or of electing senators or representatives in Congress until said insurrection in said State is suppressed or abandoned, and said inhabitants have returned to their obedience to the government of the United States, and until such return and obedience shall be declared by proclamation of the President, issued by virtue of an act to Congress hereafter to be passed, authorizing the same."

Recognizing that a state of war shall be regarded as continuing until it shall be declared no longer to exist by the President, in virtue of an act to Congress to be hereafter passed, I am glad to find by looking at the vote that the distinguished senator from Maryland [Mr. Johnson] voted for this proposition, and thus recognized the doctrine for which I am now contending; that the power to execute the guaranty is vested in Congress alone, and that it is for Congress alone to determine the status and condition of those States, and that the President has no power to proclaim peace or to declare the political condition of those States until he shall first have been thereunto authorized by an act of Congress.

I therefore, Mr. President, take the proposition as conclusively established, both by reason and authority, that this clause of the constitution can be executed only by Congress; and taking that as established, I now proceed to consider what are the powers of Congress in the execution of the guaranty, how it shall be executed, and what means may be employed for that purpose. The constitution does not define the means. It does not say how the guaranty shall be executed. All that is left to the determination of Congress. As to the particular character of the means that must be employed, that, I take it, will depend upon the peculiar circumstances of each case; and the extent of the power will depend upon the other question as to what may be required for the purpose of maintaining or guaranteeing a loyal republican form of government in each State. I use the word "loyal," although it is not used in the constitution, because loyalty is an inhering qualification, not only in regard to persons who are to fill public offices, but in regard to State governments, and we have no right to recognize a State government that is not loyal to the government of the United States. Now, sir, as to the use of means that are not prescribed in the constitution, I call the attention of the Senate to the eighteenth clause of section eight of the first article of the constitution of the United States, which declares that—

" The Congress shall have power to make all laws which shall be necessary and proper for carrying into execution the foregoing powers and all other powers vested by this constitution in the government of the United States, or any department or officer thereof."

Here is a declaration of what would otherwise be a general principle anyhow: that Congress shall have the power to pass all laws necessary to carry into execution all powers that are vested in the government under the constitution. As Congress has the power to guarantee or maintain a loyal republican government in each State, it has the right to use whatever means may be necessary for that purpose. As I before remarked, the character of the means will depend upon the character of the case. In one case it may be the use of an army; in another case perhaps it may be simply presenting a question to the courts, and having it tested in that way; in another case it may go to the very foundation of the government itself. And I now propound this proposition: that if Congress, after deliberation, after long and bloody experience, shall come to the conclusion that loyal republican State governments cannot be erected and maintained in the rebel States upon the basis of the white population, it has a right to raise up and make voters of a class of men who had no right to vote under the State laws. This is simply the use of the necessary means in the execution of the guaranty. If we have found after repeated trials that loyal republican State governments—governments that shall answer the purpose that such governments are intended to answer—cannot be successfully founded upon the basis of the white population, because the great majority of that population are disloyal, then Congress has a right to raise up a new loyal voting population for the purpose of establishing these governments in the execution of the guaranty. I think, sir, this proposition is so clear that it is not necessary to elaborate it. We are not required to find in the constitution a particular grant of power for this purpose; but we find a general grant of power, and we find also another grant of power authorizing us to use whatever means may be necessary to execute the first; and we find that the supreme court of the United States has said that the judgment of Congress upon this question shall be conclusive; that it cannot be reviewed by the courts; that it is a purely political matter, and therefore the determination of Congress, that raising up colored men to the right of suffrage·is a means necessary to the execution of that power, is a determination which cannot be reviewed by the courts and is conclusive upon the people of this country.

The President of the United States, assuming that he had the power to execute this guaranty, and basing his proclamation upon it, went forward in the work of reconstruction. It was understood at that time—it was so announced, if not by himself, at least formally by the Secretary of State, Mr. Seward—that the governments which he would erect during the vacation of Congress were to be erected as provisional only; that his plan of reconstruction and the work that was to be done under it would be submitted to Congress for its approval or disapproval at the next session. If the President had adhered to that determination, I believe that all would have been well, and that the present state of things would not exist. But, sir, the executive undertook finally to execute the guaranty himself without the co-operation of Congress. He appointed provisional governors, giving to them unlimited power until such time as the new State governments should be erected. He prescribed in his proclamation who should exercise the right of suffrage in the election of delegates. And allow me for one moment to refer to that. He says in his proclamation:

" No person shall be qualified as an elector, or shall be eligible as a member of such convention, unless he shall have previously taken and subscribed the oath of amnesty, as set forth in the President's proclamation of May 29, A.D. 1865,"

—which was issued on the same day, and was a part of the same transaction:

—" and is a voter qualified as prescribed by the constitution and laws of the State of North Carolina in force immediately before the 20th day of May, A.D. 1861."

The persons having the right to vote must have the right to vote by the laws of the State, and must, in addition to that, have taken the oath of amnesty. The President disfranchised in voting for delegates to the conventions from two hundred and fifty thousand to three hundred thousand men. His disfranchisement was far greater than that which has been done by Congress. In the proclamation of amnesty he says:

" The following classes of persons are excepted from the benefits of this proclamation: "

He then announced fourteen classes of persons:

" 1. All who are or shall have been pretended civil or diplomatic officers, or otherwise domestic or foreign agents, of the pretended Confederate government." . . .

" 13. All persons who have voluntarily participated in said rebellion, and the estimated value of whose taxable property is over twenty thousand dollars."

And twelve other classes, estimated to number at the least two hundred and fifty thousand or three hundred thousand men, while the disfranchisement that has been created by Congress does not extend perhaps to more than forty-five thousand or fifty thousand persons at the furthest. These provisional governors, under the authority of the President, were to call conventions; they were to hold the elections, and they were to count the votes; they were to exercise all the powers that are being exercised by the military commanders under the reconstruction acts of Congress. After those constitutions were formed the President went forward and accepted them as being loyal and republican in their character. He authorized the voters under them to proceed to elect legislatures, members of Congress, and the legislatures to elect senators to take their seats in this body. In other words, the President launched those State governments into full life and activity without consultation with or co-operation on the part of Congress.

Now, sir, when it is claimed that these governments are legal, let it be remembered that they took their origin under a proceeding instituted by the President of the United States

in the execution of this guaranty, when it now stands con-
fessed that he could not execute the guaranty. But even if
he had the power, let it be further borne in mind that those
constitutions were formed by conventions that were elected
by less than one third of the white voters in the States at
that time; that the conventions were elected by a small
minority even of the white voters, and that those constitutions thus formed by a very small minority have never been
submitted to the people of those States for ratification. They
are no more the constitutions of those States to-day than the
constitutions formed by the conventions now in session would
be if we were to proclaim them to be the constitutions of
those States without first having submitted them to the people for ratification. How can it be pretended for a moment,
even admitting that the President had the power to start forward in the work of reconstruction, that those State governments are legally formed by a small minority, never ratified
by the people, the people never having had a chance to vote
for them. They stand as mere arbitrary constitutions, established not by the people of the several States, but simply
by force of executive power.

And, sir, if we shall admit those States to representation on
this floor and in the other House under those constitutions,
when the thing shall have got beyond our keeping and they
are fully restored to their political rights, they will then
rise up and declare that those constitutions are not binding
upon them, that they never made them; and they will throw
them off, and with them will go those provisions which were
incorporated therein, declaring that slavery should never be
restored, and that their war debt was repudiated. Those
provisions were put into those constitutions, but they have
never been sanctioned by the people of those States, and they

will cast them out as not being their act and deed as soon as they shall have been restored to political power in this government. Therefore I say that even if it be conceded that the President had the power, which he had not, to start forward in the execution of this guaranty, there can still be no pretence that those governments are legal and authorized, and that we are bound to recognize them.

The President of the United States, in his proclamation, declared that those governments were to be formed only by the loyal people of those States; and I beg leave to call the attention of the Senate to that clause in his proclamation of reconstruction. He says:

" And with authority to exercise, within the limits of said State, all the powers necessary and proper to enable such loyal people of the State of North Carolina to restore said State to its constitutional relations with the federal government."

Again, speaking of the army:

" And they are enjoined to abstain from in any way hindering, impeding, or discouraging the loyal people from the organization of a State government as herein authorized."

Now, sir, so far from those State governments having been organized by the loyal people, they were organized by the disloyal; every office passed into the hands of a rebel; the Union men had no part or lot in those governments; and so far from answering the purpose for which governments are intended, they failed to extend protection to the loyal men, either white or black. The loyal men were murdered with impunity; and I will thank any senator upon this floor to point to a single case in any of the rebel States where a rebel has been tried and brought to punishment by the civil authority for the murder of a Union man. Not one case, I am told, can be found.

Those governments utterly failed in answering the purpose of civil governments; and not only that, but they returned the colored people to a condition of quasi-slavery; they made them the slaves of society instead of being, as they were before, the slaves of individuals. Under various forms of vagrant laws they deprived them of the rights of freemen and placed them under the power and control of their rebel masters, who were filled with hatred and revenge.

But, Mr. President, time passed on. Congress assembled in December, 1865. For a time it paused. It did not at once annul those governments. It hesitated. At last, in 1866, the constitutional amendment, the fourteenth article, was brought forward as a basis of settlement and reconstruction; and there was a tacit understanding, though it was not embraced in any law or resolution, that if the Southern people should ratify and agree to that amendment, then their State governments would be accepted. But that amendment was rejected, contemptuously rejected. The Southern people, counselled and inspired by the Democracy of the North, rejected that amendment. They were told that they were not bound to submit to any conditions whatever; that they had forfeited no rights by rebellion. Why, sir, what did we propose by this amendment? By the first section we declared that all men born upon our soil were citizens of the United States—a thing that had long been recognized by every department of this government until the Dred Scott decision was made in 1857. The second section provided that where a class or race of men were excluded from the right of suffrage they should not be counted in the basis of representation—an obvious justice that no reasonable man for a moment could deny; that if four million people down South were to have no suffrage, the men living in their midst and surrounding them and depriving them of all political rights, should not have members of Congress on their account. I say the justice of the second clause has never been successfully impugned by any argument, I care not how ingenious it may be. What was the third clause? It was that the leaders of the South, those men who had once taken an official oath to support the constitution of the United States and had afterward committed perjury by going into the rebellion, should be made ineligible to any office under the government of the United States or of a State. It was a very small disfranchisement. It was intended to withhold power from those leaders by whose instrumentality we had lost nearly half a million lives and untold treasure. The justice of that disfranchisement could not be disproved. And what was the fourth clause of the amendment? That this government should never assume and pay any part of the rebel debt; that it should never pay the rebels for their slaves. This was bitterly opposed in the North as well as in the South. How could any man oppose that amendment unless he was in favor of this government assuming a portion or all of the rebel debt, and in favor of paying the rebels for their slaves? When the Democratic party, North and South, opposed that most important and perhaps hereafter to be regarded as vital amendment, they were committing themselves in principle, as they had been before by declaration, to the doctrine that this government was bound to pay for the slaves and that it was just and right that we should assume and pay the rebel debt.

This amendment, as I have before said, was rejected, and when Congress assembled in December, 1866, they were confronted by the fact that every proposition of compromise had been rejected; every half-way measure had been spurned by the rebels and they had nothing left to do but to begin the work of reconstruction themselves; and in February, 1867, Congress for the first time entered upon the execution of the guaranty provided for in the constitution by the passage of the first reconstruction law. A supplementary bill was found necessary in March, another one in July, and I believe another is found necessary at this time; but the power is with Congress. Whatever it shall deem necessary, whether it be in the way of colored suffrage, whether it be in the way of military power—whatever Congress shall deem necessary in the execution of this guaranty, is conclusive upon the courts and upon the States.

Sir, when Congress entered upon this work it had become apparent to all men that loyal republican State governments could not be erected and maintained upon the basis of the white population. We had tried them. Congress had attempted the work of reconstruction through the constitutional amendment by leaving the suffrage with the white men, and by leaving with the white people of the South the question as to when the colored people should exercise the right of suffrage, if ever; but when it was found that those white men were as rebellious as ever, that they hated this government more bitterly than ever; when it was found that they persecuted the loyal men, both white and black, in their midst; when it was found that Northern men who had gone down there were driven out by social tyranny, by a thousand annoyances, by the insecurity of life and property—then it became apparent to all men of intelligence that reconstruction could not take place upon the basis of the white population and something else must be done.

Now, sir, what was there left to do? Either we must hold these people continually by military power or we must use such machinery upon such a new basis as would enable loyal republican State governments to be raised up; and in the last resort, and I will say Congress waited long, the nation waited long, experience had to come to the rescue of reason before the thing was done—in the last resort, and as the last thing to be done, Congress determined to dig through all the rubbish,—dig through the soil and the shifting sands, and go down to the eternal rock, and there, upon the basis of the everlasting principle of equal and exact justice to all men, we have planted the column of reconstruction; and, sir, it will arise slowly but surely, and "the gates of hell shall not prevail against it." Whatever dangers we apprehended from the introduction to the right of suffrage of seven hundred thousand men, just emerged from slavery, were put aside in the presence of a greater danger. Why, sir, let me say frankly to my friend from Wisconsin, that I approached universal colored suffrage in the South reluctantly. Not because I adhered to the miserable dogma that this was the white man's government, but because I entertained fears about at once intrusting a large body of men just from slavery, to whom education had been denied by law, to whom the marriage relation had been denied, who had been made the most abject slaves, with political power. And as the senator has referred to a speech which I made in Indiana in 1865, allow me to show the principle that then actuated me, for in that speech I said:

"In regard to the question of admitting the freedmen of the Southern States to vote, while I admit the equal rights of all men, and that in time all men will have the right to vote, without distinction of color or race, I yet believe that in the case of four million of slaves, just freed from bondage, there should be a period of probation and preparation before they are brought to the exercise of political power."

Such was my feeling at that time, for it had not then been determined by the bloody experience of the last two years that we could not reconstruct upon the basis of the white population, and such was the opinion of a great majority of the people of the North; and it was not until a year and a half after that time that Congress came to the conclusion that there was no way left but to resort to colored suffrage, and suffrage to all men except those who were disqualified by the commission of high crimes and misdemeanors.

Mr. President, we hear much said in the course of this debate and through the press about the violation of the constitution. It is said that in the reconstruction measures of Congress we have gone outside of the constitution, and the remark of some distinguished statesman of the Republican party is quoted to that effect. Sir, if any leading Republican has ever said so, he spoke only for himself, not for another. I deny the statement *in toto*. I insist that these reconstruction measures are as fully within the powers of the constitution as any legislation that can be had, not only by reason, but by authority. And who are the men that are talking so much about the violation of the constitution and who pretend to be the especial friends of that instrument? The great mass of them, only three years ago, were in arms to overturn the constitution and establish that of Montgomery in its place, or were their Northern friends, who were aiding and sympathizing in that undertaking.

I had occasion the other day to speak of what was described as a constitutional Union man—a man living inside of the federal lines during the war, sympathizing with the rebellion, and who endeavored to aid the rebellion by insisting that every war measure for the purpose of suppressing it was a violation of the constitution of the United States. Now, these men who claim to be the especial friends of the constitution are the men who have sought to destroy it by force of arms, and those throughout the country who have given them aid and comfort. Sir, you will remember that once a celebrated French woman was being dragged to the scaffold, and as she passed the statue of liberty she exclaimed: " How many crimes have been committed in thy name;" and I can say to the constitution, how many crimes against liberty, humanity, and progress are being committed in thy name by these men who, while they loved not the constitution and sought its destruction, now, for party purposes, claim to be its especial friends.

My friend from Wisconsin yesterday compared what he called the Radical party of the North to the radicals of the South, and when he was asked the question by some senator, " Who are the radicals of the South ? " he said, " They are the secessionists." Sir, the secessionists of the South are Democrats to-day, acting in harmony and concert with the Democratic party. They were Democrats during the war who prayed for the success of McClellan and Pendleton, and would have been glad to have voted for them; and they were Democrats before the war, and the men who made the rebellion. These are the radicals of the South; and my friend from Wisconsin, after all, is voting with the radicals.

The burden of his speech yesterday was that the reconstruction measures of Congress are intended to establish negro supremacy. Sir, this proposition is without any foundation whatever. I believe it was stated yesterday by the senator from Illinois [Mr. Trumbull] that in every State but two the white voters registered outnumbered the colored voters; and the fact that in two States the colored voters outnumbered the white voters is owing to the simple accident that there are more colored men in those States than there are white men. Congress has not sought to establish negro supremacy, nor has it sought to establish the supremacy of any class or party of men. If it had sought to establish negro supremacy it would have been an easy matter by excluding from the right of suffrage all men who had been concerned in the rebellion, in accordance with the proposition of the distinguished senator from Massachusetts [Mr. Sumner] in his speech at Worcester in 1865. He proposed to exclude all men who had been concerned in the rebellion, and confer suffrage only on those who were left. That would have established negro supremacy by giving the negroes an overwhelming majority in every State; and if that had been the object of Congress, it could have been readily done.

But, sir, Congress has only sought to divide the political power between the loyal and the disloyal. It has disfranchised some fifty thousand disloyal leaders, leaving all the rest of the people to vote. They have been enfranchised on both sides, that neither should be placed in the power of the other. The rebels have the right to vote so that they shall not be under the control and power of the Union men only, and the Union men have been allowed to vote so that they shall not be under the control and power of the rebels. This is the policy, to divide the political power among those men for the protection of each. Sir, the charge that we intend to create a negro supremacy or colored State governments is without the slightest foundation, for it would have been in the power of Congress to have easily conferred such supremacy by simply excluding the disloyal from the right of suffrage—a power which it had the clear right to exercise.

Now, Mr. President, allow me to consider for a moment the amendment offered by the senator from Wisconsin, and upon which his speech was made, and see what is its effect,— I will not say its purpose, but its inevitable effect,—should it become a law. I will ask the secretary to read the amendment which the senator from Wisconsin has proposed to the Senate.

[The secretary read as follows:
" Provided, nevertheless, That upon an election for the ratification of any constitution, or of officers under the same, previous to its adoption in any State, no person not having the qualifications of an elector under the constitution and laws of such State previous to the late rebellion shall be allowed to vote, unless he shall possess one of the following qualifications, namely:—

" 1. He shall have served as a soldier in the federal army for one year or more.

" 2. He shall have a sufficient education to read the constitution of the United States and to subscribe his name to an oath to support the same; or,

" 3. He shall be seized in his own right, or in the right of his wife, of a freehold of the value of $250."]

Sir, these qualifications are, by the terms of the amendment, to apply to those who were not authorized to vote by the laws of the State before the rebellion—in other words, the colored men. He proposes to allow a colored man to vote if he has been in the federal army one year, and he proposes to allow a rebel white man to vote, although he has served in the rebel army four years! He proposes that a colored man shall not vote unless he has sufficient education to read the constitution of the United States and to subscribe his name to an oath to support the same; whereas he permits a rebel white man to vote who never heard of A, and does not know how to make his mark even to a note given for whisky.

Again, sir, he proposes that the colored man shall not vote unless he shall be seized in his own right or in the right of his wife of a freehold of the value of $250; a provision which, of course, would cut off nine hundred and ninety-nine out of every thousand colored men in the South. The colored man cannot vote unless he has a freehold of $250, but the white rebel who was never worth twenty-five cents, who never paid poll-tax in his life, never paid an honest debt, is to be allowed to vote. Sir, what would be the inevitable effect of the adoption of this amendment? To cut off such a large part of the colored vote as to leave the rebel white vote largely in the ascendancy and to put these new State governments there to be formed again into the hands of the rebels. Sir, I will not spend longer time upon that.

My friend yesterday alluded to my indorsement of the President's policy in a speech in 1865. I never indorsed what is now called the President's policy. In the summer of 1865, when I saw a division coming between the President and the Republican party, and when I could not help anticipating the direful consequences that must result from it, I made a speech in which I repelled certain statements that had been made against the President, and denied the charge that by issuing his proclamation of May 29, 1865, he had thereby left the Republican party. I said that he had not left the Republican party by that act. I did show that the policy of that proclamation was even more radical than that of Mr. Lincoln. I did show that it was more radical even than the Winter-Davis bill of the summer of 1864. But, sir, it was all upon the distinct understanding that whatever the President did, that his whole policy or action was to be submitted to Congress for its consideration and decision; and, as I before remarked, if that had been done all would have been well. I did not then advocate universal colored suffrage in the South, and I have before given my reasons for it, and in doing that I was acting in harmony with the great body of the Republican party of the North. It was nearly a year after that time, when Congress passed the constitutional amendment, which still left the question of suffrage with the Southern States, left it with the white people; and it was not until a year and a half after that time that Congress came to the conclusion that we could not execute the guaranty of the constitution without raising up a new class of loyal voters.

And, sir, nobody concurred in that result more heartily than myself. I confess (and I do it without shame) that I have been educated by the great events of the war. The American people have been educated rapidly; and the man who says he has learned nothing, that he stands now where he did six years ago, is like an ancient mile-post by the side of a deserted highway. We, Mr. President, have advanced step by step. When this war began we did not contemplate the destruction of slavery. I remember well when the Crittenden resolution was passed, declaring that the war was not prosecuted for conquest or to overturn the institutions of any State. I know that that was intended as an assurance that slavery should not be destroyed, and it received the vote, I believe, of every Republican member in both houses of Congress; but in a few months after that time it was found by the events of the war that we could not preserve slavery and suppress the rebellion, and we must destroy slavery—not prosecute the war to destroy slavery, but destroy slavery to prosecute the war. Which was the better? To stand by the resolution and let the Union go, or stand by the Union and let the resolution go? Congress could not stand by that pledge, and it was " more honored in the breach than the observance."

Mr. Lincoln issued his proclamation of emancipation, setting free the slaves of the rebels. It was dictated by the

stern and bloody experience of the times. Mr. Lincoln had
no choice left him. When we began this contest, no one
thought we would use colored soldiers in the war. The distinguished senator sitting by me here [Mr. Cameron], when
in the winter of 1861 he first brought forward the proposition, as secretary of war, to use colored soldiers, was greatly
in advance of public opinion, and was thought to be visionary; but as the war progressed it became manifest to all intelligent men that we must not only destroy slavery but we
must avail ourselves of every instrumentality in our power
for the purpose of putting down the rebellion, and the whole
country accorded in the use of colored soldiers, and gallant
and glorious service they rendered. In 1864 a proposition
was brought forward in this body to amend the constitution
of the United States by abolishing slavery. We do not think
that this is very radical now, but it was very radical then;
it was the great measure of the age, and almost of modern
times, and it was finally passed; an amendment setting free
every human being within the limits of the United States.
But, sir, we were very far then from where we are now. All
will remember the celebrated Winter-Davis bill, passed
in June, 1864, which took the power of reconstruction
out of the hands of the President, where it did not in fact
belong.

I refer to Mr. Lincoln; but if that bill had passed it would
perhaps have resulted in the destruction of this government.
We can all see it now, although it was then thought to be
the most radical measure of the times. What did it propose?
It proposed to prescribe a plan, to take effect when the war
should end, by which these rebel States should be restored.
I refer to that bill simply to show how we have all travelled.
It required but one condition or guaranty on the part of the

South, and that was that they should put in their constitutions a provision prohibiting slavery. It required no other guaranty. It required no equalization of representation; no security against rebel debts, or against payment for emancipated slaves; and it confined the right of suffrage to white men. But it was thought to be a great step in advance at the time; and so it was; but events were passing rapidly, and in 1865 the President came forward with his proposition, and I am stating what is true from an examination of the documents when I say that, but for the want of power with the President, his scheme in itself considered was far more radical than that of the Winter-Davis bill: but events were rapidly teaching the statesmen of the time that we could not reconstruct upon that basis.

Still, Congress was not prepared to take a forward step until the summer of 1866, in the passage of the constitutional amendment, which we now regard as a half-way measure, necessary and vital as far as it went, but not going far enough. That was rejected, and we were then compelled to go further, and we have now fallen upon the plan of reconstruction which I have been considering. It has been dictated by the logic of events. It overrides all arguments, overrides all prejudices, overrides all theory, in the presence of the necessity for preserving the life of this nation; and if future events shall determine that we must go further, I for one am prepared to say that I will go as far as shall be necessary to the execution of this guaranty, the reconstruction of this Republic upon a right basis, and the successful restoration of every part of this Union.

Mr. President, the column of reconstruction, as I before remarked, has risen slowly. It has not been hewn from a single stone. It is composed of many blocks, painfully laid

up and put together, and cemented by the tears and blood
of the nation. Sir, we have done nothing arbitrarily. We
have done nothing for punishment—aye, too little for punishment. Justice has not had her demand. Not a man has
yet been executed for this great treason. The arch fiend
himself is now at liberty upon bail. No man is to be pun-
ished; and now, while punishment has gone by, as we all
know, we are insisting only upon security for the future.
We are simply asking that the evil spirits who brought this
war upon us shall not again come into power during this
generation, again to bring upon us rebellion and calamity.
We are simply asking for those securities that we deem necessary for our peace and the peace of our posterity.

Sir, there is one great difference between this Union party
and the so-called Democratic party. Our principles are those
of humanity; they are those of justice; they are those of
equal rights; they are principles that appeal to the hearts and
the consciences of men; while on the other side we hear appeals to the prejudice of race against race. The white man
is overwhelmingly in the majority in this country, and that
majority is yearly increased by half a million of white men
from abroad, and that majority gaining in proportion from
year to year until the colored men will finally be but a handful in this country; and yet we hear the prejudices of the
white race appealed to to crush this other race, and to prevent
it from rising to supremacy and power. Sir, there is nothing
noble, there is nothing generous, there is nothing lovely in
that policy or that appeal. How does that principle compare
with ours? We are standing upon the broad platform of the
Declaration of Independence, that "all men are created
equal; that they are endowed by their Creator with certain
inalienable rights; that among these are life, liberty, and the

pursuit of happiness." We say that these rights are not given by laws; are not given by the constitution; but they are the gift of God to every man born in the world. Oh, sir, how glorious is this great principle compared with the inhuman—I might say the heathenish—appeal to the prejudice of race against race; the endeavor further to excite the strong against the weak; the endeavor further to deprive the weak of their rights of protection against the strong.

SMITH

GOLDWIN SMITH, an English essayist and historical writer, was born at Reading, England, August 13, 1823. He was educated at Eton and Oxford; took his degree of B. A. at Magdalen College, Oxford, in 1845; became Fellow and tutor, and was called to the bar in 1850. In 1856 he was made regius professor of modern history at Oxford. In 1868 he came to the United States, having been elected professor of constitutional history in Cornell University, Ithaca, New York. In 1871 he became connected with the University of Toronto, where he has since lived. He has delivered numerous lectures upon social and political topics. Among his works are " The Study of History," delivered at Oxford (1861); " Irish History and Irish Character " (1861); " Three English Statesmen " (Pym, Cromwell, and Pitt); a " Course of Lectures on the Political History of England " (1867); " A Short History of England, down to the Reformation " (1869); " William Cowper " (1880); " Life of Jane Austen " (1890); " Canada and the Canadian Question " (1891); " The United States, 1492-1871 " (1893); " Bay Leaves " (1893); " Essays on Questions of the Day " (1893); " Oxford and her Colleges " (1894); " Guesses at the Riddle of Existence " (1897).

THE EVOLUTION OF THE DOMINION

IN Great Britain Liberalism was now in the ascendant and had carried parliamentary reform. As its envoy, and in its mantle, Lord Durham, the son-in-law of Lord Grey, the Radical aristocrat, the draftsman of the Reform Bill, came out as governor and high commissioner to report on the disease and prescribe the remedy. He overrated his position and his authority, moved about, Radical though he was, in regal state, assumed the power of banishing rebels without process of law, fell into the clutches of Brougham, with whom he was at feud, was censured and resigned. But he had brought with him Charles Buller, an expert in colonial questions, with the help of whose pen and that of Gobbon Wakefield, he framed a report which by its great ability and momentous effects forms an epoch in colonial history.

The Durham report recommends the union of the two

Provinces and the concession of responsible government, that is, of a government like the British cabinet, virtually designated by the representatives of the people and holding office by the title of their confidence. "To conduct their government," says Durham of the Canadian people, "harmoniously, in accordance with its established principles, is now the business of its rulers; and I know not how it is possible to secure that harmony in any other way, than by administering the government on those principles which have been found perfectly efficacious in Great Britain.

"I would not impair a single prerogative of the Crown; on the contrary, I believe that the interests of the people of these colonies require the protection of prerogatives, which have not hitherto been exercised. But the Crown must, on the other hand, submit to the necessary consequences of representative institutions; and if it has to carry on the government in unison with a representative body, it must consent to carry it on by means of those in whom that representative body has confidence." What Durham meant by his saving words about the prerogative is not clear; nor has he explained how supreme power could be given to the colonial Parliament without taking away prerogative from the Crown. No effect, at all events, has ever been given to those words.

"We can venture," said the Tory periodical of that day in a notice of the report, "to answer, that every uncontradicted assertion of that volume will be made the excuse of future rebellions, every unquestioned principle will be hereafter perverted into a gospel of treason, and if that rank and infectious report does not receive the high, marked, and energetic discountenance and indignation of the imperial Crown and Parliament, British America is lost."

If resignation of authority is loss of dominion, the prediction of the writer in the " Quarterly " that British America would be lost, can hardly be said, from the Tory point of view, to have proved substantially unfounded.

The avowed object of union was the extinction of French nationality, which the authors of the report hoped would be brought about without violence by the political subjection of the weaker element to the influence of the stronger.

" I entertain," says Durham, " no doubts as to the national character which must be given to Lower Canada; it must be that of the British Empire; that of the majority of the population of British America; that of the great race which must, in the lapse of no long period of time, be predominant over the whole North American continent. Without effecting the change so rapidly or so roughly as to shock the feelings and trample on the welfare of the existing generation, it must henceforth be the first and steady purpose of the British government to establish an English population, with English laws and language, in this Province, and to trust its government to none but a decidedly English legislature."

Union was accepted in Upper Canada. On the French Province, by which it would certainly have been rejected, it was imposed, the constitution there having been suspended. For the united Provinces the constitution was in form the same as it had been for each of the Provinces separately, with the governor and his executive council, a legislative council appointed by the governor and a legislative assembly elected by the people; but with " responsible government," the understanding henceforth being in Canada as in Great Britain that the governor should accept as the members of his executive council and the framers of his policy the leaders of the majority in Parliament. The upper House was afterward made, like the lower, elective with the constituencies wider than those for the lower House. The same number of members in the legislative assembly was assigned to each of the two Provinces, though the population of Quebec was at this time far the larger of the two.

The constitution thus granted to the colony was in reality far more democratic than that of the mother country, where, besides a court actually present and a hereditary upper House, there were the influences of a great land-owning gentry and other social forces of a conservative kind, as well as deep-seated tradition, to control the political action of the people.

Not without a pang or without a struggle did the colonial office or the governors finally acquiesce in responsible government and the virtual independence of the colony. Poulett Thomson, afterward Lord Sydenham, sent out as governor by the Melbourne ministry, showed some inclination to revert to the old paths, shape his own policy, and hold himself responsible to the colonial office rather than to the Canadian people; but he was a shrewd politician and took care to steer clear of rocks. His successor, Bagot, though a Conservative and appointed by a Conservative government, surprised everybody by discreet and somewhat epicurean pliancy to the exigencies of his political position. He reigned in peace.

But Metcalfe, who followed him, had been trained in the despotic government of India. Backed by the Conservative government which had sent him out, he made strenuous efforts to recover something of the old power of a governor, to shape his own course, and make his appointments himself, not at the dictation of responsible ministers. The result was a furious storm. Fiery invectives were interchanged in

Parliament and in the press. At elections stones and brick-bats flew. Canada was for several months without a government. The fatal illness of the governor terminated the strife.

Lord Elgin, when he became governor, heartily embraced the principle of responsible government, and upon the demise of the ministry sent at once for the leader of the opposition. He flattered himself that he was able to do more under that system than he could have done if invested with personal authority. That he could have done a good deal under any system by his moral influence was most likely, for he was one of the most characteristic and best specimens of imperial statesmanship. But moral influence is not constitutional power. About the last relic of the political world before responsibility was Dominick Daly, who deemed it his duty to stay in office, any changes in the ministry and principles of government notwithstanding.

The other North American colonies, Nova Scotia, New Brunswick, and Prince Edward Island, went through a similar course of contest for supreme power between the governor with the council nominated by him and the elective assembly, ending in the same way. On them also the boon of responsible government was conferred. In the case of Prince Edward Island the political problem had been complicated by an agrarian struggle with the body of grantees among whom the crown in its feudal character of supreme land-owner, had parcelled out the island.

Liberalism now gained the upper hand in the united Canada and ultimately carried its various points. Exiled rebels returned. William Lyon Mackenzie himself was, in time, again elected to Parliament, and Rolph, another fugitive, was admitted to the government. The clergy reserves were secularized, university education was made unsectarian, and religious equality became the law. The seigniories in the French Province were abolished, compensation being given to the lords.

The passions of the civil war were for a moment revived when an act was passed awarding compensation to those whose property had suffered in the suppression of the rebellion. This the Tories took to be payment of rebels. They dropped their loyalty, as Tories are apt to do when Liberals are in power, stoned the governor-general, Lord Elgin, who had assented to the bill, and burned the Parliament House at Montreal. But Lord Elgin, calmly wise, and well sustained at home, restored peace.

As an attempt to suppress the French nationality, union signally failed. The French, the mass of them at least, clung together more closely than ever, and the other race being split into factions, held the key of the political situation. They enforced the repeal of the clause in the Union act, making English the only official language. A candidate for the speakership was rejected on the ground of his ignorance of French. At most the French politicians became half Anglicized, as their successors do at present, for the purposes of the political field. It came to be recognized as a rule that government must have a majority of both sections. To the antagonism between English and French was added the strife between Orangeism, which had been imported into Canada, though rather in its political than in its religious character, and the Catholics, French or Irish.

The population of the British Province having now outgrown that of the French Province, agitation for representation by population commenced on the British side. There ensued a series of cabals, intrigues, and faction fights which lasted for about a quarter of a century, all intelligible principles of difference being lost in the struggle for place, though one question after another was taken up as a counter in the game. The only available statesmanship was address in the management of party. In this John A. Macdonald was supreme, and gained the ascendency which made him ruler of Canada for many years.

Durham, in his report, had spoken freely of the sad contrast between the wonderful prosperity of the United States and the comparative backwardness of Canada. The contrast was still more felt when, by England's adoption of free trade, Canada lost her privileges in the British market, while she was excluded from the market of her own continent. A petition signed by three hundred and twenty-five persons, including the chiefs of commerce, proposed among other remedies, " A friendly and peaceful separation from British connection, and a union upon equitable terms with the great North American Confederacy of Sovereign States."

To open a safety valve for this discontent, Lord Elgin went to Washington and negotiated a reciprocity treaty with the United States. The Democratic party, that is, the party of slavery, then dominant, would be ready enough to do whatever would prevent Canada from entering the union and turning the balance against slavery. At the same time that Canada lost her privilege in the British market, British privilege in the Canadian market was virtually given up, and the colony received fiscal independence.

Faction, cabal, intrigue, and antagonism between the British and the French Province ended in a political deadlock from which the leaders of parties, combining for the moment, agreed to escape by merging their quarrels in a confederation of all the British Provinces of North America. Into this confederation Upper or British Canada, now called Ontario, and French Canada, now called Quebec, came at once. New Brunswick came early and freely. Nova Scotia was drawn in by questionable means. Prince Edward Island came in later of her own accord. The vast Northwest was afterward purchased of the Hudson's Bay Company and added to the confederation after the American model as a set of Territories to be received, when peopled, as Provinces of the Dominion. British Columbia was ultimately incorporated by the construction of the Canadian Pacific Railway across the continent. Some of the authors of confederation would have preferred a legislative to a federal union. This was precluded by the jealous nationality of the French Province and its adherence to its own civil law.

Federation this process was called, but the form of polity comprised in the British North America act is not that of federation proper; it is that of a nation with a federal structure. There is a wide and important difference between the two. In federation proper, which has usually been the offspring of union for common defence, the several states remain sovereign. The federal government is formed of delegates from the several States. Its powers are confined to the objects of the bond, security from without and peace within; it has the power of requisition only, not of taxation; nor has it any general legislative powers.

The American colonies during their struggle for independence were a federation proper; having afterward adopted their constitution, they became a nation with a federal structure; if any doubt remained upon that point it was dispelled by the war of secession. The political parties are national; they extend into State politics, and there has been a general tendency of the national to prevail over the federal element.

In the case of Canadian confederation the national element was from the first stronger than the federal in this respect, that the residuary power which the American constitution leaves in the States was by the Canadian constitution assigned to the Dominion.

On the other hand, the geographical relations of the Canadian Provinces, which are stretched in broken line across the continent, and separated from each other by great spaces or barriers of nature, so that there is not much natural trade or interchange of population, are a bar to the ascendency of the national over the federal element. Provinces send their delegations to Ottawa charged with provincial interests, especially with reference to the outlay on public works; and it is necessary to have thirteen members in the cabinet in order to give each Province its share, while a cabinet, or to speak more properly, an administrative council of eight suffices for the population, fourteen times larger, of the United States. Political parties, however, extend over all the Provinces and generally into Provincial politics, though in the remoter Provinces, with a large element, and in British Columbia with a predominance of local objects. On the two old Canadas, now Ontario and Quebec, but chiefly on Ontario, have lain the stress and burden of confederation. Ontario has paid more than sixty per cent of the taxes.

The imperial element in the Canadian constitution is represented, besides the appointment of the governor-general and the commander of the militia, by an imperial veto on Canadian legislation, which however is becoming almost nominal; the appellate jurisdiction of the privy council, which has been partly pared away; and the subjection of Canadian relations with foreign countries to the authority of the imperial foreign office, which again is gradually giving way to Canadian autonomy, though with British responsibility and under the protection of the British army and navy; a colony having no means of asserting its claims by war.

Nor must we forget the influence of imperial titles and honors which on colonial politicians is great. The Canadian constitution, moreover, though framed in the main by Canadian politicians, is embodied in an imperial act of Parliament, subject to repeal or amendment only by the same authority by which it was passed. A community living under a constitution imposed by external authority and without the power of peace or war, can hardly be said yet to have attained the status of a nation.

The monarchical element consists of the governor-general, representing the British sovereign, and equally divested of personal power, with lieutenant-governors of Provinces appointed nominally by the governor-general, really by the prime minister, and figure-heads like their chief, the places being, in fact, retiring pensions for veteran politicians.

There is an upper House, in the shape of a Senate, the members of which are appointed for life, ostensibly by the Crown, really by the leader of the party in power. If the appointments were really in the Crown there might be some opening for the general eminence of which a model Senate would be the seat. As it is, these appointments merely form an addition to the patronage fund of party. The illusory name of the " Crown " reconciles people to the exercise, by party leaders, of powers which might otherwise be withheld. A certain number of places in the Senate is assigned to each Province; so that whatever power the Senate has may be reckoned among the federal elements of the constitution.

The Canadian constitution, with its cabinet of ministers sitting in Parliament and controlling legislation, its prerogative exercised formally by the Crown, really by the prime minister, of calling and dissolving Parliament, adapts itself to party government, for which the American constitution, with its election of a President for a stated term, and its separation of the administrative council, miscalled a cabinet, from the legislature, is a manifest misfit. Party takes its usual form and proceeds by its usual methods, though the necessity of holding together Provinces geographically and commercially disunited, so as to form a basis for the government, induces a special resort to the influence of federal subsidies for local works.

The exact relation of a colony on the footing on which Canada now is to the imperial country it would be difficult to define, though definition may presently be needful if misunderstanding is to be escaped. The Crown, by the British North America act, renounces its supreme ownership of the land by handing over the lands to the Provinces. The personal fealty of the colonists to the sovereign of Great Britain remains.

GROW

GALUSHA AARON GROW, an American party leader, was born at Ashford, Connecticut, August 31, 1823. He lost his father when but three years old, and in 1834 his mother removed with her family to Susquehanna county, Pennsylvania. For several years he labored on a farm in the summers, attending school only in the winter time till he was sent in 1837 to Franklin Academy in the same county in which he had lived. From there he went to Amherst College, graduating in 1844, and taking up the study of law not long afterward was admitted to the bar of Susquehanna County in 1847. He declined a unanimous nomination to the State legislature in August, 1850, and in the October following he was nominated and elected to the national House of Representatives to succeed David Wilmot. He sat in Congress 1851-53, 1855-57, and 1859-63, being speaker of the House during the Thirty-seventh Congress, 1861-63. After the formation of the Republican party he always acted with the Republicans, and in 1864 and again in 1868 was a delegate to the Republican convention at Baltimore. From 1871 to 1876 he lived in Texas as president of a railway company there, declining the mission to Russia which was tendered to him in the latter year. In 1894 he was elected congressman-at-large. Among important speeches of his are the speech on the Homestead Bill, February 21, 1854, the Kansas and Nebraska speech delivered in the following May, and " Free Homes for Free Men," February 29, 1860.

ON MANILA

MR. SPEAKER,—What is the duty and present responsibility of this nation to liberty and humanity? On the 21st day of April, 1898, Congress authorized and directed the President to use the army and navy of the United States to compel Spain to withdraw her flag and abandon forever her sovereignty over the island of Cuba. Never was an act of Congress more universally approved by the people.

Within ten days after this direction to the President, a squadron of the American navy, cruising in Asiatic waters, in obedience to orders received by its commander to strike the enemy wherever found and "to capture or destroy his ships," sailed into the harbor of Manila and destroyed the Pacific squadron of the Spanish navy in a victory unparalleled in the world's history of naval warfare. From that time to this the flag of the United States has floated supreme in the bay of Manila, and within one hundred days from the declaration of war by Congress it floated in triumph over Cuba, Puerto Rico, and the Philippine Islands, from all of which the flag and sovereignty of Spain was forever expelled.

Thus, by the fortunes of war, approved in its beginning almost unanimously by the people, were Puerto Rico and the Philippine Islands added to the territory of the United States. Such territory, whether desirable or not, was thenceforth to be either Spanish or American. This was the only alternative. The war, it is true, was begun on our part in behalf of liberty and humanity for a million and a half of people in the island of Cuba. Are liberty and humanity questions of latitude and longitude? Spanish rule for three hundred years in the Philippine Islands had been scarcely less cruel than in the island of Cuba. In the fortunes of war the first act against the enemy was the destruction of Spanish sovereignty over eight or ten millions of people in the far-off Philippines instead of the million and a half in Cuba.

Puerto Rico and the Philippine Islands were acquired in the fortunes of war and by a treaty of peace with Spain, in the same way that California and other territory was acquired in the fortunes of war and by a treaty of peace with Mexico; $20,000,000 was paid to Spain in concluding with her a treaty of peace; $15,000,000 was paid to Mexico in concluding with her a treaty of peace. The $20,000,000 paid to Spain was for her relinquishment of sovereignty over Cuba, Puerto Rico, and all her islands in the West Indies, and over the island of Guam and the Philippines in the Pacific Ocean.

These $20,000,000 offered by the American commission in the form of an ultimatum at the close of negotiations, before a single article of the treaty had been finally concluded, were to cover all cessions of territory and all questions in controversy as to the debts and public property of Cuba, Puerto Rico, and the Philippine Islands. The $15,000,000 paid to Mexico was for the relinquishment of her sovereignty over the territory we acquired lying west of the Louisiana purchase. The payment in both these cases was, as defined by Vattel in his " Law of Nations," the act of " an equitable conqueror."

This government has never acquired any territory outside of the original thirteen colonies without the payment of a money consideration satisfactory to the parties in interest. There is no question of forcible annexation of territory before the American people now, nor has there been. But there is a question of forcible suppression of an insurrection against the authority and sovereignty of the United States.

The flag of our fathers floats to-day over Puerto Rico and the Philippine Islands just as rightfully as over Alaska or any of the territory acquired from France or Mexico. Whether this acquisition of far-off territory is good or bad, it has fallen to us unsought and unexpected in the fortunes of war—a war that marks a new era in the history of the nations, begun in no spirit of conquest or desire for territorial expansion, but only in response to the piercing cries of a common humanity by a people doomed by their oppressors to extermination by starvation and the sword.

After American arms had triumphed on land and sea, the only alternative presented was whether the Stars and Stripes of the United States or the Castles and Lions of Spain should float over these islands.   Where is there an American heart, or one anywhere else in Christian civilization, so craven as to have justified the great Republic in giving back these islands, with their eight or ten million people, to the cruel despotism of Spain?   Such a disgraceful act on our part, under the circumstances, would have been an indelible stain through all time upon the character of the American people.

After boldly proclaiming to the world that we were fighting the battles of liberty and humanity on behalf of a people crushed by a cruel despotism, were we to sheath the sword as soon as we became apprehensive that the contest might in the end impose something of a burden not foreseen upon ourselves, and for that reason were we to remand the helpless oppressed, whom we had rescued, back to the care of the oppressor?

What shall be done with these islands and what shall be the government for their inhabitants is now a question to be settled by the Congress of the United States.

But our anti-imperialist statesmen claim that, instead of Congress, it rightfully belongs to Aguinaldo to say what kind of government shall be established for the eight or ten millions of inhabitants in the Philippine Islands.   If Aguinaldo and his little band of Tagalos drove Spain from these islands and compelled her to sue for peace, then in that case he might, as conqueror, have the right to dictate the kind of government to take the place of the Spanish government overthrown.

Whatever power destroys organized government over a people becomes morally responsible to the civilization of the age to replace the government overthrown by one equally if not more efficient for the protection of life and property.

Spain relinquished her sovereignty over the Philippine Islands to the United States of America, not to Aguinaldo. From the time that was done the United States became responsible in the forum of nations to see that an efficient government is established for these islands.

We are told by the defenders of Aguinaldo and his Tagalo insurgents, as an excuse for their acts, that one nation cannot govern another nation. The inhabitants of the Philippine Islands never were a nation and never had a government of their own. The eight or ten millions of their inhabitants, scattered over some thousand or more islands, consist of different tribes speaking different languages and of all degrees of civilization. Is not Congress just as competent to legislate for these former subjects of Spain as for the inhabitants of Alaska, former subjects of Russia, or for the people in the Territories of the Union?

Under the government of the United States, since the last amendments to the constitution, the personal, civil, and religious rights of all its inhabitants, whether near or far off, are secured to them in the language of the supreme court, " by the principles of constitutional liberty, which restrains all the agencies of government, State, and nation."

In these paramount rights the inhabitants of the Philippine Islands would be protected by Congress just the same as are the inhabitants of the District of Columbia. Will even the anti-imperialists say that the inhabitants of the District of Columbia are living under a despotic government and would therefore be justified in taking up arms against the government of the United States?

The defenders of Aguinaldo claim that he and his Tagalo insurgents are justified in warring upon the United States, which released them from Spanish despotism, just the same as they would be if they were fighting Spain, for it is only, as they say, a change of masters. Thus they malign the institutions of their own country and libel the character of the people's chosen representatives. There can be no valid legislation by Congress inconsistent with the principles of constitutional liberty. The history of Spanish rule over her colonies has always been a blood-stained record of cruelty and lawless violence. Would not the inhabitants of the Philippine Islands be under a free government when under the government of the United States? A people everywhere are justified in warring against despotism. But in this age of Christian civilization they are not justified anywhere in warring against free government.

Never was there an American gun turned upon any of the inhabitants of the Philippine Islands until its Tagalo insurgents began killing American soldiers, who in the fortunes of war came to their country not as conquerors, but as their deliverers from the cruelties of Spanish rule, while prosecuting a war for the delivery of a million and a half of Spanish subjects under the same rule in the island of Cuba.

The first great duty of the United States now is to suppress the Tagalo insurrection against its authority and to establish order in the Philippine Islands. And when that is done, to provide a government for the protection of the civil and religious rights of their inhabitants, the same as is now done for the inhabitants of the District of Columbia or the Territories of the Union.

There is no question of territorial expansion or forcible annexation to be settled. That was settled by American guns at Manila and San Juan Hill, ratified by a treaty of peace with Spain. Right or wrong, good or bad, American territory has already been expanded. Our flag, raised first by a triumph in arms and next from our unavoidable position by a treaty of peace, floats to-day over the Philippine Islands just as rightfully as over this Capitol.

Wherever on the earth's surface that flag shall once rightfully float it can never be removed, save by an act of Congress or by an order of the commander-in-chief of the army and navy in time of war. Any attempt to remove it in any other way would be an act of treason against the sovereignty of the United States, the same as it was in 1861, when General Dix said : " If any one attempts to haul down the American flag, shoot him on the spot."

The terms that General Grant fixed for all persons engaged in such attempts was " unconditional surrender." Why should any different terms be made now for Malay or Mongolian insurgents than was made then for American citizens born on American soil.

History is constantly repeating itself. Then there were those who claimed that war was Lincoln's war; now there are those who declare this war is McKinley's war; then it was copperhead; now it is anti-imperialist. Then there were self-assumed superior patriots who saw great danger to the liberties of the country in the disbanding of the two armies composed of over 2,000,000 of armed men. Now the same kind of patriots see great danger for the future of the Republic in the development of a spirit of militarism should the regular army exceed 25,000 men.

Can the liberties of the American people—now 75,000,000 and doubling in number every thirty years, scattered over a territorial area of almost 4,000,000 square miles, with forty-five independent States, to be hereafter increased in number, each fully organized with executive, judicial, and legislative powers, and each with an organized militia of its own citizens—be in danger of overthrow now, or any other time in the hereafter, by fifty or sixty thousand or any other number of citizens soldiers in the regular army? When the American people shall forget the glorious traditions of a heroic ancestry and become themselves fit subjects for slaves, then and not till then will their liberties be in danger of overthrow from any spirit of militarism within or from foreign aggression without.

This nation is not running the race the old lost nations ran, that " died of unbelief in God and wrong to man." No nation ever yet died or ever will, no matter what the extent of its territory or how vast its population, if governed by just laws and its people are imbued with a spirit of humanity as broad as the race.

Before the declaration of war with Spain the wisdom of far-off territorial acquisitions might have been a proper subject for consideration by the people of the United States. But as to the acquisition of territory in Puerto Rico and the Philippine Islands, it is a question settled by the arbitrament of the sword in the fortunes of war and by a treaty of peace recognized as valid by all nations.

There always was and probably always will be a class of " has beens " who delight in perverting the facts of history in order to put their own country in the wrong so they can have an excuse for opposing its administration, and who are always uttering warnings of danger and weeping in pathetic sorrow over the degeneracy of the times in the closing years of their own existence. So, to-day, these prophets of evil from the hilltops of a happy and prosperous republic are, Jeremiah-like, pouring out their lamentations over the extension of American free institutions. Legislative wisdom, statesmanship, and patriotism in the chosen representations of the American people will not die with this generation, and I trust will not in any other.

Over a century ago our fathers, by their heroic deeds, consecrated the Fourth of July, 1776, as the birthday of a new era in the cycles of civilization. Is there anybody that would now change, if he could, the final results as we have them of this great experiment of free constitutional government? The result has come to us only by each generation of the people boldly meeting in peace or war their responsibilities to liberty and humanity as they have been cast upon them in the providences of human events.

Let this generation, then, imitating those of the bygone, shrink not from a manly discharge of its duty and responsibilities to liberty and the rights of a common humanity, though they may have been cast upon it unexpected and unforeseen in the fortunes of a just war. Every acquisition of territory by the United States heretofore, though opposed at the time by some self-assumed superior patriots, has always received the hearty approval of the people.

From my first entry into public life I have never had any fears for the future of the republic by reason of the expansion of its territory and the extension of its free institutions. Pending the repeal of the Missouri Compromise in Congress in 1854, I then said relative to expansion:

" Who believes that the territorial expansion of the republic will not continue until it covers the whole continent? It is one of the incidents of our position, resulting from the habits of our people and the character of surrounding nationalities. While the pioneer spirit presses on into the wilderness, snatching new areas from the wild beast and bequeathing them a legacy to civilized man, it is in vain you attempt to stay his progress by meridian lines or legislative enactments.

" The habits of his life and the promptings of his nature

are stronger than the river or mountain barriers of nations.
When he has covered the whole continent with the abodes of
civilized life, seizing the standard of the Republic, he will
bear it, with the spirit and genius of free institutions, across
the mighty deep to regenerate old dynasties and breathe new
life into decaying empires. This, no matter what may be
the views of statesmen or the policy of legislation, is our
mission, our manifest destiny. For energy, intelligence,
and superior enterprise are destiny, and whoever attempts to
stay it may be borne down by the tide, but he cannot change
the current."

These words, uttered in no spirit of prophecy, and which
at the time were only a plain statement of the characteristics
of the American people and the surrounding conditions of
national existence to-day, are, by the fortunes of war,
prophecy fulfilled. But what prophetic ken can pierce the
veil of the now overhanging future? The Atlantic Ocean,
rolling between two mighty hemispheres, is a German,
French, and English sea. But the Pacific Ocean, with almost twice the area of waters washing the shores of nationalities containing two thirds the population of the globe, is
henceforth to be an American sea covered with American
ships laden with the products of American industry. The
commerce of half the world, realizing the dream of Columbus, will go westward to find the Indies.

England, facing eastward, carrying her Magna Charta of
personal rights and all her great institutions of civil and
religious liberty, and the United States of America, first-born
of these institutions, facing westward, carrying the same institutions, with the practical experience of over a hundred years
in self-government, will some day meet in the far-off Orient,
having belted the globe with institutions of civil and religious
liberty and constitutional free government for all mankind.

The white man can never lay down his burden so long as

oppression and national injustice and wrong exist among the children of men. Nations like individuals owe something to a common humanity, for they are the trustees of civilization. It is ordained in the retributions of that overruling Providence which controls in the affairs of men that nations cannot shirk their responsibilities to liberty and humanity when cast upon them in the course of human events without bitter retributions soon or late in national disasters.

" The ships will part the unknown sea,
    The march of thought will reach the strand;
The onward wave of destiny
    Will change the features of the land.

" The evil must give place to good,
    The false before the true must fade;
There is no stay in Nature's way.
    Men cannot choose or peace or war;
She sets the task, and none may ask
    What her far-reaching councils are.

" Not in the way the world would please
    The needed changes may be wrought;
When and wherever fate decrees
    The destined battles will be fought.

" The towers of strength give way at length,
    If they be not by right maintained,
And in their place a higher race
    Shall build as it has been ordained."

The American defenders of the Tagalo insurgents have no excuse for themselves in any acts of the American colonists. Our fathers in 1776 took up arms against unjust legislation and the attempt by the ministry of George III to restrict the rights and privileges of Englishmen. The colonists had governments of their own, which they were defending against encroachments by the British Parliament.

The Tagalos in attacking the American army which delivered them from Spanish despotism had no government of their own to defend, for none had ever been established; and they were not resisting unjust laws, for no laws of any kind had been passed; nor had any act of any kind been done by the American people or its army injurious or even unfriendly to the inhabitants of the Philippine Islands.

President Lincoln on the 4th of March, 1861, from the eastern portico of this Capitol, in addressing his dissatisfied fellow countrymen, said: " You can have no conflict without yourselves being the aggressors."

In like manner President McKinley through his commanding general notified the inhabitants of the Philippine Islands that they could have no conflict with the United States without they themselves being the aggressors.

General Otis, January 9, 1899, in a communication to Aguinaldo, said: " I am under strict orders of the President of the United States to avoid conflict in every way possible. There shall be no conflict of forces if I am able to avoid it."

In the evening of February 4, 1899, Aguinaldo and his Tagalos became the aggressors and opened fire along their whole entrenched line upon the American soldiers guarding Manila. The same night Agoncillo, friend and special agent of Aguinaldo, leaves Washington hastily by the midnight train for Canada, hours before any one else in Washington knew of the attack of the Tagalos upon the American army. From that time to this the Tagalo insurrection has continued in pursuance of the plans formed by Aguinaldo in August, 1898, before the capitulation of Manila, when he announced himself dictator and addressed a communication to the leading powers, asking their recognition of the independence of the Philippines, and in pursuance of his purpose to capture or drive the American army out of Manila.

The Tagalos, under Aguinaldo, took up arms to kill their benefactors, who had never done them an injury, but who had periled their lives to release them from the cruelties of

Spanish rule. At the demand of such an enemy—an enemy that knows no gratitude and whose barbarism holds prisoners of war for a money ransom—shall the flag of our fathers be lowered—a flag that never yet was lowered, save at the grave of the hero who died in its defence?

There is no justification for the American defenders of the Tagalo insurgents in anything contained in the Declaration of American Independence. The revolt of the American colonies began in a protest against unjust laws. Even after the few overzealous patriots had thrown the shipload of imported tea into the waters of Massachusetts Bay, Washington, Franklin, Adams, and Hancock, and most of their copatriots, had no idea of establishing a government independent of that of Great Britain.

The Earl of Chatham, Burke, Barre, Wilkes, and other English statesmen in advocating the cause of the colonies were defending the constitutional rights of Englishmen. And none of them ever advocated the right of the colonies to set up for themselves an independent government.

At length, after the failure of petition and protest, fifty-six bold merchants, farmers, lawyers, and mechanics, representing the organized governments of thirteen colonies, on the 4th of July, 1776, declared that their allegiance to the Crown of Great Britain was at an end. In justification of their act in severing their allegiance to the mother country, and in combating the dogma of the divine right of kingly rule they proclaimed certain self-evident truths, among which was that " The just powers of governments are derived from the consent of the governed."

Up to that time mankind had been regarded as composed of two classes—the one born to rule, the other to be ruled; the one possessing all rights in the State, the other possessing no rights save such as might be conferred by the ruling class. It was in combating this claim of the few and the old political dogma of the divine right of kingly rule that our fathers declared that governments derived their just powers from the consent of the governed.   In theory, a self-evident truth; but in actual practice then and ever since governments derive their just powers from the consent of the governed, if the governed are fitted for self-government.   Consent of the criminal classes or of the stupidly ignorant are not necessary for a just government, never has been, and never will be.

The self-evident truths of the Declaration of Independence proclaimed by our fathers in opposing the political dogmas of their times were ideals to be finally reached in the onward progress of the race to a higher and more perfect civilization, as the polar star, fixed in the heavens, is a guide for the mariner in his course to a haven of safety over tempest-tossed seas.

These ideals were not intended or expected by those who declared them to be reduced to immediate practice, for they did not themselves incorporate them into the framework of the new government which they established.   One seventh of the entire population under their new government were chattel-born slaves, bought and sold at the auction block, and continued such for almost a century after the adoption of the Declaration of Independence.   The consent of women, one half of the population to be governed, was not sought then nor since in order to give just powers to their government.

The Saviour of mankind, when on earth, bade his disciples, "Be ye perfect as your Father in heaven is perfect."   If this injunction is to be the practical test of Christian character, then there are no Christians in the world.   But a time was promised in the long-coming future when this test applied to the pilgrims on earth would not be mere theory.

The ideals of the Declaration of Independence practically apply, and were intended only thus to apply, to a people fitted for self-government. It is an absurdity to apply them in practice to a people unfitted by general intelligence or experience to carry on a free and stable government by which alone these rights can be secured to the individual.

Lafayette, years after he tendered his life with his sword to the cause of American independence, advised the crowning of Louis Philippe King of France instead of the establishment of a republic, for the reason, as he said, that the French people were not at that time as well fitted for self- would be a gross calumny upon a great nation to say that the French people were not at that time as well fitted for self-government as are the Tagalos now, or any other portion of the inhabitants of the Philippine Islands.

The American colonies had a practical experience in self-government under their respective charters from the Crown of Great Britain in township, county, and State administration for more than a hundred years, and yet not one of them adopted in practice then, nor have they since, the self-evident truth which they put in the Declaration of Independence, that governments derive their just powers from the consent of the governed. Even Massachusetts, home of Edward Atkinson and other like kindred spirits, has no provision in her organic law for ascertaining the consent of even a majority of her adult population to the constitution under which they live, or their consent to the enactment of the laws which they must obey. The legal voters anywhere are not one half of the adult population whose consent in theory is requisite for just government.

The defenders of the Tagalo insurgents, calling themselves anti-imperialists, insist that these ideals of our fathers, which have never yet been incorporated practically into any government, shall be made a part of the government to be established for the conglomerate of Malay and Mongolian population in the Philippine Islands, a population which have never had any experience in any kind of self-government and whose unfitness for such government at the present time is everywhere admitted.

But the population of these islands, under the controlling influence of the United States, with its free institutions, and their own better conditions after peace and order shall have been established, will no doubt in a short time become fitted for self-government. When that time shall come and the United States of America shall establish for these islands, with their eight or ten millions of people, a free and independent government, to be administered by themselves, it will be the gift of the great Republic to civilization of a colossal statue of liberty enlightening the world, throwing its refulgent rays from the mountain peaks overlooking the Bay of Manila, across the Chinese Sea, and over the empire of oldest time, where dwells one fourth of the present population of the globe.

Such is the mission, the manifest destiny, of this nation now, in behalf of liberty and humanity, the same as it was threescore years ago, before the pioneer settler scaled the snow-crowned summits of the Sierras or the flag of our fathers fluttered along the shores of the Pacific.

Henceforth, over whatever portion of the earth's surface the flag of the great Republic shall float, it will be the emblem of liberty, justice, and humanity, beckoning the race on to a higher and better civilization.

> Westward the course of empire takes its way;
> Time's noblest offspring is the last.

HILL

BENJAMIN HARVEY HILL, an American politician, was born in Jasper
County, Georgia, September 14, 1823. He was educated at the University of Georgia, and after studying law and being admitted to the bar began
to practise his profession at La Grange, Georgia. He entered the State
legislature in 1851 and was for ten years a leader of the Georgia Whigs.
As a member of the secession convention summoned by Georgia in January,
1861, he warmly advocated the cause of the Union, until the ordinance of
secession was actually passed, and he then acquiesced in the decision thus
made by his State. He was a prominent supporter of the Confederacy,
serving in the Confederate Senate throughout the Civil War, and in May,
1865, was arrested and for a short time imprisoned in Fort Lafayette in
New York harbor. In his " Notes on the Situation in Georgia," issued in
1867-68, he opposed the reconstruction measures of Congress, but in 1870 he
put forth " An Address to the People of Georgia " advising them to " accept
the situation." For the next two years he withdrew from public life, but
in 1872 supported the Greeley nomination for the presidency, and in 1875
entered Congress as Democratic representative. In 1877 he was elected to
the United States Senate. His death occurred at Atlanta, Georgia, August
16, 1882. Hill was noted for his eloquence both in the court-room and in
Congress, and was likewise distinguished as a constitutional lawyer of
ability. Among his best known congressional efforts are his reply in the
House to Blaine, and his speech in the Senate denouncing Mahone's coalition with the Republican party.

ON THE PERILS OF THE NATION

DELIVERED BEFORE THE YOUNG MEN'S DEMOCRATIC UNION, OCTOBER 8, 1868

PEOPLE OF THE NORTH,—In deference to the
earnest wishes of a committee from the Young Men's
Democratic Union Club, and the request of personal
friends, some of whom differ with me in political views, I
depart from my original intention not to make a speech in
the North, and appear before you this evening.

I do not come to ask any favor for the Southern people.
The representative, however, of that people who have ex-

perienced burdens of despotic power, and the insecurity of anarchy, I come, all the more earnestly, to address you in behalf of imperilled constitutional free government. Will you hear me without passion?

The South—exhausted by a long war and unusual losses—needs peace; desires peace; begs for peace. The North—distrustful, if not vindictive—demands guarantees that the South will keep the peace she so much needs.

In countries where wars have been more frequent, the important fact is well established by experiment, that magnanimity in the conqueror is the very highest guaranty of contented submission by the conquered. It is to be regretted that you seem not to have learned this lesson. A people who will not be magnanimous in victory are not worthy to be, and will not always remain, victors.

In the next place, if you of the North would only open your eyes and see the plainest truth of the century—that the Southern people fought for what they believed to be their right—you would find at once a sufficient guarantee for peace. The South believed honestly, fought bravely, and surrendered frankly; and in each of these facts she presents the most ample title to credit. Why will you not see and admit the fact which must go into history, that the Southern people honestly believed they had a right to secede? Some of the wisest framers of the constitution taught that doctrine. Many of the ablest men in the North, as well as in the South, of every generation, have taught this doctrine. Some of your own States made the recognition of that right, the recognition of their acceptance of union. Even your own Webster—your orator without a rival among you, dead or living—taught that this right existed for cause—certainly for much less cause than now exists. Will you, then, persist in saying that the Southern people are all traitors for exercising, or attempting to exercise, what such men and such States taught was a right? Will you say they did not honestly believe such teachers? Was it their intent to commit treason?

Here lies the whole cause of our continued troubles. The North will not admit what all other people know, and what all history must concede—that the South honestly believed in the right of secession. As a result of this infidelity to such plain fact, you assume that the Southern people are criminals. This idea is the sum of all your politics and statesmanship. It must be abandoned. It must be repudiated thoroughly and promptly. There can never be any peaceful and cordial reunion possible while one half the nation regard the other half as criminals. How can you trust criminals? Why should you desire Union with criminals? If the Southern people are honest, their assent to the non-secession construction of the constitution is a sufficient guarantee. If they are not honest, but criminals, no promise they could make ought to be trusted. Power is the only guaranty of fidelity in criminals, and if you cannot believe and cannot trust the South, you must, indeed, abandon the constitution and govern with power forever, or you must give up the South as unworthy to federate with you in an equal government of consent.

I speak frankly. If you cannot abandon this miserable theory and habit in your politics, in your religion, and in your schools, of regarding the Southern people as criminal traitors for attempting what good men, and wise men, and great men taught was their right, you will make peaceful reunion under free institutions utterly impossible.

You must hold them as friends, or let them go as foreign-

ers, or govern them as subjects. If you govern them as subjects you must share the penalty, for the same government
can never administer freedom to one half and despotism to
the other half of the same nation.

Rise above your passions, then, and realize that herein is
your guaranty: The South believed honestly, fought bravely,
and surrendered frankly.

Again. The exhausted condition of the South ought to
inspire you with confidence in her professions of a desire for
peace. Are you afraid for her to recover strength? Take
care lest the desperation of exhaustion prove stronger than
the sinews of prosperity. Peace is not desirable without its
blessings.

But you of the North will not try magnanimity: will insist
that the Southern people are traitors; and that an exhausted
people are dangerous, and you must have guaranties. In
your papers, from your pulpits, behind your counters, on your
streets, and along your highways, I hear the perpetual charge
that the South fought to destroy the government, committed
treason and murder, and every inhuman crime, and that she
is still intractable and rebellious, and dangerous, and insincere, and must concede and give guaranties.

Well, I am here to show you that the South has made
every concession that an honorable people would exact, or an
honest people could make. . . .

People of the North, will you not rise above passion, and
save your own honor, and our common free government by
doing plain justice to a people who accepted your pledge, and
trusted your honor?

I beg you to understand the facts of actual history before
it is too late. I repeat and beg you to note what the South
has already conceded as the results of the war:

First. The South conceded at Appomattox, that the arguments of the ablest statesmen America ever produced, in favor of the right of secession as a constitutional remedy, had been replied to in the only manner they could be effectually replied to, by physical force; and the South consented that this judgment, written by the sword, should have legal force and effect.

Second. The South, by her own act, made valid the emancipation of her slaves in the only way in which that emancipation could be made valid, and thus gave up the property the North sold her, without compensation.

Third. The South has solemnly repudiated her debts, contracted in her defence, and has agreed to pay a full share of the debt contracted for her subjugation.

Fourth. The South has permitted without hindrance, the Congress to enter her States and establish tribunals unknown to the constitution, to govern a portion of their population in a manner different from the governments of the States.

Fifth. The South has agreed to make the negroes citizens and give them absolutely equal civil rights with the whites, and to extend to them every protection of law and every facility for education and improvement which are extended to the whites.

Sixth. In a word, I repeat, the South has agreed to everything which has been proposed by the civil or military governments of the United States and by every department of that government, except the single demand to disfranchise their own best men from their own State offices, at a time when their counsels are most needed, or to consent that negroes and strangers may disfranchise them.

For this, and for this only, all their other concessions are spit upon, and they are denounced as intractable, insincere, rebellious, and unwilling to accept the results of the war! Shame upon leaders who persist in such charges; and shame upon a people who will sustain such leaders! . . .

But what will the South do? I will tell you first what the South will not do, in my opinion.

The South will not secede again. That was her great folly —folly against her own interest, not wrong against you. Mark this: That folly will not be repeated. Even if the people of the South desire the disruption of the federal government, their statesmen have the sagacity to see that that result can more effectually come of this secession of the North from the constitution. Those ominous words " outside of the constitution " are more terribly significant than those other words " secession from the Union." The former is a secession having all the vices of the latter greatly increased and none of its virtues. Certainly none of its manliness, straightforward candor, and justification. So note this: The South does not desire nor seek disunion. If she desired it she does not deem another secession necessary to bring it about. Disunion will come from Chicago, in spite of Southern opposition.

The South will not re-enslave the negro. She did not enslave him in the first instance. That was your work. The South took your slave-savage and gave him the highest civilization ever reached by the negro. You then freed him and kept the price of his slavery, and you alone hold the property that was in human flesh.

But the Southern whites will never consent to the government of the negro. Never! All your money spent in the effort to force it will be wasted. The Southern whites will never consent to social and political equality with the negro. You may destroy yourselves in the effort to force it, and then you will fail.   You may send down your armies and exhaust the resources of the whole country for a century and pile up the public debt till it lean against the skies; and you may burn our cities and murder our people—our unarmed people—but you will never make them consent to governments formed by negroes and strangers under the dictation of Congress by the power of the bayonet.   Born of the bayonet, this government must live only by the bayonet.

Now, I will tell you some things which, in my opinion, the South will do.

The South would accept the election of Mr. Seymour as a verdict of the Northern people that the general government was to be administered according to the constitution, and she would rejoice and come out of her sorrow strong, beautiful, and growing.

The South will accept the election of General Grant as a verdict by the Northern people that the constitution is a nullity and that they will that the general government be administered outside of it.   But the South will then submit passively to your laws, but in her heart hope will still cleave to the constitution.   It is her only port of safety from the storm of fanaticism, passion, and despotism.

The South surrendered secession as a constitutional remedy at Appomattox, but she did not surrender the constitution itself, nor the great principles of freedom it was intended to secure.

Whether Mr. Seymour or General Grant shall be elected, the Southern States—each State for itself—will quietly, peacefully, but firmly take charge of and regulate their own internal domestic affairs in their own way, subject only to the constitution of the United States.   What then will you of the North do?   What will President Grant do?   Will you or he send down armies to compel those States to regulate their own affairs to suit you outside of the constitution? Will you?

It is high time this people had recovered from the passions of war. It is high time that counsel were taken from statesmen, not demagogues. It is high time that editors, preachers, and stump speakers had ceased slandering the motives and purposes of the South. It is high time the people of the North and the South understood each other and adopted means to inspire confidence in each other. It is high time the people of each State were permitted to attend to their own business. Intermeddling is the crime of the century. If it was folly in the South to secede it was crime in the North to provoke it. If it was error in the South to dissolve the Union it is crime in the North to keep it dissolved.

The South yields secession and yields slavery, and yields them for equal reunion. People of the North, now is the auspicious moment to cement anew and for still greater glory our common Union. But it must be cemented in mutual good will, as between equals and under the constitution. Such a Union the South pleads for. I care not what slanderers say, what fanaticism represents, or how selfish and corrupt hate and ambition pervert; I tell you there is but one desire in the South. From every heart in that bright land, from her cotton fields and grain farms, from her rich valleys and metal-pregnant mountains, from the lullabies of her thousands of rippling streams and moaning millions of her primeval forest-trees, comes up to you but this one voice—this one earnest, united voice: Flag of our Union, wave on; wave ever! But wave over freemen, not subjects; over States, not Provinces; over a union of equals, not of lords and vassals; over a land of law, of liberty, and of peace, and not of anarchy, oppression, and strife!

People of the North, will you answer back in patriotic notes of cheering accord that our common constitution shall remain or in the discordant notes of sectional hate and national ruin that there shall be protection for the North inside of the constitution and oppression for the South outside of it?

If the latter then not only the Union, not only the constitution, but that grand, peculiar system of free federative governments so wisely devised by our fathers and known as the American system, and of which the constitution is but the instrument and the Union but the shadow—will die, must die, is dead!

Have you ever studied this American system of government? Have you compared it with former systems of free governments, and noted how our fathers sought to avoid their fatal defects? I commend this study to your prompt attention. To the heart that loves liberty it is more enchanting than romance, more bewitching than love, and more elevating than any other science. If history proves any one thing more than another it is that freedom cannot be secured in a wide and populous country except upon the plan of a federal compact for general interests, and untrammelled local governments for local interests.

Our fathers adopted this general plan with improvements in the details of profound wisdom which cannot be found in any previous system. With what a noble impulse of common patriotism they came together from distant States and joined their counsels to devise and perfect this system, henceforth to be forever known as the American system.

The snows that lodge on the summit of Mount Washington

are not purer than the motives that begot it. The fresh dew-laden zephyrs from the orange groves of the South are not sweeter than the hopes its advent inspired. The flight of its own symbolic eagle, though he blew his breath upon the sun, could not be higher than its expected destiny! Alas, are these motives now corrupted? Are these hopes poisoned? And is this high destiny eclipsed, and so soon,—aye, before a century has brought to manhood its youthful visage? Stop before the blow is given and let us consider but its early blessings.

Under the benign influences of this promising American system of government our whole country at once entered upon a career of prosperity without a parallel in human annals. The seventy years of its life brought more thrift, more success, more individual freedom, more universal happiness with fewer public burdens than were ever before enjoyed or borne by any portion of the world in five centuries. From three millions of whites we became thirty millions. From three hundred thousand blacks we became four millions—a greater relative increase than of the whites with all the aid of immigration. From a narrow peopled slope along the dancing Atlantic we stretched with wide girth to the sluggish Pacific. From a small power which a European despotism, in jealousy of a rival, patronizingly took by the hand and led to independence, we became a power whose voice united was heard throughout the world and whose frown might well be dreaded by the combined powers of earth. Our granaries fed and our factories clothed mankind. The buffalo and his hunter were gone, and cities rose in the forests of the former, and flowers grew, and hammers rang, and prayers were said, in the playgrounds of the latter. Millions grew to manhood without seeing a soldier, or hearing a cannon, or knowing the shape or place of a bayonet! And is this happy, fruitful, peaceful system dying—hopelessly dying? Has it but twenty days more to live a struggling life?

People of the North, the answer is with you. Rise above passion, throw away corruption, cease to hate and learn to trust, and this dying system will spring to newer and yet more glorious life. The stake is too great for duplicity and the danger too imminent for trifling. The past calls to you to vindicate its wisdom; the present charges you with its treasures, and the future demands of you its hopes. Forget your anger and be superior to the littleness of revenge. Meet the South in her cordial proffers of happy reunion and turn not from her offered hand.

From your great cities and teeming prairies, from your learned altars and countless cottages, from your palaces on sea and land, from your millions on the waters and your multiplied millions on the plains, let one united cheering voice meet the voice that now comes so earnest from the South, and let the two voices go up in harmonious, united, eternal, ever-swelling chorus, Flag of our Union! wave on; wave ever! Aye, for it waves over freemen, not subjects; over States, not Provinces; over a union of equals, not of lords and vassals; over a land of law, of liberty, and peace, not of anarchy, oppression, and strife!

HUGHES

THOMAS HUGHES, a noted English lawyer and author, born at Uffington, Berkshire, England, October 23, 1823, was educated at Rugby under Dr. Arnold, and at Oriel College, Oxford. He studied law and was called to the bar at Lincoln's Inn in 1848. He was an advanced Liberal in his university career and was later associated with Kingsley and Maurice in their efforts in behalf of "Christian Socialism." In trades unions and legislation regarding the relations of master and servant he took especial interest, but always deprecated the extreme measures advocated by certain of the trades unionists. From 1865 to 1868 he was member of Parliament for Lambeth, and for Frome, 1868-74. In 1869 he became queen's counsel and in the following year made a tour in the United States and aided in founding an English colony at Rugby, Tennessee. In 1882 he was made judge of the county court circuit. His death took place at Brighton, March 22, 1896. He was a warm friend of the United States and during the Civil War period spoke publicly in behalf of the cause of the Union. His published writings include "Tom Brown's School Days" (1857); "The Scouring of the White Horse" (1858); "Tom Brown at Oxford" (1861); "Religio Laici" (1861), reissued as "A Layman's Faith" (1868); "The Cause of Freedom; Which is Its Champion in America?" (1863); "Alfred the Great" (1869); "Memoir of a Brother" (1873); "The Old Church, What Shall We Do with It?" a plea against disestablishment (1878); "The Manliness of Christ," an exceedingly popular religious work (1880); "Rugby, Tennessee" (1881); "Memoir of Daniel Macmillan" (1882); "Gone to Texas" (1885); "Life of Bishop Fraser" (1887); "David Livingston" (1889); "Vacation Rambles" (1895).

THE CAUSE OF FREEDOM

DELIVERED AT EXETER HALL, JANUARY 29, 1863

LADIES AND GENTLEMEN,—I am very happy to be here to meet you this evening. It must be a great satisfaction to every man who believes as I do to find that this question, as to what is the real issue in America, is coming out more clearly and distinctly everywhere. The question which in England is now coming up clearer and

(8568)

sharper every day is, " Which is the side of freedom?" That is the only question which an Englishman has to ask himself; and that is the question which is asked now of this nation. It has been within the last fortnight answered by the "Times." [Cheers and groans for the "Times."]

Allow me to suggest, ladies and gentlemen, that as our time is limited, and as each speaker has only twenty minutes allowed to him to say all that he has to say in, there is no time for all this applause. I shall be very much obliged to you if, at any rate while I am speaking, you will be kind enough to suppress your cheering and give me the time to say what I have to say. Again I say, ladies and gentlemen, that the issue has been fairly taken by the "Times" newspaper. I hold in my hand the articles of Monday, the 19th of this month, in which the "Times" says: "The great mind of England is deeply impressed with the conviction of the truth of all this;" I leave out some sentences which are not material—" that the cause of the South gallantly defending itself against the cruel and desolating invasions of the North is the cause of freedom." [Hisses.]

Now, ladies and gentlemen, that is the point upon which we wish to take issue this evening. Let us see whether the voice of England supports that statement.

In the same article there are some remarks to which the speaker who preceded me referred—some facetious remarks and some bitter taunts—calling us who are here present to address you this evening a set of struggling obscurities. Well, gentlemen, as the speaker before me accepted that, so I accept it. I am ready to admit—though the sight before me to-night makes me doubt it—that we may be few and obscure; but that is all the more reason for us to speak out what we believe. I believe there is not a man here this evening

who won't join with me in indorsing the words of the great
American poet of freedom:

> " They are slaves who will not choose
> Scorn and hatred and abuse,
> Rather than in silence shrink
> From the truth they needs must think;
> They are slaves who will not be
> In the right with two or three."

My object to-night, then, will be to maintain before you
that the cause of the South is not the cause of freedom, but
that it is the cause of the most degrading and hateful slavery
that has been before the world for thousands of years. I shall
endeavor as much as possible to take with me your judgment
and understanding. I do not want to excite your passions. I
don't want to state anything which shall do that, and I ask
you therefore to give me a patient and quiet hearing, because
the facts that I shall have to put before you will take at least
as much time as this meeting can possibly give to me.

I propose first to take a few of the leading Southern statesmen to show you what they have done in times past, what have
been their acts, and what their words, and then to ask you to
say whether they are the sort of people who are in favor of
freedom.

The first representative man of the Southern States is Mr.
Jefferson Davis. Mr. Jefferson Davis is a planter—a Southern planter—who was educated at West Point. The first public act of his life, as far as I know, was that he raised a regiment and went to the Mexican war. The Mexican war I believe to have been as atrocious a war as has ever been waged
in this world. However, be that as it may, he came back
from that war; and what was the next public act of his life?
You know very well that a great disgrace has fallen upon
many of the States of America because they repudiated their
public debts.

Now, the next act of Mr. Jefferson Davis's life was this, that when there was a man—Mr. Walker—who came forward for the governorship of Mississippi upon the platform of making the State pay its debts, he was opposed by Mr. Jefferson Davis, who advocated repudiation of the debt. No doubt in one sense Mr. Jefferson Davis was then the advocate of freedom—the freedom of not paying debts; but that is a freedom which I don't think any Englishman will indorse.

After the Mexican war the United States got a vast tract of new territory, and the question was, what was to be done with it? Then there arose a great struggle between the Free-Soil party and the slave party. The Free-Soil party said " slavery shall not be brought into these Territories." The slave party said that any man should go where he liked with his slaves. Upon that question Mr. Jefferson Davis came out in 1850 in the debate upon what is called Bell's compromise— a compromise that was endeavored to be made by legalizing a doctrine called " squatter's sovereignty," which I may explain to you if I have time. Upon that he said in the Senate: " Never will I consent to any compromise which shall forbid slaves from being taken into the Territories at the option of their owners."

On the 23d of July, 1850, he moved " That all laws existing in the said Territory (California) which deny or obstruct the right of any citizen to remove or reside in such Territory with any species of property legally held in any State of the Union, be and are hereby declared to be null and void."

He was then appointed secretary at war to Mr. President Pierce, and as secretary at war, and throwing the force of the federal government into the struggle in Kansas, he sent troops, turned out the free legislators, and had it not been for John Brown and such men as he, slavery would have been established in Kansas by Mr. Jefferson Davis.

Then came the question of the reopening of the slave-trade; and, whatever may be said in England, I can prove to you that one of the things that is as clear as the sun at noonday is that the Southern slaveholders, whatever they may say now, have been for years in favor of the reopening of the African slave-trade. Well, upon this occasion in 1859 to which I am alluding, Mr. Jefferson Davis, though he declined to vote in the State of Mississippi for the reopening as far as that State was concerned, for fear lest Mississippi should be swamped by too much of a good thing, yet carefully guarded himself, and said, " I have no coincidence of opinion with those who prate of the inhumanity of the slave-trade." In 1860, when secession was imminent, he moved in the Senate, by way of an amendment to the constitution of the United States:

" That it shall be declared by amendment of the constitution that property in slaves, recognized as such by the local laws of any State, shall be on the same footing as any other species of property, and not subject to be divested or impaired by the local laws of any other State."

The meaning of that is that the Southern slaveholder might take his slaves into New England and that even there they should not be interfered with. Now, I have taken you shortly and rapidly through the career of this representative of the Southern States, and I say that there is not an act of his life which has not been opposed to the sacred cause of freedom.

Mr. A. H. Stephens, of Georgia, as you have been told, is the Vice-President of the Confederate States, a thoughtful man—one of the best of Southern slaveholders. Let us see

what his opinions are.   This is a portion of a speech of his in
1857 on the slave-trade:

"It is plain that unless the number of the African stock be
increased we have not the population, and might as well abandon the race with our brethren of the North in the colonization of the Territories."

I give you the very words of the celebrated statement of
Mr. Stephens, which has only been referred to by the previous
speakers.   He says:

"Our new government is founded upon exactly the opposite idea; its foundations are laid, its corner-stone rests,
upon the great truth that the negro is not equal to the white
man, that slavery—subordination to the superior race—is
his natural and normal condition.   It is upon this, as I have
stated, our social fabric is firmly planted; and I cannot permit myself to doubt the ultimate success of a full recognition
of this principle throughout the civilized and enlightened
world.   This stone, which was rejected by the first builders,
is become the chief stone of the corner in our new edifice.
It is the Lord's doing, and marvellous in our eyes."

Now, I will add nothing to that but this, that every man
who believes as I do, that there is another corner-stone for
the life of nations, must believe that that corner-stone has
always been the great enemy of slavery—aye, and will fall
upon it wherever it is found, in America or anywhere else,
and crush it to atoms.

If my time were longer I would say a little about Messrs.
Mason and Slidell and other Southern leaders, but they are
not important enough to be brought forward before this
meeting when time presses.   I will therefore only tell you
this, that Mr. Mason, who is over here in England, going
about in society and preaching the cause of the South, was
the author of the Fugitive Slave Act.   [Cries of "He is
here."]   I don't know whether he is in the room or not.

[Cries of "Turn him out."]   If he is, I would say, "Don't turn him out."

I have now a few words to say on the point, whether or not this Southern Confederacy, which we are told is the cause of freedom, is likely to reopen the African slave-trade. I will give you a few facts which I gather from documents which are as open to any of you as they are to me.   In 1857, the governor of South Carolina, in his address to the legislature, said, "Whatever our position, we must have cheap labor, which can be obtained but in one way—by the reopening of the African slave-trade."   Now I say this—and I don't believe that anybody can deny it, though I am not so certain of it as I am of the other facts, because I did not see the original draft of the Confederate constitution; but I tell you what I believe to be undoubted.   It has been stated at any rate by many Americans who ought to know that in the original draft of that constitution the reopening of the slave-trade was provided for, and that it was taken out merely as a sop to England.   I tell you why I believe so. Here is Mr. Spratt, of South Carolina—very well known in America, though perhaps many of you have not heard of him.   As a member of the convention which took South Carolina out of the Union he said, "We all know that the constitution of the Confederate States is made for the day— just for the time being—a mere tub thrown out to the whale, to amuse and entertain the public mind for a time."   That is the admission of the South Carolinian representative in a protest against the excision of the clause for reopening of the African trade.   Then comes the Baltimore convention in 1858.   At that convention the question of slavery was brought on, and Mr. Goodwin, of Georgia, said, "I am an African-trade man." and then he goes on to say:

"I want the gentlemen of this convention to visit my plantation, and I say again—if they come to see me—I will show them as fine a lot of negroes of the pure African blood as they will see anywhere. If it is right for us to go to Virginia and buy a negro, and pay $2,000 for him, it is equally right to go to Africa and pay $50."

I won't go through the speeches of the other gentlemen at that convention—a very important convention it was—but I will just read to you the resolutions which they passed. The first was "that slavery is right, and that being right, it could not be wrong to import slaves." The second was to the effect that it is expedient and proper that the African slave-trade should be reopened, and that this convention will lend its influence to promote that end. Gentlemen, I won't detain you further, except to say that in 1859—the year before secession, at Vicksburg, in Mississippi—the states convention passed a resolution for the reopening of the African slave-trade by a large majority. One more fact. In the Arkansas State legislature in the same year the motion disapproving the reopening of the African slave-trade was lost by a majority of twenty-one.

One word more as to the state of things just before secession. Every man in America, especially the men concerned in politics, saw that a great split would come unless something could be done. Accordingly, Congress appointed committees of the Senate and legislature to consider what could be done, by way of altering the constitution, so as to keep the Union together. These committees broke up hopelessly and came to no conclusion. The majority sent in a resolution, and the minority sent in a resolution; but from the beginning to the end of their proceedings there was one thing, and one thing only, considered—slavery. And to show you the temper of the South at that time—which temper has not been improved since by the war—Mr. Adams, the present minister to this country—the son and grandson of eminent men— a man as distinguished for his moderation as any man in the United States—Mr. Adams, being a member of the committee of the House of Representatives, and anxious by any means he could to retain the Union, signed at first the resolution of the majority. Finding however that no concession would do for those men, he sent in a secial report and protest alone, one part of which was:

" That no form of adjustment will be satisfactory to the recusant States which does not incorporate into the constitution of the United States a recognition of the obligation to protect and extend slavery, and to that I will never consent."

Once more, I have in my hand all the ordinances of the secession States, but I won't trouble you with them because my time is just up. But I will say this—that I have read those documents, and I tell you that not one, nor two, but all of them take up the ground, and that ground only, for seceding—that slavery was in danger and likely to be put down in the Southern States.

Now, what are the people? I have given you specimens of their leading men. I have given you specimens of the public acts of that government which we are told to recognize as a government in favor of freedom. I am sorry to say the people are quite worthy of the government and of their leaders. What said their chief judge in that accursed judgment which he pronounced in the great slave-case, known as the Dred Scott case? " That the African race are so much inferior to white men that they have no rights, and may justly be reduced to slavery for the white man's benefit." That is a decision of the chief judge of the highest court in the United States, a man who is at the head of the legal body there; and that principle seems to have been ground into the southern portion of the American people. You have all read what has been written by the special correspondent of the "Times" newspaper on this question. What does Mr. Russell say about the Southern people? That in every city dogs are employed to catch runaway slaves. He and all other trustworthy witnesses describe both the people and the government to be as deliberately hostile to freedom as any men that ever lived on the face of this earth. Of course in a meeting of this sort, and in twenty minutes, you cannot prove your case, but I only say this—I challenge any friend of the South to name one single leader there who is not pledged over and over again to slavery. I ask them to name one public act, one single Southern Confederate State, which is in favor of human freedom.

Well, I, an Englishman, find such a case as this. I, an Englishman, an inhabitant of a country of free thought, of free words, and of free men, am asked to indorse such a state of things. I am asked to indorse a people who do these acts, who have expressed these opinions, and to say that their cause is the cause of freedom. I say on the contrary, as I said when I first stood up before you, that the cause of the South is the most hateful, the most enslaving, the most debasing tyranny that has been on the face of the earth for a thousand years.

During this American contest one American has been abused, and I think more unjustly dealt by than any other man in the United States; and the cruel and unfair abuse of Americans by a portion of the press of this country accounts for the bitter feeling in America against England.

In the same " Times " article from which I read to you just now, I find this statement:

> " The stock humbug of the Northern people is a pretence of caring about slavery. Mr. Cassius Clay is much mistaken if he thinks that his neighbors could suppose that he is the real emancipator for emancipation's sake, or that he has any other object in view except that of deluding Europe with fine words."

Such words as these are enough to make any people bitter; for a more unjust, a more cruel comment on a public man was never put forward. Now, Mr. Cassius Clay has said many foolish things about this country; but just let me say a word or two about his history. He was born in Kentucky—a slave State. When he went to New England to be educated, he looked about him to see what was going on there, and the difference between that country and his own struck him, and made him think. He went back to his own State of Kentucky; and what did he do there? When he saw the state of things on one side of the Ohio—magnificent cultivation—but on the other side saw desolation and slavery, he said to himself, I will see if I cannot put an end to this, so far as I am concerned; and he emancipated every slave he had.

And what did he do then? He went about Kentucky, the most dangerous State to act such a part in in all America, and with his life in his hand he lectured against slavery. He was attacked in his lecture-room several times. At one time four men attacked him, and after a desperate fight he was left for dead on the floor. This man, who has emancipated every slave of his, who has been cut to pieces for the sake of emancipation, is the man about whom our great paper says: " Cassius Clay is much deceived in his own imagination if he thought his neighbors could imagine that he was a real emancipator for emancipation's sake."

I have done. I will only put the case to you as it has been put by the great anti-slavery poet, Mr. Lowell, in his poem called "Jonathan to John; or An Address to England:"

> " We know we've got a cause, John,
>   That's honest, right, and true;
> We thought 'twould win applause, John,
>   If nowhere else, from you.
> The South cry poor men down, John,
>   And all men up cry we,
> Black, yellow, white, and brown, John,
>   Now which is your idee?"

MAX MÜLLER

FRIEDRICH MAXIMILIAN MULLER was born at Dessau, Germany, in December, 1823. His father, the lyric poet, Wilhelm Müller, was teacher of the classical languages in the gymnasium at that town. After studying at Leipsic, Berlin and Paris, Max Müller went to England, and, having been elected a Fellow of All Souls' College, Oxford, has since resided at that university. His lectures and essays on philological subjects have gained for him remarkable distinction. In the lecture from which we subjoin an extract he opposed the Darwinian theory of the descent of man.

THE IMPASSABLE BARRIER BETWEEN BRUTES AND MAN

FROM A LECTURE DELIVERED AT THE ROYAL INSTITUTION OF GREAT BRITAIN IN 1861

IN COMPARING man with the other animals, we need not enter here into the physiological questions whether the difference between the body of an ape and the body of a man is one of degree or of kind. However that question is settled by physiologists, we need not be afraid. If the structure of a mere worm is such as to fill the human mind with awe, if a single glimpse which we catch of the infinite wisdom displayed in the organs of the lowest creature gives us an intimation of the wisdom of its Divine Creator far transcending the powers of our conception, how are we to criticise and disparage the most highly organized creatures of his creation, creatures as wonderfully made as we ourselves? Are there not many creatures on many points more perfect even than man? Do we not envy the lion's strength, the eagle's eye, the wings of every bird? If there existed animals as perfect as man in their physical structure, nay, even more perfect, no thoughtful man would ever be uneasy. His true superiority rests on different grounds. "I confess," Sydney Smith writes, "I feel myself so much at ease about the superiority of mankind—I have such a marked and decided contempt for the understanding of every baboon I have ever seen—I feel so sure that the blue ape without a tail will never rival us in poetry, painting, and music, that I see no reason whatever that justice may not be done to the few fragments of soul and tatters of understanding which they may really possess." The playfulness of Sydney Smith in handling serious and sacred subjects, has of late been found fault with by many; but humor is a safer sign of strong convictions and perfect sanity than guarded solemnity.

With regard to our own problem, no man can doubt that certain animals possess all the physical requirements for articulate speech. There is no letter of the alphabet which a parrot will not learn to pronounce. The fact, therefore, that the parrot is without a language of its own must be explained by a difference between the mental, not between the physical, faculties of the animal and man; and it is by a comparison of the mental faculties alone, such as we find them in man and brutes, that we may hope to discover what constitutes the indispensable qualification for language, a qualification to be found in man alone, and in no other creature on earth.

I say mental faculties, and I mean to claim a large share of what we call our mental faculties for the higher animals. These animals have sensation, perception, memory, will, and intellect, only we must restrict intellect to the comparing or interlacing of single perceptions. All these points can be proved by irrefragable evidence, and that evidence has never, I believe, been summed up with greater lucidity and power than in one of the last publications of M. P. Flourens, "De la Raison, du Génie, et de la Folie": Paris, 1861. There are, no doubt, many people who are as much frightened at the idea that brutes have souls and are able to think, as by "the blue ape without a tail." But their fright is entirely of their own making. If people will use such words as soul or thought without making it clear to themselves and others what they mean by them, these words will slip away under their feet, and the result must be painful. If we once ask the question, Have brutes a soul? we shall never arrive at any conclusion; for soul has been so many times defined by philosophers from Aristotle down to Hegel, that it means everything and nothing. Such has been the confusion caused by the promiscuous employment of the ill-defined terms of mental philosophy that we find Descartes representing brutes as living machines, whereas Leibnitz claims for them not only souls, but immortal souls. "Next to the error of those who deny the existence of God," says Descartes, "there is none so apt to lead weak minds from the right path of virtue, as to think that the soul of brutes is of the same nature as our own; and, consequently, that we have nothing to fear or to hope after this life, any more than flies or ants; whereas, if we know how much they differ, we understand much better that our soul is quite independent of the body, and consequently not subject to die with the body."

The spirit of these remarks is excellent, but the argument is extremely weak. It does not follow that brutes have no souls because they have no human souls. It does not follow that the souls of men are not immortal, because the souls of brutes are not immortal; nor has the major premise ever been proved by any philosopher, namely, that the souls of brutes must necessarily be destroyed and annihilated by death. Leibnitz, who has defended the immortality of the human soul with stronger arguments than even Descartes, writes: "I found at last how the souls of brutes and their sensations do not at all interfere with the immortality of human souls; on the contrary, nothing serves better to establish our natural immortality than to believe that all souls are imperishable."

Instead of entering into these perplexities, which are chiefly due to the loose employment of ill-defined terms, let us simply look at the facts. Every unprejudiced observer will admit that—

1. Brutes see, hear, taste, smell, and feel; that is to say, they have five senses, just like ourselves, neither more nor less. They have both sensation and perception, a point which has been illustrated by M. Flourens by the most interesting experiments. If the roots of the optic nerve are removed, the retina in the eye of a bird ceases to be excitable, the iris is no longer movable; the animal is blind, because it has lost the organ of sensation. If, on the contrary, the cerebral lobes are removed, the eye remains pure and sound, the retina excitable, the iris movable. The eye is preserved, yet the animal cannot see, because it has lost the organ of perception.

2. Brutes have sensations of pleasure and pain. A dog that is beaten behaves exactly like a child that is chastised, and a dog that is fed and fondled exhibits the same signs of satisfaction as a boy under the same circumstances. We can only judge from signs, and if they are to be trusted

in the case of children, they must be trusted likewise in the case of brutes.

3. Brutes do not forget, or, as philosophers would say, brutes have memory. They know their masters, they know their home; they evince joy on recognizing those who have been kind to them, and they bear malice for years to those by whom they have been insulted or ill-treated. Who does not recollect the dog Argos in the "Odyssey," who, after so many years' absence, was the first to recognize Ulysses?

4. Brutes are able to compare and distinguish. A parrot will take up a nut, and throw it down again, without attempting to crack it. He has found that it is light: this he could discover only by comparing the weight of the good nuts with that of the bad; and he has found that it has no kernel: this he could only discover by what philosophers would dignify with the grand title of a syllogism, namely, "all light nuts are hollow; this is a light nut, therefore this nut is hollow."

5. Brutes have a will of their own. I appeal to any one who has ever ridden a restive horse.

6. Brutes show signs of shame and pride. Here again any one who has to deal with dogs, who has watched a retriever with sparkling eyes placing a partridge at his master's feet, or a hound slinking away with his tail between his legs from the huntsman's call, will agree that these signs admit of but one interpretation. The difficulty begins when we use philosophical language, when we claim for brutes a moral sense, a conscience, a power of distinguishing good and evil; and, as we gain nothing by these scholastic terms, it is better to avoid them altogether.

7. Brutes show signs of love and hatred. There are well-authenticated stories of dogs following their masters

to the grave, and refusing food from any one. Nor is there any doubt that brutes will watch their opportunity till they revenge themselves on those whom they dislike.

If, with all these facts before us, we deny that brutes have sensation, perception, memory, will, and intellect, we ought to bring forward powerful arguments for interpreting the signs which we observe in brutes so differently from those which we observe in man.

Some philosophers imagine they have explained everything, if they ascribe to brutes instinct instead of intellect. But, if we take these two words in their usual acceptations, they surely do not exclude each other. There are instincts in man as well as in brutes. A child takes his mother's breast by instinct; the spider weaves its net by instinct; the bee builds her cell by instinct. No one would ascribe to the child a knowledge of physiology because it employs the exact muscles which are required for sucking; nor shall we claim for the spider a knowledge of mechanics, or for the bee an acquaintance with geometry, because we could not do what they do without a study of these sciences. But what if we tear a spider's web, and see the spider examining the mischief that is done, and either giving up his work in despair, or endeavoring to mend it as well as may be? Surely here we have the instinct of weaving controlled by observation, by comparison, by reflection, by judgment. Instinct, whether mechanical or moral, is more prominent in brutes than in man; but it exists in both, as much as intellect is shared by both.

Where, then, is the difference between brute and man? What is it that man can do, and of which we find no signs, no rudiments, in the whole brute world? I answer without hesitation: The one great barrier between the brute and man is language. Man speaks, and no brute has ever uttered a word. Language is our Rubicon, and no brute will dare to cross it. This is our matter-of-fact answer to those who speak of development, who think they discover the rudiments at least of all human faculties in apes, and who would fain keep open the possibility that man is only a more favored beast, the triumphant conqueror in the primeval struggle for life. Language is something more palpable than a fold of the brain, or an angle of the skull. It admits of no cavilling, and no process of natural selection will ever distil significant words out of the notes of birds or the cries of beasts.

Language, however, is the only outward sign. We may point to it in our arguments, we may challenge our opponent to produce anything approaching to it from the whole brute world. But if this were all, if the art of employing articulate sounds for the purpose of communicating impressions were the only thing by which we could assert our superiority over the brute creation, we might not unreasonably feel somewhat uneasy at having the gorilla so close on our heels.

It cannot be denied that brutes, though they do not use articulate sounds for that purpose, have, nevertheless, means of their own for communicating with each other. When a whale is struck, the whole shoal, though widely dispersed, are instantly made aware of the presence of an enemy; and when the grave-digger beetle finds the carcass of a mole, he hastens to communicate the discovery to his fellows, and soon returns with his four confederates. It is evident, too, that dogs, though they do not speak, possess the power of understanding much that is said to them —their names and the calls of their masters; and other animals, such as the parrot, can pronounce every articulate sound. Hence, although, for the purpose of philosophical warfare, articulate language would still form an impregnable position, yet it is but natural that for our own satisfaction we should try to find out in what the strength of our position really consists; or, in other words, that we should try to discover that inward power of which language is the outward sign and manifestation.

For this purpose it will be best to examine the opinions of those who approached our problem from another point; who, instead of looking for outward and palpable signs of difference between brute and man, inquired into the inward mental faculties, and tried to determine the point where man transcends the barriers of the brute intellect. That point, if truly determined, ought to coincide with the starting point of language; and, if so, that coincidence ought to explain the problem which occupies us at present.

I shall read an extract from Locke's "Essay Concerning Human Understanding."

After having explained how universal ideas are made, how the mind, having observed the same color in chalk, and snow, and milk, comprehends these single perceptions under the general conception of whiteness, Locke continues: "If it may be doubted whether beasts compound and enlarge their ideas that way to any degree, this, I think, I may be positive in, that the power of abstracting is not at all in them; and that the having of general ideas is that which puts a perfect distinction betwixt man and brutes, and is an excellency which the faculties of brutes do by no means attain to."

If Locke is right in considering the having general ideas as the distinguishing feature between man and brutes, and, if we ourselves are right in pointing to language as the one palpable distinction between the two, it would seem to follow that language is the outward sign and realization of that inward faculty which is called the faculty of abstraction, but which is better known to us by the homely name of reason.

ON SOME LESSONS OF ANTIQUITY

LET us remember the lessons which we have learnt from antiquity. We have learnt reading and writing from Egypt; we have learnt arithmetic from India. So much for the famous three R's.

But that is not all. If we are Egyptians whenever we read and write, and Indians whenever we do our accounts, we have only to look at our watches to see that we are Babylonians also. We must go to the British Museum to see what a cuneiform inscription is like; but it is a fact nevertheless that every one of us carries something like a cuneiform inscription in his waistcoat pocket. For why is our hour divided into sixty minutes, each minute into sixty seconds, and so forth? Simply and solely because in Babylonia there existed by the side of the decimal system of notation another system, the sexagesimal, which counted by sixties. Why that number should have been chosen is clear enough, and it speaks well for the practical sense of those ancient Babylonian merchants. There is no number which has so many divisors as sixty.

The Babylonians divided the sun's daily journey into twenty-four parasangs, or 720 stadia. Each parasang hour was subdivided into sixty minutes. A parasang is about a German mile, and Babylonian astronomers compared the progress made by the sun during one hour at the time of the equinox to the progress made by a good walker during the same time, both accomplishing one parasang. The whole course of the sun during twenty-four equinoctial hours was fixed at twenty-four parasangs, or 720 stadia, or 360 degrees. This system was handed on to the Greeks, and Hipparchus, the great Greek philosopher, who lived about 150 B.C., introduced the Babylonian hour into Europe. Ptolemy, who wrote about 150 A.D., and whose name still lives in that of the Ptolemaic system of astronomy, gave still wider currency to the Babylonian way of reckoning time. It was carried along on the quiet stream of traditional knowledge through the Middle Ages, and, strange to say, it sailed down safely over the Niagara of the French Revolution. For the French when revolutionizing weights, measures, coins, and dates, and subjecting all to the decimal system of reckoning, were induced by some unexplained motive to respect our clocks and watches and to allow our dials to remain sexagesimal, that is, Babylonian, each hour consisting of sixty minutes. Here you see again the wonderful coherence of the world and how what we call knowledge is the result of an unbroken tradition, of a teaching descending from father to son. Not more than about a hundred arms would reach from us to the builders of the palaces of Babylon and enable us to shake hands with the founders of the oldest pyramids and to thank them for what they have done for us.

And allow me to point out what I consider most important in these lessons of antiquity. They are not mere guesses or theories; they are statements resting on historical facts, on evidence that cannot be shaken. Suppose five thousand years hence, or let us be more merciful and say fifty thousand years hence, some future Schliemann were to run his shafts into the ruins of what was once called London and discover among the débris of what is now the British Museum charred fragments of newspapers, in which some Champolion of the future might decipher such names as centimetre or millimetre.

On the strength of such evidence every historian would be justified in asserting that the ancient inhabitants of London—we ourselves—had once upon a time adopted a new decimal system of weights and measures from the French, because it was in French, in primeval French only, that such words as centimetre or millimetre could possibly have been formed. We argue to-day on the strength of the same kind of evidence, on the evidence chiefly of language and inscriptions, that our dials must have come from the Babylonians, our alphabets from Egypt, our figures from India. We indulge in no guesses, no mere possibilities, but we go back step by step from the "Times" of to-day till we arrive at the earliest Babylon inscription and the most ancient hieroglyphic monuments. What lies beyond we leave to the theoretic school, which begins its work where the work of the historical school comes to an end.

I could lay before you many more of these lessons of antiquity, but the Babylonian dial of my watch reminds me that my parasang, or my German mile, or my hour, is drawing to an end, and I must confine myself to one or two only. You have heard a great deal lately of bimetallism. I am not going to inflict on this audience a lecture on that deeply interesting subject, certainly not in the presence of our chairman, the lord mayor, and with the fear of the chancellor of the exchequer before my eyes.

But I may just mention this, that when I saw that what the bimetallists were contending for was to fix and maintain in perpetuity a settled ratio between gold and silver, I asked myself how this idea arose; and, being of an historical turn of mind, I tried to find out whether antiquity could have any lessons to teach us on this subject. Coined money, as you know, is a very ancient invention. There may have been a golden age when gold was altogether unknown, and people paid with cows, not with coins. When precious metals, gold, silver, copper, or iron began to be used for payment they were at first simply weighed. Even we still speak of a pound instead of a sovereign. The next step was to issue pieces of gold and silver properly weighed and then to mark the exact weight and value on each piece.

This was done in Assyria and Babylonia, where we find "shekels," or pounds of gold and silver. The commerce of the eastern nations was carried on for centuries by means of these weights of metal. It was the Greeks, the Greeks of Phocæa in Ionia, who in the seventh century B.C. first conceived the idea of coining money, that is, of stamping on each piece their city arms, the phoca or seal, thus giving the warranty of their State for the right weight and value of those pieces. From Phocæa this art of coining spread rapidly to the other Greek towns of Asia Minor, and was thence transplanted to Ægina, the Peloponnesus, Athens, and the Greek colonies in Africa and in Italy. The weight of the most ancient gold coin in all these countries was originally the same as that of the ancient Babylonian gold shekel, only stamped with the arms of each country, which thus made itself responsible for its proper weight. And this gold shekel or pound, in spite of historical disturbances, has held its own through centuries. The gold coins of Crœsus, Darius, Philip, and Alexander, have all about the same weight as the old Babylonian gold shekel, sixty of them going to one " mina " of gold; and what is stranger still, our own sovereign, or pound, or shekel, has nearly the same weight, sixty of them going to an old Babylonian " mina " of gold. In ancient times silver drachmas, or half-shekels, went to a gold shekel, just as with us twenty silver shillings are equivalent to a sovereign. This ancient shilling was again subdivided into sixty copper coins, sixty being the favorite Babylonian figure.

Knowing therefore the relative monetary value of a gold and silver shekel or half-shekel, knowing how many silver shekels the ancient nations had to give for one gold shekel, it was possible by merely weighing the ancient coins to find out whether there was then already any fixed ratio between gold and silver. Thousands of ancient coins have thus been tested, and the result has been to show that the ratio between gold and silver was fixed from the earliest times with the most exact accuracy.

That ratio, as Dr. Brugsch has shown, was one to twelve and one half in Egypt; it was, as proved by Dr. Brandis, one to thirteen and one third in Babylonia and in all the countries which adopted the Babylonian standard. There have been slight fluctuations and there are instances of debased coinage in ancient as well as in modern times. But for international trade and tribute the old Babylonian standard was maintained for a very long time.

These numismatic researches which have been carried on with indefatigable industry by some of the most eminent scholars in Europe may seem simply curious, but, like all historical studies, they may also convey some lessons.

They prove that in spite of inherent difficulties the great political and commercial nations of the ancient world did succeed in solving the bimetallic problem and in maintaining for centuries a fixed standard between gold and silver.

They prove that this standard, though influenced no doubt by the relative quantity of the two metals, by the cost of production, and by the demand for either silver or gold in the markets of the ancient world, was maintained by the common sense of the great commercial nations of antiquity, who were anxious to safeguard the interests both of their wholesale and retail traders.

They prove lastly that though a change in the ratio between gold and silver cannot be entirely prevented, it took place in ancient time by very small degrees. From the sixteenth century B.C., or, at all events, if we restrict our remarks to coined money, from the seventh century B.C. to nearly our own time the appreciation of gold has been no more than one and two thirds, namely, from thirteen and one third to fifteen. If now within our own recollection i has suddenly risen from fifteen to twenty, have we not a right to ask whether this violent disturbance is due altogether to natural causes, or whether what we are told is the effect is not to a certain extent the cause of it—I mean the sudden resolution of certain governments to boycott for their own purposes the second precious metal of the world?

But I must not venture farther on this dangerous ground, but shall invite you in conclusion to turn your eyes from the monetary to the intellectual currency of the world, from coins to what are called the counters of our thoughts.

The lessons which antiquity has taught us with regard to language, its nature, its origin, its growth, and decay are more marvellous than any we have hitherto considered.

What is the age of Alexander and Darius, of the palaces of Babylon and the pyramids of Egypt, compared with the age of language, the age of those very words which we use every day and which forsooth we call modern? There is nothing more ancient in the world than every one of the words which you hear me utter at present.

Take the two words "there is," and you can trace them step by step from English to Anglo-Saxon, from Anglo-Saxon to Gothic; you can trace them in all the Teutonic, Celtic, Slavonic languages, in the languages of Darius and Cyrus, in the prayers of Zoroaster, finally in the hymns of the Rig Veda. Instead of "there is" the old Vedic poets said "*tatra asti.*" It is the same coin, it has the same weight, only it has suffered a little by wear and tear during the thousands of years that it has passed from hand to hand or from mouth to mouth. Those two words would suffice to prove that all the languages of the civilized races of Europe, the languages of Persia and India also, all sprang from one source; and if you place before your imagination a map of Europe and Asia you would see all the fairest portions of these two continents, all the countries where you can discover historical monuments, temples, palaces, forums, churches, or houses of parliament, lighted up by the rays of that one language which we are speaking ourselves, the Aryan language, the classical language of the past, the living language of the present, and in the distant future the true Volapük, the language of the world.

I have no time to speak of the other large streams of historical speech,—the Semitic, the Ugro-Altaic, the Chinese, the Polynesian, the African, the American. But think what a lesson of antiquity has here been thrown open to us. We learn that we are bound together with all the greatest nations of the world by bonds more close, more firm and fast than flesh, or bone, or blood could ever furnish. For what is flesh, or bone, or blood compared to language? There is no continuity in flesh, and bone, and blood. They come and go by what we call birth and death and they change from day to day. In ancient times, in the struggle of all against all, when whole tribes were annihilated, nations carried away into captivity, slaves bought and sold, and the centres of civilized life overwhelmed again and again by a deluge of barbarian invasions, what chance was there of unmixed blood in any part of the world?

But language always remained itself, and those who spoke it, whatever their blood may have been, marched in serried ranks along the highroad of history as one noble army, as one spiritual brotherhood. What does it matter whether the same blood runs in our veins and in the veins of our dark fellow men in India? Their language is the same and has been the same for thousands of years as our own language; and whoever knows what language means, how language is not only the vestment, but the very embodiment of thought, will feel that to be of the same language is a great deal more than to be of the same flesh and blood.

With the light which the study of the antiquity of language has shed on the past the whole world has been changed. We know now not only what we are, but whence we are. We know our common Aryan home. We know what we carried away from it and how our common intellectual inheritance has grown and grown from century to century, till it has reached a wealth unsurpassed anywhere, amounting in English alone to 250,000 words. What does it matter whether we know the exact latitude and longitude of that Aryan home, though among reasonable people there is, I believe,

very little doubt as to its whereabouts " somewhere in Asia."
The important point is that we know that there was such a
home and that we can trace the whole intellectual growth
of the Aryan family back to roots which sprang from a common soil. And we can do this not by mere guesses only,
or theoretically, but by facts, that is, historically. Take any
word or thought that now vibrates through our mind, and
we know now how it was first struck in countries far away and
in times so distant that hardly any chronology can reach
them. If anywhere, it is in language that we may say we
are what we have been. In language everything that is
new is old, and everything that is old is new. That is true
evolution, true historical continuity. A man who knows his
language and all that is implied by it stands on a foundation
of ages. He feels the past under his feet and feels at home
in the world of thought, a loyal citizen of the oldest and
widest republic.

It is this historical knowledge of language, and not of
language only, but of everything that has been handed down
to us by an uninterrupted tradition from father to son, it is
that kind of knowledge which I hold that our universities
and schools should strive to maintain. It is the historical
spirit with which they should try to inspire every new generation. As we trace the course of a mighty river back from
valley to valley, as we mark its tributaries and watch its
meanderings till we reach its source, or, at all events, the
watershed from which its sources spring, in the same manner the historical school has to trace every current of human
knowledge from century to century back to its fountain-head,
if that is possible, or at all events as near to it as the remaining records of the past will allow. The true interest of all
knowledge lies in its growth. The very mistakes of the

past form the solid ground on which the truer knowledge of the present is founded. Would a mathematician be a mathematician who had not studied his "Euclid?" Would an astronomer be an astronomer who did not know the Ptolemaic system of astronomy and had not worked his way through its errors to the truer views of Copernicus? Would a philosopher be a philosopher who had never grappled with Plato and Aristotle? Would a lawyer be a lawyer who had never heard of Roman law? There is but one key to the present—that is the past. There is but one way to understand the continuous growth of the human mind and to gain a firm grasp of what it has achieved in any department of knowledge—that is to watch its historical development.

No doubt it will be said there is no time for all this in the hurry and flurry of our modern life. There are so many things to learn that students must be satisfied with results, without troubling themselves how these results were obtained by the labors of those who came before us. This really would mean that our modern teaching must confine itself to the surface and keep aloof from what lies beneath, that knowledge must be what is called cut and dry, if it is to prove serviceable in the open market.

My experience is the very opposite. The cut-and-dry knowledge which is acquired from the study of manuals or from so-called crammers is very apt to share the fate of cut flowers. It makes a brilliant show for one evening, but it fades and leaves nothing behind. The only knowledge worth having and which lasts us for life must not be cut and dry, but on the contrary must be living and growing knowledge, knowledge of which we know the beginning, the middle, and the end, knowledge of which we can produce the title-deeds whenever they are called for. That knowledge

may be small in appearance, but, remember, the knowledge
required for life is really very small.

We learn, no doubt, a great many things, but what we are
able to digest, what is converted in *succum et sanguinem*,
into our very life-blood, and gives us strength and fitness
for practical life, is by no means so much as we imagine in
our youth. There are certain things which we must know
as if they were part of ourselves. But there are many other
things which we simply put into our pockets, which we can
find there whenever we want them, but which we do not
know as we must know, for instance, the grammar of a language. It is well to remember this distinction between
what we know intuitively and what we know by a certain
effort of memory only, for our success in life depends
greatly on this distinction—on our knowing what we know
and knowing what we do not know, but what nevertheless
we can find if wanted.

HIGGINSON

THOMAS WENTWORTH HIGGINSON, a distinguished American essayist and lecturer, was born in Cambridge, Massachusetts, December 22, 1823, and educated at Harvard University. After studying at the Divinity School in Cambridge he was ordained, in 1847, pastor of a Unitarian church in Newburyport, but resigned his charge in 1850 on account of his anti-slavery and abolitionist views being unacceptable to his congregation. In the same year he was an unsuccessful Free-Soil candidate for Congress. In 1852 he became the pastor of a Free church in Worcester, Massachusetts, but retired from the ministry altogether in 1858. During these years at Worcester he was active among the anti-slavery agitators, and after the beginning of the Civil War he served two years in the federal army, where as colonel of the First South Carolina volunteers he commanded the first regiment of freed slaves in the national service. He resigned from the service in 1864 on account of ill-health and resided at Newport, Rhode Island, until 1878, when he removed to Cambridge, which has been his home from that time. He has been especially prominent as an advocate of female suffrage, and has been active also in promoting the higher education of women. At the close of 1899 he delivered a course of Lowell lectures in Boston upon American oratory. His published works include besides a translation of Epictetus (1865-92), "Out-Door Papers" (1863); "Malbone," a novel (1869); "Army Life in a Black Regiment" (1870); "Atlantic Essays" (1871); "The Sympathy of Religions" (1871); "Oldport Days" (1873); "Young Folks' History of the United States" (1875); "Short Studies of American Authors" (1879); "Common Sense About Women" (1881); "Life of Margaret Fuller" (1884); "Larger History of the United States" (1885); "Travellers and Outlaws," "The Monarch of Dreams" (1886); "Hints in Writing and Speaking" (1887); "Women and Men" (1888); "An Afternoon Landscape," a collection of verse (1889); "The New World and the New Book" (1892); "Concerning All of Us" (1892); "Cheerful Yesterdays" (1898); "Book and Heart" (1897); "Tales of the Enchanted Islands of the Atlantic" (1898).

DECORATION DAY ADDRESS AT MOUNT AUBURN CEMETERY, MAY 30, 1870

WE meet to-day for a purpose that has the dignity and the tenderness of funeral rites without their sadness. It is not a new bereavement, but one which time has softened, that brings us here. We meet not around a newly-opened grave, but among those which nature has already decorated with the memorials of her love. Above every tomb her daily sunshine has smiled, her tears have wept; over the humblest she has bidden some grasses nestle, some vines creep, and the butterfly—ancient emblem of immortality—waves his little wings above every sod. To nature's signs of tenderness we add our own. Not "ashes to ashes, dust to dust," but blossoms to blossoms, laurels to the laureled.

The great Civil War has passed by—its great armies were disbanded, their tents struck, their camp-fires put out, their muster-rolls laid away. But there is another army whose numbers no presidential proclamation could reduce; no general orders disband. This is their camping-ground, these white stones are their tents, this list of names we bear is their muster-roll, their camp-fires yet burn in our hearts.

I remember this "Sweet Auburn" when no sacred associations made it sweeter, and when its trees looked down on no funerals but those of the bird and the bee. Time has enriched its memories since those days. And especially during our great war, as the nation seemed to grow impoverished in men, these hills grew richer in associations, until their multiplying wealth took in that heroic boy who fell in almost the last battle of the war. Now that roll of honor has closed, and the work of commemoration begun.

Without distinction of nationality, of race, of religion, they gave their lives to their country. Without distinction of religion, of race, of nationality, we garland their graves to-day. The young Roman Catholic convert, who died exclaiming "Mary! pardon!" and the young Protestant theological student, whose favorite place of study was this cemetery, and who asked only that no words of praise might be engraven on his stone—these bore alike the cross in their lifetime, and shall bear it alike in flowers to-day. They gave their lives that we might remain one nation, and the nation holds their memory alike in its arms.

And so the little distinctions of rank that separated us in the service are nothing here. Death has given the same brevet to all. The brilliant young cavalry-general who rode into his last action, with stars on his shoulders and his death-wound on his breast, is to us no more precious than that sergeant of sharpshooters who followed the line unarmed at Antietam, waiting to take the rifle of some one who should die, because his own had been stolen; or that private who did the same thing in the same battle, leaving the hospital service to which he had been assigned. Nature has been equally tender to the graves of all, and our love knows no distinction.

What a wonderful embalmer is death! We who survive grow daily older. Since the war closed the youngest has gained some new wrinkle, the oldest some added gray hair. A few years more and only a few tottering figures shall represent the marching files of the Grand Army; a year or two beyond that, and there shall flutter by the window the last empty sleeve. But these who are here are embalmed forever in our imaginations; they will not change; they never will seem to us less young, less fresh, less daring, than when they sallied to their last battle. They will always have the dew of their youth; it is we alone who shall grow old.

And, again, what a wonderful purifier is death! These who fell beside us varied in character; like other men they had their strength and their weaknesses, their merits and their faults. Yet now all stains seem washed away; their life ceased at its climax, and the ending sanctified all that went before. They died for their country; that is their record. They found their way to heaven equally short, it seems to us, from every battle-field, and with equal readiness our love seeks them to-day.

"What is a victory like?" said a lady to the Duke of Wellington. "The greatest tragedy in the world, madam, except a defeat." Even our great war would be but a tragedy were it not for the warm feeling of brotherhood it has left behind it, based on the hidden emotions of days like these. The war has given peace to the nation; it has given union, freedom, equal rights; and in addition to that, it has given to you and me the sacred sympathy of these graves. No matter what it has cost us individually—health or worldly fortunes—it is our reward that we can stand to-day among these graves and yet not blush that we survive.

The great French soldier, La Tour D'Auvergne, was the hero of many battles, but remained by his own choice in the ranks. Napoleon gave him a sword and the official title "First among the grenadiers of France." When he was killed, the emperor ordered that his heart should be entrusted to the keeping of his regiment—that his name should be called at every roll-call, and that his next comrade should make answer, "Dead upon the field of honor." In our memories are the names of many heroes; we treasure all their hearts in this consecrated ground, and when the name of each is called, we answer in flowers, "Dead upon the field of honor."

ORATION UPON GRANT

DELIVERED AT THE MEMORIAL SERVICES HELD IN CAMBRIDGE, MASSACHUSETTS, AUGUST 8, 1885

IT was one of the most picturesque moments of the history of Rome when, after the battle of Cannæ was lost and the Roman army almost annihilated—while Hannibal, the Carthaginian general, was measuring by bushels the gold rings of the slain Roman knights—the whole people of the city went out to greet with honor their defeated general Terentius Varro, and to bear to him a vote of thanks from the senate for " not having despaired of the republic."

The vast obsequies celebrated all over the land to-day are not in honor of a defeated general, but of a victorious one; yet the ground of gratitude is the same as in that Roman pageant. Our Civil War, like that between Rome and Carthage, began in defeat and was transformed into victory, because he whom we celebrate did not despair of the republic. From the time when his successes at Fort Donelson and Vicksburg first turned the tide of adversity until the day when he received Lee's surrender it was to him we looked.

Nor was this all. There was in all this something more than mere generalship. Generalship is undoubtedly a special gift, almost amounting to genius—a man is born to it, as he is for poetry, or chess-playing, or commerce; and as in those other vocations, so in this, his success in one direction does not prove him equally strong in all. There are many ways in which General Grant does not rank with the greatest of the sons of men. He was wanting in many of the gifts and even tastes which raise man to his highest; he did not greatly care for poetry, philosophy, music, painting, sculpture, natural science. The one art for which he had a genius is one that must be fleeting and perishable compared to these; for the human race must in its progress outgrow war. But a remarkable personal quality never can be ignored; if not shown in one way it will be shown in another; and this personal quality Grant had. Let us analyze some of its aspects.

He was great, in the first place, through the mere scale of his work. His number of troops, the vast area of his operations, surpassed what the world had before seen. When he took 15,000 prisoners at Fort Donelson, the capture was three times as large as when Burgoyne surrendered, in the only American battle thought important enough to be mentioned by Sir Edward Creasy in his " Fifteen Decisive Battles of the World."

When, on July 4, 1863, he took Vicksburg, he received what was then claimed to be the greatest capture of men and armament since the invention of gunpowder, and perhaps since the beginning of recorded history. He captured 15 generals, 31,600 soldiers and 172 cannon. For victories less than this Julius Cæsar was made dictator for ten years and his statue was carried in processions with those of the immortal gods. Cæsar at Pharsalia took but 24,000 prisoners; Napoleon at Ulm, 23,000; Hannibal at Cannæ but 20,000. Yet these in Grant's case were but special victories. How great, then, his power when at the head of the armies of the United States! Neither of these great commanders ever directed the movements of a million men. The mere coarse estimate of numbers, therefore, is the first measure of Grant's fame.

But mere numbers are a subordinate matter. He surpassed his predecessors also in the dignity of the object for which he fought. The three great generals of the world are usually enumerated—following Macaulay—as being Cæsar, Cromwell and Napoleon. Two of these fought in wars of mere conquest, and the contests of the third were marred by a gloomy fanaticism, by cruelty and by selfishness. General Grant fought to restore a nation, that nation being the hope of the world. And he restored it. His work was as complete as it was important. Cæsar died by violence; Napoleon died defeated; Cromwell's work crumbled to pieces when his hand was cold. Grant's career triumphed in its ending; it is at its height to-day.

It was finely said by a Massachusetts statesman that we did not fight to bring our opponents to our feet, but only to our side. Grant to-day brings his opponents literally to his side when they act as pall-bearers around his coffin.

The next thing remarkable about him was the spirit in which he fought. He belonged in his whole temperament to the Anglo-Saxon or Germanic type of generals, and not to the French or Latin type. It is said that in the Duke of Wellington's despatches you never find the word " glory," but always the word " duty," while in those of Napoleon Bonaparte you never find the word " duty," but always " glory." Grant was in this respect like Wellington. In his early western campaign he wrote to his father: " I will go on and do my duty to the best of my ability, and do all I can to bring the war to a speedy close. I am not an aspirant for anything at the close of the war. . . . One thing I am well aware of: I have the confidence of every man in my command." Of course he had. Once convince men that your motive is duty and their confidence is yours.

When we come to the mere executive qualities involved in fighting, we find that Grant habitually combined in action two things rarely brought together—quickness and perseverance. That could be said of him which Malcolm McLeod said of Charles Edward, the Pretender: "He is the bravest man, not to be rash, and the most cautious man, not to be a coward, that I ever saw."

He did not have the visible and conspicuous dash of Sherman or Sheridan; he was rather the kind of man whom they needed to have behind them. But in quickness of apprehension and action, where this quality was needed, he was not their inferior, if they were even his equals. He owed to it his first conspicuous victory at Fort Donelson. Looking at the knapsacks of the slain enemy, he discovered that they held three days' rations, and knew, therefore, that they were trying to get away. Under this stimulus he renewed the attack and the day was won.

Moreover, it is to be noticed that he was, in all his action as a commander, essentially original—a man of initiative, not of routine. He was singularly free from the habit of depending on others. When in Egypt an official gave him an Arabian horse and advised that, at first, he should simply pace the horse up and down, with one or two attendants to hold him, Grant, who had at West Point been the best rider in his class, said briefly, "If I can mount a horse I can ride him, and all the attendants can do is to keep away." It was the same with him through his military life; if he could mount the horse he could ride it; and what caused all to turn to him, as much as anything, was this knowledge that he was an original force, not an imitator or dependent.

And to crown all these qualities was added one more, that of personal modesty. When, at Hamburg, Germany, he was toasted as "the man who had saved the nation," he replied, "What saved the Union was the coming forward of the young men of the country." He put down the pride of the

German officers, the most self-sufficient military aristocracy of the world, by quietly disclaiming the assumption of being a soldier at all. He said to Bismarck: " I am more a farmer than a soldier. I take little or no interest in military affairs, and, though I entered the army thirty-five years ago and have been in two wars—the Mexican as a young lieutenant, and later [mark the exquisite moderation of that " and later "]—I never went into the army without regret, and never retired without pleasure." Such a remark from the greatest captain of the age disarmed even German criticism.

When we turn from the military life of Grant to his civil life, we find him at great disadvantage and entering untried on a sphere where it is, perhaps, still too early to judge him. He had been trained in the army, a bad school for civil service through this reason, that an army officer is obliged, if in command, to select his subordinates, trust a great deal to them, stand by them under attack and not interfere very much with them till they lose his confidence and he drops them. It is almost impossible for him, as can be done in a counting-room or a workshop, to watch his subordinates, check them, guide them and correct their mistakes from day to day. The chief drawbacks of President Grant's administration came from this habit, and now that it is past we can see that they left the man himself unstained. There were, undoubtedly, men of the highest character with whom he was brought in close contact whom he could not appreciate and with whom he could not well act. Thus he never did justice to Charles Sumner, but we may well admit, at this distance of time, that Sumner did not quite do justice to him.

There is no doubt, I suppose, that Grant would have died a happier man had he for a third time been raised to the Presidency. There is nothing strange in this. Nobody ever longed to be an ex-President, and anybody might honorably long to be set above even Washington by having a third Presidential term. To call this Cæsarism was idle; it was not in Grant to make one conscious step to impair the liberties of his country. Whether his third administration would not have damaged those liberties indirectly and unconsciously, we never shall know; the majority of Americans apparently either feared some such result, or found the precedent too dangerous to venture on. The step never was taken at any rate; and the nation is perhaps safer that it was not, but we must guard against connecting this ambition in Grant's case with anything base or unscrupulous.

He was never tried by this test of a third term of power; but a third term of ordeal came to him in a wholly unexpected way, and increased his hold upon us all. He told Bismarck, as we have seen, that he never entered on a war without regret or retired from it without pleasure. But he was destined to enter on just one more campaign—against pain and disease combined with sudden poverty. It was a formidable coalition. It is sometimes said that it is easier to die well than to live well; but it is harder than either to grow old, knowing that one's great period of action is past, and weighed down with the double weight of hopeless financial failure and irremediable bodily pain. Either bankruptcy or physical torture has by itself crushed many a man morally and mentally; but Grant's greatest campaign was when he resisted them both. Upon such a campaign as this he might well, as he said, shrink from entering; but having been obliged to enter upon it, he was still Grant. Thousands of Americans have felt a sense of nearness to him and a sense of pride in him during the last few months such as they never felt before. He was already a hero in war to us. The last few months have made him a hero of peace, *miles pacificus.*

It has been already said that the supreme generals of the world were Cæsar, Cromwell, and Napoleon. Grant was behind all three of these in variety of cultivation and in many of the qualities that make a man's biography picturesque and fascinating. He may be said to have seemed a little prosaic, compared with any one of these. But in moral qualities he was above them all; more truthful, more unselfish, more simple, more humane. He fell short of Washington in this, that he was not equally great in war and statesmanship; but his qualities were within reach of all; his very defects were within reach of all; and he will long be with Washington and Lincoln the typical American in the public eyes. It is this typical quality after all that is most valuable. What we need most to know is not that exceptional men of rare gifts or qualities may arise here—they may arise anywhere—but that there is such an average quality among us that when a great personal leadership is wanted it will be forthcoming, after a few experiments. This is the secret of that popular preference always so obvious for an obscure origin in ease of a great man. The preference is equally recognized among the philosophers; "the interest of history," says Emerson, "is in the fortunes of the poor." Indeed the deeper feeling of the whole world has always recognized this—it is to the proudest monarchy in Europe, the Castilian, that we owe the phrase, "the son of his own works"[1]—Grant was the son of his own works. His fame rests upon the broadest and surest of all pedestals, as broad as common humanity. He seems greatest because he was no detached or ideal hero, but simply the representative of us all.

---

[1] "El hijo de sus obras."

FOR SELF-RESPECT AND SELF-PROTECTION

[Speech at the Annual Meeting of the American Woman Suffrage Association, held at Philadelphia, Pennsylvania, November 1, 1887.]

I HAVE the sensations of a revolutionary veteran, almost, in coming back to the city of Philadelphia and remembering our early meetings here in that time of storm, in contrasting the audiences of to-day with the audiences of that day, and in thinking what are the difficulties that come before us now as compared with those of our youth. The audiences have changed, the atmosphere of the community has changed; nothing but the cause remains the same, and that remains because it is a part of the necessary evolution of democratic society and is an immortal thing.

I recall those early audiences; the rows of quiet faces in Quaker bonnets in the foreground; the rows of exceedingly unquiet figures of Southern medical students, with their hats on, in the background. I recall the visible purpose of those energetic young gentlemen to hear nobody but the women, and the calm determination with which their boot-heels contributed to put the male speakers down. I recall their too assiduous attentions in the streets outside when the meetings broke up; and if there was any of that self-sacrifice which the chairman seems to imply, it did not refer to anything that actually took place inside the hall, although even the attempt on a man's part to get to the other end of his speech was sometimes attended with difficulties. The real test of chivalry, if there was one, consisted in the subsequent escorting through the streets of Lucy Stone and Susan B. Anthony in the Bloomer dresses of those days, in the midst of a somewhat uncomplimentary and peripatetic audience of small boys.

The times have changed. Much has come and gone since then. The Southern medical students have disappeared from the room, and almost, it may be, from Philadelphia. The change of fashion has swept away the Quaker bonnets in one direction and the Bloomer trousers in another.

The grand voices that cheered us then in great measure have passed away. The heroic, changeless, firm, granite attitude of Garrison, the fascinating eloquence of Phillips, and the womanly counsel of Lucretia Mott are all only noble memories for those who recall them; but the same cause fills this hall and these hearts to-day. The same cause is ours, fresher and younger because thirty years have gone by.

We need feel no anxiety about it. It comes before us to-day with no new arguments, no new illustrations, only with new tests and new methods. It comes, not with the vague and bodiless traditions of the past, but with the twenty-six thousand women voters of Kansas to-day behind it to strengthen it. It is the cause of the future, the cause of the American people, the inevitable, logical result of all our reasons, the recognition of which alone justifies us in calling ourselves Republicans. Its future is absolutely certain. Those who join themselves with it join to something that they can hold to. It is true of this, as Frederick Douglass said years ago of another organization, " This is the deck; all else is the sea."

I consider it, Mr. Chairman, a great merit of the cause, that as the time goes on, and as it widens so greatly the sphere of its adherents, it brings in a great variety of forces to suggest new arguments; it gives different points of view; different positions. We are not now that simple homogeneous body, all united on much the same arguments, all coming to the result in much the same way, that we were at the outset. It has developed, as the anti-slavery movement developed, a great variety of angles of incidence, a great variety of points of view; and the spirit and freshness and vigor of these meetings must come in a large degree from the freedom of those who stand on this platform to speak their own thought and approach the great question in their own way.

Who of us that served in the anti-slavery ranks does not remember those conflicts of opinion on the platform that seemed at times likely to rend the whole movement asunder? I remember dear old Stephen Foster, that man of iron. I remember with delight the time when he followed me in a speech in an anti-slavery convention at Worcester. He said at the outset, " I love my friend Higginson; but if there is anything I abhor, it is such sentiments as he has been expressing."

That was the genuine thing; that was reform. Reformers are not always alike capable of that strict combination, that firm concentration, which makes conservatism so powerful. No liberal sect is ever found like the Roman Catholic Church in its power of cementing and organizing and binding. The force of reform is its individual enthusiasm, resulting from each person following out his own best view.

Reformers are like Esquimaux dogs. Do you know how Esquimaux dogs are fastened to the sledge? The owner of the dogs takes his sledge, catches his dog with difficulty, and fastens him by a single thong to the sledge. He catches another dog, puts his thong upon him and fastens him too. He has twenty dogs at last all harnessed to the sledge, each by his separate thong. Why does he waste his labor in that way? Because, whenever the experiment has been tried of putting Esquimaux dogs into a single combined harness, the trouble was, they turned around and ate each other up.

That is the trouble with reformers. If you try to make them think alike and act alike, destruction follows. Each for himself, each approaching his movement in his own way, and we have strength. I myself have tested the ability of the woman suffrage reformers to recognize this individuality of opinion; and those who know the recent history of this reform know it is a proof of the catholicity of this meeting that I have been invited to stand here among the speakers.

I believe myself that the woman suffrage reform has many points of view, and that in some points of view it is almost perilous to approach it. I believe that we never can safely rest the enfranchisement of any large number of people upon any attempt to predict with precision the specific or even the general tendency of the votes which they shall cast. I dread all prediction of that kind for the woman suffrage movement. I rejoiced to hear the first speaker [Mrs. Haggart] say this evening that if she knew that every bad woman in the country would be first at the polls, she still should advocate woman suffrage just the same.

If it were only mere policy, if it takes its chance of success only on the chance of a prediction, it is unsafe. It must rest on a principle to establish its permanent work and value.

I dare say that in many respects woman's voting would afford a better class of voters than the voters we have now, but I do not wish to enfranchise her for this reason. It might be a question then how long she would stay a better class after she had voted. I knew a man once who advocated woman suffrage on the ground that voting was necessarily demoralizing; that we had had men voting for a great while and they had brought the country to the verge of ruin; that women would unquestionably, in the course of fifty years, if enfranchised do the same thing, but that there would be fifty years in the meanwhile and that the country would last his time, which was all he cared for.

I distrust that line of argument. How do we know, it might be said, how much of the present virtue of women comes from the absence of voting? The argument proves to my mind too much. I believe that the majority of women would vote well. So we believed when we enfranchised the blacks, that the majority of them would vote well. But the thing we absolutely knew was and the only thing we knew, that whether they would vote well for the country or not the difference between their having the ballot and not having it meant for them freedom or slavery, and it was for that reason that we enfranchised them.

We took the chances of all the rest. Have they voted well? It is hard to say. They half ruined South Carolina financially. We know that. They voted against prohibition in Texas. We know that. That they would vote against civil service reform is exceedingly probable if they once knew clearly enough what it was. What we know is that because we enfranchised them they are still free, and that is enough for us to know. That stamps success upon their enfranchisement, although a thousand Senator Ingallses rise with their little voices at this late hour to protest against it and say it was a mistake.

So it is in regard to women. I believe and hope that the majority of women would vote as my friend, Mrs. Howe, thinks, for peace. But I know on the other hand that a Southern statesman said to me that the war was prolonged two years after the men would have given up, because the women of the South would not let them. That same man told me that in his opinion the practice of duelling at the South was sustained to this day not by the voices of the men but of the women.

Thus, while I believe that the vast majority of women would throw their influence for peace, I yet know the possibilities of a minority and I do not wish to rest their enfranchisement on that ground. I believe that the great majority of women would vote for honest government if they only understood it, if they would study it so as to understand it; but I cannot forget that all the ingenuity of Wall Street has never devised so perfectly ingenious and successful an instrument of fraud as the Woman's Bank of Boston, entirely the product of a woman's brain; and I do not wish to rest the demand for suffrage on the superior honesty of women.

I believe that women would be the custodians of public property, as they are the custodians of private property. You know that almost every young married man if he succeeds in making both ends meet on his limited income at the end of the first year owes it to his wife; and commonly ends in confessing that he lived more economically the first year of his marriage than the last year of his bachelorhood.

We may claim therefore that women are good, practical custodians of property; and yet I cannot forget that the Association of Collegiate Alumnæ has just published from the educated daughter of a member of Congress, a Pennsylvania woman, one of the most determined and desperate pleas in favor of German socialism that I have ever seen in print. And I cannot forget that it was a woman, Louise Michel, who uttered the other day the wish that on the day of the execu-

tion of the Chicago anarchists every court of justice in the
world might have dynamite put under it and be exploded
forever.

I do not therefore wish to claim woman suffrage on any
basis of absolute prediction of what will be. In this I do
not represent all of those who are with me. I may belong
to a more conservative class of woman suffragists. I am
sometimes told I am too conservative. I do not even dare
to rest it on the ground as many do that the superior insight of women will make them better judges of public characters and enable them to penetrate more keenly the devices
of scoundrels. I willingly believe that women may often
have a good eye for a demagogue. The women of Kansas
seem to have proved that when they disposed of Senator In-
galls.

But I am one of those who believe that in Massachusetts
a service was rendered to the nation when we finally laid
General Butler on the shelf; and I am not at all sure that
the women of Massachusetts would have done it. I think
we did a good thing, irrespective of party, when we put
President Cleveland into the presidency, and I have been
repeatedly told that if it had been left to women he never
would have been chosen.

I do not venture therefore to rest the argument for woman
suffrage on the ground that women are a race of perfectly
ideal saints.who are to step up to our voting-places and vote
a millennium as soon as we enfranchise them. I do not
know any speaker for woman suffrage who goes so far as
that, though some might go further in that direction than
I should. When George Eliot made one of her characters
say, "I am not denying that women are foolish; God Almighty made 'em to match the men," I recognize the truth

of it, and I recognize that those women, to match the men, have got to be enfranchised like the rest.

I believe, as I said, that every great extension of the franchise brings its dangers. Has there been a moment since the inauguration of our government that there has not been somebody to declare the failure of universal suffrage among men and say that our voting list was too large already? It is the price we pay for democratic government. We might have recognized it beforehand; indeed, it was recognized beforehand. Fisher Ames in comparing a monarchy and a republic, said: "A monarchy is a fine, well-built ship; it is beautiful to look at; it sails superbly. The difficulty is that sometimes it strikes a rock and then it goes down. But a republic," he said, "is a kind of a great clumsy raft. You can float anywhere on it; it will never sink but your feet are always in the water."

I have no expectation that the admission of women to the ballot will enable us to keep dry shod upon the raft, and I am as sure as I can be of anything in the future that when women are enfranchised they will have some of their own sins to answer for, and not be able to devote themselves entirely to correcting the sins of men.

So surely as you have women statesmen you will have women politicians; you will have women bosses, women wire-pullers, women intriguers. The talent that devised the Woman's Bank will be brought to bear, as far as its power goes, upon the bank of the nation. The power that advocates socialism now in the abstract would advocate it then in the concrete. All this is in the future. It is to be expected. No great extension of the suffrage, and there never was any so great as this, ever failed to bring with it risks and drawbacks on the way; but the result of those risks and drawbacks is a true republic, the result is a consistent democracy. The result is a nation in which a man can hear the glories of the republic sung, and not blush, as he has to now, at the thought that those boasts are built upon the disfranchisement of half the human race.

Why, in view of these incidental uncertainties, should women be enfranchised? That is the point where all suffragists, however they may differ as to methods or processes, come together at last. No matter how we may differ in details upon the platform you will find if you venture to take advantage of those differences that we are a good deal like those old-fashioned fighting Highlanders in Sir Walter Scott's story, of whom Bailie Nicol Jarvie declares that no matter how they may quarrel among themselves they are always ready to combine at last against " all honest folk that hae money in their pockets." Our combination is a mild one so far as the pockets go. It is incarnated in Miss Cora Scott Pond, the only person whom I have ever encountered in my long experience of reformers who could make a speech and ask for a little contribution and then take it up and make the audience feel grateful to her.[1]

That part of the duty we do well. We do well also the more strenuous and difficult parts, if, indeed, there is any part of a reform more difficult on the whole than raising money to carry it along.

I believe in woman suffrage for the sake of woman herself. I believe in it because I am the son of a woman and the husband of a woman and the father of a prospective woman. I remember that at one of the first woman suffrage meetings I ever attended one of the first speakers was an odd fellow from the neighboring town, considered

[1] Miss Pond's collection was being taken up during the speaker's remarks.

half a lunatic. That didn't make much impression in those days when we were all considered a little crazy, but he was a little crazier than the rest of us. He pushed forward on the platform, seeming impatient to speak and throwing his old hat down by his side, he said, " I don't know much about this subject nor any other ; but I know this, my mother was a woman." I thought it was the best condensed woman suffrage argument I ever heard in my life.

Woman suffrage should be urged in my opinion not from any predictions that amount to certainty, that claim anything like certainty as to what women will do with their votes after they get them, but on the ground that by all the traditions of our government, by all the precepts of its early founders, by all the axioms that lie at the foundation of all our political principles, woman needs the ballot for herself, for self-respect on the one side and for self-protection on the other.

There was a time when whatever woman studied in school the idea of teaching her the principles of government, of her studying political economy, would have seemed an absurdity ; it was hardly thought of. Her path lay outside of it. She was not brought in contact with it. There was no loss of self-respect in those days to her in finding that in every great system of government she was omitted, and that, as Tennyson says in his " Princess," in every great revolution

" Millions of throats would bawl for civil rights;
  No woman named."

How is it now ? Go into the nearest grammar school tomorrow and what may you happen upon ? A mixed class of boys and girls reciting the constitution of the United States, or some one of the various manuals upon the history of politics or the organization of our government—reciting it to-

gether, side by side, perhaps reciting it to a woman. Or
you may go even into a college sometimes and find a whole
class of young men reciting to their teacher in political economy out of a handbook written by a woman, Millicent Gar-
rett Fawcett.

After those boys and girls have attained their maturity
and voting day comes, then they separate as they come near
the voting-place, and every boy goes inside the door to put
what he has learned in the school, of that teacher, into practice; and the girls and their teacher pass along, powerless to
express in action a single one of the principles they have
been so studiously learning. I have watched that thing and
wondered how women could bear it as they do; and at last
I encountered one woman who seemed to me to take on the
whole the most sensible view I ever encountered in the matter, who told me that again and again on election day she
had gone out and walked up and down opposite the voting-
place in her ward with tears streaming from her eyes to see
every ignoramus and every drunkard in the neighborhood
going in there to cast his vote, and she, a woman, unable to
do anything to counteract it.

This is what I mean by a woman needing the ballot for
self-respect. She comes to the centennial celebrations here
—I forget just which the last one was that they had in
Philadelphia but they have them every few years—she hears
the great names cited, the great authorities, she goes home
and she looks up what those authorities said, how they defined civil government or how they defined freedom. She
takes Benjamin Franklin for instance, " that eminent Phila-
delphian," as he is called in Philadelphia; " that eminent
Bostonian who temporarily resided in Philadelphia," as they
call him in Boston. She looks in his writings and she finds

that great statesman saying, about 1770, so distinctly that
words cannot make it clearer, that " they who have no voice
nor vote in the electing of representatives do not enjoy
liberty but are absolutely enslaved to those who have votes
and to their representatives." And what is the woman to
think of that?

Fifty years ago the man who was long considered the leading jurist of the West, Judge Timothy Walker, of Cincinnati, when asked " What is the legal position of woman in
America ? " said, " Write out as best you can the definition
of legal slavery and when you have done that you have the
legal position of a woman." The woman finds that; she sees
such statements as that earlier or later. How can she feel?
How can she help feeling that same loss of self-respect
which a Jewish woman of the Jewish faith in old times could
hardly help feeling when she heard men giving thanks to
the Lord that they were not born women and heard women
with humble voices saying, " I thank thee, Lord, that thou
hast made me according to thy will ? "

How could she help feeling as she would feel in a Moham-
medan country when she found that in the great and most
sacred mosques the edict was that no idiot, lunatic, or woman
can enter here. The woman of old times who did not
read books of political economy or attend public meetings
could retain her self-respect; but the woman of modern
times with every step she takes in the higher education finds
it harder to retain that self-respect while she is in a republican government and yet not a member of it. She can study
all the books that I saw collected this morning in the political
economy alcove of the Bryn Mawr College; she can read
them all; she can master them all; she can know more about
them perhaps than any man she knows; and yet to put one

thing she has learned there in practice by the simple process of putting a piece of paper into a ballot-box—she could no more do that than she could put out her slender finger and stop the planet in its course. That is what I mean by woman's needing woman suffrage for self-respect.

Then as to self-protection. In what does protection consist for us Americans? In the power of writing a remonstrance in the newspaper when the conductor of a train does not stop as he promised or when an ash barrel is not taken at the proper moment from before our back door? Is that the power that we have for self-protection? It is indeed the beginning of power. It is power because it has the ballot behind it; because the street department and the railroad department know that they have to do with that part of the community who have votes to back up what they say. Take away those votes and how little is the power.

The woman has the voice but not the vote. We know that there have been great changes in the position of woman, great improvements in the law in regard to women. What brought about those improvements? The steady labor of women like those on this platform, going before legislatures year by year and asking those legislatures to give them something they were not willing to give, the ballot; but as a result of it to keep the poor creatures quiet some law was passed removing a restriction. The old English writer, Pepys, in his diary, after spending a good deal of money for himself, finds a little left and buys his wife a new gown because he says, " It is fit the poor wretch should have something to content her." I have seen many laws passed for the advantage of women and they were generally passed on that principle.

I remember going before the legislature of Rhode Island

once with Lucy Stone, and she unrolled with her peculiar persuasive power the wrong laws that existed in that Commonwealth in regard to women and after the hearing was over the chairman of the committee, a judge who has served for years on that committee, came down and said to her, " I have come to say to you, Mrs. Stone, that all you have said this morning is true, and that I am ashamed to think that I who have been chairman for years of this judiciary committee should have known in my secret heart that it was all true and should have done nothing to set those wrongs right until I was reminded of it by a woman."

Again and again I have seen that experience. Women with bleeding feet, women with exhausted voices, women with worn-out lives have lavished their strength to secure ordinary justice in the form of laws, which a single woman inside the State House, a single woman there armed with the position of member of the legislature and representing a sex who had votes could have got righted within two years.

Every man knows the weakness of a disfranchised class of men. The whole race of women is disfranchised and they suffer in the same way. It is not that men are so selfish. It is not that they intend to do so much wrong to women; but any of you who have served in a legislative body as I have know how difficult a thing it is to get attention for anything or any class of persons not represented on the floor; while a single person who stands on the floor clothed with his rights, with the other persons who have rights behind him, can command attention though he be in the smallest minority. A single naturalized citizen in the legislature can secure justice for all naturalized citizens. A single Roman Catholic member can secure justice for all Roman Catholic citizens; because though he may have been personally in the minority he represents votes behind him.

The woman represents no votes and she is weak. The best laws that are made for her in any State in the Union are no sure guarantee for her. They may be altered at any time so long as she is not there to speak for herself. Some Russian emperor, when he was told by an admirer, "Your Majesty, what do your people need of a constitution? Your Majesty is as good as a constitution to your people," said, "Then I am but a happy accident; that is all."

The best legislation women can get is nothing more than a happy accident unless women are there to defend it after they have got it. Again and again things have been given to them after the labor of years, and, perhaps, those same things have been taken from them.

In the legislature of New York women were vested with the power a few years ago to control their own offspring as against the will of a dead father. A year or two passed by, the law was revoked and the power was lost. For several years back in Massachusetts a married woman has had the right under the law to dispose by will of five thousand dollars' worth of real estate if held in her own name. The woman who had saved up her own earnings, who had made her own investments, who held real estate in her own name, could, to the extent of five thousand dollars, dispose of it by will.

The last legislature, as that keen observer, Mr. Sewell, tells us, by striking out a single word in a single statute, the word "intestate," took away that power and the woman no longer can dispose of her five thousand dollars. No attention was attracted, no agitation came because there was no woman there to take it up and call attention to it.

I served two years in the Massachusetts legislature and I
remember that during one of those years there came up a
bill which attracted very little attention in regard to the
right of settlement in our towns. The point seemed a little
complicated and I passed it by, being busy with other matters; but an official at the State House, Mr. H. B. Wheel-
wright, an official of the Board of State Charities, a man of
great experience, came to me and said, " Do you understand
that bill? " I said, " No. I was engaged on other matters
and paid but little attention to it." He said, " Let me explain it to you." He sat down and explained it to me and
showed me that should that bill pass hundreds of women in
our factory towns in Massachusetts would fail of obtaining, as
they had heretofore obtained under certain conditions, a
settlement in those towns.

I asked those around me if they had noticed it. They had
not. I found on investigation that the bill had come from
the representatives of a certain town and that the whole bill
was got up to meet a certain particular case. It was to relieve the overseers of the poor in that town from the duty
of disposing of a single family; and for the sake of that, by
this bill, thus quietly introduced, hundreds and perhaps thousands of women would suffer.

I took the points that he gave me, I made the statement,
becoming simply his mouthpiece in the matter, and the bill
was easily defeated. But had a single woman been on the
floor herself to take note of the bills that came up that concerned her sex do you suppose a bill like that would have
come as it did near to passage? If there is anything that is
sure in public affairs it is that we can trust people to look
after themselves.

I remember I was speaking of the ignorance of the men

recently naturalized who had been before the Bureau of State Charities, and another State House official said to me, "There is not an emigrant however ignorant he may be who after he has lived six months in Massachusetts, fails to understand three sets of laws as well as you or I do; the settlement laws, the pauper laws, and the penal laws. They understand it whether we do or not." Self-interest is what sharpens. When you get women voting and not till then will you have women substantially and permanently protected.

It is for the self-respect and self-protection of women that I want woman suffrage. If they vote for good temperance laws, so much the better. If they make property secure, so much the better. But the real need of the suffrage is for women themselves. Self-respect and self-protection, these are what the demand rests upon; and in proportion as we concede to that demand we shall have a nation that also has for its reward self-protection and self-respect.

How long will women have to point out these things? How long will men with feebler voices, because less personal and less absorbingly interested, have to aid them in pointing them out? It is not enough to have our material successes. It is not enough to have the magnificent record of our long civil war and of the period of reconstruction that has followed. This nation won the respect of the world by its career in war. What it has now before it is so to legislate for equal justice as to retain the world's respect during coming centuries of happy peace.

CURTIS

GEORGE WILLIAM CURTIS was born in Providence, Rhode Island, in 1824. After attending school at Jamaica Plain, Massachusetts, he removed to New York with his father in 1839, and was for a time engaged in mercantile pursuits. In 1842 he became a member of the Brook Farm Community in Massachusetts. Four years later he went abroad, and travelled some years in Germany, Italy, Syria and Egypt. Returning to America in 1850, he became a writer for the "New York Tribune," and two years later was made one of the editors of "Putnam's Monthly." He entered with fervor into the anti-slavery contest, speaking for the Republicans in 1856, and delivering in that year a memorable oration on the duty of the American scholar to politics. From 1857 until his death he was the editor-in-chief of "Harper's Weekly," and contributed to "Harper's Monthly" the series of papers known as the "Editor's Easy Chair." In his later years he was particularly eminent as an advocate of Civil Service Reform. In 1871 he was appointed by President Grant a member of a commission to draw up rules for the regulation of the civil service, and for some years before his death he was President of the National Civil Service Reform Association. For several years, also, he was Chancellor of the University of the State of New York. He died in 1892.

ON THE SPOILS SYSTEM AND THE PROGRESS OF CIVIL SERVICE REFORM [1]

TWELVE years ago I read a paper before this association upon reform in the Civil Service. The subject was of very little interest. A few newspapers which were thought to be visionary occasionally discussed it, but the press of both parties smiled with profound indifference. Mr. Jenckes had pressed it upon an utterly listless Con-

---

[1] An address delivered before the American Social Science Association at its meeting in Saratoga, New York, September 8, 1881.

gress, and his proposition was regarded as the harmless hobby of an amiable man, from which a little knowledge of practical politics would soon dismount him. The English reform, which was by far the most significant political event in that country since the Parliamentary Reform Bill of 1832, was virtually unknown to us. To the general public it was necessary to explain what the Civil Service was, how it was recruited, what the abuses were, and how and why they were to be remedied. Old professional politicians, who look upon reform as Dr. Johnson defined patriotism, as the last refuge of a scoundrel, either laughed at what they called the politics of idiocy and the moon, or sneered bitterly that reformers were cheap hypocrites who wanted other people's places and lamented other people's sins.

This general public indifference was not surprising. The great reaction of feeling which followed the war, the relaxation of the long-strained anxiety of the nation for its own existence, the exhaustion of the vast expenditure of life and money, and the satisfaction with the general success, had left little disposition to do anything but secure in the national polity the legitimate results of the great contest. To the country, reform was a proposition to reform evils of administration of which it knew little, and which, at most, seemed to it petty and impertinent in the midst of great affairs. To Congress, it was apparently a proposal to deprive members of the patronage which to many of them was the real gratification of their position, the only way in which they felt their distinction and power. To such members reform was a plot to deprive the bear of his honey, the dog of his bone, and they stared and growled incredulously.

This was a dozen years ago. To-day the demand for reform is imperative. The drop has become a deluge.

Leading journals of both parties eagerly proclaim its urgent necessity. From New England to California public opinion is organizing itself in reform associations. In the great custom-house and the great post-office of the country—those in the city of New York—reform has been actually begun upon definite principles and with remarkable success, and the good example has been followed elsewhere with the same results. A bill carefully prepared and providing for gradual and thorough reform has been introduced with an admirable report in the Senate of the United States. Mr. Pendleton, the Democratic Senator from Ohio, declares that the Spoils System which has debauched the Civil Service of fifty millions of people must be destroyed. Mr. Dawes, the Republican Senator from Massachusetts, summons all good citizens to unite to suppress this gigantic evil which threatens the Republic. Conspicuous reformers sit in the Cabinet; and in this sorrowful moment, at least, the national heart and mind and conscience, stricken and bowed by a calamity whose pathos penetrates every household in Christendom, cries to these warning words, "Amen! Amen!" Like the slight sound amid the frozen silence of the Alps that loosens and brings down the avalanche, the solitary pistol shot of the 2d of July has suddenly startled this vast accumulation of public opinion into conviction, and on every side thunders the rush and roar of its overwhelming descent, which will sweep away the host of evils bred of this monstrous abuse.

This is an extraordinary change for twelve years, but it shows the vigorous political health, the alert common-sense, and the essential patriotism of the country, which are the earnest of the success of any wise reform. The war which naturally produced the lassitude and indifference to

the subject which were evident twelve years ago had made
reform, indeed, a vital necessity, but the necessity was not
then perceived. The dangers that attend a vast system of
administration based to its least detail upon personal patronage were not first exposed by Mr. Jenckes in 1867, but
before that time they had been mainly discussed as possibilities and inferences. Yet the history of the old New
York council of appointment had illustrated in that State
the party fury and corruption which patronage necessarily
breeds, and Governor McKean in Pennsylvania, at the close
of the last century, had made "a clean sweep" of the places
within his power. The spoils spirit struggled desperately
to obtain possession of the national administration from the
day of Jefferson's inauguration to that of Jackson's, when
it succeeded. Its first great but undesigned triumph was
the decision of the First Congress in 1789, vesting the sole
power of removal in the President, a decision which placed
almost every position in the Civil Service unconditionally
at his pleasure. This decision was determined by the
weight of Madison's authority. But Webster, nearly fifty
years afterward, opposing his authority to that of Madison,
while admitting the decision to have been final, declared it
to have been wrong. The year 1820, which saw the great
victory of slavery in the Missouri Compromise, was also
the year in which the second great triumph of the spoils
system was gained, by the passage of the law which, under
the plea of securing greater responsibility in certain financial offices, limited such offices to a term of four years.
The decision of 1789, which gave the sole power of removal
to the President, required positive executive action to effect
removal; but this law of 1820 vacated all the chief financial
offices, with all the places dependent upon them, during the

term of every President, who, without an order of removal, could fill them all at his pleasure.

A little later a change in the method of nominating the President from a Congressional caucus to a national convention still further developed the power of patronage as a party resource, and in the session of 1825-26, when John Quincy Adams was President, Mr. Benton introduced his report upon Mr. Macon's resolution declaring the necessity of reducing and regulating executive patronage; although Mr. Adams, the last of the Revolutionary line of Presidents, so scorned to misuse patronage that he leaned backward in standing erect. The pressure for the overthrow of the constitutional system had grown steadily more angry and peremptory with the progress of the country, the development of party spirit, the increase of patronage, the unanticipated consequences of the sole executive power of removal, and the immense opportunity offered by the four-years law. It was a pressure against which Jefferson held the gates by main force, which was relaxed by the war under Madison and the fusion of parties under Monroe, but which swelled again into a furious torrent as the later parties took form. John Quincy Adams adhered, with the tough tenacity of his father's son, to the best principles of all his predecessors. He followed Washington, and observed the spirit of the Constitution in refusing to remove for any reason but official misconduct or incapacity. But he knew well what was coming, and with characteristically stinging sarcasm he called General Jackson's inaugural address "a threat of reform." With Jackson's administration in 1830 the deluge of the spoils system burst over our national politics. Sixteen years later, Mr. Buchanan said in a public speech that General Taylor would be faithless to the

Whig party if he did not proscribe Democrats. So high the deluge had risen which has ravaged and wasted our politics ever since, and the danger will be stayed only when every President, leaning upon the law, shall stand fast where John Quincy Adams stood.

But the debate continued during the whole Jackson administration. In the Senate and on the stump, in elaborate reports and popular speeches, Webster, Calhoun, and Clay, the great political chiefs of their time, sought to alarm the country with the dangers of patronage. Sargent S. Prentiss, in the House of Representatives, caught up and echoed the cry under the administration of Van Buren. But the country refused to be alarmed. As the Yankee said of the Americans at the battle of White Plains, where they were beaten, "The fact is, as far as I can understand, our folks didn't seem to take no sort of interest in that battle." The reason that the country took no sort of interest in the discussion of the evils of patronage was evident. It believed the denunciation to be a mere party cry, a scream of disappointment and impotence from those who held no places and controlled no patronage. It heard the leaders of the opposition fiercely arraigning the administration for proscription and universal wrong-doing, but it was accustomed by its English tradition and descent always to hear the Tories cry that the Constitution was in danger when the Whigs were in power, and the Whigs under a Tory administration to shout that all was lost. It heard the uproar like the old lady upon her first railroad journey, who sat serene amid the wreck of a collision, and when asked if she was much hurt, looked over her spectacles and answered, blandly, "Hurt? Why, I supposed they always stopped so in this kind of travelling." The feeling that the denunciation was only a part of the game of politics, and no more to be accepted as a true statement than Snug the joiner as a true lion, was confirmed by the fact that when the Whig opposition came into power with President Harrison, it adopted the very policy which under Democratic administration it had strenuously denounced as fatal. The pressure for place was even greater than it had been twelve years before, and although Mr. Webster as Secretary of State maintained his consistency by putting his name to an executive order asserting sound principles, the order was swept away like a lamb by a locomotive. Nothing but a miracle, said General Harrison's attorney-general, can feed the swarm of hungry office-seekers.

Adopted by both parties, Mr. Marcy's doctrine that the places in the public service are the proper spoils of a victorious party, was accepted as a necessary condition of popular government. One of the highest officers of the government expounded this doctrine to me long afterward. "I believe," said he, "that when the people vote to change a party administration they vote to change every person of the opposite party who holds a place, from the President of the United States to the messenger at my door." It is this extraordinary but sincere misconception of the function of party in a free government that leads to the serious defence of the Spoils System. Now, a party is merely a voluntary association of citizens to secure the enforcement of a certain policy of administration upon which they are agreed. In a free government this is done by the election of legislators and of certain executive officers who are friendly to that policy. But the duty of the great body of persons employed in the minor administrative places is in no sense political. It is wholly ministerial, and the political opinions of such persons affect the discharge of their duties no more than their religious views or their literary preferences. All that can be justly required of such persons, in the interest of the public business, is honesty, intelligence, capacity, industry, and due subordination; and to say that, when the policy of the government is changed by the result of an election from protection to free trade, every bookkeeper and letter-carrier and messenger and porter in the public offices ought to be a free trader, is as wise as to say that if a merchant is a Baptist every clerk in his office ought to be a believer in total immersion. But the officer of whom I spoke undoubtedly expressed the general feeling. The necessarily evil consequences of the practice which he justified seemed to be still speculative and inferential, and to the national indifference which followed the war the demand of Mr. Jenckes for reform appeared to be a mere whimsical vagary most inopportunely introduced.

It was, however, soon evident that the war had made the necessity of reform imperative, and chiefly for two reasons: first, the enormous increase of patronage, and second, the fact that circumstances had largely identified a party name with patriotism. The great and radical evil of the spoils system was carefully fostered by the apparent absolute necessity to the public welfare of making political opinion and sympathy a condition of appointment to the smallest place. It is since the war, therefore, that the evil has run riot and that its consequences have been fully revealed. Those consequences are now familiar, and I shall not describe them. It is enough that the most patriotic and intelligent Americans and the most competent foreign observers agree that the direct and logical results of that system are the dangerous confusion of the executive and legislative powers of the government; the conversion of politics into mere place-hunting; the extension of the mischief to State and county and city administration, and the consequent degradation of the national character; the practical disfranchisement of the people wherever the system is most powerful; and the perversion of a republic of equal citizens into a despotism of venal politicians. These are the greatest dangers that can threaten a republic, and they are due to the practice of treating the vast system of minor public places which are wholly ministerial, and whose duties are the same under every party administration, not as public trusts, but as party perquisites. The English-speaking race has a grim sense of humor, and the absurdity of transacting the public business of a great nation in a way which would ruin both the trade and the character of a small huckster, of proceeding upon the theory—for such is the theory of the Spoils System—that a man should be put in charge of a locomotive because he holds certain views of original sin, or because he polishes boots nimbly with his tongue—it is a folly so stupendous and grotesque that when it is fully perceived by the shrewd mother-wit of the Yankee it will be laughed indignantly and contemptuously away. But the laugh must have the method, and the indignation the form, of law; and now that the public mind is aroused to the true nature and tendency of the Spoils System is the time to consider the practicable legal remedy for them.

The whole system of appointments in the Civil Service proceeds from the President, and in regard to his action the intention of the Constitution is indisputable. It is that the President shall appoint solely upon public considerations, and that the officer appointed shall serve as long as he discharges his duty faithfully. This is shown in Mr. Jefferson's familiar phrase in his reply to the remonstrance of the merchants of New Haven against the removal of the collector of that port. Mr. Jefferson asserted that Mr. Adams had purposely appointed in the last moments of his administration officers whose designation he should have left to his successor. Alluding to these appointments, he says: "I shall correct the procedure, and that done, return with joy to that state of things when the only question concerning a candidate shall be, Is he honest? Is he capable? Is he faithful to the Constitution?" Mr. Jefferson here recognizes that these had been the considerations which had usually determined appointments; and Mr. Madison, in the debate upon the President's sole power of removal, declared that if a President should remove an officer for any reason not connected with efficient service he would be impeached. Reform, therefore, is merely a return to the principle and purpose of the Constitution and to the practice of the early administrations.

What more is necessary, then, for reform than that the President should return to that practice? As all places in the Civil Service are filled either by his direct nomination or by officers whom he appoints, why has not any President ample constitutional authority to effect at any moment a complete and thorough reform? The answer is simple. He has the power. He has always had it. A President has only to do as Washington did, and all his successors have only to do likewise, and reform would be complete. Every President has but to refuse to remove non-political officers for political or personal reasons; to appoint only those whom he knows to be competent; to renominate, as Monroe and John Quincy Adams did, every faithful officer whose commission expires, and to require the heads of departments and all inferior appointing officers to conform to this practice, and the work would be done. This is apparently a short and easy and constitutional method of reform, requiring no further legislation or scheme of procedure. But why has no President adopted it? For the same reason that the best of Popes does not reform the abuses of his Church. For the same reason that a leaf goes over Niagara. It is because the opposing forces are overpowering. The same high officer of the government to whom I have alluded said to me as we drove upon the Heights of Washington, "Do you mean that I ought not to appoint my subordinates for whom I am responsible?" I answered: "I mean that you do not appoint them now; I mean that if, when we return to the capital, you hear that your chief subordinate is dead, you will not appoint his successor. You will have to choose among the men urged upon you by certain powerful politicians. Undoubtedly you ought to appoint the man whom you believe to be the most fit. But you do not and cannot. If you could or did appoint such men only, and that were the rule of your department and of the service, there would be no need of reform." And he could not deny it. There was no law to prevent his selection of the best man. Indeed, the law assumed that he would do it. The Constitution intended that he should do it. But when I reminded him that there were forces beyond the law that paralyzed the intention of the Constitution, and which would inevitably compel him to accept the choice of others, he said no more.

It is easy to assert that the reform of the Civil Service is an executive reform. So it is. But the Executive alone cannot accomplish it. The abuses are now completely and aggressively organized, and the sturdiest President would quail before them. The President who should undertake, single-handed, to deal with the complication of administrative evils known as the Spoils System would find his party leaders in Congress and their retainers throughout the country arrayed against him; the proposal to disregard traditions and practices which are regarded as essential to the very existence and effectiveness of party organization would be stigmatized as treachery, and the President himself would be covered with odium as a traitor. The air would hum with denunciation. The measures he should favor, the appointments he might make, the recommendations of his secretaries, would be opposed and imperilled, and the success of his administration would be endangered. A President who should alone undertake thoroughly to reform the evil must feel it to be the vital and paramount issue, and must be willing to hazard everything for its success. He must have the absolute faith and the indomitable will of Luther. "Here stand I; I can no other." How can we expect a President whom this system elects to devote himself to its destruction? General Grant, elected by a spontaneous patriotic impulse, fresh from the regulated order of military life and new to politics and politicians, saw the reason and the necessity of reform. The hero of a victorious war, at the height of his popularity, his party in undisputed and seemingly indisputable supremacy, made the attempt. Congress, good-naturedly tolerating what it considered his whim of inexperience, granted money to try an experiment. The adverse pressure was tremendous. "I am used to pressure," said the soldier. So he was, but not to this pressure. He was driven by unknown and incalculable currents. He was enveloped in whirlwinds of sophistry, scorn, and incredulity. He who upon his own line had fought it out all summer to victory, upon a line absolutely new and unknown was naturally bewildered and dismayed. So Wellington had drawn the lines of victory on the Spanish Peninsula and had saved Europe at Waterloo. But even Wellington

K at Waterloo could not be also Sir Robert Peel at Westminster. Even Wellington, who had overthrown Napoleon in the field, could not also be the parliamentary hero who for the welfare of his country would dare to risk the overthrow of his party. When at last President Grant said, "If Congress adjourns without positive legislation on Civil Service reform, I shall regard such action as a disapproval of the system and shall abandon it," it was, indeed, a surrender, but it was the surrender of a champion who had honestly mistaken both the nature and the strength of the adversary and his own power of endurance.

It is not, then, reasonable, under the conditions of our government and in the actual situation, to expect a President to go much faster or much further than public opinion. But executive action can aid most effectively the development and movement of that opinion, and the most decisive reform measures that the present administration might take would be undoubtedly supported by a powerful public sentiment. The educative results of resolute executive action, however limited and incomplete in scope, have been shown in the two great public offices of which I have spoken, the New York Custom House and the New York Post-office. For nearly three years the entire practicability of reform has been demonstrated in those offices, and solely by the direction of the President. The value of such demonstrations, due to the Executive will alone, carried into effect by thoroughly trained and interested subordinates, cannot be overestimated. But when they depend upon the will of a transient officer and not upon a strong public conviction, they are seeds that have no depth of soil. A vital and enduring reform in administrative methods, although it be but a return to the constitutional intention, can be accomplished only by the commanding impulse of public opinion. Permanence is secured by law, not by individual pleasure. But in this country law is only formulated public opinion. Reform of the Civil Service does not contemplate an invasion of the constitutional prerogative of the President and the Senate, nor does it propose to change the Constitution by statute. The whole system of the Civil Service proceeds, as I said, from the President, and the object of the reform movement is to enable him to fulfil the intention of the Constitution by revealing to him the desire of the country through the action of its authorized representatives. When the ground-swell of public opinion lifts Congress from the rocks, the President will gladly float with it into the deep water of wise and patriotic action. The President, indeed, has never been the chief sinner in the Spoils System, although he has been the chief agent. Even President Jackson yielded to party pressure as much as to his own convictions. President Harrison sincerely wished to stay the flood, but it swept him away. President Grant doubtfully and with good intentions tested the pressure before yielding. President Hayes, with sturdy independence, adhered inflexibly to a few points, but his party chiefs cursed and derided him. President Garfield—God bless and restore him!—frankly declares permanent and effective reform to be impossible without the consent of Congress. When, therefore, Congress obeys a commanding public opinion, and reflects it in legislation, it will restore to the President the untrammelled exercise of his ample constitutional powers according to the constitutional intention; and the practical question of reform is, How shall this be brought about?

Now, it is easy to kill weeds if we can destroy their roots, and it is not difficult to determine what the principle of reform legislation should be if we can agree upon the source of the abuses to be reformed. May they not have a common origin? In fact, are they not all bound together as parts of one system? The Representative in Congress, for instance, does not ask whether the interests of the public service require this removal or that appointment, but whether, directly or indirectly, either will best serve his own interests. The Senator acts from the same motives. The President, in turn, balances between the personal interests of leading politicians—President, Senators, and Representatives all wishing to pay for personal service and to conciliate personal influence. So also the party labor required of the place-holder, the task of carrying caucuses, of defeating one man and electing another, as may be ordered, the payment of the assessment levied upon his salary—all these are the price of the place. They are the taxes paid by him as conditions of receiving a personal favor. Thus the abuses have a common source, whatever may be the plea for the system from which they spring. Whether it be urged that the system is essential to party organization, or that the desire for place is a laudable political ambition, or that the Spoils System is a logical development of our political philosophy, or that new brooms sweep clean, or that any other system is un-American—whatever the form of the plea for the abuse, the conclusion is always the same, that the minor places in the Civil Service are not public trusts, but rewards and prizes for personal and political favorites.

The root of the complex evil, then, is personal favoritism. This produces Congressional dictation, Senatorial usurpation, arbitrary removals, interference in elections, political assessments, and all the consequent corruption, degradation, and danger that experience has disclosed. The method of reform, therefore, must be a plan of selection for appointment which makes favoritism impossible. The general feeling undoubtedly is that this can be accomplished by a fixed limited term. But the terms of most of the offices to which the President and the Senate appoint, and upon which the myriad minor places in the service depend, have been fixed and limited for sixty years, yet it is during that very period that the chief evils of personal patronage have appeared. The law of 1820, which limited the term of important revenue offices to four years, and which was afterward extended to other offices, was intended, as John Quincy Adams tells us, to promote the election to the presidency of Mr. Crawford, who was then Secretary of the Treasury. The law was drawn by Mr. Crawford himself, and it was introduced into the Senate by one of his devoted partisans. It placed the whole body of executive financial officers at the mercy of the Secretary of the Treasury and of a majority of the Senate, and its design, as Mr. Adams says, "was to secure for Mr. Crawford the influence of all the incumbents in office, at the peril of displacement, and of five or ten times an equal number of ravenous office-seekers, eager to supplant them." This is the very substance of the Spoils System, intentionally introduced by a fixed limitation of term in place of the constitutional tenure of

efficient service; and it was so far successful that it made
the custom house officers, district attorneys, marshals, regis-
ters of the land office, receivers of public money, and even
paymasters in the army, notoriously active partisans of Mr.
Crawford. Mr. Benton says that the four-years law merely
made the dismissal of faithful officers easier, because the
expiration of the term was regarded as "the creation of a
vacancy to be filled by new appointments."   A fixed limited term for the chief offices has not destroyed or modified
personal influence, but, on the contrary, it has fostered
universal servility and loss of self-respect, because reappointment depends, not upon official fidelity and efficiency,
but upon personal influence and favor.   To fix by law the
terms of places dependent upon such offices would be like
an attempt to cure hydrophobia by the bite of a mad dog.
The incumbent would be always busy keeping his influence
in repair to secure reappointment, and the applicant would
be equally busy in seeking such influence to procure the
place, and as the fixed terms would be constantly expiring,
the eager and angry intrigue and contest of influence would
be as endless as it is now.   This certainly would not be
reform.

But would not reform be secured by adding to a fixed
limited term the safeguard of removal for cause only?   Removal for cause alone means, of course, removal for legitimate cause, such as dishonesty, negligence, or incapacity.
But who shall decide that such cause exists?   This must
be determined either by the responsible superior officer or
by some other authority.   But if left to some other authority the right of counsel and the forms of a court would be
invoked; the whole legal machinery of mandamuses, injunc-
tions, certioraris, and the rules of evidence would be put in

play to keep an incompetent clerk at his desk or a sleepy
watchman on his beat. Cause for the removal of a letter-
carrier in the post-office or of an accountant in the custom
house would be presented with all the pomp of impeachment
and established like a high crime and misdemeanor. Thus
every clerk in every office would have a kind of vested interest in his place because, however careless, slovenly, or
troublesome he might be, he could be displaced only by
an elaborate and doubtful legal process. Moreover, if the
head of a bureau or a collector, or a postmaster were
obliged to prove negligence, or insolence, or incompetency
against a clerk as he would prove theft, there would be no
removals from the public service except for crimes of which
the penal law takes cognizance. Consequently, removal
would be always and justly regarded as a stigma upon
character, and a man removed from a position in a public
office would be virtually branded as a convicted criminal.
Removal for cause, therefore, if the cause were to be decided by any authority but that of the responsible superior
officer, instead of improving, would swiftly and enormously
enhance the cost, and ruin the efficiency, of the public service, by destroying subordination, and making every lazy
and worthless member of it twice as careless and incompetent as he is now.

If, then, the legitimate cause for removal ought to be
determined in public as in private business by the responsible appointing power, it is of the highest public necessity
that the exercise of that power should be made as absolutely honest and independent as possible. But how can
it be made honest and independent if it is not protected so
far as practicable from the constant bribery of selfish interest and the illicit solicitation of personal influence? The

experience of our large patronage offices proves conclusively that the cause of the larger number of removals is not dishonesty or incompetency; it is the desire to make vacancies to fill. This is the actual cause, whatever cause may be assigned. The removals would not be made except for the pressure of politicians. But those politicians would not press for removals if they could not secure the appointment of their favorites. Make it impossible for them to secure appointment, and the pressure would instantly disappear and arbitrary removal cease.

So long, therefore, as we permit minor appointments to be made by mere personal influence and favor, a fixed limited term and removal during that term for cause only would not remedy the evil, because the incumbents would still be seeking influence to secure reappointment, and the aspirants doing the same to replace them. Removal under plea of good cause would be as wanton and arbitrary as it is now, unless the power to remove were intrusted to some other discretion than that of the superior officer, and in that case the struggle for reappointment and the knowledge that removal for the term was practically impossible would totally demoralize the service. To make sure, then, that removals shall be made for legitimate cause only, we must provide that appointment shall be made only for legitimate cause.

All roads lead to Rome. Personal influence in appointments can be annulled only by free and open competition. By that bridge we can return to the practice of Washington and to the intention of the Constitution. That is the shoe of swiftness and the magic sword by which the President can pierce and outrun the protean enemy of sophistry and tradition which prevents him from asserting his power. If you say that success in a competitive literary examination

does not prove fitness to adjust customs duties, or to distribute letters, or to appraise linen, or to measure molasses,
I answer that the reform does not propose that fitness shall
be proved by a competitive literary examination. It proposes to annul personal influence and political favoritism
by making appointment depend upon proved capacity. To
determine this it proposes first to test the comparative general intelligence of all applicants and their special knowledge of the particular official duties required, and then to
prove the practical faculty of the most intelligent applicants
by actual trial in the performance of the duties before they
are appointed. If it be still said that success in such a competition may not prove fitness, it is enough to reply that
success in obtaining the favor of some kind of boss, which
is the present system, presumptively proves unfitness.

Nor is it any objection to the reformed system that many
efficient officers in the service could not have entered it had
it been necessary to pass an examination; it is no objection,
because their efficiency is a mere chance. They were not
appointed because of efficiency, but either because they were
diligent politicians or because they were recommended by
diligent politicians. The chance of getting efficient men in
any business is certainly not diminished by inquiry and
investigation. I have heard an officer in the army say that
he could select men from the ranks for special duty much
more satisfactorily than they could be selected by an examination. Undoubtedly he could, because he knows his men,
and he selects solely by his knowledge of their comparative
fitness. If this were true of the Civil Service, if every appointing officer chose the fittest person from those that he
knew, there would be no need of reform. It is because
he cannot do this that the reform is necessary.

It is the same kind of objection which alleges that competition is a droll plan by which to restore the conduct of the public business to business principles and methods, since no private business selects its agents by competition. But the managers of private business are virtually free from personal influence in selecting their subordinates, and they employ and promote and dismiss them solely for the interests of the business. Their choice, however, is determined by an actual, although not a formal, competition. Like the military officer, they select those whom they know by experience to be the most competent. But if great business houses and corporations were exposed to persistent, insolent, and overpowering interference and solicitation for place such as obstructs great public departments and officers, they too would resort to the form of competition, as they now have its substance, and they would resort to it to secure the very freedom which they now enjoy of selecting for fitness alone.

Mr. President, in the old Arabian story, from the little box upon the sea-shore, carelessly opened by the fisherman, arose the towering and haughty demon, ever more monstrous and more threatening, who would not crouch again. So from the small patronage of the earlier day, from a Civil Service dealing with a national revenue of only $2,000,000, and regulated upon sound business principles, has sprung the un-American, un-Democratic, un-Republican system which destroys political independence, honor, and morality, and corrodes the national character itself. In the solemn anxiety of this hour the warning words of the austere Calhoun, uttered nearly half a century ago, echo in startled recollection like words of doom: "If you do not put this thing down it will put you down." Happily it is the historic faith of the race from which we are chiefly sprung, that eternal vigilance is the price of liberty. It is that faith which has made our mother England the great parent of free States. The same faith has made America the political hope of the world. Fortunately removed by our position from the entanglements of European politics, and more united and peaceful at home than at any time within the memory of living men, the moment is most auspicious for remedying that abuse in our political system whose nature, proportions, and perils the whole country begins clearly to discern. The will and the power to apply the remedy will be a test of the sagacity and the energy of the people. The reform of which I have spoken is essentially the people's reform. With the instinct of robbers who run with the crowd and lustily cry "Stop thief!" those who would make the public service the monopoly of a few favorites denounce the determination to open that service to the whole people as a plan to establish an aristocracy. The huge ogre of patronage, gnawing at the character, the honor, and the life of the country, grimly sneers that the people cannot help themselves and that nothing can be done. But much greater things have been done. Slavery was the Giant Despair of many good men of the last generation, but slavery was overthrown. If the Spoils System, a monster only less threatening than slavery, be unconquerable, it is because the country has lost its convictions, its courage, and its common-sense. "I expect," said the Yankee as he surveyed a stout antagonist, "I expect that you're pretty ugly, but I cal'late I'm a darned sight uglier." I know that patronage is strong, but I believe that the American people are very much stronger.

HIS SOVEREIGNTY UNDER HIS HAT[1]

Gentlemen of the Convention:

A REPUBLICAN and a free man I came into this convention; by the grace of God a Republican and a free man will I go out of this convention. Twenty-four years ago I was here in Chicago. Twenty-four years ago I took part with the men of this country who nominated the man who bears the most illustrious name in the Republican party, and the brightest ray in whose halo of glory and immortality is that he was the great emancipator. In that convention, sir, a resolution was offered in amendment of the platform. It introduced into that platform certain words from the Declaration of Independence. That man was voted down in that convention, and Joshua R. Giddings, of Ohio, rose from his seat and was passing out of the convention. As he went to pass by my chair, I, well nigh a boy and unknown to him, reached out my hand and said: "Sir, where are you going?" He said to me: "Young man, I am going out of this convention, for I find there is no place in a Republican convention for an original anti-slavery man like me." Well, gentlemen, after this he stopped and again took his seat, and before the convention concluded the Republican party declared no word, no deed, no sign should ever be made in a Republican convention that in the slightest degree reflected upon the honor or the

---

[1] Delivered in the Republican National Convention, at Chicago, June 4, 1884, on the resolution offered by Mr. Hawkins, of Tennessee: "*Resolved*, As the sense of this convention, that every member of it is bound in honor to support its nominee, whoever that nominee may be, and that no man should hold a seat here who is not ready to so agree."

loyalty of the men who took part in that convention, and upon their adhesion to liberty. The gentleman who was last upon the floor dared any one upon this floor to vote against that resolution. I say to him in reply that the presentation of such a resolution in such a convention as this is a stigma, an insult, upon every man who stands here. The question is no question at all. Precisely the same motion was brought up at the last convention, and a man from West Virginia (I honor his name!) said in the face of the roaring galleries: "I am a Republican who carries his sovereignty under his own hat."

Now, Mr. Chairman, Mr. Campbell's position in that convention agreed with the wise reflection, the afterthought of the Republican convention of 1880, under the direction of that great leader whose face fronts us there, James A. Garfield, of Ohio. Under the lead of Garfield, I remind you, my friend from California, that convention, taking its action, induced the gentleman who presented the resolution to withdraw it from consideration. Now, sir, in the light of the character of the Republican party; in the light of the action of the last Republican convention, the first convention I have known in which such a pledge was required of the members; I ask this convention, mindful of all that hangs upon the wisdom, the moderation, the tolerance, and the patriotism of our action—mindful of it all I beg this convention to remember Lincoln, to remember Garfield, to remember the most vital principle of the Republican party, and assume that every man here who is an honorable man will vote this resolution down, as something which should never have appeared in a Republican convention, and as unworthy to be ratified by the concourse of free men I see before me.

THE DUTY OF THE AMERICAN SCHOLAR

DELIVERED BEFORE THE LITERARY SOCIETIES OF THE WESLEYAN
UNIVERSITY, AUGUST 5, 1856

GENTLEMEN,—The summer is our literary festival.
We are not a scholarly people, but we devote to the
honor of literature some of our loveliest days.
When the leaves are greenest, and the mower's scythe sings
through the grass; when plenty is on the earth, and splendor
in the heavens, we gather from a thousand pursuits to celebrate the jubilee of the scholar.

No man who loves literature, or who can in any way claim
the scholar's privilege, but is glad to associate the beauty of
the season with the object of the occasion; and grace with
flowers and sunshine, and universal summer, the homage
which is thus paid to the eternal interest of the human mind.

We are glad of it as scholars, because the season is the
symbol of the character and influence of scholarly pursuits.
Like sunshine, a spirit of generous thought illuminates the
world.   Like trees of golden fruit in the landscape, are the
philosophers and poets in history.   Happy the day! Happy
the place! The roses and the stars wreathe our festival with
an immortal garland.

Too young to be your guide and philosopher, I am yet old
enough to be your friend.   Too little in advance of you in
the great battle of life to teach you from experience, I am
yet old enough to share with you the profit of the experience
of other men and of history.   I do not come to-day a
mounted general.   I hurry at your call to place myself beside
you, shoulder to shoulder, a private in the ranks.   We are all

young men; we are all young Americans; we are all young American scholars. Our interests and duties are the same. I speak to you as to comrades. Let us rest a moment that we may the better fight. Here, in this beautiful valley, under these spreading trees, we bivouac for a summer hour. Our knapsacks are unslung and our arms are stacked. We give this tranquil hour to the consideration of our position and duties.

The occasion prescribes my theme; the times determine its treatment.

That theme is the scholar; the lesson of the day is the duty of the American scholar to politics.

I would gladly speak to you of the charms of pure scholarship; of the dignity and worth of the scholar; of the abstract relation of the scholar to the State. The sweet air we breathe, and the repose of mid-summer, invite a calm ethical or intellectual discourse. But, would you have counted him a friend of Greece who quietly discussed the abstract nature of patriotism on that Greek summer day through whose hopeless and immortal hours Leonidas and his three hundred stood at Thermopylæ for liberty? And, to-day, as the scholar meditates that deed, the air that steals in at his window darkens his study and suffocates him as he reads. Drifting across a continent and blighting the harvests that gild it with plenty from the Atlantic to the Mississippi, a black cloud obscures the page that records an old crime, and compels him to know that freedom always has its Thermopylæ, and that his Thermopylæ is called Kansas.

Because we are scholars of to-day, shall we shrink from touching the interests of to-day? Because we are scholars shall we cease to be citizens? Because we are scholars shall we cease to be men?

Gentlemen, I am glad that, speaking of the duty of the American scholar to the times, I can point to one who fully understands that duty, and has illustrated it, as Milton did. Among fellow countrymen, that scholar falls defending the name and rights of his countrymen; and one of those countrymen stares at him as he lies insensible, and will not raise him lest his motives be misunderstood; and another turns his back upon the bleeding colleague because for two years he has not been upon speaking terms with him. Gentlemen, the human heart is just, and no traitor to humanity escapes his proper doom. Sacred history hands down to endless infamy the priest and the Levite who passed by on the other side. Among gentlemen this scholar pleads the cause dear to every gentleman in history, and a bully strikes him down. In a republic of free men this scholar speaks for freedom, and his blood stains the senate floor. There it will blush through all our history. That damned spot will never out from memory, from tradition, or from noble hearts. Every scholar degrades his order and courts the pity of all generous men who can see a just liberty threatened, without deserting every other cause to defend liberty. Of what use are your books? Of what use is your scholarship? Without freedom of thought, there is no civilization or human progress; and without freedom of speech liberty of thought is a mockery.

I know well that a conventional prejudice consecrates this occasion to dull abstractions and timid, if not treacherous, generalities. It would allow me to speak of the scholar, and of the American scholar, in his relation to Greek roots and particles, but would forbid me to mention his duties to American topics and times. I might speak of him as a professor, a dialectician, a dictionary, a grammar, but I must not speak

of him as a man. I know that a literary orator is held to be
bound by the same decencies that regulate the preacher.
But what are those decencies? Is the preacher to rebuke
the sins of Jerusalem, or of Philadelphia? Is he to say in
general, " be good," when he sees in what particulars we are
bad, and counsel silence and peace, when silence and peace
are treason to God and man? Are the liars to cry to the
preacher, " It is not your business to denounce lying; we pay
you to preach against sin?" But the preacher's master
cried, " Woe unto you, Scribes and Pharisees, hypocrites, for
ye devour widows' houses." He specified sins and classified
sinners. In our day the hot adjuration to a clergyman not
to soil his pulpit with politics is merely the way in which the
nineteenth century offers him the thirty pieces of silver.

What are politics but the divine law applied to human
government? Politics are the science of the relation of men
in human society; and as the founder of Christianity taught
peace and good will to men, how can the Christian preacher
better fulfil his office than by showing how peace and good
will may be introduced among men, and by exposing, in all
the terror of truth, those whose policy fosters war and hatred
among men? Why does the pulpit command so little comparative respect but because it does not apply truth to life?
When the American people has great sins to account for, the
smooth preacher touches with the dull edge of his reproof
the sins of the Jewish people. Therefore, with us, the
lecture-room is more thronged than the church, because the
lecturer addresses the moral sense of the people upon their
moral interests, and the most popular lecturers are the
preachers who are most faithful in their pulpits to God and
man—for their cause is one.

What is true of the preacher is true of the orator. I

GEORGE WILLIAM CURTIS

Orations—Volume twenty

should insult your manhood, I should forget my own, if, in addressing you to-day, and here, I did not say what I conceive to be the duty of the scholar to-day, and here.

Of the scholar. The popular idea of the scholar makes him a pale student of books, a recluse, a valetudinarian, an unpractical and impracticable man. He is a being with an endless capacity of literary and scientific acquisition. He is only a consumer, not a producer; or, if so, only a producer of useless results. Learning is supposed to be put into him, not as vegetables into the ground, whence, as they spring again covering the earth with beauty and feeding the race, so learning is to flower into heroic deeds and consoling thoughts; but it is absorbed by him, as vegetables are thrown into a cellar, where they lie buried, not planted, producing only some poor, pallid, useless shoot, as his learning only germinates into some treatise upon the ablative absolute.

In the old plays and romances we have the same picture of an absent pedant, the easy prey of every knave, the docile husband of a termagant; who, because he could read a tragedy of Æschylus, could not tie his shoes. He belonged to great establishments as an encyclopædia, in the same way that the fool belonged to them as a jestbook. Scholars were popularly ranked with women, having all their weakness and none of their charms.

This estimate grew naturally out of their exceptional character as monks; for, at the beginning of modern history, learning came out of the monasteries with the ecclesiastics. By religious vows the monks were separated from all secular interests, including the family relation. The reputation of the scholar arose from the character of the monk. The monk was a man who dealt professionally with ideas rather than men. He was therefore held to know nothing of men.

Dreamer, poet, vagabond, and scholar, grew to be synony-
mous names. But while the mass of monks undoubtedly
justified this judgment, it is in the few and not in the mass
that their characteristics are to be sought; they were accused
of not knowing men, but Gregory was a monk, and they
belonged to the most sagacious organization in human
history. They were called pedants and moles, but Abèlard
and Martin Luther were churchmen and scholars. To call
grammarians, formalists, and swollen sponges of learning
scholars, is to call a parish clerk a statesman. To call
Bentley and Parr scholars is to insult Johnson and Milton.
Sydney Smith tells of Dr. George, who, hearing the great
king of Prussia highly praised, said that he had his doubts
whether the king, with all his victories, knew how to conjugate a Greek verb in *mi*. If you call Dr. George, and
Wolff, and Heyne scholars, what name have you for Goethe
and Schiller?

In any just classification of human powers and pursuits,
the scholar is the representative of thought. Devoted to the
contemplation of truth, he is, in the state, a public conscience
by which public measures may be tested; the scholarly class,
therefore, to which now, as of old, the clergy belong, is the
upper house in the politics of the world.

Now there is a constant tendency in material prosperity,
when it is the prosperity of a class and not of the mass, to
relax the severity of principle. Therefore we find that the
era of noble thought in national history is not usually coinci-
dent with the greatest national prosperity. Greece was not
greatest when rumors of war had ceased. Rome was not
most imperial in the voluptuous calm of Constantinopolitan
decay. The magnificent monotony of Bourbon tyranny in
France, and the reign of its shopkeeping king, were not the

grand eras of French history. Holland began as generously as America, and Holland has sunk into the inbeeile apathy of commercial prosperity, without art, without literature, without a noble influence in the world, and with no promise of the future.

When Napoleon reviled England as a nation of shop-keepers, it was not an idle phrase Napoleon knew that, both historically and in the nature of the case, it was the tendency of a long peace to foster trade and that it is the inevitable tendency of trade, which is based upon self-interest, to destroy moral courage, because trade demands peace at any price, and peace is often to be purchased only by principle. When he said a nation of shop-keepers, he meant a nation whose ruling principle was private gain, rather than public good; and the sagacious ruler knew that corruption and cowardice are twins.

The tendency of selfish trade is demoralizing, because its eagerness for peace constantly lowers the moral ideal. The private pocket inevitably becomes the arbiter of public policy. Plausibility supplants honesty; sophistication takes the place of simplicity, and the certain evils of the existing condition are resolutely preferred to the splendid possibilities of progress.

Thus it arises that the very material success for which nations, like individuals, strive, is full of the gravest danger to the best life of the state, as of the individual. But as in human nature itself are found the qualities which best resist the proclivity of an individual to meanness and moral cowardice; as each man has a conscience, a moral mentor which assures him what is truly best for him to do, so has every state a class, which, by its very character, is dedicated to eternal and not to temporary interests, whose members are priests of the mind, not of the body, and who are necessarily the conservative party of intellectual and moral freedom.

This is the class of scholars. This elevation and correction of public sentiment is the scholar's office in the state.

To the right discharge of this duty all his learning is merely subsidiary; and if he fail to devote it to this end he is recreant to his duty. The end of all scholarly attainment is to live nobly. If a man read books merely to know books, he is a tree planted only to blossom. If he read books to apply their wisdom to life, then he is a tree planted to bear glorious fruit. He does not think for himself alone, nor hoard a thought as a miser a diamond. He spends for the world. Scholarship is not only the knowledge that makes books, but the wisdom which inspires that knowledge. The scholar is not necessarily a learned man, but he is a wise man. If he be personally a recluse, his voice and influence are never secluded. If the man be a hermit, his mind is a citizen of the world.

If, then, such be the scholar, and the scholar's office, if he be truly the conscience of the state, the fundamental law of his life is liberty. At every cost, the true scholar asserts and defends liberty of thought and liberty of speech. Of what use to a man is a thought that will help the world, if he cannot tell it to the world? Such a thought comes to him as Jupiter came to Semele. He is consumed by the splendor that secretly possesses him. The inquisition condemns Galileo's creed. *Pur muove*—still it moves—replies Galileo in his dungeon. Tyranny poisons the cup of Socrates; he smilingly drains it to the health of the world. The church, towering vast in the midst of universal superstition, lays its withering finger upon the freedom of the human mind, and its own child, leaping from its bosom, denounces to the world his mother's madness.

I speak, of course, of the ideal scholar, of what the scholar ought to be, rather than of the historical men who have been called scholars; and yet I think we shall find the man whom we should select from history as the scholar, as also the man who most nearly fulfils the conditions I have mentioned.

In English history, which is also our history, who is the scholar? Is it Roger Ascham, a pedant and a school-master? Is it Ben Jonson with his careless, cumbrous ease, borrowing his shilling, fighting his duel, writing his plays and his stately verses, and lighting up the " Mermaid " with his witty revelry? Is it either of the churchmen—even Jeremy Taylor, whose written wisdom breathes like organ-music through English literature; or George Herbert, whose life shone with the beauty of holiness? Is it the sad Swift, the versatile Addison, the keen Pope, or the fastidious Gray, noting when crocuses opened, and roses bloomed, leaving one poem and the record of a life as inoffensive as that of a college cat; or Bentley, or Porson, or Parr, who made valuable notes on valuable Greek classics; or Dr. Johnson, gravely supporting an aristocratic public policy, while he powerfully and pathetically rebuked aristocratic private conduct? Let the name of Dr. Johnson never be mentioned among scholars without a sad respect; but is he, distinctively, the scholar in English history?

There is one man, gentlemen, I have not mentioned. Your hearts go before my tongue to name him. Technical scholarship begins in a dictionary, and ends in a grammar. The sublime scholarship of John Milton began in literature and ended in life.

Graced with every intellectual gift, he was personally so

comely that the romantic woods of Vallambrosa are lovelier
from their association with his youthful figure sleeping in
their shade. He had all the technical excellences of the
scholar. At eighteen he wrote better Latin verses than have
ever been written in England. He replied to the Italian
poets who complimented him in purer Italian than their own.
He was profoundly skilled in theology, in science, and in the
pure literature of all languages.

These were his accomplishments, but his genius was vast
and vigorous. While yet a youth, he wrote those minor
poems, which have the simple perfection of productions of
nature; and, in the ripeness of his wisdom and power, he
turned his blind eyes to heaven, and sang the lofty song
which has given him a twin glory with Shakespeare in English renown.

It is much for one man to have exhausted the literature of
other nations and to have enriched his own. But other men
have done this in various degrees. Milton went beyond it
to complete the circle of his character as the scholar.

You know the culmination of his life. The first scholar
in England, and in the world at that time, fulfilled his office.
His vocation making him especially the representative of
liberty, he accepted the part to which he was naturally called,
and, turning away from all the blandishments of ease and
fame, he gave himself to liberty and immortality.

Is the scholar a puny, timid, conforming man? John
Milton showed him to be the greatest citizen of the greatest
commonwealth. Disdaining to talk of the liberty of the
Shunammites when the liberty of Englishmen was imperilled,
he exposed the details of a blind tyranny in words which are
still the delight and refuge of freedom; and whose music is
majestic as the cause they celebrate. The radiance of those

principles is still the glory of history. They still search out and expose the wiles of tyranny, as the light of a great beacon, flashing at midnight upon the mountain top, reveals the tents of the enemy skulking on the plain.

While the men of Norfolk, and of the fens, were mustering to march away for liberty—to return no more—he did not stay to conjugate Greek verbs in *mi*, nor conceive that the scholar's library was his post of honor. In words that are the eternal rebuke of every scholar, of every literary man, of every clergyman, who, in a day when human liberty is threatened, does not stand for liberty, but cringes under the courtesies of position, Milton cries to us across two hundred years, with a voice of multitudinous music, like that of a great wind in a forest: "I cannot praise a fugitive and cloistered virtue, unexercised and unbreathed, that never sallies out and sees her adversary, but slinks out of the race where that immortal garland is to be run for, notwithstanding dust and heat."

Can you not fancy the parish beadles getting up and walking rapidly away from such sentiments? Can you not fancy all the noble and generous hearts in the world shouting through all the centuries, "amen, amen!"

Gentlemen, the scholar is the representative of thought among men, and his duty to society is the effort to introduce thought and the sense of justice into human affairs. He was not made a scholar to satisfy the newspapers or the parish beadles, but to serve God and man. While other men pursue what is expedient, and watch with alarm the flickering of the funds, he is to pursue the truth, and watch the eternal law of justice.

But if this be true of the scholar in general, how peculiarly is it true of the American scholar, who, as a citizen of a Republic, has not only an influence by his word and example, but, by his vote, a direct agency upon public affairs. In a Republic which decides questions involving the national welfare by a majority of voices, whoever refuses to vote is a traitor to his own cause, whatever that cause may be; and if any scholar will not vote, nor have an opinion upon great public measures, because that would be to mix himself with politics, but contents himself with vague declamation about freedom in general, knowing that the enemies of freedom always use its name, then that scholar is a traitor to liberty, and degrades his order by justifying the reproach that the scholar is a pusillanimous trimmer.

The American scholar, gentlemen, has duties to politics in general; and he has, consequently, duties to every political crisis in his country; what his duties are in this crisis of our national affairs I shall now tell you as plainly as I can. The times are grave, and they demand sober speech. To us young men the future of this country is intrusted. What names does history love, and every honest man revere? The names of those who gave their youth and strength to the cause which is waiting for us to serve it.

The object of human government is human liberty. Laws restrain the encroachment of the individual upon society in order that all individuals may be secured the freest play of their powers. This is because the end of society is the improvement of the individual and the development of the race. Liberty is therefore the condition of human progress, and, consequently, that is the best government which gives to men the largest liberty and constantly modifies itself in the interest of freedom.

The laws of society, indeed, deprive men of liberty, and even of life, but only when by crime they have become injurious to society. The deprivation of the life or liberty of the individual under other circumstances is the outrage of those rights which are instinctively perceived by every man, but are beyond argument or proof.

Human slavery annihilates the conditions of human progress. Its necessary result is the destruction of humanity; and this not only directly by its effect upon the slave, but indirectly by its effect upon the master. In the one it destroys the self-respect which is the basis of manhood, and is thus a capital crime against humanity. In the other it fosters pride, indolence, luxury, and licentiousness, which equally imbrute the human being. Therefore, in slave States there is no literature, no art, no progressive civilization.

Manners are fantastic and fierce; brute force supplants moral principle; freedom of speech is suppressed because the natural speech of man condemns slavery; a sensitive vanity is called honor, and cowardly swagger, chivalry; respect for woman is destroyed by universal licentiousness; lazy indifference is called gallantry, and an impudent familiarity, cordiality. To supply by a travesty of courage the want of manly honor, men deliberately shoot those who expose their falsehoods. Therefore they go armed with knives and pistols, for it is a cardinal article of a code of false honor that it is possible for a bully to insult a gentleman. Founded upon crime, for by no other word can manstealing be characterized, the prosperity of such a people is at the mercy of an indignant justice. Hence a slave society has the characteristics of wandering tribes, which rob, and live, therefore, insecure in the shadow of impending vengence. There is nothing admirable in such a society but what its spirit condemns; there is nothing permanent in it but decay. Against nature, against reason, against the human instinct, against the divine law, the institution of human slavery is the most dreadful that philosophy contemplates or the imagination conceives.

Certainly, some individual slaveholders are good men, but the mass of men are never better than their institutions; and certainly some slaves are better fed and lodged than some free laborers; but so are many horses better fed and lodged than some free laborers; is, therefore, a laborer to abdicate his manhood and become a horse; and, certainly, as it exists, God may, in a certain sense, be said to permit it; but in the same way God permitted the slaughter of the innocents in Judea, and he permitted the awful railway slaughter not a month ago near Philadelphia. Do you mean that as comfort for the mothers of Judea and the mothers of Pennsylvania?

History confirms what philosophy teaches. The eastern nations and the Spanish colonies, Rome in her decline, and the southern States of America, display a society of which the spirit is similar however much the phenomena may differ. Moral self-respect is the first condition of national life, as labor is the first condition of national prosperity; but the laborer cannot have moral respect unless he be free.

The true national policy therefore is that which enobles and dignifies labor. Cincinnatus, upon his farm, is the ideal of the citizen. But slavery disgraces labor by making the laborer a brute, while it makes the slaveholder the immediate rival of the free laborer in all the markets of the world. Hence, Tiberius Gracchus, one of the greatest of Roman citizens, early saw that in a state where an oligarchy at the same time monopolized and disgraced labor, there must necessarily be a vast demoralized population who would demand support of the state and be ready for the service of the demagogue, who is always the tyrant.   Gracchus was killed, but the issue proved the prophet.

The canker which Rome cherished in her bosom ate out the heart of Rome, and the empire whose splendor flashed over the whole world fell like a blighted tree.   Not until slavery had barbarized the great mass of the Romans did Rome fall a prey to the barbarians from abroad.

Gentlemen, it is a disgrace for all of us, that in this country, and in this year of our history, the occasion should require me to state such principles and facts as these.   History seems to be an endless iteration.   But it is not so.   Do not lose heart.   It only seems so because there has been but one great cause in human affairs—the cause of liberty.   In a thousand forms, under a thousand names, the old contest has been waged.   It divided the politics of Greece and Rome, of England, France, America, into two parties; so that the history of liberty is the history of the world. . . .

Do you ask me our duty as scholars?   Gentlemen, thought, which the scholar represents, is life and liberty.   There is no intellectual or moral life without liberty.   Therefore, as a man must breathe and see before he can study, the scholar must have liberty, first of all; and as the American scholar is a man and has a voice in his own government, so his interest in political affairs must precede all others.   He must build his house before he can live in it.   He must be a perpetual inspiration of freedom in politics.   He must recognize that the intelligent exercise of political rights which is a privilege in a monarchy, is a duty in a republic.   If it clash with his ease, his retirement, his taste, his study, let it clash, but let him do his duty.   The course of events is incessant, and when the good deed is slighted, the bad deed is done.

Young scholars, young Americans, young men, we are all

called upon to do a great duty. Nobody is released from it. It is a work to be done by hard strokes, and everywhere. I see a rising enthusiasm, but enthusiasm is not an election; and I hear cheers from the heart, but cheers are not votes. Every man must labor with his neighbor, in the street, at the plough, at the bench, early and late, at home and abroad. Generally we are concerned in elections with the measures of government. This time it is with the essential principle of government itself. Therefore, there must be no doubt about our leader. He must not prevaricate, or stand in the fog, or use terms to court popular favor, which every demagogue and traitor has always used. If he say he favors the interest of the whole country, let him frankly say whether he think the interest of the whole country demands the extension of slavery. If he declares for the Union, let him say whether he means a Union for freedom or for slavery. If he swear by the constitution, let him state, so that the humblest free laborer can hear and understand, whether he believes the constitution means to prefer slave labor to free labor in the national representation of the Territories. Ask him as an honest man, in a great crisis, if he be for the Union, the constitution, and slavery extension, or for "Liberty and union, now and forever, one and inseparable."

Scholars, you would like to loiter in the pleasant paths of study. Every man loves his ease—loves to please his taste. But into how many homes along this lovely valley came the news of Lexington and Bunker Hill, eighty years ago, and young men like us, studious, fond of leisure, young lovers, young husbands, young brothers, and sons, knew that they must forsake the wooded hillside, the river meadows, golden with harvest, the twilight walk along the river, the summer Sunday in the old church, parents, wife, child, mistress, and go away to uncertain war. Putnam heard the call at his plough, and turned to go, without waiting. Wooster heard it and obeyed.

Not less lovely in those days was this peaceful valley, not less soft this summer air. Life was dear, and love as beautiful, to those young men as it is to us, who stand upon their graves. But because they were so dear and beautiful those men went out bravely to fight for them and fall. Through these very streets they marched, who never returned. They fell and were buried; but they can never die. Not sweeter are the flowers that make your valley fair, not greener are the pines that give your river its name, than the memory of the brave men who died for freedom. And yet, no victim of those days, sleeping under the green sod of Connecticut, is more truly a martyr of liberty than every murdered man whose bones lie bleaching in this summer sun upon the silent plains of Kansas.

Gentlemen, while we read history we make history. Because our fathers fought in this great cause, we must not hope to escape fighting. Because, two thousand years ago, Leonidas stood against Xerxes we must not suppose that Xerxes was slain, nor thank God that Leonidas is not immortal. Every great crisis of human history is a pass of Thermopylæ, and there is always a Leonidas and his three hundred to die in it if they cannot conquer. And so long as liberty has one martyr, so long as one drop of blood is poured out for her, so long from that single drop of bloody sweat of the agony of humanity shall spring hosts as countless as the forest leaves, and mighty as the sea.

Brothers! the call has come to us. I bring it to you in these calm retreats. I summon you to the great fight of freedom. I call upon you to say, with your voices, whenever the occasion offers, and with your votes, when the day comes, that upon these fertile fields of Kansas, in the very heart of the continent, the upas tree of slavery, dripping death-dews upon national prosperity, and upon free labor, shall never be planted. I call upon you to plant there the palm of peace, the vine, and the olive of a Christian civilization. I call upon you to determine whether this great experiment of human freedom, which has been the scorn of despotism, shall, by its failure, be also our sin and shame. I call upon you to defend the hope of the world.

The voice of our brothers who are bleeding, no less than of our fathers who bled, summons us to this battle. Shall the children of unborn generations, clustering over that vast western empire, rise up and call us blessed or cursed? Here are our Marathon and Lexington; here are our heroic fields. The hearts of all good men beat with us. The fight is fierce — the issue is with God. But God is good.

ORATION AT CONCORD

DELIVERED AT THE CENTENNIAL CELEBRATION, APRIL 19, 1875

WE ARE fortunate that we behold this day. The heavens bend benignly over, the earth blossoms with renewed life, and our hearts beat joyfully together with one emotion of filial gratitude and patriotic exultation. Citizens of a great, free, and prosperous country, we come hither to honor the men, our fathers, who, on this spot and upon this day, a hundred years ago, struck the first blow in the contest which made that country independ-

ent.   Here beneath the hills they trod, by the peaceful river
on whose shores they dwelt, amidst the fields that they sowed
and reaped, proudly recalling their virtue and their valor,
we come to tell their story, to try ourselves by their lofty
standard to know if we are their worthy children; and, standing reverently where they stood and fought and died, to
swear before God and each other, in the words of him upon
whom in our day the spirit of the revolutionary fathers
visibly descended, that government of the people, by the
people, for the people, shall not perish from the earth.

This ancient town with its neighbors who share its glory,
has never failed fitly to commemorate this great day of its
history.   Fifty years ago, while some soldiers of the Concord fight were yet living—twenty-five years ago, while still
a few venerable survivors lingered—with prayer and eloquence and song you renewed the pious vow.   But the last
living link with the Revolution has long been broken.
Great events and a mightier struggle have absorbed our own
generation.   Yet we who stand here to-day have a sympathy
with the men at the old North Bridge which those who preceded us here at earlier celebrations could not know.   With
them war was a name and a tradition.   So swift and vast
had been the change and the development of the country
that the revolutionary clash of arms was already vague and
unreal, and Concord and Lexington seemed to them almost
as remote and historic as Arbela and Sempach.   When they
assembled to celebrate this day they saw a little group of
tottering forms, eyes from which the light was fading, arms
nerveless and withered, thin white hairs that fluttered in the
wind—they saw a few venerable relics of a vanished age,
whose pride was that before living memory they had been
minute-men of American Independence.

But with us how changed! War is no longer a tradition half romantic and obscure. It has ravaged how many of our homes! it has wrung how many of the hearts before me! North and South we know the pang. Our common liberty is consecrated by a common sorrow. We do not count around us a few feeble veterans of the contest, but are girt with a cloud of witnesses. We are surrounded everywhere by multitudes in the vigor of their prime—behold them here to-day sharing in these pious and peaceful rites, the honored citizens, legislators, magistrates—yes, the chief magistrate of the Republic—whose glory it is that they were minute-men of American liberty and union. These men of to-day interpret to us with resistless eloquence the men and the times we commemorate. Now, if never before, we understand the Revolution. Now we know the secret of those old hearts and homes. We can measure the sacrifice, the courage, the devotion, for we have seen them all. Green hills of Concord, broad fields of Middlesex, that heard the voice of Hancock and of Adams, you heard also the call of Lincoln and of Andrew, and your Ladd and Whitney, your Prescott and Ripley and Melvin, have revealed to us more truly the Davis and the Buttrick, the Hosmer and the Parker, of a hundred years ago.

The story of this old town is the history of New England. It shows us the people and the institutions that have made the American Republic. Concord was the first settlement in New England above tide-water. It was planted directly from the mother country, and was what was called a mother town, the parent of other settlements throughout the wilderness. It was a military post in King Philip's war, and two hundred years ago—just a century before the minute-men whom we commemorate—the militia of Middlesex were organized as minute-men against the Indians. It is a Concord tradition that in those stern days, when the farmer tilled these fields at the risk of his life, Mary Shepard, a girl of fifteen, was watching on one of the hills for the savages, while her brothers threshed in the barn. Suddenly the Indians appeared, slew the brothers and carried her away. In the night while the savages slept, she untied a horse which they had stolen, slipped a saddle from under the head of one of her captors, mounted, fled, swam the Nashua river and rode through the forest home. Mary Shepard was the true ancestor of the Concord matrons who share the fame of this day—of Mrs. James Barrett, of the widow Brown, of Mrs. Amos Wood, and Hannah Burns, with the other faithful women whose self-command and ready wit and energy on this great morning, show that the mothers of New England were like the fathers, and that equally in both their children may reverence their own best virtues.

A little later than Philip's war, one hundred and eighty-six years ago last night, while some of the first settlers of Massachusetts Bay still lingered, when the news came that King James II had been dethroned, a company marched from this town and joined that general uprising of the colony which the next day — this very day — with old Simon Bradstreet at its head, deposed Sir Edmund Andros, the King's governor, and restored the ancient charter of the colony. We demand only the traditional rights of Englishmen, said the English nobles as they seated William and Mary upon the throne. We ask nothing more, said the freemen of Concord as they helped to dissolve royal government in America, and returned to their homes. Eighty-five years later the first Provincial Congress which had been called to meet at Concord if for any reason the general court at Salem were ob-

structed, assembled in the old meeting house on the 11th of
October, 1774, the first independent legislature in Massachusetts and America; and from that hour to this, the old
mother town has never forgotten the words nor forsworn the
faith of the Revolution which had been proclaimed here six
weeks before: "No danger shall affright, no difficulties intimidate us; and if in support of our rights we are called to
encounter even death, we are yet undaunted, sensible that he
can never die too soon who lays down his life in support of
the laws and liberties of his country."

But the true glory of Concord, as of all New England, was
the town meeting, the nursery of American Independence.
When the Revolution began, of the eight millions of people
then living in Old England only one hundred and sixty thousand were voters, while in New England the great mass of
free male adults were electors. And they had been so from
the landing at Plymouth. Here in the wilderness the settlers
were forced to govern themselves. They could not constantly refer and appeal to another authority twenty miles
away through the woods. Every day brought its duty that
must be done before sunset. Roads must be made, schools
built, young men trained to arms against the savages and the
wildcat, taxes must be laid and collected for all common purposes, preaching must be maintained, and who could know
the time, the means, and the necessity so well as the community itself? Thus each town was a little and a perfect
republic, as solitary and secluded in the New England wilderness as the Swiss cantons among the Alps. No other practicable human institution has been devised or conceived to
secure the just ends of local government so felicitous as the
town meeting. It brought together the rich and the poor,
the good and the bad, and gave character, eloquence, and

natural leadership full and free play. It enabled superior experience and sagacity to govern, and virtue and intelligence alone are rulers by divine right. The Tories called the resolution for committees of correspondence the source of the rebellion; but it was only a correspondence of town meetings. From that correspondence came the confederation of the colonies. Out of that arose the closer majestic union of the constitution, the greater phœnix born from the ashes of the lesser, and the national power and prosperity to-day rest securely only upon the foundation of the primary meeting. That is where the duty of the citizens begins. Neglect of that is disloyalty to liberty. No contrivance will supply its place, no excuse absolves the neglect; and the American who is guilty of that neglect is as deadly an enemy of his country as the British soldier a century ago.

But here and now I cannot speak of the New England town meeting without recalling its great genius, the New Englander in whom the Revolution seemed to be must fully embodied, and the lofty prayer of whose life was answered upon this spot and on this day. He was not eloquent like Otis, nor scholarly like Quincy, nor all-fascinating like Warren, yet bound heart to heart with these great men, his friends, the plainest, simplest, austerest among them, he gathered all their separate gifts and adding to them his own, fused the whole in the glow of that untiring energy, that unerring perception, that sublime will, which moved before the chosen people of the colonies a pillar of cloud by day, of fire by night. People of Massachusetts, your proud and grateful hearts outstrip my lips in pronouncing the name of Samuel Adams. Elsewhere to-day, nearer the spot where he stood with his immortal friend Hancock a hundred years ago this morning, a son of Massachusetts who bears the name of a friend of Samuel Adams, and whose career has honorably illustrated the fidelity of your State to human liberty, will pay a fitting tribute to the true American tribune of the people—the father of the Revolution, as he was fondly called. But we also are his children and must not omit our duty.

Until 1768 Samuel Adams did not despair of a peaceful issue of the quarrel with Great Britain. But when in May of that year the British frigate " Romney " sailed into Boston harbor, and her shotted guns were trained upon the town, he saw that the question was changed. From that moment he knew that America must be free or slave, and the unceasing effort of his life, by day and night, with tongue and pen, was to nerve his fellow colonists to strike when the hour should come. On that gray December evening, two years later, when he rose in the Old South, and in a clear, calm voice, said, " This meeting can do nothing more to save the country," and so gave the word for the march to the tea ships, he comprehended more clearly, perhaps, than any man in the colonies, the immense and far-reaching consequences of his words. He was ready to throw the tea overboard because he was ready to throw overboard the King and Parliament of England.

During the ten years from the passage of the Stamp Act to the fight at Lexington and Concord, this poor man in an obscure provincial town beyond the sea was engaged with the British ministry in one of the mightiest contests that history records. Not a word in Parliament that he did not hear, not an act in the cabinet that he did not see. With brain and heart and conscience all alive, he opposed every hostile Order in Council with a British precedent, and arrayed against the government of Great Britain the battery of principles impregnable with the accumulated strength of centuries of British conviction. The cold Grenville, the brilliant Townsend, the obsequious North, the reckless Hillsborough, the crafty Dartmouth, all the ermined and coroneted chiefs of the proudest aristocracy in the world, derided, declaimed, denounced, laid unjust taxes, and sent troops to collect them; cheered loudly by a servile Parliament, the parasite of a headstrong King—and the plain Boston Puritan laid his finger on the vital point of the tremendous controversy, and held to it inexorably King, Lords, Commons, the people of England and the people of America. Intrenched in his own honesty, the King's gold could not buy him. Enshrined in the love of his fellow citizens, the King's writ could not take him. And when on this morning the King's troops marched to seize him, his sublime faith saw beyond the clouds of the moment the rising sun of the America that we behold, and careless of himself, mindful only of his country, he exultingly exclaimed, " Oh! what a glorious morning! "

Yet this man held no office but that of clerk of the assembly, to which he was yearly elected, and that of constant moderator of the town meeting. That was his mighty weapon. The town meeting was the alarm bell with which he aroused the continent. It was the rapier with which he fenced with the ministry. It was the claymore with which he smote their counsels. It was the harp of a thousand strings that he swept into a burst of passionate defiance, or an electric call to arms, or a proud pæan of exulting triumph — defiance, challenge, and exultation all lifting the continent to independence. His indomitable will and command of the popular confidence played Boston against London, the provincial town meetings against the royal Parliament, Faneuil Hall against St. Stephen's. And as long as the American town meeting is known, its great genius will be revered, who with the town meeting overthrew an empire. So long as Faneuil Hall stands, Samuel Adams will not want his most fitting monument, and when Faneuil Hall falls, its name with his will be found written as with a sunbeam upon every faithful American heart.

The first imposing armed movement against the colonies on the 19th of April, 1775, did not of course take by surprise a people so prepared. For ten years they had seen the possibility, for five years the probability, and for at least a year the certainty, of the contest. They quietly organized, watched, and waited. The royal governor, Gage, was a soldier, and he had read the signs of the times. He had fought with provincial troops at the bloody ambuscade at Braddock, and he felt the full force of the mighty determination that exalted New England. He had about four thousand effective troops, trained veterans, with brilliant officers who despised and ridiculed the Yankee militia. Massachusetts had provided for a constitutional army of fifteen thousand men. Minute companies were everywhere organized, and military supplies were deposited at convenient towns. Everybody was on the alert. Couriers were held ready to alarm the country should the British march, and wagons to remove the stores. In the early spring Gage sent out some of his officers as spies, and two of them came in disguise as far as Concord. On the 22d of March the Provincial Congress met in this town, and made the last arrangements for a possible battle, begging the militia and minute-men to be ready, but to act only on the defensive.

As the spring advanced it was plain that some movement would be made, and on Monday, the 17th of April, the Committee of Safety ordered part of the stores deposited here to be removed to Sudbury and Groton, and the cannon to be secreted. On Tuesday, the 18th, Gage, who had decided to send a force to Concord to destroy the stores, picketed the roads from Boston into Middlesex to prevent any report of the intended march from spreading into the country. But the very air was electric. In the tension of the popular mind every sound and sight was significant. It was part of Gage's plan to seize Hancock and Adams, who were at Lexington, and on the evening of the 18th the Committee of Safety at Cambridge sent them word to beware, for suspicious officers were abroad. A British grenadier in full uniform went into a shop in Boston. He might as well have proclaimed that an expedition was on foot. In the afternoon one of the governor's grooms strolled into a stable where John Ballard was cleaning a horse. John Ballard was a Son of Liberty; and when the groom idly remarked, in nervous English, that " there would be hell to pay to-morrow," John's heart leaped and his hand shook, and asking the groom to finish cleaning the horse, he ran to a friend, who carried the news straight to Paul Revere, who told him he had already heard it from two other persons.

That evening, at ten o'clock, 800 British troops, under Lieutenant-Colonel Smith, took boat at the foot of the Common and crossed to the Cambridge shore. Gage thought that his secret had been kept, but Lord Percy, who had heard the people say on the Common that the troops would miss their aim, undeceived him. Gage instantly ordered that no one should leave the town. But Dr. Warren was before him, and as the troops crossed the river Ebenezer Dorr, with a message from Warren to Hancock and Adams, was riding over the neck to Roxbury, and Paul Revere was rowing over the river farther down to Charlestown, having agreed with his friend Robert Newman to show lanterns from the belfry of the Old North Church—

"One, if by land, and two, if by sea"—

as a signal of the march of the British. Already the moon was rising, and while the troops were stealthily landing at Lechmere Point their secret was flashed out into the April night, and Paul Revere, springing into the saddle upon the Charlestown shore, spurred away into Middlesex.

"How far that little candle throws his beams!"

The modest spire yet stands, reverend relic of the old town of Boston, of those brave men and of their deeds. Startling the land that night with the warning of danger, let it remind the land forever of the patriotism with which that danger was averted, and for our children as for our fathers still stand secure, the pharos of American liberty.

It was a brilliant April night. The winter had been unusually mild and the spring very forward. The hills were already green. The early grain waved in the fields, and the air was sweet with blossoming orchards. Already the robins whistled, the bluebird sang, and the benediction of peace rested upon the landscape. Under the cloudless moon the soldiers silently marched, and Paul Revere swiftly rode, galloping through Medford and West Cambridge, rousing every house as he went, spurring for Lexington and Hancock and Adams, and evading the British patrols who had been sent out to stop the news. Stop the news! Already the village churches were beginning to ring the alarm, as the pulpits beneath them had been ringing for many a year. In the awakening houses lights flashed from window to window. Drums beat faintly far away and on every side. Signal guns flashed and echoed. The watch-dogs barked, the cocks crew. Stop the news! Stop the sunrise! The murmuring night trembled with the summons so earnestly expected, so dreaded, so desired. And as long ago the voice rang out at midnight along the Syrian shore, wailing that great Pan was dead, but in the same moment the choiring angels whispered, " Glory to God in the highest, for Christ is born," so, if the stern alarm of that April night seemed to many a wistful and loyal heart to portend the passing glory of British dominion and the tragical chance of war, it whispered to them with prophetic inspiration, " Good-will to men; America is born !"

There is a tradition that long before the troops reached Lexington an unknown horseman thundered at the door of Captain Joseph Robbins in Acton, waking every man and woman and the babe in the cradle, shouting that the regulars were marching to Concord, and that the rendezvous was the Old North Bridge. Captain Robbins's son, a boy of ten years, heard the summons in the garret where he lay, and in a few minutes was on his father's old mare, a young Paul Revere, galloping along the road to rouse Captain Isaac Davis, who commanded the minute-men of Acton. He was a young man of thirty, a gunsmith by trade, brave and thoughtful, and tenderly fond of his wife and four children. The company assembled at his shop, formed and marched a little way when he halted them and returned for a moment to his house. He said to his wife, " Take good care of the children," kissed her, turned to his men, gave the order to march and saw his home no more. Such was the history of that night in how many homes! The hearts of those men and women of Middlesex might break, but they could not waver. They had counted the cost. They knew what and whom they served;

and as the midnight summons came they started up and answered, " Here am I ! "

Meanwhile the British bayonets glistening in the moon moved steadily along the road. Colonel Smith heard and saw that the country was aroused, and sent back to Boston for reinforcements, ordering Major Pitcairn with six companies to hasten forward and seize the bridges at Concord. Paul Revere and Dorr had reached Lexington by midnight and had given the alarm. The men of Lexington instantly mustered on the green, but as there was no sign of the enemy they were dismissed to wait his coming. He was close at hand. Pitcairn swiftly advanced, seizing every man upon the road, and was not discovered until half-past four in the morning, within a mile or two of Lexington meeting house. Then there was a general alarm. The bell rang, drums beat, guns fired, and sixty or seventy of the Lexington militia were drawn up in line upon the green, Captain John Parker at their head. The British bayonets glistening in the dawn moved rapidly toward them. Pitcairn rode up, and angrily ordered the militia to surrender and disperse. But they held their ground. The troops fired over their heads. Still the militia stand. Then a deadly volley blazed from the British line, and eight of the Americans fell dead and ten wounded at the doors of their homes and in sight of their kindred. Captain Parker seeing that it was massacre, not battle, ordered his men to disperse. They obeyed, some firing upon the enemy. The British troops, who had suffered little, with a loud huzza of victory pushed on toward Concord, six miles beyond.

Four hours before Paul Revere and Ebenezer Dorr had left Lexington to rouse Concord, and were soon overtaken by Dr. Samuel Prescott of that town, who had been to Lex-

ington upon a tender errand. A British patrol captured
Revere and Dorr, but Prescott leaped a stone wall and dashed
on to Concord. Between one and two o'clock in the morning
Amos Melvin, the sentinel at the court house, rang the bell
and roused the town. He sprang of heroic stock. One of
his family thirty years before had commanded a company at
Louisburg and another at Crown Point, while four brothers
of the same family served in the late war; and the honored
names of the three who perished are carved upon your soldiers' monument. When the bell rang, the first man that
appeared was William Emerson, the minister, with his gun
in his hand. It was his faith that the scholar should be the
minute-man of liberty, a faith which his descendants have
piously cherished and illustrated before the world. The
minute-men gathered hastily upon the Common. The citizens, hurrying from their homes, secreted the military stores.
Messengers were sent to the neighboring villages, and the
peaceful town prepared for battle. The minute-men of Lincoln, whose captain was William Smith, and whose lieutenant
was Samuel Hoar, a name not unknown in Middlesex, in
Massachusetts, and in the country, and wherever known still
honored for the noblest qualities of the men of the Revolution, had joined the Concord militia and minute-men, and
part of them had marched down the Lexington road to recon-
noitre. Seeing the British, they fell back toward the hill
over the road at the entrance of the village, upon which stood
the liberty pole.

It was now seven o'clock. There were perhaps two hundred men in arms upon the hill. Below them, upon the
Lexington road, a quarter of a mile away, rose a thick cloud
of dust, from which, amidst proudly rolling drums, eight hundred British bayonets flashed in the morning sun. The

Americans saw that battle where they stood would be mere butchery, and they fell gradually back to a rising ground about a mile north of the meeting house, the spot upon which we are now assembled. The British troops divided as they entered the town, the infantry coming over the hill from which the Americans had retired, the marines and grenadiers marching by the high road. The place was well known to the British officers through their spies, and Colonel Smith, halting before the court house, instantly sent detachments to hold the two bridges, and others to destroy the stores. But so carefully had these been secreted that during the two or three hours in which they were engaged in the work the British merely broke open about sixty barrels of flour, half of which was afterward saved, knocked off the trunnions of three cannon, burned sixteen new carriage wheels and some barrels of wooden spoons and trenchers; they threw some five hundred pounds of balls into the pond and wells, cut down the liberty-pole and fired the court house.

The work was hurriedly done, for Colonel Smith, a veteran soldier, knew his peril. He had advanced twenty miles into a country of intelligent and resolute men, who were rising around him. All Middlesex was moving. From Acton and Lincoln, from Westford, Littleton, and Chelmsford, from Bedford and Billerica, from Stow, Sudbury, and Carlisle, the sons of Indian fighters and of soldiers of the old French war poured along the roads, shouldering the fire-locks and fowling-pieces and old king's arms that had seen famous service when the earlier settlers had gone out against King Philip, or the later colonists had marched under the flag on which George Whitefield had written "*Nil desperandum Cristo Duce*"— Never despair while Christ is captain—and those words the children of the Puritans had written on their hearts. As

the minute-men from the other towns arrived they joined the
force upon the rising ground near the North Bridge, where
they were drawn into line by Joseph Hosmer of Concord,
who acted as adjutant. By nine o'clock some five hundred
men were assembled, and a consultation of officers and chief
citizens was held.

That group of Middlesex farmers, here upon Punkatasset,
without thought that they were heroes, or that the day and
its deeds were to be so momentous, is a group as memorable
as the men of Rutli on the Swiss Alps, or the barons of the
meadow of Runnymede. They confronted the mightiest empire in the world, invincible on land, supreme on the sea,
whose guns had just been heard in four continents at once,
girdling the globe with victory. And that empire was their
mother-land, in whose renown 'they had shared—the land
dear to their hearts by a thousand ties of love, pride and
reverence. They took a sublime and awful responsibility.
They could not know that the other colonies, or even their
neighbors of Massachusetts, would justify their action.
There was as yet no Declaration of Independence, no continental army. There was, indeed, a general feeling that a
blow would soon be struck, but to mistake the time, the place,
the way, might be to sacrifice the great cause itself and to
ruin America. But their conscience and their judgment assured them that the hour had come. Before them lay their
homes, and on the hill beyond the graveyard in which
their forefathers slept. A guard of king's troops opposed their
entrance to their own village. Those troops were at that
moment searching their homes, perhaps insulting their wives
and children. Already they saw the smoke as of burning
houses rising in the air, and they resolved to march into the
town and to fire upon the troops if they were opposed. They

resolved upon organized, aggressive, forcible resistance to
the military power of Great Britain, the first that had been
offered in the colonies. All unconsciously every heart beat
time to the music of the slave's epitaph in the graveyard that
overhung the town:

> " God wills us free; man wills us slaves;
> I will as God wills; God's will be done."

Isaac Davis of Acton drew his sword, turned toward his
company, and said, " I haven't a man that's afraid to go."
Colonel Barrett of Concord gave the order to march. In
double file and with trailed arms the men moved along the
causeway, the Acton company in front, Major John Buttrick
of Concord, Captain Isaac Davis of Acton, and Lieutenant-
Colonel John Robertson of Westford leading the way. As
they approached the bridge the British forces withdrew across
it and began to take up the planks. Major Buttrick ordered
his men to hasten their march. As they came within ten
or fifteen rods of the bridge a shot was fired by the British
which wounded Jonas Brown, one of the Concord minute-
men, and Luther Blanchard, fifer of the Acton company. A
British volley followed, and Isaac Davis of Acton, making a
way for his countrymen like Arnold von Winkelried at Sempach, fell dead, shot through the heart. By his side fell his
friend and neighbor, Abner Hosmer, a youth of twenty-two.
Seeing them fall, Major Buttrick turned to his men, and raising his hand, cried, " Fire, fellow soldiers! for God's sake,
fire! " John Buttrick gave the word. The cry ran along
the line. The Americans fired. The Revolution began! It
began here. Let us put off the shoes from off our feet, for
the place whereon we stand is holy ground.

One of the British was killed, several were wounded, and
they retreated in confusion toward the centre of the village.

The engagement was doubtless seen by Smith and Pitcairn from the graveyard hill that overlooked the town, and the shots were heard by all the searching parties, which immediately returned in haste and disorder. Colonel Smith instantly prepared to retire, and at noon, one hundred years ago at this hour, the British columns marched out of yonder square. Then and there began the retreat of British power from the American colonies. Through seven weary and wasting years it continued. From Bunker Hill to Long Island; from Princeton, Trenton and Saratoga; from the Brandywine, Monmouth and King's Mountain; through the bloody snow at Valley Forge; through the treachery of Arnold and Lee; through cabals and doubt and poverty and despair; but steadily urged by one great heart that strengthened the continent — the heart of George Washington — the British retreat went on from Concord Bridge and Lexington Green to the plains of Yorktown and the King's acknowledgment of American independence.

Of the beginning of this retreat, of that terrible march of the exhausted troops from this square to Boston, I have no time fitly to tell the tale. Almost as soon as it began all Massachusetts was in motion. William Prescott mustered his regiment of minute-men at Pepperell and Timothy Pickering at Salem and Marblehead. Dedham left no man behind between the ages of sixteen and seventy. The minute-men of Worcester marched out of the town one way as the news went out the other, and flying over the mountains sent Berkshire to Bunker Hill. Meanwhile the men of Concord and the neighborhood, following the British over the bridge, ran along the heights above the Lexington road and posted themselves to await the enemy. The retreating British column with wide sweeping flankers advanced steadily and slowly. No drum beat, no fife blew. There was the hushed silence of intense expectation. As the troops passed Merriam's Corner, a little beyond Concord, and the flank guard was called in, they turned suddenly and fired upon the Americans. The minute-men and militia instantly returned the fire, and the battle began that lasted until sunset.

When Colonel Smith ordered the retreat, although he and his officers may have had some misgivings, they had probably lost them in the contempt of regulars for the militia. But from the moment of the firing at Merriam's Corner they were undeceived. The landscape was alive with armed men. They swarmed through every wood-path and by-way, across the pastures and over the hills. Some came up in order along the roads, as from Reading and Billerica, from East Sudbury and Bedford, and John Parker's company from Lexington waited in a woody defile to avenge the death of their comrades. The British column marched steadily on, while from trees, rocks and fences, from houses, barns, and sheds, blazed the withering American fire. The hills echoed and flashed. The woods rang. The road became an endless ambuscade of flame. The Americans seemed to the appalled British troops to drop from the clouds, to spring from the earth. With every step the attack was deadlier, the danger more imminent. For some time discipline and the plain extremity of the peril sustained the order of the British line. But the stifling clouds of dust, the consuming thirst, the exhaustion of utter fatigue, the wagons full of wounded men moaning and dying, madly pressing through the ranks to the front, the constant falling of their comrades, officers captured and killed, and through all the fatal and incessant shot of an unseen foe, smote with terror that haughty column, which, shrinking, bleeding, wavering, reeled through Lexington panic-stricken and broken. The officers, seeing the dire extremity, fought their way to the front and threatened the men with death if they advanced. The breaking line recoiled a little, and even steadied under one of the sharpest attacks of the day. For not as yet were Hessians hired to enslave Americans, and it was English blood and pluck on both sides. At two o'clock in the afternoon, a half-mile beyond Lexington meeting house, just as the English officers saw that destruction or surrender was the only alternative, Lord Percy with a reinforcement of twelve hundred men came up, and opening with two cannons upon the Americans, succored his flying and desperate comrades, who fell upon the ground among Percy's troops, their parched tongues hanging from their mouths.

The flower of General Gage's army was now upon the field, but its commander saw at once that its sole hope of safety was to continue the retreat. After half an hour's delay the march was resumed, and with it the barbarities as well as the sufferings of war. Lord Percy threw out flanking parties, which entered the houses upon the line of march plundering and burning. The fields of Menotomy or Arlington, through which lay the road, became a plain of blood and fire. But the American pursuit was relentless, and beyond Lexington the lower counties and towns came hurrying to the battle. Many a man afterward famous was conspicuous that day, and near West Cambridge Joseph Warren was the inspiring soul of the struggle. It was now past five o'clock. The British ammunition was giving out. The officers, too much exposed in the saddle, alighted and marched with the men, who as they approached Charlestown, encountered the hottest fire of the day. General Gage had learned the perilous extremity of his army from a messenger sent by Percy and had issued a proclamation threatening to lay Charlestown in ashes if the troops were attacked in the streets. The town hummed with the vague and appalling rumors of the events of the day, and just before sunset the excited inhabitants heard the distant guns, and soon saw the British troops running along the old Cambridge road to Charlestown Neck, firing as they came. They had just escaped the militia, seven hundred strong, from Salem and Marblehead — the flower of Essex,— and as the sun was setting they entered Charlestown and gained the shelter of their frigate guns. Then General Heath ordered the American pursuit to stop and the battle was over. But all that day and night the news was flying from mouth to mouth, from heart to heart, rousing every city, town, and solitary farm in the colonies; and before the last shot of the minute-men on the British retreat from Concord bridge was fired, or the last wounded grenadier had been rowed across the river, the whole country was rising; Massachusetts, New England, America, were closing around the city, and the siege of Boston and the war of American independence had begun.

Such was the opening battle of the Revolution — a conflict which, so far as we can see, saved civil liberty in two hemispheres, saved England as well as America, and whose magnificent results shine through the world as the beacon light of free popular government. And who won this victory? The minute-men and militia, who in the history of our English race have been always the vanguard of freedom. The minute-man of the Revolution — who was he? He was the husband and father who, bred to love liberty, and to know that lawful liberty is the sole guarantee of peace and progress, left the plow in the furrow and the hammer on the bench, and kissing wife and children, marched to die or to be free. He was the son and lover, the plain shy youth of the singing school and the village choir, whose heart beat to arms for his country, and who felt, though he could not say with the old English cavalier:

"I could not love thee, dear, so much,
Loved I not honor more."

The minute-man of the Revolution! He was the old, the middle-aged, and the young. He was Captain Miles of Concord, who said that he went to battle as he went to church. He was Captain Davis of Acton, who reproved his men for jesting on the march. He was Deacon Josiah Haynes of Sudbury, eighty years old, who marched with his company to the South Bridge at Concord, then joined in the hot pursuit to Lexington, and fell as gloriously as Warren at Bunker Hill. He was James Hayward of Acton, twenty-two years old, foremost in that deadly race from Concord to Charlestown, who raised his piece at the same moment with a British soldier, each exclaiming, "You are a dead man!" The Briton dropped, shot through the heart. James Hayward fell mortally wounded. "Father," he said, "I started with forty balls; I have three left. I never did such a day's work before. Tell mother not to mourn too much; and tell her whom I love more than my mother that I am not sorry I turned out."

This was the minute-man of the Revolution, the rural citizen trained in the common school, the church, and the town meeting, who carried a bayonet that thought, and whose gun, loaded with a principle, brought down not a man, but a system. Him we gratefully recall to-day — him, in yon manly figure wrought in the metal which but feebly typifies his inexorable will, we commit in his immortal youth to the reverence of our children. And here among these peaceful

fields; here in the county whose children first gave their
blood for American union and independence, and eighty-six
years later gave it first also for a truer union and a larger
liberty; here in the heart of Middlesex county, of Lexington
and Concord, and Bunker Hill, stand fast, Son of Liberty!
as the minute-man stood at the old North Bridge. But
should we or our descendants, false to liberty, false to justice
and humanity — betray in any way their cause — spring into
life as a hundred years ago, take one more step, descend, and
lead us, as God led you, in saving America, to save the hopes
of man.

At the end of a century we can see the work of this day as
our fathers could not; we can see that then the final movement began of a process long and unconsciously preparing,
which was to intrust liberty to new forms and institutions that
seemed full of happy promise for mankind. And now for
nearly a century what was formerly called the experiment of
a representative republic of imperial extent and power has
been tried. Has it fulfilled the hopes of its founders and
the just expectations of mankind? I have already glanced at
its early and fortunate conditions, and we know how vast and
splendid were its early growth and development. Our material statistics soon dazzled the world. Europe no longer
sneered but gazed in wonder, waiting and watching. Our
population doubled every fifteen years, and our wealth every
ten years. Every little stream among the hills turned a mill;
and the great inland seas, bound by the genius of Clinton to
the ocean, became the highway of boundless commerce, the
path of unprecedented empire. Our farms were the granary
of other lands. Our cotton fields made England rich. Still
we chased the whale in the Pacific Ocean and took fish in the
tumbling seas of Labrador. We hung our friendly lights

along thousands of miles of coast to tempt the trade of every clime; and wherever, on the dim rim of the globe there was a harbor, it was white with American sails. Meanwhile at home the political foreboding of federalism had died away, and its very wail seemed a tribute to the pacific glories of the land.

> "The ornament of beauty is suspect,
> A crow that flies in heaven's sweetest air."

The government was felt to be but a hand of protection and blessing; labor was fully employed; capital was secured; the army was a jest; enterprise was pushing through the Alleghanies, grasping and settling the El Dorado of the prairies, and still braving the wilderness, reached out toward the Rocky Mountains, and reversing the voyages of Columbus, rediscovered the Old World from the New. America was the Benjamin of nations, the best beloved of heaven, and the starry flag of the United States flashed a line of celestial light around the world, the harbinger of freedom, peace, and prosperity.

Such was the vision and the exulting faith of fifty years ago. "Atlantis hath risen from the ocean!" cried Edward Everett to applauding Harvard; and Daniel Webster answered from Bunker Hill, "If we fail, popular governments are impossible." So far as they could see, they stood among the unchanged conditions of the early republic. And those conditions are familiar. The men who founded the republic were few in number, planted chiefly along a temperate coast, remote from the world. They were a homogeneous people, increasing by their own multiplication, speaking the same language, of the same general religious faith, cherishing the same historic and political traditions, universally educated, hardy, thrifty, with general equality of fortune, and long and intelligent practice of self-government, while the slavery that existed among them, inhuman in itself, was not seriously defended, and was believed to be disappearing. But within the last half century causes then latent, or wholly incalculable before, have radically changed those conditions, and we enter upon the second century of the republic with responsibilities which neither our fathers nor the men of fifty years ago could possibly foresee.

Think, for instance, of the change wrought by foreign immigration, with all its necessary consequences. In the State of Massachusetts to-day the number of citizens of foreign birth who have no traditional association with the story of Concord and Lexington is larger than the entire population of the State on the day of battle. The first fifty years after the battle brought to the whole country fewer immigrants than are now living in Massachusetts alone. At the end of that half century, when Mr. Everett stood here, less than three hundred thousand foreign immigrants had come to this country, but in the fifty years that have since elapsed that immigration has been more than nine millions of persons. The aggregate population in the last fifty years has advanced somewhat more than threefold, the foreign immigration more than thirtyfold, so that now immigrants and the children of immigrants are a quarter of the whole population. This enormous influx of foreigners has added an immense ignorance and entire unfamiliarity with republican ideas and habits to the voting class. It has brought other political traditions, other languages and other religious faiths. It has introduced powerful and organized influences not friendly to the republican principle of freedom of thought and action. It is to the change produced by immigration that we owe the first serious questioning of the public school system, which was the nursery of the early republic, and which is to-day the palladium of free popular government.

Do not misunderstand me. I am not lamenting even in thought the boundless hospitality of America. I do not forget that the whole European race came hither but yesterday, and has been domesticated here not yet three hundred years. I am not insensible of the proud claim of America to be the refuge of the oppressed of every clime, nor do I doubt in her maturity her power, if duly directed, to assimilate whole nations, if need be, as in her infancy she achieved her independence, and in her prime maintained her unity. But if she has been the hope of the world, and is so still, it is because she has understood both the conditions and the perils of freedom, and watches carefully the changing conditions under which republican liberty is to be maintained. She will still welcome to her ample bosom all who choose to be called her children. But if she is to remain the mother of liberty, it will not be the result of those craven counsels whose type is the ostrich burying his head in the sand, but of that wise and heroic statesmanship whose symbol is her own heaven-soaring eagle, gazing undazzled even at the spots upon the sun.

Again, within the century steam has enormously expanded the national domain, and every added mile is an added strain to our system. The marvellous ease of communication both by rail and telegraph tends to obliterate conservative local lines and to make a fatal centralization more possible. The telegraph, which instantly echoes the central command at the remotest point, becomes both a facility and a temptation to exercise command, while below upon the rail the armed blow swiftly follows the word that flies along the wire. Steam concentrates population in cities. But when the government was formed the people were strictly rural, and there were but six cities with eight thousand inhabitants or more. In 1790 only one thirtieth of the population lived in cities, in 1870 more than one fifth. Steam destroys the natural difficulties of communication; but those very difficulties are barriers against invasion, and protect the independence of each little community, the true foundation of our free republican system. In New England the characteristic village and local life of the last century perishes in the age of steam. Meanwhile the enormous accumulation of capital engaged in great enterprises, with unscrupulous greed of power, constantly tends to make itself felt in corruption of the press which molds public opinion, and of the legislature which makes the laws. Thus steam and the telegraph tend to the concentration of capital and the consolidation of political power, a tendency which threatens liberty, and which was wholly unknown when the Republic began, and was unsuspected fifty years ago. Sweet Liberty is a mountain nymph, because mountains baffle the pursuer. But the inventions that level mountains and annihilate space alarm that gracious spirit, who sees her greater insecurity. But stay, heaven-eyed maid, and stay forever! Behold, our devoted wills shall be they invincible Alps, our loyal hearts thy secret bower, the spirit of our fathers a cliff of adamant that engineering skill can never pierce nor any foe can scale!

But the most formidable problem for popular government which the opening of our second century presents springs from a source which was unsuspected a hundred years ago, and which the orators of fifty years since forbore to name. This was the system of slave labor which vanished in civil war. But slavery had not been the fatal evil that it was, if with its abolition its consequences had disappeared. It holds us still in mortmain. Its dead hand is strong, as its living power was terrible. Emancipation has left the Republic exposed to a new and extraordinary trial of the principles and practices of free government. A civilization resting upon slavery, as formerly in part of the country, however polished and ornate, is necessarily aristocratic and hostile to republican equality, while the exigencies of such a society forbid that universal education which is indispensable to wise popular government. When war emancipates the slaves and makes them equal citizens, the ignorance and venality which are the fatal legacies of slavery to the subject-class, whether white or black, and the natural alienation of the master-class, which alone has political knowledge and experience, with all the secret conspiracies, the reckless corruption, the political knavery, springing naturally from such a situation, and ending often in menacing disorder that seems to invite the military interference and supervision of the government — all this accumulation of difficulty and danger lays a strain along the very fibre of free institutions. For it suggests the two-fold question whether the vast addition of the ignorance of the emancipated vote to that of the immigrant vote may not overwhelm the intelligent vote of the country, and whether the constant appeal to the central hand of power, however necessary it may seem, and for whatever reason of humanity and justice it may be urged, must not necessarily destroy that local self-reliance which was the very seed of the American Republic, and fatally familiarize the country with that employment of military power which is inconsistent with free institutions, and bold resistance to which has forever consecrated the spot on which we stand.

These are some of the more obvious changes in the conditions under which the Republic is to be maintained. I mention them merely; but every wise patriot sees and ponders them. Does he therefore despond? Heaven forbid! When was there ever an auspicious day for humanity that was not one of doubt and of conflict? The robust moral manhood of America confronts the future with steadfast faith and indomitable will, raising the old battle-cry of the race for larger liberty and surer law. It sees clouds, indeed, as Sam Adams saw them when this day dawned. But with him it sees through and through them, and with him thanks God for the glorious morning. There is, indeed, a fashion of scepticism of American principles even among some Americans, but it is one of the oldest and worst fashions in our history. There is a cynicism which fondly fancies that in its beginning the American Republic moved proudly toward the future with all the splendid assurance of the Persian Xerxes descending on the shores of Greece, but that it sits to-day among shattered hopes, like Xerxes above his ships at Salamis. And when was this golden age? Was it when John Adams appealed from the baseness of his own time to the greater candor and patriotism of this? Was it when Fisher Ames mourned over lost America like Rachel for her children, and would not be comforted? Was it when William Wirt said that he sought in vain for a man fit for the Presidency or for great responsibility? Was it when Chancellor Livingston saw only a threatening future because Congress was so feeble? Was it when we ourselves saw the industry, the commerce, the society, the church, the courts, the statesmanship, the conscience of America seemingly prostrate under the foot of slavery? Was this the golden age of these sentimental sighs, this the region behind the north wind of these reproachful regrets? And is it the young nation which with prayer and faith, with untiring devotion and unconquerable will, has lifted its bruised and broken body from beneath that crushing heel, whose future is distrusted?

Nay, this very cynicism is one of the foes that we must meet and conquer. Remember, fellow citizens, that the impulse of republican government, given a century ago at the old North Bridge, has shaken every government in the world, but has been itself wholly unshaken by them. It has made monarchy impossible in France. It has freed the Russian serfs. It has united Germany against ecclesiastical despotism. It has flashed into the night of Spain. It has emancipated Italy and discrowned the Pope as king. In England, repealing the disabilities of Catholic and Hebrew, it forecasts the separation of church and state, and step by step transforms monarchy into another form of republic. And here at home how glorious its story! In a tremendous war between men of the same blood — men who recognize and respect each other's valor — we have proved what was always doubted, the prodigious power, endurance and resources of a republic, and in emancipating an eighth of the population we have at last gained the full opportunity of the republican principle. Sir, it is the signal felicity of this occasion that on the one hundredth anniversary of the first battle of the war of American independence, I may salute you, who led to victory the citizen soldiers of American liberty, as the first elected President of the free Republic of the United States. Fortunate man! to whom God has given the priceless boon of associating your name with that triumph of freedom which will presently bind the East and the West, the North and the South, in a closer and more perfect union for the establishment of justice and the security of the blessings of liberty than these States have ever known.

Fellow citizens, that union is the lofty task which this hallowed day and this sacred spot impose upon us. And what cloud of doubt so dark hangs over us as that which lowered above the colonies when the troops of the King marched into this town, and the men of Middlesex resolved to pass the bridge? With their faith and their will we shall win their victory. No royal governor, indeed, sits in yon stately capital, no hostile fleet for many a year has vexed the waters of our coasts, nor is any army but our own ever likely to tread our soil. Not such are our enemies to-day. They do not come proudly stepping to the drum-beat, with bayonets flashing in the morning sun. But wherever party spirit shall strain the ancient guarantees of freedom, or bigotry and ignorance shall lay their fatal hands upon education, or the arrogance of caste shall strike at equal rights, or corruption shall poison the very springs of national life, there, minute-men of liberty, are your Lexington Green and Concord Bridge, and as you love your country and your kind, and would have your children rise up and call you blessed, spare not the enemy! Over the hills, out of the earth, down from the clouds, pour in resistless might. Fire from every rock and tree, from door and window, from hearth-stone and chamber; hang upon his flank and rear from noon to sunset, and so through a land blazing with holy indignation hurl the hordes of ignorance and corruption and injustice back, back, in utter defeat and ruin.

EULOGY OF WENDELL PHILLIPS

DELIVERED BEFORE THE MUNICIPAL AUTHORITIES OF BOSTON,
APRIL 18, 1884

MASSACHUSETTS is always rich in fitting voices to commemorate the virtues and services of her illustrious citizens, and in every strain of affectionate admiration and thoughtful discrimination, the legislature, the pulpit, and the press — his old associates, who saw the glory of his prime — the younger generation which cherishes the tradition of his devoted life—have spoken the praise of Wendell Phillips. But his native city has justly thought that the great work of his life was not local or limited; that it was as large as liberty and as broad as humanity, and that his name, therefore, is not the treasure of a State only, but a national possession. An orator whose consecrated eloquence, like the music of Amphion raising the wall of Thebes, was a chief force in giving to the American Union the impregnable defence of freedom, is a common benefactor; the West may well answer to the East, the South to the North, and Carolina and California, Minnesota and New York, mingle their sorrow with that of New England, and own in his death a common bereavement.

At other times, with every mornful ceremony of respect, the commonwealth and its chief city have lamented their dead sons, conspicuous party leaders, who, in high official place, and with the formal commission of the State, have worthily maintained the ancient renown and the lofty faith of Massachusetts. But it is a private citizen whom we commemorate to-day, yet a public leader; a man always foremost in political controversy, but who held no office, and belonged to no political party; who swayed votes, but who seldom voted, and never for a mere party purpose; and who, for the larger part of his active life, spurned the constitution as a bond of iniquity, and the Union as a yoke of oppression. Yet, the official authority which decrees this commemoration — this great assembly which honors his memory — the press, which from sea to sea has celebrated his name — and I, who at your summons stand here to speak his eulogy, are all loyal to party, all revere the constitution and maintain the Union, all hold the ballot to be the most sacred trust, and voting to be the highest duty of the citizen.

As we recall the story of that life, the spectacle of to-day is one of the most significant in our history. This memorial rite is not a tribute to official service, to literary genius, to scientific distinction; it is homage to personal character. It is the solemn public declaration that a life of transcendent purity of purpose, blended with commanding powers, devoted with absolute unselfishness, and with amazing results, to the welfare of the country and of humanity, is, in the American republic, an example so inspiring, a patriotism so lofty, and a public service so beneficent, that, in contemplating them, discordant opinions, differing judgments, and the sharp sting of controversial speech, vanish like frost in a flood of sunshine.

It is not the Samuel Adams who was impatient of Washington, and who doubted the constitution, but the Samuel Adams of Faneuil Hall, of the Committee of Correspondence, of Concord and Lexington — Samuel Adams, the father of the Revolution, whom Massachusetts and America remember and revere.

The revolutionary tradition was the native air of Wendell Phillips. When he was born in this city, seventy-three years ago last November, some of the chief revolutionary figures still lingered. John Adams was living at Quincy, and Thomas Jefferson at Monticello; Elbridge Gerry was governor of the State, James Madison was President, and the second war with England was at hand. Phillips was nine years old when, in 1820, the most important debate after the adoption of the constitution, the debate of whose tumultuous culmination and triumphant close he was to be the great orator, began, and the second heroic epoch of our history, in which he was a master figure, opened in the long and threatening contest over the admission of Missouri. Unheeding the transactions which were shaking the land and setting the scene of his career, the young boy, of the best New England lineage and prospects, played upon Beacon Hill, and at the age of sixteen entered Harvard College. His classmates recall his manly pride and reserve, with the charming manner, the delightful conversation, and the affluence of kindly humor, which was never lost. He sauntered and gently studied; not a devoted student, not in the bent of his mind, nor in the special direction of sympathy, forecasting the reformer, but already the orator and the easy master of the college platform; and still, in the memory of his old companions, he walks those college paths in unfading youth, a figure of patrician port, of sovereign grace — a prince coming to his kingdom.

The tranquil years at the university ended, and he graduated in 1831, the year of Nat. Turner's insurrection in Virginia; the year, also, in which Mr. Garrison issued the "Liberator," and, for unequivocally proclaiming the principle of the Declaration of Independence was denounced as

a public enemy. Like other gently nurtured Boston boys,
Phillips began the study of law, and, as it proceeded, doubtless the sirens sang to him, as to the noble youth of every
country and time.

If, musing over Coke and Blackstone, in the full consciousness of ample powers and of fortunate opportunities, he sometimes forecast the future, he doubtless saw himself succeeding Fisher Ames, and Harrison Gray Otis, and Daniel
Webster, rising from the bar to the legislature, from the
legislature to the senate, from the senate — who knew
whither ? — the idol of society, the applauded orator, the brilliant champion of the elegant repose and the cultivated conservatism of Massachusetts.

The delight of social ease, the refined enjoyment of taste
in letters and art, opulent leisure, professional distinction,
gratified ambition — all these came and whispered to the
young student. And it is the force that can tranquilly put
aside such blandishments with a smile, and accept alienation,
outlawry, ignominy, and apparent defeat, if need be, no less
than the courage which grapples with poverty and outward
hardship, and climbs over them to worldly prosperity, which
is the test of the finest manhood. Only he who fully knows
the worth of what he renounces gains the true blessing of
renunciation.

The time during which Phillips was studying law was the
hour of the profoundest moral apathy in the history of this
country. The fervor of revolutionary feeling was long since
spent, and that of the final anti-slavery contest was but just
kindled. The question of slavery, indeed, had never been
quite forgotten. There was always an anti-slavery sentiment
in the country, but there was also a slavery interest, and the
invention of the cotton-gin in 1789 gave slavery the most

powerful and insidious impulse that it had ever received. At once commercial greed was allied with political advantage and social power, and the active anti-slavery sentiment rapidly declined.

Ten years after the invention of the cotton-gin, the General Convention of the Abolition Societies deplored the decay of public interest in emancipation. Forty years later, in 1833, while Phillips was still studying law, the veteran Pennsylvania Society lamented that since 1794 it had seen one after another of those societies disband, until it was left almost alone to mourn the universal apathy.

When Wendell Phillips was admitted to the bar in 1834, the slave interest in the United States, entrenched in the constitution, in trade, in the church, in society, in historic tradition, and in the prejudice of race, had already become, although unconsciouⁿly to the country, one of the most powerful forces in the world. The English throne in 1625, the old French monarchy in 1780, the English aristocracy at the beginning of the century, were not so strong as slavery, in this country fifty years ago. The grasp of England upon the American colonies before the Revolution was not so sure, and was never so menacing to liberty upon this continent, as the grasp of slavery upon the Union in the pleasant days when the young lawyer sat in his office careless of the anti-slavery agitation, and jesting with his old college comrades over the clients who did not come.

But on an October afternoon in 1835, while he was still sitting expectant in his office, the long-awaited client came, but in what an amazing form! The young lawyer was especially a Boston boy. He loved his native city with that lofty pride and intensity of local affection which are peculiar to her citizens. " I was born in Boston," he said long after-

ward, " and the good name of the old town is bound up with
every fibre of my heart." In the mild afternoon his windows
were open and the sound of unusual disturbance drew him
from his office. He hastened along the street, and suddenly,
a stone's throw from the scene of the Boston massacre, in the
very shadow of the old State House, he beheld in Boston
a spectacle which Boston cannot now conceive. He saw
American women insulted for befriending their innocent
sisters, whose children were sold from their arms. He saw
an American citizen assailed by a furious mob in the city of
James Otis for saying with James Otis that a man's right to
liberty is inherent and inalienable.

Himself a citizen-soldier, he looked to see the majesty of
the people maintaining the authority of law; but, to his own
startled surprise, he saw that the rightful defenders of law
against the mob were themselves the mob. The city whose
dauntless free speech had taught a country how to be independent he saw raising a parricidal hand against its parent—
Liberty.

It was enough. As the jail doors closed upon Garrison
to save his life, Garrison and his cause had won their most
powerful and renowned ally. With the setting of that
October sun vanished forever the career of prosperous ease,
the gratification of ordinary ambition, which the genius and
the accomplishment of Wendell Phillips had seemed to fore-
tell. Yes, the long-awaited client had come at last. Scarred,
scorned, and forsaken, that cowering and friendless client
was wronged and degraded humanity. The great soul saw
and understood.

> " So nigh is grandeur to our dust,
> So near is God to man,
> When duty whispers low, Thou must,
> The youth replies, I can."

Already the Boston boy felt what he afterward said: " I love inexpressibly these streets of Boston over which my mother led my baby feet, and if God grants me time enough I will make them too pure for the footsteps of a slave."

And we, fellow citizens, who recall the life and the man, the untiring sacrifice, the complete surrender, do we not hear in the soft air of that long-vanished October day, far above the riot of the stormy street, the benediction that he could not hear, but whose influence breathed always from the ineffable sweetness of his smile and the gracious courtesy of his manner, " Inasmuch as thou hast done it to the least of these my brethren, thou hast done it unto me."

The scene of that day is an illustration of the time. As we look back upon it it is incredible. But it was not until Lovejoy fell, while defending his press at Alton, in November, 1837, that an American citizen was killed by a raging mob for declaring in a free State the right of innocent men and women to their personal liberty. This tragedy, like the deadly blow at Charles Summer in the Senate chamber, twenty years afterward, awed the whole country with a sense of vast and momentous peril.

The country has just been startled by the terrible riot at Cincinnati, which sprang from the public consciousness that by crafty legal quibbling crime had become secure. But the outbreak was at once and universally condemned because, in this country, whatever the wrong may be, reform by riot is always worse than the wrong. The Alton riot, however, had no redeeming impulse. It was the very frenzy of lawlessness, a sudden and ghastly glimpse of the unquenchable fires of passion that were burning under the seeming peace and ¬rosperity of the Union. How fierce and far-reaching those passions were was seen not only in the riot itself, but in the refusal of Faneuil Hall for a public meeting to denounce the appalling wrong to American liberty which had been done in Illinois, lest the patriotic protest of the meeting should be interpreted by the country as the voice of Boston.

But the refusal was reconsidered, and never since the people of Boston thronged Faneuil Hall on the day after the massacre in State street had that ancient hall seen a more solemn and significant assembly. It was the more solemn, the more significant, because the excited multitude was no longer, as in the revolutionary day, inspired by one unanimous and overwhelming purpose to assert and maintain liberty of speech as the bulwark of all other liberty. It was an unwonted and foreboding scene. An evil spirit was in the air.

When the seemly protest against the monstrous crime had been spoken, and the proper duty of the day was done, a voice was heard, the voice of the high officer solemnly sworn to prosecute in the name of Massachusetts every violation of law, declaring, in Faneuil Hall, sixty years after the battle of Bunker Hill, and amid a howling storm of applause, that an American citizen who was put to death by a mad crowd of his fellow citizens for defending his right of free speech, died as the fool dieth.

Boston has seen dark days, but never a moment so dark as that. Seven years before Webster had said, in the famous words that Massachusetts binds as frontlets between her eyes, " There are Boston and Concord, and Lexington and Bunker Hill, and there they will remain forever." Had they already vanished? Was the spirit of the Revolution quite extinct? In the very cradle of liberty did no son survive to awake its slumbering echoes? By the grace of God such a son there was. He had come with the multitude, and he had heard with sympathy and approval the speeches that condemned the wrong; but when the cruel voice justified the murderers of Lovejoy the heart of the young man burned within him. This speech, he said to himself, must be answered. As the malign strain proceeded the Boston boy, all on fire, with Concord and Lexington tugging at his heart, unconsciously murmured, " Such a speech in Faneuil Hall must be answered in Faneuil Hall."

" Why not answer it yourself? " whispered a neighbor who overheard him.

" Help me to the platform and I will "—and pushing and struggling through the dense and threatening crowd the young man reached the platform, was lifted upon it, and, advancing to speak, was greeted with a roar of hostile cries. But riding the whirlwind undismayed, as for many a year afterward he directed the same wild storm, he stood upon the platform in all the beauty and grace of imperial youth — the Greeks would have said a god descended—and in words that touched the mind and heart and conscience of that vast multitude, as with fire from heaven, recalling Boston to herself, he saved his native city and her cradle of liberty from the damning disgrace of stoning the first martyr in the great struggle for personal freedom.

" Mr. Chairman," he said, " when I heard the gentleman lay down principles which placed the rioters, incendiaries, and murderers of Alton side by side with Otis and Hancock, and Quincy and Adams, I thought those pictured lips would have broken into voice to rebuke the recreant American— the slanderer of the dead."

And even as he spoke the vision was fulfilled. Once more

its native music rang through Faneuil Hall. In the orator's own burning words those pictured lips did break into immortal rebuke. In Wendell Phillips, glowing with holy indignation at the insult to America and to man, John Adams and James Otis, Josiah Quincy and Samuel Adams, though dead, yet spake.

In the annals of American speech there had been no such scene since Patrick Henry's electrical warning to George III. It was that greatest of oratorical triumphs when a supreme emotion, a sentiment which is to mold a people anew, lifted the orator to adequate expression.

Three such scenes are illustrious in our history. That of the speech of Patrick Henry at Williamsburg, of Wendell Phillips in Faneuil Hall, of Abraham Lincoln in Gettysburg —three, and there is no fourth. They transmit, unextinguished, the torch of an eloquence which has aroused nations and changed the course of history, and which Webster called "noble, sublime, God-like action." The tremendous controversy indeed inspired universal eloquence. As the cause passed from the moral appeal of the Abolitionists to the political action of the Liberty party, of the Conscience Whigs and Free-Soil Democrats, and finally of the Republican party, the sound of speech, which in its variety and excellence had never been heard upon the continent, filled the air.

But supreme over it all was the eloquence of Phillips, as over the harmonious tumult of a great orchestra, one clear voice, like a lark high-poised in heaven, steadily carries the melody. As Demosthenes was the orator of Greece against Philip, and Cicero of Rome against Catiline, and John Pym of England against the Stuart despotism, Wendell Phillips was distinctively the orator, as others were the statesmen, of the anti-slavery cause.

When he first spoke at Faneuil Hall some of the most renowned American orators were still in their prime. Webster and Clay were in the Senate, Choate at the bar, Edward Everett upon the academic platform. From all these orators Phillips differed more than they differed from each other. Behind Webster and Everett and Clay there was always a great organized party or an entrenched conservatism of feeling and opinion.

They spoke accepted views. They moved with masses of men, and were sure of the applause of party spirit, of political tradition, and of established institutions. Phillips stood alone. He was not a Whig nor a Democrat, nor the graceful panegyrist of an undisputed situation. Both parties denounced him. He must recruit a new party. Public opinion condemned him. He must win public opinion to achieve his purpose. The tone, the method of the new orator, announced a new spirit. It was not a heroic story of the last century, nor the contention of contemporary politics; it was the unsuspected heroism of a mightier controversy that breathed and burned in his words. With no party behind him, and denouncing established order and acknowledged tradition, his speech was necessarily a popular appeal for a strange and unwelcome cause, and the condition of its success was that it should both charm and rouse the hearer, while, under cover of the fascination, the orator unfolded his argument and urged his plea. This condition the genius of the orator instinctively perceived, and it determined the character of his discourse.

He faced his audience with a tranquil mien and a beaming aspect that was never dimmed. He spoke, and in the measured cadence of his quiet voice there was intense feeling, but no declamation, no passionate appeal, no superficial and

feigned emotion. It was simple colloquy—a gentleman conversing. Unconsciously and surely the ear and heart were
charmed. How was it done?—Ah! how did Mozart do it,
how Raphael?

The secret of the rose's sweetness, of the bird's ecstasy,
of the sunset's glory—that is the secret of genius and of eloquence. What was heard, what was seen, was the form of
noble manhood, the courteous and self-possessed tone, the
flow of modulated speech, sparkling with matchless richness
of illustration, with apt allusion, and happy anecdote and
historic parallel, with wit and pitiless invective, with melodious pathos, with stinging satire, with crackling epigram and
limpid humor, the bright ripples that play around the sure
and steady prow of the resistless ship. Like an illuminated
vase of odors he glowed with concentrated and perfumed fire.
The divine energy of his conviction utterly possessed him,
and his

> " Pure and eloquent blood
> Spoke in his cheek, and so distinctly wrought,
> That one might almost say his body thought."

Was it Pericles swaying the Athenian multitude? Was it
Apollo breathing the music of the morning from his lips?—
No, no! It was an American patriot, a modern son of liberty,
with a soul as firm and as true as was ever consecrated to
unselfish duty, pleading with the American conscience for the
chained and speechless victims of American inhumanity.

How terribly earnest was the anti-slavery contest this
generation little knows. But to understand Phillips we must
recall the situation of the country. When he joined the
Abolitionists, and for more than twenty years afterward,
slavery sat supreme in the White House and made laws in
the capitol. Courts of justice were its ministers and legislatures its lackeys.

It silenced the preacher in the pulpit, it muzzled the editor at his desk, and the professor in his lecture-room. It set a price upon the head of peaceful citizens, robbed the mails, and denounced the vital principle of the Declaration of Independence as treason. In States whose laws did not tolerate slavery, slavery ruled the club and the drawing-room, the factory and the office, swaggered at the dinner table, and scourged, with scorn, a cowardly society.

It tore the golden rule from school books, and from the prayer book the pictured benignity of Christ. It prohibited in the free States schools for the hated race, and hunted women who taught children to read. If forbade a free people to communicate with their representatives, seized territory to extend its area and confirm its sovereignty, and plotted to steal more to make its empire impregnable and the free Republic of the United States impossible. Scholars, divines, men and women in every church, in every party, raised individual voices in earnest protest. They sighed against a hurricane. There had been such protest in the country for two centuries—colonial provisions and restrictions—the fiery voice of Whitfield in the south—the calm persuasion of Woolman in the middle colonies—the heroism of Hopkins in Rhode Island—the eloquence of Rush in Pennsylvania. There had been emancipation societies at the North and at the South, arguments and appeals and threats in the congress of the confederation, in the constitutional convention, in the Congress of the Union; there had been the words and the will of Washington, the warning of Jefferson, the consenting testimony of the revered fathers of the government; always the national conscience somewhere silently pleading, always the finger of the world steadily pointing in scorn.

But here, after all the protest and the rebuke and the

endeavor, was the malign power, which, when the constitution was formed, had been but the shrinking Afrite bound in the casket, now towering and resistless. He had kicked his casket into the sea, and, haughtily defying the conscience of the country and the moral sentiment of mankind, demanded absolute control of the Republic as the price of union — the Republic, anxious only to submit and to call submission statesmanship.

If, then, the work of the Revolution was to be saved, and independent America was to become free America, the first and paramount necessity was to arouse the country. Agitation was the duty of the hour. Garrison was certainly not the first Abolitionist; no, nor was Luther the first Protestant. But Luther brought all the wandering and separate rays of protest to a focus, and kindled the contest for religious freedom. So, when Garrison flung full in the face of slavery the defiance of immediate and complete abolition, slavery, instinctively foreseeing its doom, sprang to its feet and joined with the heroism of despair in the death-grapple with liberty, from which, after a generation, liberty arose unbruised and victorious.

It is hard for the survivors of a generation to which Abolitionist was a word suggesting the most odious fanaticism — a furious declamation at once nonsensical and dangerous, a grotesque and sanctimonious playing with fire in a powder-magazine—to believe that the names of the representative Abolitionists will be written with a sunbeam, as Phillips says of Toussaint, high over many an honored name. But history, looking before and after, readjusts contemporary judgments of men and events. In all the essential qualities of heroic action Luther, nailing his challenge to the church upon the church's own door, when the church was supreme in

Europe, William Tell, in the romantic legend, serenely scorning to bow to the cap of Gesler, when Gesler's troops held all the market-place, are not nobler figures than Garrison and Phillips, in the hour of the complete possession of the country by the power of slavery, demanding immediate and unconditional emancipation.

A tone of apology, of deprecation or regret, no more becomes an American in speaking of the Abolitionists than in speaking of the Sons of Liberty in the Revolution, and every tribute of honor and respect which we gladly pay to the illustrious fathers of American independence is paid as worthily to their sons, the pioneers of American freedom.

That freedom was secured, indeed, by the union of many forces. The Abolition movement was moral agitation. It was a voice crying in the wilderness. As an American movement it was reproached for holding aloof from the American political method. But in the order of time the moral awakening precedes political action. Politics are founded in compromise and expediency, and had the Abolition leaders paused to parley with prejudice and interest and personal ambition, in order to smooth and conciliate and persuade, their duty would have been undone. When the alarm-bell at night has brought the aroused citizens to the street they will organize their action.

But the ringer of the bell betrays his trust when he ceases to startle. To vote was to acknowledge the constitution. To acknowledge the constitution was to offer a premium upon slavery by granting more political power for every slave. It was to own an obligation to return innocent men to unspeakable degradation and to shoot them down if, with a thousandfold greater reason than our fathers, they resisted oppression. Could Americans do this? Could honest men do this? Could a great country do this and not learn, sooner or later, by ghastly experience, the truth which George Mason proclaimed—that Providence punishes national sins by national calamities? The Union, said Wendell Phillips, with a calmness that enchanted while it appalled—the Union is called the very ark of the American covenant; but has not idolatry of the Union been the chief bulwark of slavery, and in the words and deeds and spirit of the most vehement " Union saviours " who denounce agitation, can any hope of emancipation be described?

If, then, under the sacred charter of the Union, slavery has grown to this stupenduous height, throwing the shadow of death over the land, is not the Union as it exists the foe of liberty, and can we honestly affirm that it is the sole surviving hope of freedom in the world? Long ago the great leaders of our parties hushed their voices and whispered that even to speak of slavery was to endanger the Union. Is not this enough? Sons of Otis and of Adams, of Franklin and of Jay, are we ready for union upon the ruins of freedom? *Delenda Carthago! Delenda Carthago!*

Even while he spoke there sprang up around him the marshalled host of an organized political party which, raising the constitution as a banner of freedom, marched to the polls to make the Union the citadel of liberty. He, indeed, had rejected the constitution and the Union as the bulwark of slavery. But he and the political host, widely differing, had yet a common purpose, and were confounded in a common condemnation. And who shall count the voters in that political army, and who the generous heroes of the actual war, in whose young hearts his relentless denunciation of the Union had bred the high resolve that, under the protection of the constitution and by its own lawful power, the slave

Union which he denounced should be dissolved in the fervid glory of a new Union of freedom?

His plea, indeed, did not persuade his friends, and was furiously spurned by his foes. "Hang Phillips and Yancey together, hang the Abolitionist and the fire-eater and we shall have peace," cried mingled wrath and terror as the absorbing debate deepened toward civil war. But still, through the startling flash and over the thunder-peal with which the tempest burst, that cry rang out undismayed, *Delenda Carthago!*—The awful storm has rolled away. The warning voice is stilled forever. But the slave Union whose destruction he sought to dissolve, and the glorious Union of freedom and equal rights which his soul desired, is the blessed Union of to-day. . . .

When the war ended, and the specific purpose of his relentless agitation was accomplished, Phillips was still in the prime of his life. Had his mind recurred to the dreams of earlier years, had he desired, in the fulness of his fame and the maturity of his powers, to turn to the political career which the hopes of the friends of his youth had forecast, I do not doubt that the Massachusetts of Sumner and of Andrew, proud of his genius and owning his immense service to the triumphant cause, although a service beyond the party line, and often apparently directed against the party itself, would have gladly summoned him to duty. It would, indeed, have been a kind of peerage for this great Commoner. But not to repose and peaceful honor did this earnest soul incline. "Now that the field is won," he said gayly to a friend, "do you sit by the camp-fire, but I will put out into the underbrush." The slave, indeed, was free, but emancipation did not free the agitator from his task. The client that suddenly appeared before him on that memorable October day was

not an oppressed race alone; it was wronged humanity; it
was the victim of unjust systems and unequal laws; it was the
poor man, the weak man, the unfortunate man, whoever and
whatever he might be. This was the cause that he would
still plead in the forum of public opinion. " Let it not be
said," he wrote to a meeting of his old Abolition friends, two
months before his death, " that the old Abolitionist stopped
with the negro, and was never able to see that the same
principles claimed his utmost effort to protect all labor, white
and black, and to further the discussion of every claim of
humanity."

Was this the habit of mere agitation, the restless discontent that followed great achievement? There were those
who thought so. But they were critics of a temperament
which did not note that with Phillips agitation was a principle, and a deliberately chosen method to definite ends.
There were still vast questions springing from the same
root of selfishness and injustice as the question of slavery.
They must force a hearing in the same way. He would not
adopt in middle life the career of politics, which he had re-
nounced in youth, however seductive that career might be,
whatever its opportunities and rewards, because the purpose
had grown with his growth and strengthened with his
strength, to form public opinion rather than to represent
it, in making or in executing the laws. To form public
opinion upon vital public questions by public discussion, but
by public discussion absolutely fearless and sincere, and conducted with honest faith in the people to whom the argument
was addressed—this was the service which he had long performed, and this he would still perform, and in the familiar
way.

His comprehensive philanthropy had made him, even

during the anti-slavery contest, the untiring advocate of other great reforms. His powerful presentation of the justice and reason of the political equality of women, at Worcester, in 1857, more than any other single impulse launched that question upon the sea of popular controversy. In the general statement of principle, nothing has been added to that discourse. In vivid and effective eloquence of advocacy it has never been surpassed. All the arguments for independence echoed John Adams in the Continental Congress; all the pleas for applying the American principle of representation to the wives and mothers of American citizens echo the eloquence of Wendell Phillips at Worcester. His, also, was the voice that summoned the temperance voters of the Commonwealth to stand up and be counted; the voice which resolutely and definitely exposed the crime to which the busy American mind and conscience are at last turning—the American crime against the Indians. Through him the sorrow of Crete, the tragedy of Ireland, pleaded with America. In the terrible experience of the early anti-slavery debate, when the church and refined society seemed to be the rampart of slavery, he had learned profound distrust of that conservatism of prosperity which chills human sympathy and narrows the conscience. So the vast combinations of capital, in these later days, with their immense monopolies and imperial power, seemed to him sure to corrupt the government and to obstruct and threaten the real welfare of the people. He felt, therefore, that what is called the respectable class is often really, but unconsciously and with a generous purpose, not justly estimating its own tendency, the dangerous class. He was not a party politician; he cared little for party or for party leaders. But any political party which in his judgment represented the dangerous tendency was a party to be defeated in the interest of the peace and progress of all the people.

But his judgment, always profoundly sincere, was it not sometimes profoundly mistaken? No nobler friend of freedom and of man than Wendell Phillips ever breathed upon this continent, and no man's service to freedom surpasses his. But before the war he demanded peaceful disunion— yet it was the Union in arms that saved liberty. During the war he would have superseded Lincoln—but it was Lincoln who freed the slaves. He pleaded for Ireland, tortured by centuries of misrule, and while every generous heart followed with sympathy the pathos and the power of his appeal, the just mind recoiled from the sharp arraignment of the truest friends in England that Ireland ever had. I know it all; but I know also, and history will remember, that the slave Union which he denounced is dissolved; that it was the heart and conscience of the nation, exalted by his moral appeal of agitation, as well as by the enthusiasm of patriotic war, which held up the hands of Lincoln, and upon which Lincoln leaned in emancipating the slaves, and that only by indignant and aggressive appeals like his has the heart of England ever opened to Irish wrong.

No man, I say, can take a pre-eminent and effective part in contentions that shake nations, or in the discussion of great national policies, of foreign relations, of domestic economy and finance, without keen reproach and fierce misconception. "But death," says Bacon, "bringeth good fame." Then, if moral integrity remain unsoiled, the purpose pure, blameless the life, and patriotism as shining as the sun, conflicting views and differing counsels disappear, and, firmly fixed upon character and actual achievement, good fame rests secure. Eighty years ago, in this city, how un-

JOSEPH R. HAWLEY

sparing was the denunciation of John Adams for betraying and ruining his party, for his dogmatism, his vanity, and ambition, for his exasperating impracticability—he, the Colossus of the Revolution! And Thomas Jefferson? I may truly say what the historian says of the Saracen mothers and Richard Cœur de Lion, that the mothers of Boston hushed their children with fear of the political devil incarnate of Virginia. But, when the drapery of mourning shrouded the columns and overhung the arches of Faneuil Hall, Daniel Webster did not remember that sometimes John Adams was imprudent and Thomas Jefferson sometimes unwise. He remembered only that John Adams and Thomas Jefferson were two of the greatest American patriots — and their fellow citizens of every party bowed their heads and said, Amen. I am not here to declare that the judgment of Wendell Phillips was always sound, nor his estimate of men always just, nor his policy always approved by the event. He would have scorned such praise. I am not here to eulogize the mortal, but the immortal. He, too, was a great American patriot; and no American life — no, not one — offers to future generations of his countrymen a more priceless example of inflexible fidelity to conscience and to public duty; and no American more truly than he purged the national name of its shame, and made the American flag the flag of hope for mankind.

Among her noblest children his native city will cherish him, and gratefully recall the unbending Puritan soul that dwelt in a form so gracious and urbane. The plain house in which he lived — severely plain, because the welfare of the suffering and the slave were preferred to books and pictures and every fair device of art; the house to which the North Star led the trembling fugitive, and which the unfortunate and the friendless knew; the radiant figure passing swiftly through these streets, plain as the house from which it came, regal with a royalty beyond that of kings; the cease-less charity untold; the strong sustaining heart of private friendship; the sacred domestic affections that must not here be named; the eloquence which, like the song of Orpheus, will fade from living memory into a doubtful tale; that great scene of his youth in Faneuil Hall; the surrender of ambi-tion; the mighty agitation and the mighty triumph with which his name is forever blended; the consecration of a life hidden with God in sympathy with man — these, all these, will live among your immortal traditions, heroic even in your heroic story. But not yours alone! As years go by, and only the large outlines of lofty American characters and careers remain, the wide Republic will confess the benedic-tion of a life like this, and gladly own that if with perfect faith and hope assured America would still stand and " bid the distant generations hail," the inspiration of her national life must be the sublime moral courage, the all-embracing humanity, the spotless integrity, the absolutely unselfish de-votion of great powers to great public ends, which were the glory of Wendell Phillips.

COX

SAMUEL SULLIVAN COX, an American congressman, was born at Zanesville, Ohio, September 30, 1824, and educated at Ohio State University and Brown University. After practising law for a short period he became in 1853 the editor of the "Statesman," a journal published in Columbus, Ohio. After serving for a year as secretary of legation at Lima, Peru, he entered the lower house of Congress in 1857, serving there continuously until March, 1865. During this time he supported the policy of the administration in voting supplies and men to carry on the war for the Union, but frequently criticized its course in various other matters. He removed to New York city in 1866 and two years later was sent to Congress as representative from New York, retaining his seat at this time for twelve years. He introduced and secured the passage of the bill creating the life-saving service, and also brought forward the bill for increasing the pay of the letter carriers, who in after years erected a bronze statue of their benefactor in New York city. In 1885-86, he was minister to Turkey and subsequently served another term in Congress as representative. His death took place in Washington city September 10, 1889. Cox was a very popular as well as effective speaker, and won an extensive reputation as a humorist. He travelled extensively and wrote much concerning his travels. His published works include "The Buckeye Abroad" (1851); "Puritanism in Politics" (1863); "Eight Years in Congress" (1865); "A Search for Winter Sunbeams" (1870); "Why We Laugh" (1876); "Free Land and Free Trade" (1876); "Arctic Sunbeams" (1882); "Orient Sunbeams" (1882); "Memorial Eulogies" (1883); "Three Decades of Federal Legislation" (1885); "A Diplomat in Turkey" (1887); "The Isles of the Princes" (1887); "The Four New States" (1889).

THE BEAUTIES OF DIPLOMACY

FROM SPEECH DELIVERED IN THE HOUSE OF REPRESENTATIVES, FEBRUARY 9, 1876

NOW, gentlemen, I will go to Greece although there is hardly a grease spot left! However there is something very interesting in connection with Greece which I would like to refer to. I do not think it has been exhausted altogether. The gentleman from Illinois [Mr. Springer] anticipated me a little as I was the first man to find out the interesting letters which he has quoted. My friend, Judge Holman, also anticipated me but he did not find, read, nor comment on the most interesting epistles. Here is one:

Legation of the United States,
Athens, March 8, 1875.
(Received April 5.)

Sir.—A magnificent ball took place at the palace on the 3d instant. On that occasion the American minister had the honor to be selected to lead a contra-dance with the queen.

Now that is something that I like. It makes me wish to defend in one sense the minister to Greece. I will defend anybody that has been so abused as this minister. Why what do we not owe to Greece? Think of it! The land where " burning Sappho loved and sung," and all the rest of Byron's fine ode, which you, Mr. Chairman, rehearsed in your boyhood. Think of Athens—the eye of Greece and the Piræus which has been called the " eyesore of Greece." Think of the arts of war and peace which Greece illustrated two thousand years ago! Think of Marathon and Salamis, and the " ships by thousands " which used to lay below, but which do not lay around there at all now, especially with our starry flag at their mast!

Think of Thermopylæ and her three hundred, of the Pyrrhic phalanx and Anacreon, Suli's rock and Sunium's marbled steep; and then, swan-like, die for love of Greece, after Byron's draught of Samian wine! Think of the Acropolis. Think of those old heroes that modern Greeks name their children after—Æschylus, Thersites, Agamemnon, and Ulysses—never forget Ulysses,—Epaminondas, and Pericles, and Sophocles, and Alcibiades, and Themistocles, and Euripides, and all the other D D's belonging to the early days of ancient Greece.

Yet, sir, as my friend from Indiana [Mr. Holman] well

said, our representatives, when they go to Greece go to the tomb of departed greatness. Greece gave art, science, logic, and poetry to the ages. She is entitled to a minister from the United States of America, not on account of any special living people that are there, or any special commerce which they have with us, for they only send us, I believe, from two to ten thousand pounds of Zante currants every year; but Greece has a nomadic population of goat-herds, and we ought to improve on a certain kind of goat that we have in this country.

Is there here any man who will not assist us to protect and raise Greece to her ancient fame? Let him read Clay and Webster, if not Plato and Aristotle. Let him read the catalogue of the Homeric heroes! True, her streams are dried up, her soil barren, her olive-trees cut up by the roots for fuel, and her very grass made the food of her nomadic goats; but is it not Greece? Some cynic may ask before voting appropriations for our minister, who honors the dead past and the great heroes of that dead past, " What is Cithera's isle to the grasshopper-despoiled West? What is Milos, from whence the famous statue of Venus came, or Salamis with the fame of Themistocles, when Mississippi is under the ban and its plantations are overgrown with sedge-grass? What the Piræus, where Socrates questioned the sailors, or what the academy under whose olive-trees the divine Plato sat while the bees of Hymettus settled on his lips, when the Texas border is ravaged by greasers and American cattle driven to Cortina's ranches by the thousand?

What are Morea's hills with their golden and purple sunsets, when beyond our sunset, contractors cheat the government and Indians on meat and flour? What the violet-wreathed city of Minerva, when in the great metropolis of

New York, "farther west," the tenement houses teem with skeleton starvelings? Let imagination paint in rainbow colors the verdureless and yellow isles of Greece and sing them again in Byron's muse, but what are these to the demoralized and overflowed bacon of Alabama? When there is sung the glories of Bacchus and the mazy dance of the Bacchantes, who is to tell the mysteries of the crooked juices of the maize of Illinois, Wisconsin, and Missouri?

And if further the same cynic asks why King George of Greece plays with his pet birds while the bandits prowl, plunder, and murder; if it is said that Greece is the land of ruins, brigands, and beggars, and the little kinglet of Schleswig-Holstein is held on his throne by other powers, may we not respond, " It is Greece, the Greece of Aristotle and Homer to which we send expensive ambassadors ? "

We ought to go further in our pride and protection for this grave of greatness. We ought to bring out of the ruins of the Acropolis some of those rare works of art that were left by Lord Elgin when he surreptitiously carried off so many to the British museum. I plead as well for art as for the poor inhabitants of Greece. They ought to be in some way or other protected by our minister.

There are many new members here who probably do not know that two years ago we had an executive document, No. 54 of the second session of the Forty-second Congress, sent here by a Colonel Steinberger, who went to what is called the Navigator islands. He was on a special mission from our government. I do not know just what it was for. Perhaps there was a land job in it. *Omne ignotum pro mirifico.*[1] But he went out to these islands and there he was soon hand and glove with King Lunalilo. He is now premier. There

---

[1] Every unknown is regarded as marvellous.

he is now, sitting under the bread-fruit trees, with the little
monkey clinging with prehensile grip to their limbs, and he
(I do not mean the monkey) wrapped around with the Star
Spangled Banner of our country; only seventy-five hundred
miles from San Francisco, eight thousand miles from China
and four thousand miles from Juan Fernandez! There our
banner floats!

O, how proud we were when we knew that our banner was
floating over those basaltic rocks, washed by the waves as
they rolled over coral reefs, with fishes among them of all
kinds and colors! Then to think that away off, where no
good man had ever gone, except some of the Botany Bay
shipwrecked convicts to convert the natives to our religion,
how beautiful it was in this centennial year to feel that General Grant had sent out Colonel Steinberger to bring those
islands within our own influence and confederacy! If we
can do so much for people who are so far off, why not jump
from Samoa sixteen thousand miles to Greece, and there revive through our diplomacy its ancient glories under our centennial tutelage.

In Greece we have a minister whom I like. I do not want
to see him dismissed. He is a man that can dance a contra-
dance with the Queen, and such a queen as Queen Olga—a
grand duchess of Russia! And Russia may almost be called
the leading power of Europe. We should be proud to think
of such a minister! How did they dance it?

> " Hands across and down the middle
> To the tune of flute and fiddle."

Mr. Chairman, I have seen such promiscuous dancing.
Byron referred to the Pyrrhic dances of classic Greece, but
that dance is obsolete. I have seen the Kabyles in northern
Africa with their strange swaying dances. I have seen some

dancing in the aisles of this House that forcibly reminded
me of the dervishes of the East. I have seen some ravish-
ing dancing by the señoritas of Seville.

But, sir, I pause. We have here a gentle professor [Mr.
Monroe], at one time a very good professor at Oberlin, and
a good man. He is, or was, a very religious man. He is well
educated, but did he know when he was speaking for Greece
and its minister the other day and quoting its history—did
he know that our minister there had been dancing a contra-
dance? Did he know that he was thus desecrating the old
religious Presbyterian principles? No, sir, I repudiate such
an idea. How can he vote against Greece in this bill?

Sir, the letter which the gentleman from Illinois sent up
to be read was not exactly read by the clerk in the proper
tones. I proceed to read it through:

"The spacious salons were filled at half-past nine, and
the festivities continued until half-past five in the morning.
The arrangements throughout were of the most admirable
character. An elaborate supper for eight hundred guests
was laid in the royal *salle à manger* and in the two large
adjoining rooms, while the ministers of state and the diplomatic corps were entertained by the king and queen in the
beautiful private apartments of their majesties."

I would like to know what they had to eat on that festive
occasion. What did they drink? Was it champagne or was
it Burgundy? Did they have imported from Spain the rare
Montillado? Did they have Rüdesheimer, or did they have
Hochheimer or some other "heimer" from the Rhine?
What were they drinking? Was it the Vin D'Asti from
Italy or Tokay from Hungary? What was their *menu?* Was
it drawn from Apicius or the "mouth officers" of Lucullus?
Was it inspired by Brillat Savarin or Delmonico? I think

some man on the Republican side of the House who is interested in retrenchment ought to have the question raised and inquiry made as to what was going on on that occasion in respect to the edibles and drinking; for I hold that the first duty of an American diplomat is to drink nothing but pure old American Bourbon whiskey.

Moreover, the utility of this wonderful diplomatic system which I am now defending, for I think it will prove of great utility, is the right to have inquiry as to the peculiar diplomatic dress our minister wore when he danced with the Queen of Greece.

Did he wear a spike-tailed coat; were his hands covered with graceful kids; were they of the Alexandrine pattern, and was his hair parted in the middle? How was the Queen dressed? How did she manage that white-satin dress so as not to take the color from her cheeks as represented in another interesting dispatch? We want to know all about it; how long was her train; and, if not, why not?

Now, Mr. Chairman, I had the other day a little troublesome matter with my friend from Maine [Mr. Hale], as to which I wish to express my regret. I called him by an endearing epithet, but I felt a little bad about it. I went to the Corcoran Art Gallery on Saturday to relieve myself from this feeling.

I never felt the necessity of keeping a minister at Greece until I walked, thoughtful, silent, among the mutilated plaster casts of the Corcoran Gallery on Saturday. There were orators without lungs, statesmen without brains, soldiers without arms, and Venuses without robes. Here was a torso Demosthenes and a one-eyed Homer; there was a Theseus garrotting a spavined Centaur. The gentleman from Kentucky will understand what a spavined Centaur is. All about were the fauns, satyrs, Apollos, and Dianas which Greece gave to art and art to the ages: although the only art of modern Greece consists in the ransoming of travellers from brigands, and the farming out of revenues for the sick man of the Levant, and feeding goats. Yet that is a strong reason for a minister to look after art, brigands, and revenue.

If the British Queen—whose empire is based on the wisdom and the rocks of ages, and whose star and course of empire is eastward through her newly acquired Suez canal to her hundreds of millions in India, and whose footsteps of empire are marked at Malta, Corfu, and in the isles of Greece—could not protect her subjects from brigandage and murder within sight of the Acropolis, does it not become our duty, as the mighty limb of her magnificent trunk, to throw our shadow over that sterile soil where Marathon looks on the sea? Is not this our bounden duty this centennial year? Are we not inviting all the nations to our carnival of industry and jubilee of freedom? What would that interesting occasion be without a wooden horse from Greece within thy gates, O city of brotherly love!

Moreover, do we not reach out to other isles than those of Greece and other lands remote? Does not Massachusetts, through an honored son and an ex-member of Congress, give law to the realm of King Kalakaua? Has not our vessel with our proud starry flag borne a Pennsylvanian, Colonel Steinberger, to the distant Samoan group of the southwestern seas, eight thousand miles from our coast, near the tropic of Capricorn? Has he not there eaten of the bread-fruit with the kings of the group and a group of kings, made himself premier over their councils and king of the ex-cannibal islands? If we can do this in the isles of King Lunalilo amid the ancient vesicular lava-beds, amagladaloids, and basalt, where, over coralline ledges, amid which disport fish banded and spotted with green and crimson, the wild waves are singing our everlasting glory hallelujah; why may we not reach out from Pago-Pago and the slopes of Upolu and Savaii to the land where Homer ruled as his demesne and Sappho sang her sad refrain to the Ægean, into whose bosom she sprang and from whose bosom her favorite deity arose.

If we can use the contingent fund as we have to reach Pago-Pago and its interesting converts to polygamous Christianity why may we not extend an enterprising rule and roving into that land where Pericles ruled, Demosthenes spoke, Sophocles sang, and even Paul preached? Did we not last year to gratify an Ohio member, appropriate thousands for a new survey of Judea? And if so why may not Mars Hill have its geologist and the Morea its photographs?

Gentlemen may tell us that we have no commerce with Greece, and therefore require no minister there. Gentlemen may say that our ships and clippers no longer plow the historic waves rendered classic by the prows of Ulysses and the pinnaces of Agamemnon. True, our ship-building is a myth; but Greece is the land of myths. True, the decadence of our shipping calls for little or no men-of-war; but what an interesting study for our minister are the men-of-war who went out to take Troy forty-five hundred years ago and besought and besieged that city till the young men went west! But is it not a strong reason for the encouragement of our navigation? If we had our olden commerce, there would be no need of its fostering. We must have ancient Greece to teach us the art of navigation and revive our shipping.

REVIVAL OF AMERICAN SHIPPING

[The House having under consideration the bill (H. R. 6937) to authorize the purchase of foreign-built ships by citizens of the United States for use in the foreign carrying trade, Mr. Cox, of New York, said:]

M R. SPEAKER,—In most cases, either of social or physical grievance or disease, the way to reach the remedy is to study the causes so as to remove them. The sickness even unto death of our marine is a partial exception to this mode of treatment. Many of the causes which produced the effect which we deplore have done their worst and have expired as active energies. To their operation have been added new causes which congressional supineness and injurious policies have intensified. So that indeed it may be said that if our navigation and commerce are to be restored the remedy must be as heroic as the case is desperate.

We are progressing somewhat in the search for remedies. We are eliminating delusive proposals, such as subsidies. It is not necessary to discuss subsidies, so called, any more. Subsidy is an obsolete and disgraced system.

While referring to a generous postal service as one of the fair methods of supporting our marine, I do not ask that the Treasury should be an eleemosynary institution for the running of ships. No one of the minority of the committee has proposed to create for our decrepit navigation charity hospitals.

In presenting a petition for a special committee on shipping revival to the Senate in last July the Senator from Maine [Mr. Frye] was at a loss where to send it. "There is no committee that takes the slightest interest in it," he exclaimed, " no head of department has jurisdiction over the subject.   It is an orphan, without any orphan's court or guardian.   It is a waif without a home.   It is a tramp to whom nobody is bound to give cold victuals even."

At last it found sheltering arms in the committee whose report is before us.   We, at least, give it the benefit of many repealing and a few enacting statutes.

It is beyond doubt that the origin of our navigation laws was a compact with slavery.   This David A. Wells has shown most vividly in his volume on the " Mercantile Marine." New England was engaged in shipping and in transporting and selling slaves to the South.   She desired to hold the monopoly of that trade.   This she procured for a period by the extension of the time for the extinction of the slave-trade to 1808.   The compact was completed by the navigation laws of 1790 and 1792.   Tonnage dues and imposts gave to the American the entire commerce and prohibited foreign ship-owners from engaging in our trade.   Again, in 1816, 1817, and 1820 the odious British navigation laws against which our fathers rebelled were re-enacted by Congress.   Every discrimination possible was made against foreigners.

These laws, whose origin is found in the horrors of the middle passage and whose history is a part of the most disgraceful experience of our country, have ceased to protect American shipping.

Although there is an apparent concurrence by all the committee in the bill reported, some of the committee reserved the right to differ.   They prefer some modes to others.   Besides, it is a question, since the burdens now sought to be removed existed when shipping interests were prosperous, whether their removal will revive those interests.

There is so much contrariety of opinion between those interested that it is a wonder that even an approximation has been made to some partial relief.

Indeed the protection of these laws by the whirligig and revenges of time is given to the foreigner, to the Briton. We drive to him the carrying of our persons and property; load him with largesses of freight and fare, and forbid our own people from enjoying even a share in the hundred and odd millions which our laws transfer out of our produce and producers to the pocket of the foreigner! If this be done to protect our ship-builder it fails; if it be done to protect our ship-owner it fails. The owner if he would build here must do it at a loss of fifteen or thirty per cent. If he would buy, he must buy ships only thus built. Thus builder and owner are burdened by the clinging of this Old Man of the Sea. If we can build as cheap here as abroad we need no protection; if we cannot build as cheap here as abroad, who can afford to buy? The sea is open field, where the guerdon falls to him who can procure his vessel in the best market.

This open competition as to purchase and use of ships of all kinds has changed, or ought to change, the laws which govern our marine. The laws of eighty years ago are not suited to our changed condition. Those laws suited sail, not iron or steam. As soon think of returning to the stage-coach or the footman for land conveyance, or to the skin boat of the Esquimaux, or junk of the Chinese for sea transportation, as to run the ocean fleet of to-day under the ancient laws. Nay, as well think of discarding the new motors of physics and their energies as return even to the wooden paddles of the early Cunarder, with its petty 1,200 tonnage and its little subsidy.

Thus the very causes which produced our disasters are as

obsolete and inoperative as the slave-trade itself. The very model upon which our navigation laws was moulded has been shattered, and our shipping to-day, with all these restrictions, guards, and prohibitions, is as useless and uninteresting as the "fat weed that rots on Lethe's wharf."

It matters, therefore, little to examine into the causes which produced the decay of our marine. When we see other nations improving their marine by liberal policies while our government has neglected to adopt them, the solution is easy. As well expect the boor of Russia, with his old modes of farming his wheat, to compete with the American farmer with his new implements of labor and time-saving, as the United States rival Germany and England in shipping without the marine instrumentalities which these nations employ.

Another and kindred reason for the loss of our carrying trade and the failure to restore it, is that other countries have laid hands on that which slipped from us in our preoccupation during the civil war. For others, vessels are now at work; for others, vessels are being built on the best models. The seamen, the skill, the capital, and the enterprise of others hold the lines of sea adventure. Possession, with its concomitant advantages, is not ours. We have to struggle valiantly for what others have already.

So that, Mr. Speaker, to remove this mountain in our path we must remodel the whole industrial system of our own half-hemisphere, and we must turn and overturn natural laws of supply and demand in other spheres of labor and locality. This being impossible, what remains for us except tentative legislation, the repeal of burdens on navigation here, of a liability on a ship-owner there, a reasonable compensation for mails, in many directions; and as the best thing, in the judgment of our wisest economists and merchants, freedom for all stores and materials and liberty to purchase vessels wherever we please to buy.

If these remedies fail, then the country must await some catastrophe in the shape of a great foreign war, which, like the Crimean, calls our marine into being and activity; but even then we must have the right to buy freely, else it will be useless to regard the opportunity. Or perhaps some exceptional progress may be made in the building of ships or the motive power of its enginery. This may give us a fresh start and added momentum, such as England received in her iron-ship building. . . .

The relief, whatever it is, must come as well to the ship-using as to the ship-building interest. Even if we remove all the burdens upon the use of ships it will avail nothing so long as the ships cannot be bought or made as cheaply at home as abroad.

If, therefore, our tariff laws will not allow us to build or our navigation laws to buy, of what use is the bill of the majority? What is the necessity of taking burdens from the running of vessels which we have not and can not buy or build?

Hence the minority report explicitly says that—

" While the committee are generally agreed upon the measures proposed the minority are constrained to notice the fact that the most vital and prominent relief, by the freedom of materials for ships from custom dues and the right to purchase ships abroad is utterly ignored in the majority report. In the opinion of the minority nothing could be more futile, not to say absurd, than to deal with a vital disease by remedies which only affect the superficial ailments whose removal would leave the patient in as dangerous a plight as ever."

N

Go on, gentlemen! Modify your shipping laws, remove burdens, extend privileges, copy the British code! We will aid you in the experiment as far as you go and would bid you go further, to fare better. Compensate for mail service; make ship-supplies free; adapt your rules to the new class of seamen; make a new and inexpensive consular code for their discharge and return home; prohibit the advance wages and "blood money;" allow a Norwegian or Italian to be an American mate; limit the liability of ship-owners; reduce the hospital tax; modify the tonnage tax, or repeal it altogether; erase from every State statute the local taxation on shipping; ay, even erect a bureau like the British Board of Trade as the special cherub to keep watch over poor Jack; do all these as your committee suggests. Do more! Out of your treasury or out of the tonnage fund, mostly collected from foreign shipping, make a sort of allowance for the use of certain American materials in building ships; and yet like the young man in Scripture, one thing ye will lack. You may copy the English statutes as liberalized in 1849 in allowing Englishmen to buy ships where they pleased, and in 1854, when they opened their coasting trade to all the world. "Begin," as your majority say Great Britain did, "begin a complete revision of the merchant-shipping statutes, so as to remove every obstacle and give every facility," and then you may have some dim hope of the resurrection of our wrecked marine!

We now pay our own steamships the same rates we pay to foreigners. The British line to China receives the same and no more than the Pacific Mail Company; and the British steamers, three lines of them running from New York to Rio de Janeiro, take letters at two cents. Of the vast number of British steamships in the trans-Atlantic trade but one in twenty has a special mail contract, and none of the German ships have any. Nevertheless, both the majority and minority agree that the compensation for mail-carrying ought to be a *quantum meruit,* not a subsidy; and we are ready to indorse an amendment based on fair postage paid for similar service on established routes upon the inland.

The following is a summary of burdens to which an American ship of 1,000 tons is subjected beyond such a ship under a foreign flag in a year: From three months' extra pay, $100; from transportation of disabled sailors, $100; from hospital tax, $32; from consular fees, $40; from duty on stores, $100; a total of $372.

A first-class iron sailing ship of 1,000 tons would cost in Scotland $62,000. Such a ship built here would cost $80,000; a difference of $18,000. On this sum, interest at 6 per cent.; insurance, 7 per cent.; wear and tear, 7 per cent.; in all 20 per cent., entailing a yearly loss in sailing of $3,600, which is vastly more against us than the paltry $372 of infinitesimal " burdens."

In a steamship the difference is greater still. When we had to compete with England in wooden ships of a less cost than hers, we could beat her, as she beats us now that her ships cost less than ours. That is the whole story as to the cost of running our ships and the relief we obtain by this bill on these smaller items, counting it in dollars and cents. . . .

I pause here, Mr. Speaker, to ask first what are our navigation laws? Wherein do they obstruct the revival of our shipping?

Briefly they are: That a vessel of the United States engaged in the foreign trade must be registered to entitle it to the rights and privileges of a vessel of the United States;

and to be so registered must be built within the United
States and belong wholly to citizens of the United States or
be captured in war and condemned as a prize, or be adjudged
forfeited for breach of the laws of the United States, being
wholly owned by citizens of the United States. No vessel
can be registered, or if registered, entitled to the benefits
and privileges of a vessel of the United States, if owned in
whole or in part by any citizen of the United States who
usually resides in a foreign country, during the continuance
of such residence, unless he be a consul of the United States
or agent for a partner in some house of trade consisting of
citizens of the United States, actually carrying on trade
within the United States, or if owned in whole or in part by
any naturalized citizen of the United States who resides more
than one year in the country from which he came, or for
more than two years in any foreign country, unless he be a
consul or agent of the United States. No vessel registered
as a vessel of the United States licensed or authorized to sail
under a foreign flag and to have the protection of any
foreign government during the existence of the rebellion can
be deemed or registered as a vessel of the United States, or
to have the rights and privileges of such vessels, except under
provisions of law especially authorizing such register. A
register may be issued to a vessel built in a foreign country
when such vessel shall be wrecked in the United States and
be purchased and repaired by a citizen of the United States,
if the repairs equal three fourths of the cost of such vessel
when repaired.

The navigation laws are practically dead for the purpose
of their being. Let us—

" Rise on stepping stones
Of their dead selves to higher things."

Is it not, Mr. Speaker, marvellous that in this majority report the confession is naively made that our merchant shipping laws remain the same as they were originally framed more than fourscore years ago, and that they were all that were needed so long as the English laws were the same? And yet the majority stop short of the one prominent and majestic feature of the newly constituted English system: Liberty to build and buy! The majority say that "our error was in not imitating England in so modifying our laws as to give the American marine the same advantages in this respect that English shipping was given under English laws;" and yet it would perpetuate the error by a blindly selfish persistence in the very laws which England repealed! Well, sir, if England is to be our exemplar, if her maritime success is a sign that her laws worked beneficently, then let the obstructions which she removed be removed by us. This the minority propose in the amendments for free materials and free ships.

Without, therefore, arguing at length any of the lesser propositions in the majority report, it is enough to say that the acquiescence in most of the measures proposed was hearty and earnest by the whole committee; while the reluctance as to one proposition, the "drawback," so called, was somewhat mitigated by the belief that the amendment for free materials might prove more acceptable. And if, as the minority hope, both should be adopted little harm could result as the nullification of the bad consequences of the one would be nearly perfect by the adoption of the other. Or if there should be an option allowed the builder to choose either the "drawback" or free materials under my amendment, the adoption of the drawback thus coupled would not be without some utility. But if no compromise be tendered in the interest of freedom of materials or ships, I want no allowance fixed on the treasury, no leech to draw its blood such as this drawback will then be. . . .

Adroitly recognizing " the stimulus given by the tariff to all protected domestic industries, and especially to American labor," California reminds us that " her shipping business has been thereby ruined, sacrificed to the general good; her property rendered worthless without compensation for the benefit of the public at large." The irony of this appeal is so very elusive and delicate that one must quote it for full appreciation:

" For while the protected domestic market recoups the high cost and guarantees a profit on all protected articles of American manufacture, the cost of building our vessels is raised by the same means, but our market is not likewise protected. On the contrary, our shipping in the foreign trade must compete without any possible protection from our government in the free, open market of the world, which of course hires vessels where it can hire cheapest. If high interest on high cost, high wages, taxes, fees, repairs, etc., make $1,000 per month the cost of running an American ship, while low interest on low cost, low wages, and the absence of taxes, fees, or repairs bring down the cost of running an English ship to $500 per month, who does not perceive that the English vessel will make money where the American owner must soon become bankrupt? Yet this is the actual condition of the shipping business now, and such it has been since the enactment of our present high tariff.

" That under these circumstances common justice to our injured class, regard for the national honor abroad, as well as for the national economy which requires the retention in our own country of the enormous freights paid on American exports to other nations, and the national safety in case of foreign war—all these motives justify us in the demand that we should be placed as far as possible in such a position as if there were no tariff; and that such legislation should be promptly enacted as will place American ship-owners on an equality with those of England. Unloose the fetters; remove the weights imposed on us by our ill-fitting and outgrown laws; leave us free, as are the English, to utilize our abundant materials, our energy and skill, and doubt not American mechanics and sailors will soon again overtake their rivals on the seas.

" The foreign carrying trade has been struck with a deadly mildew."

Exclaims a leading journal of Portland, Maine:

" The decadence of her shipping interests is the sacrifice Maine pays to give 15 to 20 per cent. dividends to other branches of industry. She has paid it that Maine's shipping interests shall receive the protection which the wolf gives to the lamb."

The saddest part of this plaint is that Maine by her own members here mildewed her own interests; and while not confessing the blighting policy of protection, still joins California in begging for federal aid.

In urging this measure the San Francisco traders evidently felt the orphanage of navigation and the hopelessness of asking for a repeal of the navigation laws. Which way soever they looked they saw the image of protection, like Pluto's countenance—iron and inexorable. Piteously they pleaded that their plan was " not a subsidy levied on many industries to benefit a few, but simply the payment of a debt due by the many enterprises which are prospering by means of the tariff to the one which has been ruined by it." They pleaded as those who owned the cargo which was jettisoned to save the vessel, and that they should be made good by a general average contribution.

In this rhetorical masquerade they meant to say: " Behold us, the victims of your robbery! True, you may have robbed us under pleasing disguises; your self-seeking may have made your larcenies unwitting; still as pirates of the land you have destroyed our fair and free trade upon the water. And as you have thriven upon this piracy, be generous to your despoiled victims, as you have in your coffers the loot you stole from us. Be patriotic and devoted in this paramount matter and in our death agony! No longer continue to help Great Britain at our expense after rifling us for the general welfare!"

It is upon such reasoning as this that we are asked to allow this drawback; and if there be, as Bastiat held, a reciprocity in brigandage, let us steal back from those who stole from us, that we may have some compensation for our losses by the restoration of something of our own. Let us cultivate a mutuality in rascality! . . .

If it be said again that the repeal of the navigation laws will destroy our ship-yards, we reply that there is nothing on our stocks of much general consequence in iron ship-building; and since the business will not remunerate without subsidies or bounties or general taxes on all the people for one interest let us try the experiment which other nations have tried successfully, namely: buy abroad, since we cannot build at home.

It is argued that because a great many poor ships are built in England, those are the ships that we would buy if we could! Undoubtedly there are many poor carriages built in England. We are at liberty to import land vehicles, while we cannot import vehicles to be used on the water. When we do import carriages we import the best. The Americans are not fools. Let the buyer of a horse or a ship beware. Why should not trade and labor be left a little to natural laws? Are there not regulations more powerful than Congress can make? Repeal burdens and restraints; stop the talk about stimulation; practise non-intervention—these are maxims only less radical and wholesome than the natural prescripts which ordain them.

Could we have seen ten or twenty years ago to-day what others saw we might have had to-day a splendid fleet of screw steamers under our flag. The earnings might have been saved to us. We relied on our own ship-yards, and in 1881 but eight of the 44,463 tons of steamers built on our seaboard were for the ocean, or only one per cent. of the British tonnage built the same year. Our citizens, had they been allowed, would have bought the ships of iron and steel we could not build. One of the oldest ship-builders and owners of the United States, formerly a member here, writes me that had we had the privilege of buying iron ships there would to-day have been two hundred of them under our flag; and he says:

" I do not believe there would have been many more ships in the world than at present, only we should have had our share; our sons would have had employment and our country would have been so much richer. I have three sons, masters of ships. I shall never build another wooden ship; but I would if I could go into the iron ships; they last longer. There have been great improvements in them the past five years, and we would have received the benefit of them."

Why not allow the merchant, if he thinks he can do it, to get his ship abroad and try at least to run it? He will not charge the treasury for his failure and loss.

In time, as in Germany, the ownership leads to repair, and repair to building. The number of ship-yards and workshops increases and the tonnage leaps up under this impulse. That which seemed a mustard-seed becomes a mighty tree. Every nation has tried the free-ship experiment but the

United States, and we are lowest to-day in our proportionate share of the navigation of the world. No one can say it is a failure until it is tried. All other schemes—and especially its opposite, protection—have been tried and failed. The commercial eminence of Great Britain, not to speak of Germany, France, Italy, and Norway, is supreme logic for the trial of the experiment. Germany is the best illustration; she has not as good coal and iron as we have, but she began to buy her ships on the Clyde, as we might have done a score of years ago. She is now building her own iron steamships. She builds now more than she buys. She has never sub-sidized. Her tonnage in 1856-57, when ours began to decline, was but 166,000 tons; last year she had 950,000; ours in eleven years dropped from 4,400,000 to 600,000, and all its vast income was lost.

Last week I read that a new steel steamship, the Rugia, of 6,500 tons, was turned out for our trade from the Vulcan Works at Stettin, warranted for the safety of 1,200 passengers, with steel life-boats and steam steering-gear and a refinement in the reversal of her engines in seven seconds. German growth has been in iron screw-steamers, which she began to buy abroad. They could not afford to wait, this phlegmatic people, for their own ship-yards to arise, but began to repair in the blacksmith shops and little foundries of their "free towns," and now where the little furnace glowed mighty engines are made to mate the ocean in its wildest tempest!

Even Japan has a fleet of fifty-seven iron steamers, and China leaves us laggard and unprogressive. Fifty years of Cathay—nay, twenty years—is worth more than a century of our experience.

Twenty years ago Norway and Sweden traded with us and

had but 20,000 tons in the trade; now they have 850,000. The Viking is abroad and we are stupidly looking on. Everybody is making money out of our carrying and commerce but ourselves. What avails it that ours is the largest carrying trade of any nation since we do not do the work? It adds to the humiliation.

It makes the humiliation worse to consider the losses in money as well as the prestige at sea.

The gentleman from Pennsylvania [Mr. Randall] has called upon the treasury for the amount of ocean freights on exports and imports during the year ending June 30, 1882. Much loose understatement will be set at rest by the report. It may be reached by the average percentage on the values. . . .

Looking at the wall of adamant which shuts us in from all the world and shuts the world out from us in this once famous enterprise of ours, can we draw hope from the prospect? The gigantic results of an hundred years of national existence and energy are not discouraging. Over mountains and through valleys, upon rivers, across continents and under oceans, our enterprises by rail and telegraph have developed our resources. They astound by their marvels. And yet halting on the shores of two vast oceans we have said to the land, or rather the voice of either ocean has said to these enterprises and products of the mine and field: "Thus far, but by our help no farther. The illimitable ocean is beyond and its trident is in another's grasp." Upon the west we face the Orient, rich in the elements of commerce. We had hoped once that the Pacific would have been an American lake. That hope is dead. On the east we almost touch Europe, with its teeming industries, peoples, and civilizations; but they come to us in their own vessels and bear away our produce. In this we have no pay, part, nor lot. On the south we were reaching across gulf and sea to the tropics at our doors and to the republics of our continent. Once we had mutual relations with the Dominion on our north; but this and all such visions of material supremacy and splendor have faded. The ocean coast still gives us its thunderous line of breakers, its seven thousand miles and more indented with harbors of safety and bays of wondrous beauty. The net-work of our hundred thousand miles of railway still trembles with its immense freight, the garnered opulence of our sky, sun, soil, and mine. Cotton, corn, and petroleum —the triumvirate of our common weal—head the stately procession in which a thousand forms of labor and graces of art move and chant their praises to our smiling and copious land.

The time was when amid the glory and pride of our country our models of ships and adventure at sea were the theme of lyre and the praise of eloquence. It was comfort and wealth in peace, hope and safety in war.

It was the horn of plenty and the nursery of seamen for the maintenance of our independence and rights. Why should America not have her part in these glories of the sea? Was she not discovered by the genius, daring, and devotion of Columbus? Were not our colonies created into commonwealths by the men who braved the dangers of the sea to found here new empires? Our country is born of the sea! Its freedom is of the wind and wave.

Shall these praises be forever an echo of the past? Are we to take no part in the enlightenment and progress in science and art, of which commerce is the procreant cause and infallible gauge? Has the sea rolled back and away from us at the command of the insolent monarchs of capital?

To one born inland the sea has a weird and wondrous mystery. I have studied its moods as a lover those of his mistress. Through the generosity of my fellow legislators here we have been able to mitigate somewhat of its terrors. Its enchantment has led me over liquid leagues on leagues to remotest realms. Not alone does it enchant because of its majestic expanse, its resistless force, its depth and unity, its cliffs, bays, and fiords, its chemical qualities, its monstrous forms, its riches and rocks, its tributes, its graves, its requiem, its murmur of repose and mirror of placid beauty, but for its wrath, peril, and sublimity. These have led adventurous worthies of every age, by sun, star, and compass over its trackless wastes, and returned them for their daring untold wealth and the eulogy of history.

But it is for its refining, civilizing, elevating influences upon our kind that the ocean lifts its mighty minstrelsy. Unhappy that nation which has no part in the successes of the sea. Happy in history those realms like Tyre, Sidon, Carthage, Greece, Italy, Spain, and Norway, whose gathered glories are symboled in the trident. Happy in the present are those nations who, under the favoring gales of commerce, the fostering economies of freedom, and the unwavering faith in the guidance of Providence, bear the blessings of varied industry to distant realms and bring back to their own the magnificent fruits of ceaseless interchange. Happy that nation whose poet can raise his voice to herald the hope and humanity of its institutions in the grandeur of the familiar symbol of Longfellow:

> " Sail on, O Union, strong and great!
> Humanity with all its fears,
> With all the hopes of future years,
> Is hanging breathless on thy fate! "

Amid this divided marine dominion, in which one power alone has half the rule of the ocean, shall America sit scepterless and forlorn—dethroned, ignoble, dispirited, and disgraced? The ensign of our nationality takes its stars from the vault of heaven. By them brave men sail. It is now an unknown emblem upon the sea. We welcome every race to our shores in the vessels of other nations. Our enormous surplus, which feeds the world, is for others to bear away. We gaze at the leviathans of commerce entering our harbors and darkening our sky with the pennons of smoke; but the thunder of the engines is under another flag and the shouting of the captains is in an alien tongue. Others distribute the produce, capitalize the moneys, gather the glories, and elevate their institutions by the amenities and benignities of commerce, and we, boasting of our invention, heroism, and freedom, allow the jailers of a hated and selfish policy to place gyves upon our energy, and when we ask for liberty to build and for liberty to buy imprison our genius in the sight of these splendid achievements.

Mr. Speaker, if you would that we should once more fly our ensign upon the sea, assist us to take off the burdens from our navigation and give to us the first, last, and best—the indispensable condition of civilization by commerce—liberty.

KING

THOMAS STARR KING, a distinguished American orator and clergyman, was the son of a Universalist clergyman and was born in New York city December 17, 1824. After the death of his father he was for some time a clerk in a store in Charlestown, Massachusetts, but in 1840 was appointed an assistant teacher in a school in that town. In 1842, while principal of a school in West Medford, Massachusetts, he studied for the Universalist ministry under Hosea Ballou, and after a few years spent in preaching in and about Boston was ordained pastor of the Hollis Street Unitarian church in Boston, where he remained eleven years. During this period his remarkable eloquence made him one of the most popular preachers in Boston, while on the lecture platform he was equally successful. Among his lectures those on " Substance and Show," " Socrates," and " Sight and Insight " were perhaps the most generally popular. In 1860 he accepted a call to a Unitarian church in San Francisco, where he met with extraordinary success. In the political canvass of 1860 he urged with great eloquence the paramount duty of supporting the Union cause and to his patriotic efforts the preservation of California to the Union at that time was largely due. While the civil war was in progress he was active in behalf of the sanitary commission. He was an enthusiastic lover of nature and was one of the first to direct public attention to the beauties of the White Mountains of New Hampshire and of the Yosemite Valley. His death occurred in San Francisco March 4, 1864, and in 1889 his statue was erected in the Golden Gate Park in that city. He was the author of " The White Hills: their Legends, Landscape, and Poetry " (1859); " Patriotism and Other Papers " (1865); " Christianity and Humanity " (1877); " Substance and Show and Other Lectures " (1877).

ON THE PRIVILEGE AND DUTIES OF PATRIOTISM

FROM AN ADDRESS BEFORE THE "SUMMER LIGHT GUARD,"
NOVEMBER 18, 1862

LET us waste no words in introduction or preface. I am to speak to you of the privilege and duties· of American patriotism.

First the privilege. Patriotism is love of country. It is a privilege that we are capable of such a sentiment. Self-love is the freezing point in the temperature of the world. As the heart is kindled and ennobled it pours out feeling and

(8748)

interest, first upon family and kindred, then upon country, then upon humanity. The home, the flag, the cross,—these are the representatives or symbols of the noblest and most sacred affections or treasures of feeling in human nature.

We sometimes read arguments by very strict moralists which cast a little suspicion upon the value of patriotism as a virtue, for the reason that the law of love, unrestricted love, should be our guide and inspiration. We must be cosmopolitan by our sympathy, they prefer to say. Patriotism if it interferes with the wider spirit of humanity is sectionalism of the heart. We must not give up to country " what is meant for mankind."

Such sentiments may be uttered in the interest of Christian philanthropy but they are not healthy. The divine method in evoking our noblest affections is always from particulars to generals. God " hath set the solitary in families," and bound the families into communities, and organized communities into nations; and he has ordained special duties for each of these relationships and inspired affections to prompt the discharge of them and to exalt the character.

The law of love is the principle of the spiritual universe, just as gravitation is the governing force of space. It binds each particle of matter to every other particle, but it attracts inversely as the square of the distance and thus becomes practically a series of local or special forces, holding our feet perpetually to one globe, and allowing only a general unity which the mind appropriates through science and meditation with the kindred but far-off spheres. The man that has most of the sentiment of love will have the most intense special affections. You cannot love the whole world and nobody in particular. If you try that it will be true of you as of the miser who said, " what I give is nothing to nobody."

However deep his baptism in general good will a man must look with a thrill that nothing else can awaken into the face of the mother that bore him; he cannot cast off the ties that bind him to filial responsibilities and a brother's devotion; and Providence has ordained that out of identity of race, a common history, the same scenery, literature, laws, and aims,—though in perfect harmony with good will to all men,—the wider family feeling, the distinctive virtue, patriotism, should spring.

If the ancient Roman could believe that the yellow Tiber was the river dearest to heaven; if the Englishman can see a grandeur in the Thames which its size will not suggest; if the Alpine storm-wind is a welcome home-song to the Swiss mountaineer; if the Laplander believes that his country is the best the sun shines upon; if the sight of one's own national flag in other lands will at once awaken feelings that speed the blood and melt the eyes; if the poorest man will sometimes cherish a proud consciousness of property in the great deeds that glow upon his country's annals and the monuments of its power,—let us confess that the heart of man, made for the Christian law, was made also to contract a special friendship for its native soil, its kindred stock, its ancestral traditions,—let us not fail to see that where the sentiment of patriotism is not deep, a sacred affection is absent, an essential element of virtue is wanting, and religion barren of one prominent witness of its sway.

But why argue in favor of patriotism as a lofty virtue? History refuses to countenance the analytic ethics of spiritual dreamers. It pushes into notice Leonidas, Tell,. Cincinnatus, Camillus, Hampden, Winkelried, Scipio, Lafayette, Adams, Bolivar, and Washington, in whom the sentiment has become flesh, and gathered to itself the world's affections and honors.

It asks us, " What do you say of these men ? These are among the brighter jewels of my kingdom. Thousands of millions fade away into the night in my realm, but these souls shine as stars, with purer lustre as they retreat into the blue of time. Is not their line of greatness as legitimate as that of poets, philosophers, philanthropists, and priests ? "

Nay, the Bible is opened for us, to stimulate and increase our love of country. Patriotism is sanctioned and commended and illustrated there by thrilling examples: by the great patriot-prophet Moses, who, during all those wilderness-years bore the Hebrew people in his heart; by Joshua who sharpened his sword on the tables of stone till its edge was keen as the righteous wrath of heaven and its flame fierce as a flash from Sinai, as it opened a path through an idolatrous land for the colonization of a worthier race and a clean idea; (O that there were enough of that steel in America to-day to make a sword for the leader of the Union armies!) by the great statesman Samuel, to whom every Jew may point with pride as the Hebrew Washington; by David, who, for the glory of his nation wielded the hero's sword and tuned the poet's harp, by the long line of the fire-tongued prophets whose hearts burned for their country's redemption while they proclaimed the " higher law;" by the lyric singers of the exile, like him who chanted the lament, which seems to gush from the very heart of patriotism, " How shall we sing the Lord's song in a strange land ? If I forget thee, O Jerusalem, let my right hand forget her cunning. . . . Let my tongue cleave to the roof of my mouth if I prefer not Jerusalem above my chief joy ! "

Yes, and when we pass higher up than these worthies of the older inspiration to him the highest name, him from whom we have received our deepest life, him whose love embraced the whole race in its scope, the eternal and impartial love made flesh, who pronounced the parable of the good Samaritan and shed the warmth of that spirit through his life into the frosty air of human sentiment, do we not read that he felt more keenly the alienation of his countrymen according to the flesh than he felt the spear-point and the nails, and paused over the beautiful city of David to utter a lament whose burden swept away the prospect of his own lowering destiny,—" O Jerusalem, Jerusalem, . . . how often would I have gathered your children together, even as a hen gathereth her chickens under her wings, and ye would not. Behold your house is left unto you desolate."

Although the highest office of revelation is to point to and prepare us for " a better country, even a heavenly," no one can rightly read the pages of the Bible without catching enthusiasm for his earthly country, the land of his fathers, the shelter of his infancy, the hope of his children.

It is a privilege of our nature, hardly to be measured, that we are capable of the emotion of patriotism, that we can feel a nation's life in our veins, rejoice in a nation's glory, suffer for a nation's momentary shame, throb with a nation's hope. It is as if each particle of matter that belongs to a mountain, each crystal hidden in its darkness, each grass-blade on its lower slopes, each pebble amid its higher desolation, each snowflake of its cold and tilted fields could be conscious all the time of the whole bulk and symmetry and majesty and splendor of the pile,—of how it glows at evening, of how it blazes at the first touch of morning light, of its pride when it overtops the storm, of the joy it awakens in hearts that see in it the power and glory of the Creator. It is as if each could exult in feeling—I am part of this organized majesty; I am an element in one flying buttress of it, or its firm-poised peak; I contribute to this frosty radiance; I am ennobled by the joy it awakens in every beholder's breast!

Think of a man living in one of the illustrious civilized communities of the world and insensible to its history, honor, and future,—say of England! Think of an intelligent inhabitant of England so wrapped in selfishness that he has no consciousness of the mighty roots of that kingdom, nor of the toughness of its trunk, nor of the spread of its gnarled boughs! Runnymede and Agincourt are behind him, but he is insensible to the civil triumph and the knightly valor. All the literature that is crowned by Bacon, Shakespeare, and Milton, the noblest this earth ever produced from one national stock, awakens in him no heart-beat of pride. He reads of the study blows in the great rebellion, and of the gain to freedom by the later and more quiet revolution, and it is no more to him than if the record had been dropped from another planet.

The triumphs of English science over nature, the hiss of her engines, the whirl of her wheels, the roar of her factory drums, the crackle of her furnaces, the beat of her hammers, the vast and chronic toil that mines her treasures, affect him with no wonder and arouse no exultant thrill of partnership. And he sees nothing and feels nothing that stirs his torpid blood in the strokes and sweep of that energy before which the glory of Waterloo and Trafalgar is dim, which has knit to the English will colonies and empires within a century which number nearly one fourth of the inhabitants of the globe.

The red flag of England hung out on all her masts, from all her house-tops, and from every acre of her conquests and possessions, would almost give this planet the color of Mars if seen through a telescope from a neighboring star.

What a privilege to be a conscious fibre of that compacted force! If I were an Englishman I should be proud every hour of every day over my heritage. I believe I should now and then imitate the man who sat up all night to hate his brother-in-law, and sit up all night to exult in my privilege. And as an Englishman I should keep clear of the pollution of sympathy with the American rebellion. The man who is dead to such pride ought not to be rated as a man.

And is it any less a privilege to be an American? Suppose that the continent could turn towards you to-morrow at sunrise and show to you the whole American area in the short hours of the sun's advance from Eastport to the Pacific! You would see New England roll into light from the green plumes of Aroostook to the silver stripe of the Hudson; westward thence over the Empire State, and over the lakes, and over the sweet valleys of Pennsylvania, and over the prairies, the morning blush would run and would waken all the line of the Mississippi; from the frosts where it rises, to the fervid waters in which it pours, for three thousand miles it would be visible, fed by rivers that flow from every mile of the Alleghany slope and edged by the green embroideries of the temperate and tropic zones; beyond this line another basin, too, the Missouri, catching the morning, leads your eye along its western slope till the Rocky Mountains burst upon the vision and yet do not bar it; across its passes we must follow as the stubborn courage of American pioneers has forced its way till again the Sierra and their silver veins are tinted along the mighty bulwark with the break of day; and then over to the gold fields of the western slope, and the fatness of the California soil, and the beautiful valleys of Oregon, and the stately forests of Washington the eye is drawn as the globe turns out of the night-shadow, and when the Pacific waves are crested with radiance you have the one blending picture, nay, the reality of the American domain! No such soil, so varied by climate, by products, by mineral riches, by forest and lake, by wild heights and buttresses, and by opulent plains,—yet all bound into unity of configuration and bordered by both warm and icy seas,—no such domain was ever given to one people.

And then suppose that you could see in a picture as vast and vivid the preparation for our inheritance of this land: Columbus haunted by his round idea and setting sail in a sloop to see Europe sink behind him, while he was serene in the faith of his dream; the later navigators of every prominent Christian race who explored the upper coasts; the " Mayflower " with her cargo of sifted acorns from the hardy stock of British Puritanism, and the ship whose name we know not that bore to Virginia the ancestors of Washington; the clearing of the wilderness and the dotting of its clearings with the proofs of manly wisdom and Christian trust; then the gradual interblending of effort and interest and sympathy into one life, the congress of the whole Atlantic slope to resist oppression upon one member, the rally of every State around Washington and his holy sword, and again the nobler rally around him when he signed the constitution, and after that the organization of the farthest west with north and south into one polity and communion; when this was finished, the tremendous energy of free life under the stimulus and with the aid of advancing science, in increasing wealth, subduing the wilds to the bonds of use, multiplying fertile fields, and busy schools, and noble workshops, and churches hallowed by free-will offerings of prayer, and happy homes, and domes dedicated to the laws of States that rise by magic from the haunts of the buffalo and deer, all in less than a long lifetime; and if we could see also how, in achieving this, the flag which represents all this history is dyed in traditions of exploits by land and sea that have given heroes to American annals whose names are potent to conjure with, while the world's list of thinkers in matter is crowded with the names of American inventors and the higher rolls of literary merit are not empty of the title of our " representative men;" if all that the past has done for us and the present reveals could thus stand apparent in one picture, and then if the promise of the future to the children of our millions under our common law and with continental peace could be caught in one vast spectral exhibition, the wealth in store, the power, the privilege, the freedom, the learning, the expansive and varied and mighty unity in fellowship, almost fulfilling the poet's dream of

" The parliament of man, the federation of the world,"

you would exclaim with exultation, " I, too, am an American!"

You would feel that patriotism next to your tie to the divine love is the greatest privilege of your life; and you would devote yourselves out of inspiration and joy to the obligations of patriotism, that this land so spread, so adorned, so colonized, so blessed, should be kept forever against all the assaults of traitors, one in polity, in spirit, and in aim!

Gentlemen, this is what we ought to do, what we should try to do; we should seize by our imagination the glory of our country, that our patriotism may be a permanent and a lofty flame. Patriotism is an imaginative sentiment. Imagination is essential to its vigor; not imagination which distorts facts, but which sweeps a vast field of them and illumines it. It comprehends hills, streams, plains, and valleys in a broad conception, and from traditions and institutions, from the life of the past and the vigor and noble tendencies of the present, it individualizes the destiny and personifies the spirit of its land, and then vows its vow to that.

It is of the very essence of true patriotism, therefore, to be earnest and truthful, to scorn the flatterer's tongue, and strive to keep its native land in harmony with the laws of national thrift and power. It will tell a land of its faults as a friend will counsel a companion. It will speak as honestly as the physician advises a patient. And if occasion requires, an indignation will flame out of its love like that which burst from the lips of Moses when he returned from the mountain and found the people to whom he had revealed the austere Jehovah and for whom he would cheerfully have sacrificed his life worshipping a calf.

We condense all the intimations of these last thoughts in saying that true patriotism is pledged to the idea which one's native country represents. It does not accept and glory in its country merely for what it is at present and has been in the past, but for what it may be. Each nation has a representative value. Each race that has appropriated a certain latitude which harmonizes with its blood has the capacity to work out special good results and to reveal great truths in some original forms.

God designs that each country shall bear a peculiar ideal physiognomy, and he has set its geographical characteristics as a bony skeleton and breathed into it a free life spirit, which, if loyal to the intention, will keep the blood in health, infuse vigor into every limb, give symmetry to the form, and carry the flush of a pure and distinct expression to the countenance. It is the patriot's office to study the laws of public growth and energy, and to strive with enthusiastic love to guard against every disease that would cripple the frame, that he may prevent the lineaments of vice and brutality from degrading the face which God would have radiant with truth, genius, and purity.

He was the best patriot of ancient Greece who had the widest and wisest conception of the capacities and genius of Greece, and labored to paint that ideal winningly before the national mind, and to direct the flame of national aspiration, fanned by heroic memories, up to the noblest possibilities of Grecian endeavor. The truest patriot of England would be the man whose mind should see in the English genius and geography what that nation could do naturally and best for humanity, and, seizing the traditional elements that are in harmony with that possibility, should use them to enliven his own sympathies and to quicken the nation's energy. We might say the same of Russia and of Italy. The forward look is essential to patriotism.

And how much more emphatically and impressively true is this when we bring our own country into the foreground! We have been placed on our domain for the sake of a hope. What we have done and what has been done for us is only preparation, the outline sketching of a picture to be filled with color and life in the next three centuries. Shall the sketch be blurred and the canvas be torn in two? That is what we are to decide in these bitter and bloody days.

Our struggle now is to keep the country from falling away from the idea which every great patriot has recognized as the purpose towards which our history, from the first, has been moving. God devised the scheme for us of one republic. He planted the further slope of the Alleghanies at first with Saxon men; he has striped the Pacific coast with the energy of their descendants, protecting thus both avenues of entrance to our domain against European intrusion; but the great wave of population he has rolled across the Alleghanies into the central basin.

That is the seat of the American polity. And an imperial river runs through it to embarrass and to shame and to balk all plans of rupture. The Mississippi bed was laid by the Almighty as the keel of the American ship, and the channel of every stream that pours into it is one of its ribs. We have just covered the mighty frame with planking, and have divided the hull into State compartments. And the rebels say, " Break the ship in two." They scream, " We have a right to, on the ground of the sovereignty of the compartments and the principles of the Declaration of Independence; we have a right to, and we will! " The loyal heart of the nation answers, " We will knock out all your Gulf compartments and shiver your sovereign bulkheads, built of ebony, to pieces, and leave you one empty territory again before you shall break the keel." This is the right answer. We must do it, not only for our own safety, but to preserve the idea which the nation has been called to fulfil, and to which patriotism is called and bound to be loyal. Ay, even if there were one paragraph or line in the Declaration of Independence that breathed or hinted a sanction of the rebellion! Geology is older than the pen of Jefferson; the continent is broader than the Continental Congress, and they must go to the foundations to learn their statesmanship.

The Procrustes bed of American patriotism is the bed of the Mississippi, and every theory of national life and every plan for the future must be stretched on that; and woe to its wretched bones and sockets if it naturally reaches but halfway!

Providence made the country, too, when the immense basin

should be filled with its fitting millions, to show the world the beauty and economy of continental peace. It is a destiny radically different from that of Europe, with its four millions of armed men, that has been indicated for us. By the interplay of widely different products into one prosperity—cotton and cattle, tobacco and corn, metals and manufactures, shipyards and banking-rooms, forests and fields,—and all under one law, and all enjoying local liberty,—sufficient centralization, but the mildest pressure on the subordinate districts and the personal will—Providence designed to bless us with immense prosperity, to develop an energy unseen before on this globe, and to teach the nations a lesson which would draw them into universal fraternity and peace.

The rebels have tried to frustrate this hope and scheme. Patriotism, which discerns the idea to which the nation is thus called, arms to prevent its defeat. They say that there shall not be such unified prosperity and all-embracing peace for the future hundreds of millions on our domain. We say that there shall. And we arm to enforce our vision.

But is not that a strange way to establish peace, by fighting on such a scale as the Republic now witnesses? Is it not a novel method to labor for economy of administration and expense in government by a war which will fetter the nation with such a debt? We answer, the rebellion gave the challenge, and now victory at any cost is the only economy. Carnage, if they will it, is the only path to peace.

> " For our own good
> All causes shall give way; we are in blood
> Stept in so far, that, should we wade no more,
> Returning were as tedious as go o'er."

Yes, if we return, all our blood and treasure are wasted. The peace we gain by victory is for all the future, and for uncounted millions. The debt we incur by three years' fighting will be nothing compared with the new energy and security aroused, nothing to the next hundred years. And it will establish the idea to which the land was dedicated.

But do you say that if we conquer the rebellious area, we must hold it in subjection by a standing army which will be very costly and is contrary to the American idea? Very, well, if we do not conquer, if the rebels gain a strong and arrogant independence, we must keep up an immense standing army. It would cost more to watch them than it will to hold them. For we should be obliged in watching them to watch Europe too. We prefer to pay money to hold rather than to watch; and if we pay our money I suppose we can take our choice.

Patriotism says, and says it in the interest of peace and economy and final fraternity, " Fight and conquer even at the risk of holding them for a generation under the yoke." Fight, though, on such a scale that there will be no need of holding them; that they will gladly submit again to the rule which makes the Republic one and blesses all portions with protection and with bounty. Fight till they shall know that they kick against fate and the resistless laws of the world! Patriotism calls on the cabinet and the head of the nation and the generals who give tone to the campaign to forget the customs and interests of peace till we shall gain it by the submission of the rebels and the shredding of their last banner into threads.

The stake is worth this style of fighting. For it is the peace of our grandchildren, the interblended prosperity of the continent, the economy of centuries, the abolition of standing armies for a thousand years, the indefinite postponement of war, the idea of America, that we are to bend up thus " each corporal agent " to secure. Fight with hosepipes and lavender water if you want perpetual hatred and indefinite slaughter; fight with sheets of schrapnel and red-hot shot if you want to see the speedy dawn again of American peace and good will!

And Providence still further dedicated this land as the better home for labor, and to a polity that honors and blesses labor. Not equal rights so much as new honor to the workman is the idea which our polity is divinely called to emblazon and to guard. For this and to help this our immense fields were shrouded in darkness until a race should be ready who would bring a free ballot-box with them, and an untitled church, and a free Bible, and the seed of public schools, and a spirit that should shake at last the "glittering generalities" of the Declaration of Independence into literature like dew-drops in the morning from a tree. Into whatever movement or conceptions the doctrine of the sacredness of man and the worth of labor flows, there patriotism discerns the proper march of the tide of American thought and spirit.

Whatever denies and cramps and opposes, that is hostile to the call and destiny of the younger continent. For whatever in America blasphemes the rights of labor and bars the education of the workman smites the soil to that extent with blight, degrades literature, drains public spirit, chains the wheel of progress, insults the New Testament, and flouts the nobler traditions of the land.

I need not tell you that the rebellion is guilty of this too. It sins against the Mississippi; it sins against the coast line; it sins against the ballot-box; it sins against oaths of allegiance; it sins against public and beneficent peace; and it sins worse than all against the corner-stone of American progress and history and hope,—the worth of the laborer, the rights of man. It strikes for barbarism against civilization.

We have taken the carbon of labor from Europe and tried to promote it into the diamond.   Under the true American system a journeyman machinist in his striped shirt becomes General Nathaniel P. Banks.   The rebel idea is hostile to all this crystallization.   Keep all labor in its grimy and carbon state, they say; and so they choose it and perpetuate it of a color that will fulfil their arrogant conception.

Patriotism calls us to brace our sinews against this hideous apostasy and to see that the land is not severed by it.   Our unity gone, our economical peace broken up, standing armies imposed on us forever, European intrigue and antagonism our law,—and all for the doctrine that labor may rightfully be trodden into the mire,—what a close of the book of our national story!   What a robbery of the crown from our once proud forehead!

Gentlemen, it is a privilege that we can feel a patriotism which sets our present struggle in such relations and coolly sees that our country has been dedicated to a mission and a service so vast and eminent.   The duties correspond to the privilege.   One great duty is to feel the privilege more keenly, and by the inspiration of it stand strong for the country's unity.

Especially against any intimation from foreign powers of intervention to stop our war and break our integrity.   If France tries it we will arm as France armed against the intervention of Europe in her great Revolution, and hurled the circling armies back!   If England tries it we will say to her as Macaulay said with admirable vigor and eloquence in the House of Commons when the secession of Ireland was threatened: " The Repeal of the Union we regard as fatal to the empire and we never will consent to it; never, though the country should be surrounded by dangers as great as those which threatened her when her American colonies, and France, and Spain, and Holland were leagued against her, and when the armed neutrality of the Baltic disputed her maritime rights; never, though another Bonaparte should pitch his camp in sight of Dover castle; never, till all has been staked and lost; never, till the four quarters of the world have been convulsed by the last struggle of the great English people for their place among the nations." It was an island utterly disjoined from England and separated more widely by blood and belief than by the chafing sea, of whose threatened secession these words were spoken by the most widely read English orator of this generation. How much more fitly and honorably can we urge the spirit of them if England should attempt to break our hold upon integral portions of our empire, the very courses of our rivers, the very land for which we have paid our millions and our blood! Let the spirit sweep through our loyal millions which Macaulay thus uttered; let us become such a battery that fervor and determination of that temperature shall leap out whenever the thought of foreign intervention is breathed. Then Europe will be careful enough how she touches the awful galvanic pile. Patriotism of that temper will be a peace-preserver.

And another duty of patriotism now is to call for the declaration of a new policy in the war.

Many of you have heard of the eloquent sailor preacher of Boston, Father Taylor. No man is more patriotic; no man is more powerful in prayer. A few weeks ago he prayed thus for our excellent chief magistrate in Boston: (those of you who have heard him will conceive with what vitality and emphasis he shot out the adjectives) " O Lord, guide our dear President, our Abraham, the friend of God

like old Abraham! Save him from those wriggling, in-
triguing, politic, piercing, slimy, boring keel-worms; don't
let them go through the sheathing of his integrity!"

Now we ought to begin to beseech Abraham, and to pray
heaven in his behalf and ours, that the " keel-worms " shall
not through his delay or scruples bore through the sheathing of the nation's integrity.

The time has come when we must look more at the actual
constitution of the nation than at the paper constitution
through which the rebel chiefs have struck their daggers.
The time has come when it should be said and known and
proclaimed with the trumpet of the President that we strike
to exterminate the power of the slave-aristocracy of the rebel
region.

The slave-oligarchy of the rebel States, if the war is to
end in our favor, must be shorn of all their power for mischief. Otherwise the war, though we conquer, does not end
in our favor. By the necessity of their position they stand
thus hostile. Hostility to the American spirit steams like
an intellectual malaria from their plantations. They breathe
it invisibly and perforce. They are enemies by fate to all
that as loyal Americans we honor and all that we are fighting to save.

In the now rebellious States there are less than three hundred thousand of them. We must crush their power. Any
other issue to the war is simply chopping off the rattles from
the snake instead of drawing the fangs. And to crush their
power, we must strike the fetters from their bondmen. And
we must say soon that our purpose is nothing less than this,
that we shall hold on until we accomplish this.

Some would do this as a crusade in favor of the freedom
of the black race. I would do it as a wise and statesmanlike

blow for the permanent interest of all the white race in our empire, and to insure the unity and peace of the continent for centuries. Thus we make America homogeneous. . . . Thus we give the war a principle. Thus we strike at the root of our differences, our dangers, our sorrows, and our mighty wrong. The rebel aristocracy have staked their power upon this challenge. If they fail they have lost, and we must see that they both fail and lose. . . .

O, that the President would soon speak that electric sentence,—inspiration to the loyal North, doom to the traitorous aristocracy whose cup of guilt is full! Let him say that it is a war of mass against class, of America against feudalism, of the schoolmaster against the slave-master, of workmen against the barons, of the ballot-box against the barracoon. This is what the struggle means. Proclaim it so, and what a light breaks through our leaden sky! The war-wave rolls then with the impetus and weight of an idea.

> "The sword!—a name of dread!—yet when
> Upon the freeman's thigh 't is bound,—
> While for his altar and his hearth,
> While for the land that gave him birth,
> The war-drums roll, the trumpets sound,—
>   How sacred is it then!
>
> Whenever for the truth and right
> It flashes in the van of fight,—
> Whether in some wild mountain pass,
> As that where fell Leonidas;
> Or on some sterile plain and stern,—
> A Marston or a Bannockburn;
> Or mid fierce crags and bursting rills,—
> The Switzer's Alps, gray Tyrol's hills;
> Or, as when sunk the Armada's pride,
> It gleams above the stormy tide;—
> Still, still, whene'er the battle's word
> Is Liberty,—when men do stand
> For Justice and their native land,—
> Then Heaven bless the sword!"

Yes, gentlemen, then Heaven will bless the sword!